Grenville Mellen Dodge
in the Civil War

ALSO BY JAMES PATRICK MORGANS

*The Underground Railroad on the Western Frontier:
Escapes from Missouri, Arkansas, Iowa and the Territories of Kansas,
Nebraska and the Indian Nations, 1840–1865* (McFarland, 2010)

*John Todd and the Underground Railroad:
Biography of an Iowa Abolitionist* (McFarland, 2006)

# Grenville Mellen Dodge in the Civil War

*Union Spymaster, Railroad Builder and Organizer of the Fourth Iowa Volunteer Infantry*

JAMES PATRICK MORGANS

McFarland & Company, Inc., Publishers
*Jefferson, North Carolina*

LIBRARY OF CONGRESS CATALOGUING-IN-PUBLICATION DATA

Names: Morgans, James Patrick, author.
Title: Grenville Mellen Dodge in the Civil War : union spymaster, railroad builder and organizer of the Fourth Iowa Volunteer Infantry / James Patrick Morgans.
Description: Jefferson, North Carolina : McFarland & Company, Inc., Publishers, 2016. | Includes bibliographical references and index.
Identifiers: LCCN 2016007849 | ISBN 9780786470693 (softcover : acid free paper) ∞
Subjects: LCSH: Dodge, Grenville M., 1831–1916. | United States—History—Civil War, 1861–1865—Biography. | Generals—United States—Biography. | United States. Army. Iowa Infantry Regiment, 4th (1861–1865) | United States—History—Civil War, 1861–1865—Secret service.
Classification: LCC E467.1.D6 M67 2016 | DDC 355.0092—dc23
LC record available at http://lccn.loc.gov/2016007849

BRITISH LIBRARY CATALOGUING DATA ARE AVAILABLE

ISBN (print) 978-0-7864-7069-3
ISBN (ebook) 978-1-4766-2142-5

© 2016 The Estate of James Patrick Morgans. All rights reserved

*No part of this book may be reproduced or transmitted in any form or by any means, electronic or mechanical, including photocopying or recording, or by any information storage and retrieval system, without permission in writing from the publisher.*

Front cover: *inset* Portrait of Maj. Gen. Grenville M. Dodge, officer of the Federal Army (Library of Congress); Central Pacific Transcontinental Railroad, Tunnel No. 39, Milepost 180.95, Cisco, Placer County, California (Library of Congress)

Printed in the United States of America

*McFarland & Company, Inc., Publishers*
*Box 611, Jefferson, North Carolina 28640*
*www.mcfarlandpub.com*

To my
Grandson Benjamin Patrick Kuehler
and
Granddaughter Elizabeth Joy Kuehler

The joy and happiness you have given
your grandmother and me is immeasurable.

—James Patrick Morgans,
December 25, 1946–August 11, 2015.

# Acknowledgments

I am grateful that Michael Irvin of Shenandoah, Iowa,
read the manuscript and made suggestions.
Thanks go to my wife, Judith A. Morgans, for her help on this project.
I wish to acknowledge the help of my son, Patrick James Morgans,
and daughter, Meredith Joy Kuehler, in finding research materials.
I would additionally like to extend my gratitude
to the staff at the State Historical Society of Iowa
for their help in finding research materials.
I am appreciative to the many people who encouraged me
to write and research this book.

# Table of Contents

*Acknowledgments* vi
*Preface* 1
*Introduction* 3

**1.** War Comes to the Prairies 7
**2.** "Who were those black-coated devils?" 42
**3.** Battle Tested 75
**4.** "The last full measure" 117
**5.** Postbellum 159

*Chapter Notes* 173
*Bibliography* 183
*Index* 189

# Preface

Major-General Grenville M. Dodge was the most famous Iowan to come out of the Civil War. In recognition of his contributions during the Civil War, the State of Iowa named the Iowa National Guard training site Camp Dodge in his honor. Dodge, besides being a skilled field commander, created the largest and most effective spy network in the Western Theater of operations in the Civil War. During the Civil War, Dodge had few equals in building railroads, and after the war, he became recognized as one of the world's greatest railroad industrialists.

Dodge also organized the 4th Iowa Volunteer Infantry Regiment, which became one of the best fighting Union regiments in the Civil War. This was an amazing feat. The 4th Iowa was recruited mostly over a sprawling 17-county area of southwest Iowa that covered almost 12,000 square miles. Most of the recruits had not been born in Iowa or had not gone to school in Iowa. Many were new arrivals to the state. They were strangers to each other. Some had arrived so near the start of the Civil War that they did not even know in what Iowa county they resided. The recruiter would take a guess at what congressional district the recruit lived in and write that down as his home residence. If you had asked many of the soldiers in the newly recruited 4th Iowa where they were from, many would have said Ohio, Indiana, Pennsylvania or some other state or foreign country. A number had not lived in the state long enough to consider themselves Hawkeyes. Dodge would soon change this. He created an atmosphere of camaraderie, trust, courage, sacrifice and unshakeable loyalty.

Right after the Civil War, Captain Addison A. Stuart wrote short biographies of most of the men who obtained the rank of colonel in Iowa regiments. He also wrote regimental histories of the various Iowa units. Probably no man knew more about Iowa's efforts during the Civil War than Stuart. He wrote, "During the present war, no officer, whether of the regular or volunteer service, has made a better record than Major-General Dodge." Stuart went on to write, "If Iowa has been honored by her troops in the field, she has been equally honored by her general officers; and in this respect she is indebted to no one more than to General Dodge." Of the 4th Iowa Volunteer Infantry he wrote, "To no Iowa regiment is the state more largely indebted for its military renown."

There have been two biographies written about Grenville Dodge; one was penned in 1929 and the other in 1967. While both biographies have their strengths, neither does Dodge justice for his service during the Civil War. The Civil War made Dodge's reputation and made him not only a collogue of General Ulysses S. Grant, General

William T. Sherman and General Philip Sheridan but also a confidant and friend. Abraham Lincoln looked upon Dodge as an expert on the transcontinental railroad. These men would go on to shape much of the history of the United States in the 19th century.

I felt it was necessary to revisit Dodge's life and service during the Civil War. I also felt that a more detailed history of the 4th Iowa Volunteer Infantry was in order. After Dodge's and the 4th Iowa's heroic efforts at the Battle of Pea Ridge in Arkansas, Dodge was promoted from colonel to brigadier-general then eventually to major-general. Dodge went on to become a divisional, corps and department commander and did not have direct command over the 4th Iowa after the Battle at Pea Ridge. The regimental colonelcy of the 4th Iowa fell to Colonel James A. Williamson, who eventually through Dodge's efforts became a brigadier-general. Williamson became one of Dodge's closest friends, his protégé and lifelong confidant.

# Introduction

This book begins with Chapter 1, "War Comes to the Prairies," with an introduction to Grenville Mellen Dodge, who was a railroad-surveyor-turned-businessman from Council Bluffs, Iowa. Dodge, along with the other Iowa Republicans, backed Abraham Lincoln in the election of 1860. It was now February of 1861, and the Iowa delegation was going to Washington, D.C., to Lincoln's inauguration. Most in the delegation wanted plum political jobs from the Lincoln administration. Dodge had a chance meeting with Lincoln in 1859, and they discussed the building of the transcontinental railroad. Dodge's only interest in the Lincoln administration was in the building of this railroad or, if there was to be war, a high officer ranking in the Union army. The chapter goes on to discuss the Dodge family history and Dodge's college years at Norwich University, where he received a top-notch military education. Norwich University would supply more Union officers than any other institution besides the military academy at West Point. Dodge's business associates wanted him to keep out of the fight and make the enormous profits that were to be had by supplying the Union war machine. Dodge's wife also wanted him to steer clear of the military. However, Dodge wanted to be in this fight. At first, his interest in high command was rebuffed by Iowa governor Kirkwood, who had many high-ranking politicians and important people in Iowa clamoring for the officers' slots. However, by Dodge's energy and pluck, he managed to secure a colonelcy and raised a regiment from southwestern Iowa, to be known as the 4th Iowa Volunteer Infantry.

The second chapter opens with a biography of James A. Williamson. Williamson was born in a southern state and was the head of the Democratic Party in Iowa. He became Dodge's chief of staff. Williamson was very intelligent and industrious, but some of the officers in the 4th Iowa did not like him and petitioned Dodge to have him removed. Dodge ignored the petition and stayed loyal to Williamson. After a while the men saw Williamson's value and withdrew the petition. The 4th Iowa, stationed in Rolla, Missouri, chased Confederate army regulars and Confederate guerrilla fighters all over southern Missouri. John C. Frémont was the department head in Missouri, and things were a complete chaotic mess. Dodge finally got uniforms, arms, military equipment and back pay for his men. Dodge also bought his regiment non-government-issued black overcoats for the wintertime. These coats gave his regiment a distinctive look. Dodge began using spies and scouts to gain information about the enemy's whereabouts. Dodge became good friends with Philip Sheridan, and as quartermaster Sheridan appreciated the help Dodge and the 4th Iowa Infantry rendered to him. Samuel

Curtis took over command of the Army of the Southwest and, though outnumbered by the Confederate army in front of them, marched on Springfield, Missouri, and recaptured the town for the Federals. At Pea Ridge, General Curtis set up his defensive positions as if the Rebels were going to attack from the south to the north. Dodge, who was now commanding a brigade, found out through his intelligence network that the Confederate army was going around Union lines on the Bentonville Detour Road to attack Curtis' rear and right flank. Dodge told Curtis this, but he dismissed Dodge's information. Curtis didn't even send out pickets on his right flank on the roads to see if there was any Rebel troops movement. Dodge on his own initiative felled trees on the Bentonville Detour to slow the Confederate advance. Later Confederate generals Sterling Price and Earl Van Dorn mention how these felled trees upset their plan of attack. Dodge disobeyed Curtis' orders and pulled the 4th Iowa out of his defensive position so they could meet the Rebel army attacking from the rear. The 4th Iowa and their black overcoats made an impression on the Confederates, and they stemmed the tide of the Confederate attack. Dodge and the 4th were all over the battlefield, with the 4th Iowa sustaining some of the highest casualty rates of any Union unit at Pea Ridge. After the battle Curtis gave the 4th Iowa its due, and Dodge was promoted to brigadier-general.

Chapter 3 begins with a biography of Alonzo Gaston, a soldier in the 4th Iowa Infantry. Gaston's parents were abolitionists and were deeply involved in the Underground Railroad, but they forbade their son Alonzo from joining the Union army. They wanted him to finish his education at Oberlin College. Alonzo went against his parents' wishes and joined the 4th Iowa. Alonzo fought in the battles at Chickasaw Bayou and at Fort Hindman. After these engagements, Alonzo became very ill. Alonzo did not die in a blaze of glory on the field of battle, but of disease, as did a majority of Civil War soldiers. The 4th Iowa became involved in bottling up the Confederates forces in Vicksburg. Dodge's corps was busy building and protecting the railroad along the Tennessee River Valley. Brigadier-General Dodge began to assemble the largest spy network on the Western frontier. His headquarters looked like a modern-day war room, with updated maps and constant military information being brought to Dodge. Dodge had as many as 120 spies in his network. He used civilians and soldiers in his network. He used males and females, blacks and whites, as spies. He even had spies in the Confederate army. Grant also wanted Dodge's corps to shield Braxton Bragg's army so they could not join up with the defenses at Vicksburg. Grant put a siege on at Vicksburg, and the 4th Iowa acted as sappers, a very dangerous job. Vicksburg fell, and the Union won at Gettysburg, and it looked as if the Federal army was on its way to ultimate victory. However, General Rosecrans' disastrous defeat at Chickamauga Creek and the Confederate siege of Chattanooga were major setbacks for the Union army. The 4th Iowa Infantry and Dodge's XVI Corps were sent to eastern Tennessee to claim back that portion of the Confederacy for the Union.

Chapter 4 begins with the 4th Iowa and Dodge's XVI Corps following the rail line south to Atlanta, through the Georgia towns of Ringgold, Dalton, Resaca, Kingston, Marietta and then Atlanta. The movement of the Confederate army to the south was accomplished by a series of Union flanking maneuvers. Dodge sent his super-spy, Philip Henson, on an important mission, but his luck finally ran out, and he was captured and finally jailed. The 4th Iowa, now in Williamson's "Iowa Brigade," started to receive attention as a superior fighting unit. One of Dodge's spies in Atlanta brought the news that John Bell Hood had replaced Joe Johnston as commander of the Confederate forces in Atlanta. Sherman decided to use Hood's natural aggressive behavior against him. Disaster struck the Union army when popular Union general James McPherson was killed. The Union won what was known as the Battle of Atlanta. However, the Rebels moved into Atlanta and fortified that city. A heavy artillery bombardment of Atlanta had little to do with this Confederate stronghold. Dodge had trouble with General Sweeny, the commander of his 2nd Division. He managed to get Sweeny removed from his command. Sherman tried to cut off Hood's supply lines from the south but was unsuccessful. General Dodge was severely wounded with a bullet to the head. He was unconscious for several days, and a chunk of his scalp peeled off. He had to take several months to recuperate. During this convalescence period, Dodge visited Grant in the Eastern Theater and President Lincoln. Another flanking maneuver dislodged the Rebels from Atlanta. Later, during the Battle of Jonesboro, 4th Iowa corporal Amos Ames was captured by the Confederate soldiers. He spent the rest of the war in a series of Rebel prison camps including Andersonville. The rest of the 4th Iowa was involved in Sherman's March to the Sea. After capturing Savannah, Georgia, Sherman's armies invaded South Carolina and then North Carolina, where the war ended. The 4th Iowa was mustered out in Louisville, Kentucky, after performing provost duties. After Dodge recovered, he was given command of the Department of Missouri, where he was only partly successful in pacifying the guerrilla warfare in the state. Dodge was then given command of the Department of Kansas, where he had control of much of the Western territories. After the cowardly attacks of Colonel Chivington, whole tribes of native peoples from the Arkansas River to the Canadian border were conducting war against the whites. Telegraph lines from Omaha to Denver were destroyed, mail routes disrupted, and white wagon trains and settlements attacked. Within 40 days during the dead of winter, Dodge had restored telegraph service and the mail routes and had stopped many of the attacks on wagon trains and white settlements. Using Pawnee scouts, Dodge's subordinate, General Connor, used some questionable means to subdue native warrior attacks. However, Dodge tried to protect "friendly tribesmen" from dishonest whites, and he championed keeping treaties made with native tribesmen. Dodge stayed in the U.S. Army until May of 1866, when he took the position of chief engineer for the Union Pacific Railroad.

Chapter 5 tells of the post–Civil War lives of some of the members of the 4th Iowa, including General James A. Williamson. Much of the chapter summarizes the life of General Grenville M. Dodge after the war, his tremendous career as a railroad builder and business mogul and his election to the United States Congress. As one of the youngest major-generals in the Civil War, Dodge was also feted as a hero of the Civil War clear into the 20th century. Also, Dodge was asked his advice on the fighting in the Spanish-American War and the formation of the Iowa National Guard.

For anyone interested in how people such as Grenville Dodge lived during the Victorian age, I would wholly recommend a tour of the Dodge House in Council Bluffs, Iowa.

# Chapter 1

# War Comes to the Prairies

Grenville Mellen Dodge was a very busy man. Besides his railroading interests, his banking business and his mercantile trade, Dodge had just helped elect a president. After the euphoria of electing Abraham Lincoln in November of 1860 had worn off, the realities of the fragile political situation of the United States had been exposed. South Carolina seceded from the Union in December of 1860. The states of Mississippi, Florida, Alabama, Georgia, and Louisiana seceded in January of 1861. Texas followed them in February of 1861. All the states that seceded allowed slavery within their borders.

Dodge was going to travel from his home in Council Bluffs, Iowa, to the state capital of Iowa in Des Moines. He was to meet follow Republican friends and go to the Lincoln inauguration. It was in February when Dodge departed on his trip, intending to reach Washington, D.C., by March 4, 1861, Lincoln's inauguration date. Jefferson Davis had already been inaugurated as the provisional president of the Confederate States at Montgomery, Alabama, on February 18, 1861.[1]

A bitter plains snowstorm disrupted the 125-mile trip from Council Bluffs to Des Moines. The snowdrifts were so high that they buried cattle and the frozen bodies of would-be gold miners headed for Colorado. It took Dodge three arduous days to reach Iowa's capital city, sometimes fighting through snowdrifts higher than a two-story building. In Des Moines, Dodge joined Republican friends for the Washington trip. The trip to the nation's capital proved less dramatic than the one from Council Bluffs to Des Moines. The atmosphere in the District of Columbia in March of 1861 was both tense and intoxicating.

Dodge had hoped war would be averted. He thought Lincoln's inaugural address soared and was conciliatory to the South but at the same time had "backbone."[2] Abraham Lincoln was glad to see Dodge and his Iowan friends in Washington. One of Lincoln's biographers, Carl Sandburg, said, "The people of Washington (D.C.) were almost all politically opposed to him.... Yet there came familiar faces, Iowa men who had gone the limit to nominate him at Chicago [including] Grenville Dodge, whom he had last talked with in Council Bluffs about the best Pacific-railway route."[3] Dodge was able to visit with Lincoln after the inaugural speech. The president assured Dodge and his friends, "I shall bring the country out all safe." Lincoln also told Dodge of his continued interest in a transcontinental railroad. Later in March, Dodge would testify before a congressional committee on railroad matters.[4]

One of the friends with Dodge when he talked to Lincoln was Peter Dey. Dey was a railroad surveyor for the Chicago and Rock Island Railroad; Dodge had at one time been Dey's surveyor's rodman.[5] Dey had applied to become the governor of the Territory of Nevada. He would not get the post; James Warren Nye was appointed. Another transplanted Iowan, Orion Clemens, would get the post of secretary of the Nevada Territory, a real political plum. Clemens, originally from Hannibal, Missouri, had moved to Muscatine, Iowa, and then Keokuk, Iowa, after his newspaper venture in Hannibal had failed. Clemens had stumped for Lincoln in northern Missouri during the election of 1860, a very brave thing to do as many thought Clemens was an abolitionist and Lincoln only received a small amount of votes in pro-slavery Missouri. Orion Clemens had read for law with Edward Bates in St. Louis. It was Bates, a powerful Missouri politician, who had helped secure the appointment as secretary for Clemens. Bates would become Lincoln's attorney general.[6] Clemens took his younger brother Sam out to Nevada. Sam had hoped to become the secretary to the secretary of Nevada but found that the post paid nothing. Sam Clemens' nom de plume was Mark Twain. Twain wrote of many of his Nevada adventures in the book *Roughing It*. Nevada and her silver and gold strikes would become very important to the Union in paying for the Civil War.

The dean of the Dodge group at this time was John A. Kasson, an attorney from Des Moines. Kasson was a free-soiler New Englander who had come out West to Missouri to seek his fame and fortune. Kasson practiced in a crackerjack St. Louis law firm with J. B. Crockett. Crockett later became a California Supreme Court judge. Also in the firm were Gratz Brown and Henry S. Geyer, who would go on to become United States senators. More importantly, Edward Bates also practiced at this firm. Bates would become a Kasson supporter. Kasson later would form his own law firm. St. Louis doubled in size during the time Kasson was there. Real estate boomed during this time, with plenty of legal work for attorneys trying to decipher ownership of plots of land that had at one time been owned by the Spanish, the French and now the Americans. Kasson became a minor cog in St. Louis society with his striking, urbane looks, his commanding voice and his ability to give talks to eager St. Louis audiences on a variety of subjects. At this time Kasson was making the equivalent of a million dollars a year in present-day dollars. Not all of this money was made doing legal work. The banking system in the United States at this time was rudimentary. Men of means like Kasson, in

**John Kasson was a free-soiler from New England who moved to St. Louis, Missouri, and made a small fortune practicing law. In 1857, Kasson moved to Des Moines and prospered, becoming a leader in Republican politics in Iowa. While in Congress, Kasson championed Grenville Dodge's promotion from brigadier-general to major-general. The two would later become bitter political rivals (Library of Congress).**

a boom town like St. Louis, could make piles of money, if careful, loaning money out at rates as high as 12 percent. It would seem that Kasson could do no wrong.

However, despite the money, Kasson and his wife were miserable. Their Yankee ways didn't fit in with the Southern sensibilities of the St. Louis elites. As one might imagine, Kasson worked all hours, while his wife was lonely in a strange city. Kasson even bought and owned a slave in St. Louis. But they never really fit in. In 1856 Kasson and his wife could afford to take a whole year off, and they traveled Europe. When they came back to St. Louis in 1857 they had decided to leave this city. They freed their slave and left for the free soil of Iowa.

Kasson liked to write that when he came to the frontier town of Des Moines, Iowa, his wagon broke down and he had to walk in a sea of mud to his house. Kasson also told of establishing himself in the new capital city by taking payments in vegetables from Hawkeye farmers. But it didn't take the patrician-like Kasson long to figure out that if he wanted the kind of money he was used to in St. Louis, his clients would have to be the wealthier people and businesses in the Hawkeye state. He quickly upgraded his clientele and continued in the loan business. In a few short years he became one of the richest men in Des Moines. Kasson also became very active in Republican politics in Iowa and was an enthusiastic supporter of Abraham Lincoln.

In 1860 Kasson wrote the pro-railroad and other planks into the platform of the Republican Party Convention. Montgomery Blair, whom Kasson had known as a judge in Missouri, became postmaster general and with a good word from Edward Bates, Kasson became the assistant postmaster general in Lincoln's administration. In the next few months, Kasson became very busy replacing all of the Democratic postmasters with loyal Unionists and Republicans. Kasson became a much-sought-out person for these plum political patronage positions. On one occasion Kasson replaced some 600 postmasters in a day. Some of these postal replacements were because of politics and some for disloyalty to the Union. It would also fall to Kasson during the Civil War to develop the large and at times daunting military postal system that would be needed during that great conflict. In 1863, Kasson would call for an international postal reform conference in Paris, France. Kasson would go on to have a lengthy career as a Republican congressman and politician and international ambassador and diplomat.[7]

As a congressman Kasson sponsored the Metric Act of 1866 or, as some called it, the Kasson Act. Some states in the United States forbade the use of the metric system for anything, including the use or manufacturing of equipment using the metric system. However, many in the scientific community clamored for the metric system in measuring for scientific purposes. Also, companies such as the Fairbanks scale company were developing and expanding export markets in countries such as France and needed to be able to produce metric instruments. Kasson was able to husband the bill through the Congress, and it greatly helped the American business and scientific communities. Later Kasson became minister to Austria-Hungry and to Germany and also took on other diplomatic posts. However, after the Civil War, Kasson and Dodge would become bitter political enemies over Kasson's congressional seat.[8]

In the Dodge group, the almost exact opposite of the elegant John A. Kasson was Herbert "Hub" Hoxie. Hoxie was a rough-hewn man, the exact type of person you would expect to gravitate to the frontier. Before the Civil War, it was said, Hoxie was often unemployed and never made more than $800 in any year. However, he became the chairman of the Republican State Committee in Iowa, often having Republican faithful ask him for job opportunities when he himself didn't have employment. Hoxie had hoped that his political connections would help his financial situation. Hoxie's friendship with Grenville Dodge did this. Dodge acquainted Hoxie with the world of railroading. Before the Civil War Hoxie didn't have a dime to his name. After the Civil War during his tenure as a highflying railroad executive, Hoxie would return to Des Moines in his own palatial railroad car.

Born in New York State, Hub Hoxie moved with his family to Des Moines when there was just a fort and trading post at that location. Hoxie and his father engaged in farming and trading with the Native Americans in central Iowa. In the 1850s Hoxie had ventured out West to look for gold but, like so many, he returned home empty-handed. Hoxie then figured like many others of the time that politics and the world of business connections were surer paths to riches than panning for gold. Hoxie was a very energetic man, and when he came back from the gold fields he immersed himself in politics. Hoxie became a lawyer but was never able to come close to the success of Kasson in the courtroom.

After his foray into the gold fields of California, Hoxie came back to Iowa and married a young lady, the niece to Thomas Mitchell. "Uncle Tommy" Mitchell was a central Iowa politician who knew the ins and outs of politics in the Hawkeye state. Hoxie and Mitchell ran a hotel together and became a political force in the new Republican Party in Iowa. Also, Uncle Tom Mitchell and Hoxie and his new wife's family were also deeply involved in the Underground Railroad in Iowa. The central and southern parts of Iowa were interwoven with Underground Railroad connections and advanced hundreds of fugitive slaves from Missouri, Kansas, Arkansas and the Indian Nations of Oklahoma to Chicago and Canada.[9]

Hoxie threw himself into the world of the Underground Railroad. Hoxie and Mitchell would send runaway slaves up the line to J.B. Grinnell, founder of Grinnell, Iowa. Although Grinnell was a Congregational minister he was also one of the largest wool merchants in Iowa. Hoxie and Mitchell used the terminology of the wool merchant to alert Grinnell of possible "passengers" coming along the Underground Railroad line. One time Hoxie wrote to Grinnell to alert him of fugitive slaves being sent to Grinnell. He wrote: "Dear Grinnell: Uncle Tom says if the roads are not too bad you can look for those fleeces of wool by to-morrow. Send them on to test the market and price, and no back charges. Yours, Hub."[10]

After Lincoln was elected, the emerging Republican machine rewarded Hoxie with a position as the United States marshal of Iowa. If the Confederacy hadn't formed, or had not fired on Fort Sumter and performed other hostile acts, and had adopted a wait-and-see attitude towards the Lincoln administration, the fugitive slave movement might eventually have had a dramatic effect on the institution of slavery. The backbone to the enforcement of the Fugitive Slave Act of 1850, sometimes called the "bloodhound law," in the Millard Fillmore, Franklin Pierce and James Buchanan administrations was the corps of United States marshals in the northern states and the territories of Kansas and Nebraska. The U.S. marshals in these three presidential administrations cajoled and threaten local county sheriffs and city marshals to enforce the act. These local northern lawmen were reminded that if they did not enforce the act and hunt down and capture fugitive slaves and return them to their Southern masters, they could be arrested and fined under the provisions of this draconian Federal Law. With men like Hub Hoxie as U.S. marshals, the Fugitive Slave Act of 1850 would have been largely ignored. The steady stream of runaway slaves from Missouri, Arkansas, and the Indian Nations of Oklahoma passing through Iowa might have turned into a torrent of fugitive bondspersons headed North for freedom.[11]

On August 11, 1859, Abraham Lincoln had visited Council Bluffs, Iowa. Lincoln was treated as a distinguished visitor. Although Lincoln had lost the Illinois senatorial race in 1858 to Stephen A. Douglas, the Lincoln-Douglas debates had captured the attention of the nation. Lincoln had become a rising star in the growing galaxy of the upstart Republican Party.

The Republican-leaning Council Bluffs *Nonpareil* newspaper, in its August 13, 1859, edition, implored its readers to go to the Council Bluffs Concert Hall and listen to the issues of the day being discussed and "hear Old Abe." The *Nonpareil* in the same issue declared its confidence that Lincoln's celebrity would insure a "full house" at the Concert Hall. A week later the *Nonpareil* said of Lincoln's speech that it was "clear and lucid ... [and] set forth the true principals of the republican party." The article went on to note "the dexterity with which he applied the political scalpel to the democratic carcass.... The speaker fully and fairly sustained the great reputation he acquitted in the memorable Illinois campaign." The Democratic-leaning newspaper in the city, the Council Bluffs *Bugle*, saw things differently. The *Bugle* opinioned, "He [Lincoln] then, with many excuses and a lengthy explanation, as if conscious of the nauseous nature of the black republican rostrum ... entered into a lengthy and ingenious analysis of the 'nigger' question." A black Republican was a person who believed not only that black people should not be slaves but also that they were to enjoy full social and political standing in the United States. However, even the *Bugle* had to admit that Lincoln's speech was "in reality as good a speech as could have been made for the interest of the Democracy. He was listened to with much attention, for his Waterloo defeat by Douglas has magnified him into quite a lion here."[12]

Although by 1859 Lincoln had become a celebrity, his reason for visiting Council Bluffs was business. Grenville Dodge had been the main surveyor for the Mississippi and Missouri Railroad. The Mississippi and Missouri Railroad was to be a railroad line across Iowa. The railway was supposed to stretch from Davenport, Iowa, on the east side of the state on the Mississippi River to Council Bluffs, Iowa, on the west side of the state on the Missouri River. However, this was never accomplished. Dodge had purchased land in what was known as the Riddle Tract for the Mississippi and Missouri Railroad in Council Bluffs. The land was to be used for the future company railroad shops and a rail yard. The extra lots in the tract were to be sold for town lots and businesses and put on the market for sale. Many people were interested in purchasing these lots for speculation to be sold to businesses who wanted to be near the rail yards.

At this time Norman Judd was a friend of Lincoln.[13] Judd had been Lincoln's campaign manager and would later convince Dodge to come to the Republican Convention in Chicago in 1860 to help nominate Lincoln for the office of the presidency. Judd had also been a lawyer for the M&M Railroad, and he had purchased 17 of these town lots in Council Bluffs for a total of $3,500. The lots were not selling because railroad building had stalled out in eastern Iowa. However, at this date in August of 1859, Judd needed money. He had asked Lincoln to borrow $3,000, a large sum of money for the time, using the town lots in Council Bluffs as collateral. Being a prudent man, Lincoln came out to Council Bluffs to look at the real estate collateral.[14]

The Mississippi and Missouri Railroad had never completed the rail line from eastern Iowa to western Iowa; in fact, the railroad had never even made it as far as Des Moines in the middle of the state.[15] At this time, in the last year of the decade of the 1850s, Dodge was using his considerable energy to build up his banking and mercantile business in Council Bluffs. Lincoln had railroaded to St. Joseph, Missouri, then visited Kansas. He then travelled to Council Bluffs in 1859 via a steamboat up the Missouri River from St. Joseph.[16]

Lincoln had former friends from Springfield, Illinois, now living in Council Bluffs. When Lincoln went to visit these friends, they told Lincoln of the surveyor, Grenville Dodge, and his proposed route to the Pacific Ocean. The two visionaries, Dodge and Lincoln, met at the Pacific Hotel in Council Bluffs to talk of the viability of a transcontinental railroad. Dodge expressed the viewpoint that the best route out West was through the Platte River Valley, following roughly along the 42nd parallel. Dodge reasoned that the flat land in the Platte River Valley would make for rapid speed in the laying of the railroad track and would position the track for access to mountain passes in the Rockies. Like most of Dodge's comments, this was not idle talk but backed by sound experience and reasoning.

In 1857 and into 1858 Grenville Dodge had been sent on a surveying mission to find the best route out West across the Great Plains and into the Rocky Mountains. Henry Farnam and Thomas C. Durant had financed the expedition as directors of the Mississippi and Missouri and also the Chicago and Rock Island railroads. Dodge had also conferred with his boyhood friend Frederick W. Lander—now an explorer and surveyor—as to the best route through the South Pass to the West Coast. Nevertheless, the Panic of 1857 and the collapse of many banks in the United States made the raising of funds for such a project, a railroad to the West Coast, not feasible, and the plan was put on the back burner.[17]

Dodge noted Lincoln's quick grasp of the facts and the lanky Illinoisan's penetrating questions. Lincoln thought the building of a rail line to the Pacific coast of utmost importance. Dodge

This is how Abraham Lincoln looked when he visited Council Bluffs, Iowa, in August of 1859. After a meeting during the visit, Dodge became one of Lincoln's experts on the transcontinental railroad (Library of Congress).

later wrote, "He virtually shelled my words, getting all the secrets that were later to go to my employers." The two men would never forget their meeting and the information shared at the Pacific Hotel. Later, with great irony Dodge would note that the town lots in Council Bluffs that Lincoln held as collateral would be adjoined by town lots owned by Ohio congressman Clement L. Vallandingham. Vallandingham would become one of the Lincoln administration's harshest critics and a leader of the Copperhead movement. Things were so bad during the Civil War that Vallandingham was arrested by General Ambrose Burnside, tried and convicted of treason. However, Lincoln, not wishing to make a martyr of the Ohio congressman, commuted his prison sentence and he was sent to live in the Confederacy during the Civil War. However, Vallandingham made his way to Canada, crossed the border into the United States and spent much of his time in the North during the Civil War. Vallandingham tried to seek political office in Ohio during and after the Civil War but was unsuccessful.[18]

In the spring of 1861 everyone was waiting for the other shoe to drop. Would there be civil war in the United States or not? In April of 1861 the answer became clear. On the 12th of that month, Confederate forces fired on federal positions at Fort Sumter in the harbor of Charleston, South Carolina. Abraham Lincoln responded three days later with a call-up of 75,000 men to end the rebellion.

Closer to home for Grenville Dodge, pro–Confederate men numbering about 200 from Clay, Lafayette and Jackson counties in Missouri had stormed the small Federal arsenal at Liberty, Missouri, and taken guns and field pieces and ammunition from this facility on April 20, 1861. This was only nine days after the firing on Fort Sumter and six days after Lincoln's call-up of 75,000 troops. Liberty, Missouri, was only some 100 miles, as the crow flies, from the southern border of Iowa. There would be war. The much larger Federal arsenal in St. Louis, Missouri, would be an even larger prize for the Confederate forces in Missouri.[19]

Being a businessman Dodge and his considerable circle of friends wrote to each other about how the states of Iowa and Kansas and the territory of Nebraska would be supplied during the war and what war materials would be coming through the region. Everyone, both North and South, thought the conflict would be over quickly, and they knew those that were well connected could make a considerable profit during this conflict. Dodge's friend Hoxie even advised Dodge, "Don't enlist or take command of a company. There will be plenty that will want to go. Keep clear of that." Even though Hoxie was now a U.S. marshal he was ever on the lookout for business opportunities he and Dodge could exploit. Dodge's wife Anne also wished him to stay clear of the military. Other business and political associates, William B. Allison and Pete Reed, also implored Dodge to secure contracts from the government. However, Dodge was more interested in raising a regiment and getting a commission as a high-ranking officer. Dodge had no intention of just becoming a well-connected businessman during the Civil War. Dodge wanted into this fight.[20]

Grenville Dodge decided to have his old friend Peter Dey, who had been elected mayor of Iowa City, Iowa, in 1860, call upon Iowa governor Samuel J. Kirkwood.[21] Dodge wanted Dey to see if he couldn't get Dodge a colonelcy from Kirkwood so he could raise a regiment in western Iowa. At this time Grenville Dodge was 30 years old; he was known in railroad circles but not in the political realm. Dodge was a smallish man and was what some would call common-looking and ungainly. Years of looking through a surveyor's transit had given Dodge a stooped look; some even said Dodge looked sickly. Dexter Bloomer, a lawyer in Council Bluffs at this time, said of Dodge that he looked "a very ordinary man, small in stature, narrow in figure, with a small head on narrow shoulders.... I had no reason to anticipate for him much higher distinction. Still, he was self-asserting, and in some measure egotistical."[22] Dexter Bloomer wouldn't achieve much fame himself, but his wife Amelia Bloomer, did. Amelia became a leader in the woman's movement in 19th century America, and although she didn't invent them her name was attached to a certain style of woman's clothing of the time, "bloomers." These "bloomers" were long, baggy pants narrowing to a cuff at the ankles. They were usually worn below a skirt. They preserved the Victorian era's idea of decency but they allowed woman more unfettered movement underneath the long, full skirts of the Victorian period.

Kirkwood had many important Iowa politicians who wanted the brigadier-general slot and four colonelcies he had available. Kirkwood frankly didn't think Dodge had the stuff to be a top field commander. With Dodge being relatively unknown, how could he appoint Dodge when he had so many well-connected Iowa politicians clamoring for positions? Dey pointed out what a wonderful soldier Dodge would make, but the governor was unimpressed.[23]

Kirkwood had been elected governor of Iowa on the Republican ticket. He had gained the allegiance of all the abolitionists and members of the Underground Railroad in Iowa when he interfered with the extradition of Barclay Coppoc. Barclay Coppoc and his brother Edwin Coppoc had gone with John Brown on his infamous raid into the Federal Arsenal at Harper's Ferry, Virginia, in October of 1859. Brown and his men were trying to take the weapons at the arsenal, give them to the black slaves in the South, and create a slave insurrection whose ultimate goal was to end slavery in the southern United States. Edwin had been captured with Brown in the engine room of the arsenal, and he was tried immediately. On December 16, 1859, Edwin Coppoc was hanged.[24]

His brother, Barclay Coppoc, had managed to escape capture at Harper's Ferry. He went to Canada and came back home to Springdale, Iowa. Springdale was a hotbed of abolitionists and helpers on the Underground Railroad who regularly aided escaping slaves to freedom. The governor of Virginia tried to have Barclay Coppoc extradited to Virginia for trial, but Iowa governor Kirkwood refused on some technicalities of the extradition papers. The governor of Virginia corrected these technicalities, but after the new extradition papers were issued, Kirkwood claimed he could not find Barclay Coppoc. Barclay Coppoc was never brought to trial for the Harper's Ferry assault.[25]

Kirkwood was a good example of the new type of Republican politician elected in Iowa in the latter part of the 1850s. Iowa became a territory in 1838, encompassing the present state of Iowa and parts of Minnesota and North and South Dakota, although the Iowa territorial constitution forbids slavery. It wasn't common to see slaves, but enslaved humans were found in the Hawkeye territory before and after it had achieved territorial status. Usually the owners of these slaves were the wealthy and powerful, and no one wanted to charge them with owning slaves. Over half of the members of the first Iowa territorial legislature hailed from states that allowed slavery. Iowa's second territorial governor, John Chambers, appointed by President William Henry Harrison, owned slaves. Chambers had been an aide to Harrison during the War of 1812. Chambers, a former congressman from Kentucky, and his secretary both owned seven or eight slaves that they brought to the territory of Iowa.[26]

Most of the slaves in territorial Iowa were domestic slaves to their Southern-born masters. However, some slaves worked in the mines around Dubuque, and others worked in agricultural endeavors in the territory. Slaves were not common in territorial Iowa, but the several dozen who found themselves as slaves were supplying labor to the sparsely settled territory. Free black persons were a very small minority in the Iowa territory, and for the most part they were not welcomed. The whites in Iowa were very capricious when it came to the black population, whether they were slave or free. On one occasion, a slave miner who had made an agreement to buy his freedom from his Missouri master was being forced back to that slave state. The whites fought back, and the Missouri slave was allowed to stay in the Hawkeye state as a free man. On another occasion a free black man was killed when it was thought he had stolen something. When a doctor proclaimed they were killing the black man with their excessive whip lashings, the doctor was told to mind his own business or he would be next. The black man was killed; however, no evidence was ever produced that he had taken anything. The white mob members were never punished for this murder. The Iowa territory was somewhat similar to the majority of slave and free states and territories when it came to free blacks: Free blacks were only granted as much "freedom" as the local whites would permit. In some localities the whites were very tolerant to the free blacks, while in others they were very intolerant.

The Iowa territorial legislature made it clear in no uncertain terms that free blacks were not welcomed in the Iowa territory. Meeting for the first time in Burlington, Iowa, the assembly in 1839 quickly passed "An Act to Regulate Blacks and Mulattoes." This law required mulattoes and blacks to obtain from a court a certificate proving they were free within 20 days of entering the state. They then had to post a $500 bond.[27]

Any sheriff capturing a runaway slave had to return the person to his or her master. Southern masters could bring their slaves into the Iowa territory with impunity. The territorial legislature passed laws that only white males could vote, only white children could be educated in Iowa schools, and only white males could serve in the state militia. The statutes read that "a negro, mulatto, or Indian" could not be a witness in any case against a white person. At the second session of the territorial assembly, the members passed legislation that no black person could marry a white person. This was a matter that had been overlooked during the first meeting of the legislature.[28]

These statutes left little doubt in anyone's mind that white males would be the ruling class in territorial Iowa. Territorial Iowa, as would the future state of Iowa, had the longest border with a slave state (Missouri) that had no natural impediments such as rivers, mountains or rugged escarpments to keep fleeing slaves from entering the territory or state. The southern border between Iowa and Missouri was generally flat land, easily walked over. The lawmakers in territorial Iowa wanted to keep all fleeing slaves out of the "for whites only" state.

When Iowa became a state in 1846, attitudes were still much the same. The state constitution forbade slavery but also tried to keep free blacks out of the state. A $500 bond was supposed to be posted by a free black person to live in the state. A $500 bond would have been two years' working wages to many whites and blacks in Iowa, so this bond kept most free blacks out.

Iowa's first United States senators, George Wallace Jones and Augustus Caesar Dodge, were both racist and pro-slavery. Augustus Caesar Dodge was born in slave state Missouri and apparently was no close relative of Grenville's.

When Iowa was still a territory, George Wallace Jones brought slaves with him into the territory. Although born in Indiana, Jones had lived in slave state Missouri and was educated in slave state Kentucky. Jones quickly adjusted to slave society and bought human beings. In 1837 Jones was a delegate from the territory of Wisconsin, which included the area of what would become the state of Iowa. Jones sought to have Iowa recognized as its own territory and then eventually as a state. Former vice president John C. Calhoun of South Carolina, one of the most powerful men in Congress and a great proponent of slavery, blocked Jones' request to have the Iowa territory recognized. Calhoun predicted that Iowa would become a haven for abolitionists. Jones protested that he knew of no abolitionists in the state and even boasted of owning a dozen slaves himself. Calhoun predicted with some accuracy, "Wait until western Ohio, New York and New England shall pour their population into that section, and you will see Iowa some day grow to be the strongest abolitionist State in the Union."[29]

Calhoun would never know how close he was to the truth. However, men such as George Wallace Jones and Augustus Caesar Dodge from the fledgling state would fight to keep slavery alive and well in the nation and keep free blacks out of the Hawkeye state. The infamous Fugitive Slave Act of 1850 would give George Wallace Jones and Augustus Caesar Dodge a chance to show their true colors. This act made it compulsory for all Northerners to actively chase down fugitive slaves when they reached the Northern states. It also compelled Northern sheriffs to actively hunt and capture Southern fugitive slaves or face jail time or fines. G.W. Jones and A.C. Dodge and one other Northern senator were the only three senators from Northern states to vote for this horrific act.[30]

Grenville Dodge left Washington to make an appeal directly to Kirkwood in Iowa. But the governor had too many congressmen, other important state legislators, and influential businessmen in the state clamoring for colonelcies and the brigadier-general slot to give any high position to Dodge. Dodge then offered the service of the Council Bluffs Guards, which had been formed in Pottawatamie County in 1856. Dodge had been elected captain of that group when it looked as though an attack by hostile Native Americans was possible in western Iowa. Kirkwood told Dodge that he could serve the state better if he went back to Council Bluffs and captained his home guards to protect the western border of Iowa from any possible Indian attacks and its southern border from any invasion from pro-confederate Missourians. Dodge was bitterly disappointed. Dodge told Kirkwood he would go back to Washington and talk to Secretary of War Simon Cameron to see if he could obtain a high-ranking officer's position.

Kirkwood saw an opening. When the war first broke out, Kirkwood had borrowed money from friends to pay for equipment for Iowa soldiers. However, as thousands of

Iowans were joining Iowa units, this was no longer a practical way of equipping Iowa's regiments. The governor had been deeply frustrated by Iowa's senators and congressmen and their lack of success in obtaining guns, ammunition and other equipment for Iowa. Iowa was fast raising regiments, but many of them went weaponless for lack of arms. Iowa was still a frontier state vulnerable from the South from Rebel invasions and the West from hostile Native American attacks. Kirkwood had written to Secretary of War Cameron on April 29, 1861:

> I can raise 10,000 [troops] in this State in twenty days, but the state has not any arms.... Daily receiving letters from our northwestern frontier expressing alarm on account of Indians.... Don't ask for anything but arms, accouterments, and ammunition.... We have plenty of men willing to use them.... For God's sake, send us some.[31]

Kirkwood commissioned Dodge to obtain arms for Iowa to stop any hostile raids on the state. Also, Kirkwood had become very alarmed at the exposure of the southern border of Iowa to slave state Missouri. He appointed Judge Caleb Baldwin, then a justice of the Iowa Supreme Court, in charge of the military companies guarding Iowa's southern border. Kirkwood also named Dodge, Baldwin's adjutant. Besides Dodge's Council Bluffs Guards, other companies began patrolling Iowa's southern border, such as the Page County Rangers, the Frontier Guards and the Constitutional Guards.[32]

Later in the Civil War, Grenville Dodge became the best spymaster in the Western Theater during that conflict. Many others would fail at this spy game, even the great private eye Allan Pinkerton. In pursuing guns for the state of Iowa, Dodge showed the thoroughness and competency he would later develop in gathering intelligence. First he went to Fort Leavenworth in Kansas and was told there were no extra guns there. In St. Louis, Dodge had heard that there were some 3,000 muskets located at Fort Kearney in the Nebraska Territory. However, Dodge found out these arms were not available. Next Dodge went to St. Louis; the commander there, General Harney, told Dodge he thought some arms could be found at the Allegheny Arsenal near Pittsburgh, Pennsylvania.

Dodge headed to Washington, D.C., to call on Secretary of War Simon Cameron. But first Dodge spoke to the influential New York *Tribune* reporter in Washington, Fitz Henry Warren. Warren was a transplanted Iowan, and Dodge wanted to understand the political situation in the District. Warren offered the opinion that there were no arms to be found anywhere, as the states had already spoken for them. Warren called on Secretary of War Cameron and introduced him to Dodge. Dodge asked about getting arms for Iowa, but Cameron insisted that it was impossible to find any arms anywhere. Then Dodge politely asked whether, if he could find any arms anywhere, could he keep them for the Hawkeye state. Cameron replied, "Yes."

Dodge had a friend in the ordnance department, and he hurried over there. Dodge told the friend to check with the Allegheny Arsenal to see if they had any arms. The friend reported back that the arsenal had 6,000 smooth-bore Springfield muskets that had not been issued to any military unit. Dodge placed a man in charge of the muskets.

The Iowan went back to Secretary Cameron and told him of the Springfields at Allegheny Arsenal, saying he would hold the secretary to his word. Cameron at first hesitated, but he finally relented and gave Dodge the 6,000 Springfield arms. Cameron then asked Dodge to be a captain in the 15th U.S. Regular Infantry. Dodge told Cameron he had to go to an Iowa unit. Cameron then offered Dodge the colonelcy of the 4th Iowa Volunteer Infantry, which he eventually accepted. Governor Kirkwood was wired, and Kirkwood accepted the situation.[33]

The energetic Dodge then headed north to New York City to buy supplies for his troops. In New York, Dodge met up with Ezekiel Clark, a prominent banker in Iowa City, Iowa. Dodge and Clark went to procure supplies for the Iowa troops but quickly found out the state had no money and had issued no bonds for arms or supplies. The merchants in the Big Apple were reluctant to give Iowa any credit. So not only did the merchants demand paper from the state of Iowa; they also demanded that Dodge and Clark personally co-sign for the goods. Dodge noted that this was the first time he knew of when a personal signature had meant more than that of a state. Dodge went out on a limb and personally outfitted part of what would become the 4th Iowa regiment, hoping for some sort of reimbursement at a later date. Even by early October of 1861, Governor Kirkwood would write to "His Excellency the President" asking him, "Can you help us in the way of arms?" Kirkwood admitted to Lincoln in a postscript, "I forgot to say that by reason of our failure to sell our state bonds I have been and am wholly unable to buy arms for the State."[34]

When Dodge got back to Iowa, Camp Kirkwood had already been established just north of Mosquito Creek near Council Bluffs. One thousand men were already pouring into the camp. These would be the soldiers of the 4th Iowa Volunteer Infantry.[35]

As expected, when news reached the offices of the appointment of Grenville Dodge as a colonel of the 4th Iowa Volunteer Infantry, the politically unfriendly Council Bluffs *Bugle* said, "Notwithstanding our political hostilities towards him, we will do him the justice to say that as neighbor and citizen; we entertain the highest respect for him." The *Bugle* went on to state, incorrectly, that Dodge was a graduate of West Point Military Academy.[36]

The Council Bluffs *Nonpareil* stated, "We hazard nothing in saying that Col. Dodge will make as efficient and accomplished an officer as any one of the many men who have been called from the civil pursuits of life into the army raised for the purpose of asserting the supremacy of this Government." The *Nonpareil* correctly reported that Dodge had graduated from the Norwich (Vermont) Military School and had additional military training under Captain Partridge.[37]

Samuel J. Kirkwood was known as Iowa's wartime governor (1860–1864). Early in his governorship Kirkwood showed his commitment to the anti-slavery and abolitionist cause. When Dodge applied to become a colonel of an Iowa regiment, Kirkwood demurred; however, after seeing Dodge's energy, grit and intelligence, Kirkwood relented and made Dodge the regimental colonel and organizer of the 4th Iowa Volunteer Infantry Regiment. In time, Kirkwood became a big supporter and ally of Dodge (Library of Congress).

## 1. War Comes to the Prairies 19

Dodge kept hearing from his business associates who wanted to make deals with the war pending. Charles W. Durant was disappointed that Dodge had left New York. He wrote Dodge, "Had you remained here [in New York] we could have made something out of war contracts. There has undoubtedly been and will still be good pickings. If this war should be protracted there will be plenty of good chances and if we should make up our minds that it would last one or two years. I think it would pay us to spend some time in Washington and see what could be done. Write me what you think of it." However, Grenville Dodge had more pressing matters on his mind than war contracts. He had a mob of raw recruits to train and turn into a professional fighting force. Dodge also didn't have a lot of time in which to do this.[38]

In the beginning, almost all the soldiers joining the 4th Iowa Volunteer Infantry were from the western and southwestern Iowa region. Company A was filled with recruits from Mills, Fremont, Warren and Madison counties. At this time, the covered wooden bridges had not even been built in Madison County that would bring them so much fame in Robert James Waller's bestselling novel *The Bridges of Madison County* a hundred-plus years later. Company B was made up of men from Pottawattamie, Harrison, Cass and Shelby counties. Many of the men in Dodge's old Council Bluffs Guards unit were in this company. Company C saw Guthrie and Dallas counties represented. Company D was filled with recruits from Decatur and Clarke counties. Company E had men from Polk, Warren and Dallas counties. Polk was the county where the state capital, Des Moines, was located. Company F was represented by the men from Madison County. Company G was filled by men from Ringgold County. Company H had recruits from Adams and Union counties. Company I was made up of men from Wayne County. Company K was made up of men from Page, Montgomery and Taylor counties.

After the unit had been in the field for some time, replacements came from different parts of Iowa but still mainly the western and southwestern region. There were a few men who came from outside of Iowa to join the 4th. Some good Union men from the state of Missouri joined; 20 of the men were foreign-born. Only 15 of the 1,005 men originally recruited by the 4th were born in Iowa. Most had migrated to the state of Iowa before the war started. The states of Ohio, Indiana and Pennsylvania were the birthplace of 70 percent of the men originally recruited. One of the few men in the unit to be born in Iowa was 18-year-old Aden King. King was residing in Batesville, Arkansas, when the war started. The average age of the soldiers in the regiment originally recruited was 24.[39]

Dodge waited for the 6,000 Springfields he had procured in Washington, D.C., from the Allegheny Arsenal to train the 4th Iowa Infantry and others who were at Camp Kirkwood. But to his dismay, these arms were hijacked by other regiments in Keokuk, Iowa. The 1st Iowa Infantry Regiment and the 2nd Iowa Infantry Regiment were being organized in Keokuk, and they received these muskets. These weapons never got to Dodge, so the 4th Iowa Infantry had to drill with old Prussian-made muskets that some said were more dangerous at the butt than at the muzzle.

Grenville Dodge, ever since his college military training at Norwich, had been interested in artillery. He got permission to raise an artillery battery. The battery became known as the Dodge Battery. Dodge made Nelson T. Spoor the battery's captain and J.R. Reed its first lieutenant. One of the enlisted men in the Dodge Battery was 17-year-old Lewis F. Phillips. Two of Lewis Phillips' sons, Frank Phillips and Lee Eldas Phillips, struck it rich in the oil fields of Oklahoma after the turn of the century. In 1917, they formed the Phillips Petroleum Company, which became better known as Phillips 66. However, Lincoln's secretary of war, Cameron, wrote to Iowa governor Kirkwood and said, "Dodge's artillery battery cannot be attached to any particular regiment." What was known as Dodge's Battery became known as the 2nd Battery Iowa Light Artillery. Grenville Dodge was quickly learning the ways of the army. Sometimes the cool logic of a surveyors' transit didn't always resonant with the military bureaucrats in Washington, D.C.[40]

As a newly appointed colonel, Grenville Dodge began to train the 4th Iowa Volunteers, and his men noticed something. Dodge trained right alongside his men. This would be a wartime trait of Dodge's. Dodge was a hands-on type of leader. When the bullets started flying, he would be right there with his men, not in some headquarters tent miles away from the front. The men of the 4th Iowa Volunteers didn't know it at this time, but Grenville Dodge was one of the best military leaders in the Union army. Unlike many in command positions in the Union army, Dodge had actually had military training.

Grenville Mellen Dodge was born in Danvers, Essex County, Massachusetts, on April 12, 1831.[41] Dodge's parents were Sylvanus and Julia Theresa (Phillips) Dodge, who were married in 1827.[42] The house Grenville was born in was already 100 years old when his birth occurred. The original house had been over 200 years old but had been destroyed by fire. Another family, the Putnams, persons of some distinction, lived in the other half of the house. Sylvanus Dodge moved his growing family from South Danvers (later to be known as Peabody, Massachusetts) several times, including to Salem, Lynn, and Tapleyville.[43]

In his typewritten autobiography Grenville insists that he was the second son born to his parents. However, he never gives the name of the first son born to Sylvanus and Julia Dodge. Dodge's brother Nathan Phillips Dodge, named after his mother's father, was born in South Danvers on August 20, 1837. A daughter was born to Sylvanus and Julia Dodge on January 17, 1843, in Tapleyville. The Dodges named their only daughter Julia Mary.[44]

Sylvanus and Julia Dodge had also named their first son Grenville Mellen Dodge. This infant only lived from his birth date on September 23, 1829, to October 6, 1829. It was not unusual, at this time, to give the name of an infant who had passed away to another child born later into the family. This practice was often done to keep family names alive or to honor a much-revered relative. It was, however, a little unusual to give the exact name of a deceased infant to the next child born.[45]

Although Grenville describes his father as a merchant, the constant moving would indicate that his business ventures proved to be none too successful. In 15 years, the Dodge family moved nine times. It was during one of these moves, to Salem, Massachusetts, that Sylvanus came into contact and became friends with Nathaniel Hawthorne. Sylvanus Dodge had amassed debts, and two severe bouts with typhoid fever seemed to sap his strength. Many old-timers in the Danvers area said that mother Julia Dodge was the rock that kept the family together. Friends of the family remember Sylvanus asking to borrow money. However, after supporting Democrat James K. Polk for president in 1844, Sylvanus Dodge was named postmaster for South Danvers. Sylvanus' 10-year stint as postmaster finally provided much-needed financial stability to his family. While postmaster, Sylvanus also opened a bookstore in the back of the post office. Sylvanus saw himself as a promoter of literature, and he liked to point out that he was a friend of Nathaniel Hawthorne.[46]

Grenville Dodge stated that the Dodge family, Richard Dodge and his brother William, had emigrated from England on the *Lion's Whelp* in 1629 and settled in Essex County in Massachusetts. In his usual optimistic style, Grenville portrayed his father and mother and other relatives as idyllic. Grenville stated that his father was "a man with much natural talent, a ready talker, an original thinker, generous almost to a fault, filling many positions of honor and trust." Grenville goes on to say that his mother "was a beautiful woman, brilliant and very quick at repartee; had a very kind heart, very energetic and very tenacious of her opinion, very active and almost always accomplished whatever she undertook."

Grenville describes his grandfather Captain Solomon Dodge as being "truly a public benefactor, always ready to help the poor and needy and to aid in every charitable work." Dodge goes on to say that his grandfather was an innovator. His grandfather was a miller and market man. All the others brought their goods to the markets in Salem, Massachusetts, in carts and saddle bags. Solomon was the first to use a four-wheeled wagon.

Grenville Dodge was very proud of his great-uncle William B. Dodge. William was a school teacher in Salem, Massachusetts. William taught at the first "colored school" in the area. Grenville Dodge stated that the churches in Salem were "closed against" Uncle William because "it was considered a desecration to their pulpit to plead the cause of the slave." Dodge went on to say that William was considered "a Christian gentleman of the old puritanical school of Orthodox, very popular in all his ideas, except in his sympathy for the poor and oppressed." Dodge's mother Julia (Phillips) claimed that she was related to Wendell Phillips, the noted abolitionist.[47]

Grenville Dodge was a bright child, but he, as did others, only attended school during the winter months so as to accommodate the agricultural seasons of work. Dodge went to labor in his father's butcher business at age eight; his grandfather Solomon Dodge also conducted a door-to-door butcher trade. Sylvanus' butcher business ended when he was appointed postmaster. Grenville found himself in the summer working at another butcher shop for a Mr. Fairfield. During the wintertime Grenville began working in his father's book shop and clerking in the grocery store of Lambert and Merrill.[48]

Grenville then went to work at a large farming operation run by Mrs. Eliza Lander from 1846 to 1848. The Landers were very wealthy and were considered to be royalty in that part of Massachusetts. On the maternal side, Eliza (West) Lander was a member of one of the wealthiest families of the young United States. Her grandfather Elias Haskett Derby had loaned ships and supplies to the young revolutionaries in America. He had also made a bundle as a privateer against the British Crown. A privateer was in actuality a pirate authorized by the United States government to attack and rob British vessels of their cargo. After the Revolutionary War, Derby had opened trade with India and made Salem, Massachusetts, one of the great mercantile ports in young America.

Derby had turned Salem from a sleepy little village, with an embarrassing past of hanging unfortunates whom they claimed to be witches, into the sixth largest city in the United States at that time. Eliza's mother Elizabeth had married a dashing privateer, Nathaniel West, who captained the *Black Prince*. When Elias Derby passed away, in 1799, he left a fortune to his son-in-law Nathaniel West and his daughter Elizabeth.

Elizabeth (Derby) West shocked New England society, in 1806, when she sued Nathaniel West for divorce. Apparently Nathaniel West had been unfaithful to his wife, and Elizabeth in open court told of West's wanderings into the "Brothels of Boston" and his meetings with the "vile wretches" of the underbelly of that city. Elizabeth was able to regain her father's fortune from her wayward husband. The fourth child of Captain West and Elizabeth was Eliza. Eliza had married Edward Lander in 1813, a merchant whose family had impressive roots in the young United States.[49]

Through his intelligence and energy young Grenville was put in charge of all the fruits, vegetables and milk products on the farm that were sold in Salem. During the evenings and any free time Grenville had, he studied to take college courses. The association with the Lander family would prove to be life-changing for Grenville.

One of Mrs. Lander's sons, Frederick, had been a cadet and civil engineer at Norwich University in Vermont. Another son, Charles, was buying up old meeting houses in that area of Massachusetts, moving them to Wenham Lake and turning them into ice houses. To aid in the ice business, a very important and profitable business for the time, Frederick was building a short rail line from the ice houses to the Eastern Railroad. Grenville took part in the surveying of this line, and he realized this could become his life's work. Frederick also encouraged Grenville to go to Norwich University, get a degree in civil engineering and learn the ways of the military.[50]

Frederick W. Lander was certainly someone the young Dodge could look to for inspiration. Lander was smart, handsome, and tall, and had incredible strength. In 1858, Lander was out West; he surveyed and constructed the first federally funded road west of the Mississippi at the Lander cut-off in Wyoming. This road was still in use some 54 years later—until 1912, in fact—and was a great help in getting pioneers to the West Coast and other locations in the West. Frederick W. Lander had Lander, Wyoming and Lander counties in Nevada named after him.[51]

In 1860, in true storybook fashion, the golden boy Frederick W. Lander married a beautiful English actress, Jean Margaret Davenport. Lander and Davenport settled in California on a large ranch. Davenport was a child actress who at the early age of eight had graced America stages. She would go on to gain renown in most of the major cities in America, England and Ireland playing a wide variety of roles, including her much praised role of Lady Macbeth. During the Civil War Davenport and her mother would become well-known nurses to the Union army.[52]

At the beginning of the Civil War, Frederick W. Lander left California and joined the 19th Massachusetts, where he rose to the rank of brigadier-general. He was with McClellan's army and stationed in Western Virginia. On October 22, 1861, at Edwards Ferry, Lander was wounded in the leg in what was considered a non-life-threatening situation. Lander stayed in command of his troops and drove himself very hard. On the 2nd of March 1862, Lander finally succumbed to complications from this leg wound.

Most of McClellan's command officers were stunned by the death of Lander. Lander was the man General Winfield Scott called the "Great Natural American Soldier."[53]

Dodge started to formulate a plan for his life, but knew he wasn't ready for the academic rigors of college. During the winter of 1847–48, Dodge went to the Academy at Durham, New Hampshire, to prepare for Norwich University. Grenville's mother noted his somewhat shabby clothes and suggested her son should buy himself a new coat. However, Dodge reasoned that he would be better off saving his money for college instead of worrying about his wardrobe. He was saving $14 a month for college. At this time, Norwich University cost $49 a year for tuition, room and board. Incidentals were extra. In September of 1848, Dodge entered Norwich University, located at that time in Norwich, Vermont.[54]

Norwich University was a unique institution, founded by Captain Alden Partridge. Partridge had at one time been the superintendent at the military academy in West Point. He tried to develop what he called the "American System of Education." He met with resistance for his system at West Point, so in 1819 Partridge formed what would become Norwich University, the oldest private military college (later university) in the United States. He believed a liberal arts education would provide the nation with well-rounded individuals. He also believed students should be knowledgeable in the military arts so that if called on by the military for service, they could be useful to the young nation. Partridge believed in citizen-soldiers. Partridge believed his college prepared youth "to discharge, in the best possible manner, the duties they owe to themselves, to their fellow-men, and to their country." Partridge felt a large standing army was a danger to the republic. He felt a cadre of civilian officers should be available who understood the military arts but were also educated in the elements of government, business and agriculture.[55]

At the time Dodge attended Norwich it only had seven faculty members and had 60 students enrolled. Grenville would later assert that he learned disciple and obedience at Norwich. However, several entries in his personal diaries indicate he was somewhat rebellious and even obnoxious. One night Dodge and several of his classmates went after hours to a dance. For this, they were disciplined for three months by being sent to the strict Methodist Thetford College in Newbury, Vermont. While at Thetford College, Dodge and his fellow exiled Norwich cadets delighted in fisticuffs with the locals. Dodge would later say in his dairy, "How we used to gum the Profs and cheat the buttery, steal marches on the steward and sneak around at night with those vixens will often be told in times to come."[56]

Dodge was allowed back into Norwich in the fall of 1849. He tended to his studies, but there were times when the boys from neighboring Dartmouth College and the Norwich cadets would tangle. Dodge always seemed to have an eye out for the fairer sex, and the young ladies of Vermont and New England seemed to be impressed by the cadets' uniforms. Dodge reported on several occasions in his dairies that he took "French leave" from the college to attend a dance and stir up a fuss. However, as money from home came less frequently, Dodge was forced to do all sorts of odd jobs around the Norwich campus to keep himself in school. He even became the assistant janitor at one of the college buildings.

In 1850, Norwich University was hardly an abolitionist stronghold, even though many high-ranking Civil War Union army and naval officers would eventually graduate from Norwich. At this time, they were not advocating the end of slavery and certainly were not for equal rights for black people. In addition, among many Protestants, because they feared the large number of Catholic immigrants from Ireland due to the potato famine and from Germany, there was a concern that Catholicism and other so-called undesirable foreign elements were taking over the country. In his diary he tells of an anti-slavery Englishman who spoke in Springfield, Massachusetts; Dodge felt the Englishman should be run out of the country. In addition, in his diary Dodge tells of heckling a fugitive slave, along with other Norwich cadets, who came to Norwich to speak of the horrors of slavery. Dodge relates another incident in his diary of eating in a Boston, Massachusetts, restaurant. The server in the restaurant was a young black man, who Dodge calls a "nigger" in his diary. Apparently, the young server looked at Dodge's brass buttons too long; this irritated Dodge, so he pushed a plate of stewed oysters into the unfortunate man's face. Dodge says the other white patrons eulogized him for his actions.[57] Fortunately, by the time Dodge joined the Republican Party in Iowa in the late 1850s, many of his views on race had changed. Certainly during the Civil War Dodge's views about Catholics and foreign-born Americans would change. Many Irish- and German-born units carried the Union banner.[58]

Grenville plunged into his studies even though it was hard paying the tuition and other college costs. Railroad construction was booming in America at this time, and civil engineers were much in demand by this industry. Many students came to Norwich University, took the minimum amount of engineering classes, and left school before graduating. These former students would quickly find high-paying civil engineering jobs with the railroads, as the demand was so great.[59]

However, Grenville was determined to graduate from Norwich University, and he did. Despite his sometimes mischievous behavior, Dodge graduated from Norwich University with good grades during the midwinter term of 1850–1851. Dodge had earned a degree in civil and military engineering and graduated in the scientific course of that institution. Dodge then enrolled in Captain Alden Partridge's private school with special emphases on field military instruction. This course lasted from January until June of 1851.[60]

Captain Alden Partridge's Norwich University would always hold a special place in Grenville M. Dodge's heart. When Professor William Arba Ellis wanted to publish his large, three-volume work *Norwich University 1819–1911, Her History, Her Graduates, Her Roll of Honor*, Grenville Dodge paid for the publishing of this important book of Norwich University's history.[61]

While at Norwich, Grenville had another meeting with a well-connected family that would serve him well on his career path. Dodge while at Norwich had boarded with Mrs. Truman B. Ransom. Mrs. Ransom was the widow of Truman B. Ransom, who at one time had been the president of Norwich University. When the Mexican War came along Truman B. Ransom became a major in the 9th United States Infantry or, as it was sometimes known, the New England Regiment. Ransom then ascended to the rank of colonel when future President Franklin Pierce was promoted from colonel to brigadier-general.

Guarding the way to Mexico City, the prize the American Army was trying to capture during the Mexican War in 1847, lay the fortress at Chapultepec. This castle was atop a 200-foot embankment and housed the Mexican Military Academy. Mexican general Antonio Lopez de Santa Anna knew Chapultepec was one of the keys to the defense of Mexico City. General Winfield Scott opened up a barrage of artillery fire on the fortress, but to no avail. The castle would have to be stormed with a direct assault. The assault was successful, but Colonel Truman B. Ransom lost his life in the attack. Colonel Truman B. Ransom gave the ultimate sacrifice and became a real-life model for the ideals of Norwich University and her concept of citizen-soldiers.[62]

While boarding at the Ransom house, Grenville Dodge became a friend of Truman B. Ransom's three sons. Two of the Ransom brothers headed out West to be with their uncle George W. Gilson in Peru, Illinois. Gilson was well connected in Illinois. Gilson was an associate of Stephen Douglas; he was a surveyor, he had connections in the railroad world and he was a member of the Illinois legislature. The Ransom brothers wrote back to Grenville of opportunities in the West for men like him. After graduating from Captain Partridge's military class Grenville decided he would head to Illinois. The Dodge family was somewhat dismayed that Grenville was not going to stay in the New England area, but Grenville became convinced that the West was where he should seek his fortune.

If Dodge had a crystal ball he could not have picked a better place than Illinois in the 1850s to start his career as a surveyor and railroad builder. Chicago, then a town of 30,000 with three railroads in its midst, would grow within the decade four times over, with more than a dozen railroads using this location as their hub. Railroads were spreading like a web over the Illinois prairies. Senator Douglas had made sure railroads such as the Illinois Central would receive millions of acres of land in exchange for development of their tracks. The Illinois Central became the first land-grant railroad in the United States. After Illinois, no state needed a railroad system more than its neighbor Iowa, the Hawkeye state. With the Mississippi River on its eastern border and the Missouri River on its west, Iowa was in dire need of reliable transportation to ensure the settlement of the interior of that state, especially after the state capital was moved to Des Moines, in the central part of the state in 1857. The people of Illinois and Iowa both understood that railroads were the keys to their settlement and success.[63]

Dodge's trip to Peru, Illinois, was not without incident. Dodge made his way to Niagara Falls, New York, where he visited friends. These friends asked him to escort the unmarried niece of Levi Woodbury, an associate justice of the United States Supreme Court, to Cleveland where she was to meet relatives. They made their way to Buffalo, where they took passage on the steamer *Bay State*, bound for Cleveland. The boat was overflowing with passengers, as were many of the conveyances out to the West, and a stormy night proved the ship's undoing. The upper part of the ship split apart, but the hull was still intact. There was much consternation amongst the passengers, but Dodge noted that his female charge was taking the incident in stride. The *Bay State* seemed incapable of making it into the harbor at Cleveland. Another boat attempted to tow the *Bay State* into harbor using a hawser, but this boat capsized and all on it were lost. Finally, the *Bay State* made it into the harbor at Cleveland under its own power, and Dodge was able to deliver his charge to her relatives in Cleveland.

From Cleveland Dodge went by steamer to Detroit and then railroaded across

Michigan. From Michigan City, he took the steamer *Baltimore* to Chicago. This steamer too was vastly overbooked, and Dodge had to sleep on top of a cabin dining table. When Dodge awoke in the morning, he found two feet of water in the dining room and learned that the *Baltimore* had sunk at the dock in Chicago. From Chicago Dodge went on a small ship that ran on the canal from Chicago to LaSalle, Illinois. Dodge noted that there was a curious crowd on this boat. They spent most of their time up on the deck shooting at bull snakes that lay sunning themselves on the rocks through which the canal had been dug. Dodge also noted the bad shooting, as very few snakes were being hit. Grenville had learned to be a good shot at Norwich and he went down below, got out his pistol, and hit a snake on his first shot. The other passengers were duly impressed. It took a day and a night to make it to LaSalle. Peru, Illinois lay a short distance from LaSalle.

Dodge then went to ask the skipper of the boat, a Captain Wheeler, about the best way to get to Peru. Captain Wheeler was talking in a rather animated fashion to a man when another man came up and shot the man Wheeler had been talking with. Dodge noted that this shooting did not seem to create much excitement. Grenville had enough sense to quickly exit the scene and make his way to Peru via an omnibus. Once in Peru, Dodge quickly made it to Mr. Gilson's office. On the way, Dodge noted a party of men on the Illinois River pulling the dead body of a soldier out of the river. He went down to the river to investigate. Dodge began to wonder what kind of a country he now resided in. In his hometown of Danvers, Massachusetts, these incidents of death would have brought out the whole town but in the West, they barely caused a stir.

After conversing with Gilson and the Ransom boys Dodge found himself surveying town lots in Peru. Working for two dollars a day, Grenville showed he had an aptitude for working outside in difficult conditions. In the past three years, Peru, Illinois, had become a boomtown, and people were buying up lots as fast as they could be surveyed. One night when Dodge came home from work a prairie fire swept across the farms around Peru. Grenville was impressed by the destruction these fires wrought on the local farmsteads.[64]

While at Peru Grenville got his first real taste of railroad surveying. Ironically, it was with the Illinois Central, which was running a line from LaSalle to Dixon, Illinois. Dodge's benefactor Gilson had connections with the Rock Island Railroad, but by this time, Dodge had gained enough experience to go out on his own.

Dodge started in January of 1852. It was a bitterly cold winter, and the chief surveyor stayed inside in the warmth and let Dodge run the crew in the elements. Dodge became upset with this situation, and when the surveying job was done, he gave them his resignation and left the employment of the Illinois Central. Years later Grenville learned that the division engineer was surprised at Dodge's action; was greatly impressed with Dodge's work and had been prepared to make him the head of the surveying party.

When Dodge lived in Peru the town, although it had a population of only about 2,000, felt it would surpass Chicago in importance some day. There was a lively social scene there, and Dodge spent some time going to dances and such. He met a young lady there, Ruth Anne Brown, to whom he took a liking. Ruth Anne usually went by the name of Anne. Miss Brown, like many other young ladies of the West, could ride a horse and shoot with the best of them. Miss Brown was the daughter of a banker, and she could claim ancestry clear to William Bradford on her mother's side. (Bradford had sailed for America on the *Mayflower* and had become governor of the Plymouth Colony.) Miss Brown had brown hair and blue eyes, and Dodge was proud to say most considered her pretty and—not withstanding her proficiency in firearms and as an equestrian—completely feminine.

With Ned Ransom, Dodge found a couple of old cannons. They cleaned them up, made them operational, and formed an artillery squad. When a construction crew on the Illinois Central went on strike, Dodge brought out the artillery squad and forced the construction crew to go back to work.[65]

Dodge's mind was always active on the topic of making money. Dodge had noticed that the land through which the railroads were building was doubling, tripling or sometimes quadrupling in value. He wrote to his father Sylvanus Dodge to buy up old Mexican War warrants from widows and orphans for $100. With each warrant he could purchase 160 acres of land in Illinois and quickly sell it for several times more than it had been purchased for. However, Sylvanus did not have any extra money to buy up these warrants. Nevertheless, Dodge was able to avail others of this moneymaking scheme, and they made a nice profit.[66]

Dodge went back to work for Gilson. However, soon after, in the fall of 1852, he was hired by the Rock Island Railroad for surveying work. This would have a profound effect on Dodge's career and life. The Illinois Central Railroad had been mainly interested in running its rails from Chicago in the north to points in southern Illinois. The Rock Island Railroad was interested in developing its line to the west of Chicago through Illinois and into the Hawkeye state. Also, at the Rock Island Railroad was Peter Dey. Dey was one of the best civil engineers in the United States, and he developed extreme confidence in Dodge's abilities. Dey would become extremely influential in railroad circles and in politics in Iowa.

Dey eventually put Dodge in charge of his own surveying crew. When Joseph Sheffield, Henry Farnam and others of the Rock Island Railroad organized the Mississippi and Missouri Railroad to survey across Iowa for the purpose of laying tracks, Peter Dey was named chief engineer. Dey then named Dodge as his principal assistant.[67]

On May 17, 1853, Dodge and others moved across the Mississippi River at Rock Island for the purpose of moving into the Hawkeye state. Almost immediately, Dodge ran into opposition. Antoine Le Claire, a large man of 300 pounds, was a trader of French and Native American heritage. Le Claire objected to Dodge's running his railroad through his property. Dodge protested that the bridge across the Mississippi River dictated where the railroad tracks were to be laid. Le Claire, who was used to getting his way, went over Dodge's head to Peter Dey. However, Dey backed Dodge's survey. Le Claire was mollified when the value of his land increased by a considerable sum due to its proximity to the railroads. Dodge and his surveying crew went from Davenport on the Iowa side to Iowa City, a distance of 54 miles. Dodge had a crew of two wagons, fourteen men and six horses. His expenses were $1,000 a month, a large amount for this time.

However, Dodge and the Rock Island and the Mississippi and Missouri railroads were not alone in wanting to push a rail line across the state of Iowa. The Lyon and Iowa Central Line also wanted to bring the iron horse to the Hawkeye plains. Sam

Curtis, who would become Dodge's commanding officer at the battle of Pea Ridge, headed the Iowa Central. Iowa Central had a two-week advance start on Dodge, but Dodge soon caught up with them.

When Dodge got to the spot where Grinnell, Iowa, would be located, he erected a flagpole there. Dodge then pushed the survey crew onto Des Moines, then only a small village. He purchased some forty acres for a depot grounds and then pushed the survey west of Des Moines.[68]

Josiah Bushnell Grinnell became an important figure in Iowa history. Although a Congregational minister, Grinnell's ambition was much broader than herding a church's flock. Grinnell became one of the largest wool merchants in Iowa. He studied law, became a licensed attorney, and eventually became a United States congressman.[69]

Grinnell's wife was wealthy, and she had inherited a large farm of 640 acres in Marion County, Missouri, near Hannibal. After a conversation with railroad executive Henry Farnam, who advised Grinnell to seek his fortune in free state Iowa rather than slave state Missouri, Grinnell sought out Grenville Dodge, the main surveyor, as to the best spot for a town on the railway line. Dodge advised Grinnell of the place where he had put a flagpole. Grinnell erected a town on that spot. He became involved in the Underground Railroad and also started a college, which still bears his name today.[70]

West of Des Moines the Dodge crew moved the line 12 miles on the north side of the Raccoon River to where a relative of Daniel Boone lived. The autumn colors of west-central Iowa were putting on their annual show for the Dodge crew, with blazing sumac, yellow willows, colorful hard maples, silvers wild grasses and tall cottonwoods. However, even this fall show could not keep Dodge's crew from becoming ill. The crew was shrinking due to sickness with fevers and the ague. During the weeks out on the open prairies, some of Dodge's survey crew began to contract the ague, a fever-like malady, and they were in no condition to work. Dodge had to resort to hiring local workers to fill in the gaps on his survey crew.

There was one young man in particular who watched Dodge and his crew, a local lad named Wiley Lane. However, he was only 16 years old. Dodge asked Lane if he would like to join the survey crew, and the boy said yes—if it was okay with his mother. Dodge went personally to see Lane's mother to ask her if Wiley could join the survey crew. His mother consented, and Wiley Lane became an important member of the crew. Lane was an excellent axe man and well versed in all manner of woodcraft. However, his true hidden talent was in following bees to their hives and extracting their honey. Young Lane kept the Dodge survey crew in honey all the way to the Missouri River. Honey was considered a luxury food item to those on the open prairie, and Dodge's men felt they were blessed with the addition of Wiley Lane and his ability to locate honey.

West of Des Moines, the Hawkeye state was lightly settled. The Dodge crew pressed on, following the Raccoon River to Beaver Creek, then on to Troublesome Creek, finally reaching the East Nishnabotna River. The East and West Nishnabotna rivers were branches of one of the main rivers in western and southwestern Iowa. When his party got to Cuppy's Grove, Dodge realized they were out of meat, and he went looking for a deer. Grenville still considered himself to be one of the best shots in his survey party. When Dodge was near the Boone cabin, he had killed a panther that came near him.

Dodge almost mistook Ad Cuppy, the owner of the grove, for a deer. Cuppy hollered out, "For God's sake don't shoot me." Cuppy then gave Dodge good intelligence about this lightly settled area of Iowa.[71]

Peter Dey, the head engineer and Dodge's immediate superior, had started out from Iowa City with a team and a wagon. Dey had much-needed provisions and mail for Dodge's crew. Dey brought with him a young tenderfoot by the name of Bacon. Bacon had graduated from Yale University and was the son of a noted minister, the Reverend Dr. Bacon. Bacon was now a correspondent for the New York *Tribune* newspaper; he wished to tell the readers back East of this new country in Iowa. Dey and Bacon had all sorts of trouble on the open prairie, most of all crossing the rivers and streams, most of which had no bridges. Dodge and his survey crew had made good time and were much farther west than Dey had thought. To catch up with Dodge, Dey parked the wagon and took the team of horses. He and Bacon threw blankets over them and rode.

The next morning Bacon, not used to riding a horse, was very sore and lame. Bacon told Dey to go on without him. Dey told Bacon to follow the stakes of the survey crew and catch up with them as soon as he recovered. Dey proceeded on and caught up with Dodge's survey crew. However, after some time had passed Dey became very concerned that Bacon was still not in camp.

Dodge offered to go back and try to find Bacon, and started out. At every stream and river crossing, Dodge yelled at the top of his lungs for Bacon, but to no avail. Dodge ran into a band of Otoe Native Americans who had been south in Missouri, hunting hogs. Their ponies were loaded with the hog meat. For a few tense moments, the Otoe thought Dodge might have been a Missouri farmer whose hogs they had slaughtered and was chasing them into Iowa. However, after looking each other over, the Otoe and Dodge departed, each convinced the other was not interested. When Dodge reached the point on Indian Creek where Dey said he had left Bacon, Dodge became convinced that Bacon was lost. Dodge went back to camp and decided the whole crew must go on a search for the lost newspaperman.

Dodge and the survey crew made a systematic search for Bacon. A teamster named Thompson found Bacon staggering out on the prairie some twenty miles south of the survey line. The newspaperman had been three days without food. Instead of heading west, Bacon had veered to the south. The fact that it was Thompson who found Bacon was ironic, because in Iowa City Thompson had taken his watch into a watch repair shop to have it fixed. When the watch repairman had found out Bacon was headed out to resupply the Dodge survey crew, he gave Bacon Thompson's repaired watch to give it to him. This was how things were done on the frontier. After Bacon had recovered, he gave the readers of the New York *Tribune* a graphic account of being lost and then found. Bacon stayed with the survey crew but got lost again when they reached the Missouri River Valley. Dodge heard later that Bacon returned to the East, probably figuring he was not cut out for this country. Bacon became a prominent lawyer in Rochester, New York.

Dodge and Dey took off the next day to scout for a new campsite. They followed Pigeon Creek. They ran into a camp of Otoe Indians—a different group from the ones with the Missouri hog meat. This band of Otoe had just returned from a fight with the powerful Sioux. Dodge and Dey found a suitable campsite near a deserted Mormon house.[72]

Five days later on November 22, 1853, Dodge had pushed his crew to Kanesville, Iowa, on the banks of the Missouri River. Kanesville had recently changed its name to Council Bluffs. Council Bluffs had grown to be the largest settlement in southwestern Iowa. The bluffs of Council Bluffs were actually a part of the Loess Hills. The Loess Hills are a geological phenomenon made of windblown silt, much of it lightweight, porous material tightly packed between grains of quartz, feldspar, mica and other material. The Loess Hills rise 200 feet from the Missouri River bottoms and run approximately 200 miles parallel with the Missouri River in northern Missouri to northern Iowa.[73]

The Council Bluffs area had always been an active area for Native Americans. Twenty miles to the south of Council Bluffs in pre–Columbian times, approximately from A.D. 1000 to A.D. 1400, a large community of Native Americans lived who built earthen lodges. Almost 1,000 of these earthen lodges were built and at one time, it is believed that 10,000 people lived in this community. They farmed the bottomlands of the Missouri River and lived in their earthen lodges, which were located in the Loess Hills. The center of this community was near the confluence of the Platte and Missouri rivers.[74]

By 1838 Sauganash, also known as Billy Caldwell, led some 2,000 Potawatomi tribesmen to live at the present site of Council Bluffs. Sauganash had signed treaties giving up the area where Chicago now stands, and he and his band were to move west. Soon Father Pierre-Jean De Smet founded the St. Joseph Mission in the Council Bluffs area to convert the Potawatomi to Christianity. De Smet, however, had little success in this endeavor. United States dragoons built a small fort, Fort Croghan, in the area. More and more tribes of Native American were being pushed into this general region, a profitable and illegal whiskey trade sprang up, and the fort tried to keep this activity in check.

By 1846 after continuing violence against them in Nauvoo, Illinois, Mormons began settling in the Council Bluffs region. Thomas Leipe Kane, although not a Mormon, became a champion for this group. He helped form the Mormon Battalion that marched from Council Bluffs to San Diego during the Mexican War. Kane also secured the rights for refugee Mormons to live on Potawatomi and Omaha tribal lands in what is now Council Bluffs. In appreciation for his work for them, the Mormons named this community Kanesville.

It is estimated that almost 32,000 Mormons came through Kanesville on their way west to Utah. On December 6, 1847, a large Mormon tabernacle was built in Kanesville. Over 200 men helped build the tabernacle, and it was built in two and a half weeks. After gold was discovered in California, Kanesville saw some 10,000 gold-seekers pass through the community.[75]

However, by 1852, the Mormon influence in the city had waned and the city changed its name from Kanesville to Council Bluffs. When Dodge and Dey reached the city, they were treated like royalty. Council Bluffs certainly understood the importance of a railroad coming to the city. Grenville Dodge's brother Nathan described early Council Bluffs as "composed mostly of log cabins [which] commenced filling up with people mostly of that class who were going from one part to another of the frontier."[76]

The people of Council Bluffs even entertained Dey and Dodge with a formal ball. About a week after Dey and Dodge made it to Council Bluffs, the rival Lyon and Iowa Central Railroad survey party made it to the Bluffs. This party was under the supervision of Sam Curtis.

The rival railroad survey parties held a public meeting in Council Bluffs. A large contingent of the citizenry of the Bluffs attended and were addressed by Peter A. Dey and Samuel Curtis. The people of this area were very interested in bringing a railroad to the area. However, the Civil War would be over, some 14 years later, before the rail lines reached Council Bluffs.

Dey and Dodge had completed their survey for the Mississippi and Missouri Railroad. They had surveyed from the eastern edge of the Hawkeye state on the Mississippi River to the western edge of the state on the Missouri River. However, it did not take long for new orders to be given to Dey and Dodge. They were to cross the Missouri River into what would become the Nebraska Territory and survey the Platte River Valley. It was thought this could be the beginning of a transcontinental railway.

Dey and Dodge crossed the Missouri River where Omaha now stands. They followed Saddle Creek, eventually making it to the Elkhorn River Valley. Dodge was out in front of Dey and the main body of the survey crew by some 25 miles, scouting locations for the survey party. He took a flatbed boat down the Elkhorn River. He also took his horse with him. One night while sleeping in a ravine that opened out to the Elkhorn River, he was awakened by the neighing of his horse. The sleepy-eyed Dodge then spotted his horse being led off by a member of the Pawnee tribe. Dodge grabbed his rifle and hollered at the Pawnee tribesman. Dodge's horse was not cooperating with the tribesman and was pulling back. The Pawnee tribesman eventually dropped the horse's reins, jumped into the Elkhorn River, and swam away to make his escape.

Dodge then made his way to the main camp and found the cooks were feeding a large contingent of Omaha tribesmen. Fearing that they would run out of supplies, Dodge chased these tribesmen off. Dodge and the crew ascertained that these Omaha tribesmen wished them no harm, but they were drastically cutting into their food supply. Dey and Dodge surveyed a little farther west and then made their way back to Council Bluffs.[77]

During February of 1854, Sylvanus Dodge came out West to file land claims in the Nebraska Territory near Fort Calhoun. Dodge had been writing letters to his family about these Western lands of Iowa and Nebraska. How he wished they would move out to be closer to him. Sylvanus then went back East. Grenville in May of 1854 asked for a leave of absence. He went back to Massachusetts to marry the young lady, Anne Brown, whom he had met in Peru, Illinois. They were married on May 28, 1854, in Salem, Massachusetts, by a Universalist minister. By July of 1854, Grenville was back in Iowa, having dropped his new bride off in her hometown of Peru, Illinois.[78]

Also in July, Dodge met up with Frederick Lander, who was coming back from a survey expedition on the West Coast. Lander and Dodge discussed the best route for a transcontinental railroad.[79]

However, bad news was on the horizon. Economic conditions in the United States worsened. Although the Panic of 1854 directly affected banks in the East, one of the collateral damages to this panic was the collapse of railroad building in Iowa. Almost all of the railroad building in the Hawkeye state had stopped. All the Iowa survey crew for the M&M Railroad were let go. However, Dodge was kept on the payroll for a nice sum of $1,500 a year. Though this was far above the average salary in Council Bluffs, Dodge noted that the city was becoming expensive to live in.

Dodge got a peek into the sometimes less-than-perfect business of railroad financing. Henry Farnam was in the railroading contracting business with the Durant brothers, Dr. Thomas C. Durant and his brother Charles. Dr. Thomas Durant was a medical doctor who had a flair for railroad building. Farnam and Durant thought railroad builders such as themselves should have access to huge government subsidies when they built railroads. They allowed Dodge to supplement his income by locating land warrants for the Farnam and Durant Company. This proved to be very lucrative for Dodge. The Durants and Farnam become huge kingpins in the railroad building industry in America. Thomas Durant would become exceedingly deceitful in his business practices, culminating in the Credit Mobiler railroad-building scandal. Henry Farnam as time went by became alarmed at the Durants' business practices and ended his business dealings with the Durant brothers.[80]

Dodge had decided to settle in the Nebraska Territory. Samuel Fifield, a friend from Massachusetts and a student at Norwich University with Dodge, had decided to throw his lot in with Dodge. Dodge had a lot of money from people back East wanting to file land claims in Iowa. As Dodge and Fifield made their way across Iowa, Dodge filed these claims. They crossed the Missouri River and found that Sylvanus and Fifield's claims near Fort Calhoun had been jumped. They then went to Elkhorn, close to where Dodge had proposed railroad tracks be built, and entered claims for Dodge, his father, his brother Nathan and Mr. Fifield. Shortly after this Dodge ran into some Omaha tribesmen who had done battle with the Pawnee tribesmen. In January of 1855 the Nebraska territorial legislature voted to make Omaha its territorial capital. Elkhorn lay about 17 miles west of Omaha, and Elkhorn looked like a good place to settle in the Nebraska Territory.

Samuel Fifield was courageous to the point of being reckless. He was one of the best shots Dodge had ever seen. At Norwich Fifield fired a cannon during a Fourth of July celebration and blew off his left hand. Sometime later, after he had lost his left hand, while hunting Fifield had shot himself in his left arm, causing a loss of an additional portion of that limb.[81]

In February of 1855, Dodge brought his wife and the rest of his family out to the Elkhorn claims. This claim was for 320 acres. Some settlers noted that the Elkhorn River was a pretty yet very crooked river. Dodge was soon contacted by the railroads to do some business for them. Dodge then surveyed the present city of Columbus, Nebraska. In between railroad work and surveying, Grenville farmed his claim. All during the late spring and summer, the Pawnee tribesmen were trying to get the whites to move out of their lands. They would ride up at full gallop, in full warrior garb, bodies painted and adorned with feathers, and bearing guns, bows and arrows. They would ride up to the two-story cabin Dodge had built, go in and harass the inhabitants. Dodge and Fifield took an aggressive attitude towards these Pawnee, and they were left alone. Others were not so lucky. However, Dodge and Fifield did go into a nearby Pawnee village and become friends with some of the inhabitants. They did this hoping to ease the tensions in the area with the Pawnee.

However, when Fifield gave their sick chief, Ish-got-up, some medicine to take, this backfired. Fifield knew the chief would die and gave him some medicine that would make his final days more comfortable. Dodge had made a map at this time using information from maps made by Frémont, Warren and others. He also added information he had gathered from the Mormons about their Western travels plus intelligence from Frederick Lander and other emigrants. The map showed camping places, fords, and where water and wood could be found. The map was published by the citizens of Council Bluffs hoping to make Council Bluffs the premier jumping-off or gateway spot to California, Oregon, Utah and Colorado by emigrants heading West. Dodge was very proud of this map and its influence on the Western expansion of the United States.

The Pawnee were at war with the Ponca tribe and accused the whites around Elkhorn of hiding the Poncas in their log cabins. This was not true, and Dodge knew it was just a ruse to search their cabins for things they deemed valuable. When Ish-got-up finally died, the Pawnee blamed Fifield's medicine and claimed it was poison. They called Dodge to their village, and a terrible sight of wailing and grief greeted Dodge. To prove the medicine was poison, one of the sub-chiefs made Dodge drink the rest of it. Dodge did so without hesitation and of course showed no ill effects. However, the Pawnee still were not completely convinced the medicine was not poison.

The Sioux killed a white man around the Elkhorn area, causing much concern. Unknown tribesmen killed a couple of other white settlers, and all the Elkhorn settlers moved to the much larger settlement in Omaha for safety. Only Dodge and Fifield stayed in the Elkhorn Valley. They knew their position was untenable, and they too moved to safety. Dodge moved to a residence in Council Bluffs mainly so Anne could deliver their first child without threat of an attack by Native Americans. Anne delivered Grenville his first child, Lettie, while they lived in Council Bluffs.[82]

The Omaha tribe had mostly been friendly to the settlers around Elkhorn. This was mainly due to the influence of Logan Fontenelle. Fontenelle was the child of a French-Creole trader from New Orleans named Lucien Fontenelle. Lucien had taken as his wife an Omaha tribal princess, Me-um-bane, the daughter of tribal chief Big Elk. All the whites thought Logan was a chief in the Omaha tribe, which was incorrect. He acted as an interpreter, however, and had great influence in the tribe. Logan had influenced the tribe to cede huge amounts of tribal lands to the whites in eastern Nebraska in exchange for protection from the warlike and dominate tribe of the Plains, the Sioux. Logan Fontenelle along with another Omaha tribesman went on to build very profitable ferries along the rivers near the site of present-day Columbus and Fremont, Nebraska. Fontenelle later sold these ferries at a nice profit to English settlers. Logan, along with other Omaha tribesmen, were on a buffalo hunt when members of the Brule Sioux tribe attacked them. Logan could have escaped, but he chose to stay and fight with his rifle to save as many of his people as possible. Logan was able to kill a number of the Sioux, but they eventually overran Logan's position and he and five Omahas were killed. Logan was scalped and his body mutilated, but the Omaha tribal elders were able to recover his remains, which they showed to anyone who would look at them. The Omaha tribesmen claimed this was the way the white men protected the Omaha tribe from the Sioux. After this, the Pawnee and other tribesmen in eastern Nebraska became very restless.

They were all afraid of being attacked by the much larger tribe of Sioux, and they had great doubt that the firepower of the whites would protect them.[83]

Dodge and Fifield, not wishing to give up on their Elkhorn claims, returned to them. They noticed that the Pawnee were very hostile and belligerent towards them. The Pawnee tribesmen began killing the cattle of the settlers who had left their livestock behind in the Elkhorn Valley. Some of the tribesmen placed the heads of the killed cattle on mounds with their horns facing the white settlements in Elkhorn. Dodge understood this to be an act of defiance.

The sheriff of Douglas County, in which Omaha and Elkhorn were located, came out to the Elkhorn Valley with about thirty white men to punish the Pawnee and any others who had been killing their cattle. Among the white men were people who had lived in Elkhorn and others, including the sheriff, who lived in Omaha but who had cattle and claims in the Elkhorn region. The sheriff pleaded with Dodge and Fifield to accompany them to punish the Pawnees. Dodge told the sheriff that the tribesmen were in no mood to be trifled with, and if his posse wasn't careful they all would be killed. The best thing the sheriff's posse could do was to head back to Omaha. The sheriff and posse were very upset with Dodge and Fifield but vowed they would get "cattle or blood" from the Pawnee. Fifield ferried the men across the Elkhorn River on his conveyance.

The sheriff and his posse ran into a trap when about 500 Pawnee tribesmen surrounded the posse. The white men were stripped of their clothing, firearms and possessions and some were beaten. The tribesmen finally allowed the white men to escape. They ran and stumbled in their underwear across the prairie as fast as they could to get back to the town of Omaha. When they came to Fifield's ferry they asked Fifield to hurry them across the Elkhorn River to put a barrier between them and the Pawnee. Fifield, seeing the sheriff in his underwear, asked the sheriff which he got, the "cattle or blood?"[84]

The situation with the Native Americans began to deteriorate even more around Elkhorn, so Dodge left for good and resided in Omaha. It is interesting to note that when Dodge was sent back to the plains to fight hostile Native Americans during the end of the Civil War, he hired some of these same Pawnee to act as scouts for him: the same Pawnee who had tried to run him out of the Elkhorn Valley and the Pawnee tribesman who had tried to steal his horse. In addition, when Dodge built the transcontinental railroad and needed scouts, he hired many of these same Pawnee. Dodge was never one to let a grudge keep him from hiring the best man for the job.

Never one to stay idle, Dodge became very active while living in Omaha. He went to Chicago to have a conference with Harry Farnam, Peter Dey and the rest of the men of the M&M Railroad. He went to Iowa City and accompanied his mother and sister to the Dodge homestead. Now his family was completely together. His mother Julia became home sick for Massachusetts. Dodge now considered himself a man of the West, with all its possibilities, and could not understand why anybody would think the East superior. His mother, however, finally became content with life on the frontier.

In the fall of 1855, Dodge went into the banking and land business with John T. Baldwin. They opened their doors for business in February of 1856. The firm became known as Baldwin, Dodge and Co. Grenville's brother Nathan was hired to keep the books. Baldwin was a huge man for the time, 6'4" and weighing over 300 lbs. Baldwin had in 1854 been elected to the Iowa House of Representatives and had connections all over the state because of this. Baldwin's younger brother Caleb became the firm's lawyer. Caleb was also huge 6'6" and over 400 lbs. Caleb would eventually become a member of the Iowa Supreme Court and its chief justice and very influential in Iowa politics. Caleb would be invaluable to Dodge in helping to push Dodge's career forward. Later another man by the name of Benjamin R. Pegram would become a partner in the firm. Pegram had set up a store in Council Bluffs to supply the Mormons as they went to the Great Salt Lake Valley in Utah, and he had experience in banking. He was elected treasurer of Council Bluffs. However, Pegram was extremely aggressive and at times could become outright dishonest. In the summer of 1856 Dodge spent a lot of his time back East signing up people who wished to own land and invest in Iowa. Dodge did especially well in Massachusetts around the old Dodge family stomping grounds of Peabody, Danvers and Rowley.[85]

During the winter of 1853–1854, a drunken white trader by the name of Lott had killed the chief of a band of the Santee Sioux, Sintominaduta, near Fort Dodge, Iowa (the name of Fort Dodge has nothing to do with Grenville Dodge or his family). Sintominaduta had been decapitated. Lott then went on to murder other defenseless members of Sintominaduta's family, including children. Lott tried to make the murders look as though the Sac and Fox tribe had committed these crimes. Lott then fled Iowa with his stepson, who may have aided him in this horrible offense. Sintominaduta's brother Inkpaduta and several others discovered these crimes. Inkpaduta went to the white authorities about the murders, and they assured him they would find the perpetrators.

Inkpaduta was described as being industrious, tall, and slender with a marked face due to a bout of smallpox as a child. A grand jury impaneled in Polk County, Iowa, some eighty miles south of Fort Dodge, indicted Lott for this crime, but little was done to find him. A coroner's jury was impaneled, but it was turned into a farce by the prosecuting attorney when he nailed Sintominaduta's decapitated head to a post over his house. It became obvious to Inkpaduta and other members of his band that the whites had no intention of finding the murderer of his brother and his family.

Inkpaduta, after his brother's death, became chief of this band of Santee Sioux. Sintominaduta and Inkpaduta also had another grievance with the whites in Iowa. Wishing to clear the various

After sparring with Iowa governor Kirkwood over getting his own regiment, Dodge (above) was finally given the rank of colonel and was given permission in 1861 to organize the 4th Iowa Volunteer Infantry for service in the Civil War. He created an atmosphere of camaraderie, trust, courage, sacrifice and unshakeable loyalty among his recruits (courtesy State Historical Society of Iowa, Des Moines).

bands of Sioux out of northwest Iowa, the white government had signed a treaty with various members of the Sioux tribe. As was often the case, these signatories were Native Americans who held no positions of authority in the Sioux tribe. Sintominaduta never signed this treaty.

After this, raids were conducted against white settlers in Iowa. No one was killed, but it was thought that Inkpaduta and possibly other bands of Sioux who resided in southern Minnesota and northern Iowa were responsible for these raids. In 1855, Iowa governor James Grimes made an appeal to the Iowa legislature that Iowa was in no position to protect itself if these Indian raids escalated. Grimes instructed the legislature to ask for help from the United States Congress, and Grimes even made an appeal to President Franklin Pierce. However, nothing was ever done.[86]

Because these bands of Sioux could cover a great amount of area, the citizens of Council Bluffs became alarmed at the potential for an attack by the Sioux on their city. They turned to Grenville Dodge to raise a company of men to protect them against any attack. Dodge raised a company of about 50 men in July of 1856. They were called the Council Bluffs Guards. The men were armed with muskets and had uniforms and other accouterments of the military. Undoubtedly the raising of this citizen army in Council Bluffs was a good dress rehearsal for the eventual time when Dodge would need to raise, drill, and command a regiment during the Civil War. Dodge's brother Nathan was in this company, as well as John Baldwin. Dodge noted that the cost of the muskets and uniforms was around $1,500. The men were supposed to pay for their own muskets and uniforms but many could not afford this, so Dodge ended up paying for most of the arms and uniforms out of his own pocket. The men often paraded at events around the area.[87]

By February of 1857, Inkpaduta and his band were as close as 75 miles to the north of Council Bluffs in Smithland, Iowa. He had some 30 warriors and a total of 70 in his band. Some of the white settlers in the Smithland area would come into Council Bluffs to get supplies for their farmsteads. Inkpaduta and his band headed north to the lakes region in northern Iowa, where they committed what was known as the Spirit Lake Massacre. A total of 32 whites were killed in that newly settled area, and four teenage white girls were taken captive. Inkpaduta and his band then went north into Minnesota, where eight more whites were killed. Although only one settler from Spirit Lake was killed, the papers back East called this the Spirit Lake Massacre. Inkpaduta was never captured or brought to justice for these crimes. Black Elk, a relative of Crazy Horse, later said Inkpaduta was present at the Battle of the Little Big Horn on June 25–26, 1876, for what is known as Custer's Last Stand. Lieutenant Colonel George Armstrong Custer and 268 of his men in the 7th United States Cavalry were completely wiped out by several thousand members of the Sioux and Northern Cheyenne Native Americans tribes led by Crazy Horse and Sitting Bull. Inkpaduta was too old, blind and unwell to have participated in the actual battle. However, two of Inkpaduta's sons fought at the Little Big Horn against the 7th Cavalry.[88]

By the fall of 1856, Dodge had received good news from Peter Dey that they would need Dodge's services for a survey party for the M&M Railroad. They wanted them to remake a survey from a fork in the Raccoon River to Council Bluffs. However, by this time a couple of the prominent men in the M&M Railroad line had made land acquisitions in the town of Florence, a community a few miles north of Omaha in the Nebraska Territory. They wanted the terminus to be in Florence, Nebraska Territory, not Council Bluffs, Iowa. When the citizens of Omaha, now a rival to Council Bluffs in size, heard of this possibility of a railroad terminus in the area, they wanted in on the action and they made noise to have the railroad terminus in Omaha. However, Dey and Dodge thought the approach to Council Bluffs made the most sense, and they lobbied for that city to be the terminus. They won out.

Dodge and his survey crew were then sent back to Iowa City, Iowa, to survey the land between that city and Des Moines during the winter of 1856–57. Dodge noted that it was extremely cold that winter, with the thermometer dropping to eight to ten degrees below zero. At this time one of the directors of the M&M Railroad wanted to give his nephew a job. Dodge set him to work on a simple task of carrying stakes. Dodge had warned his men to be careful crossing small streams, as the snow had crusted across them and there was always the possibility of breaking through the snow crust and the small streams not being completely frozen over. This young nephew paid no attention to Dodge's advice and crossed a small stream, broke through the snow, and fell through a thin coating of ice into the stream. Dodge thought the young man might die, as all his clothes were wet and the temperature extremely low. Dodge stripped the young man of all his wet clothing and rolled him in the snow. Then each man in the crew took off one piece of his dry clothing until the nephew was fully clothed. The young man survived. In the days following, Dodge noted that the young man stayed in camp and became very despondent. The stage line back to Iowa City ran by the proposed railway survey line. One day Dodge came into camp and found a short note from the director's nephew. The nephew said the M&M Railroad and Dodge could go to hell, and he was going back to New York City. Dodge thought that the young man apparently had had all of the surveying he cared for.

In early January of 1857, the citizens of Council Bluffs and Omaha became alarmed that the terminus of the railroad might be moved to another location. Harry Farnam and Grenville Dodge went back to these two cities and made a proposal. If Pottawattamie County, of which Council Bluffs was the county seat, would vote $300,000 in bonds and if Douglas County in the Nebraska Territory would raise $200,000 in bonds, Farnam would make sure the grading of the M&M Railroad began in Council Bluffs. Both counties came through, and Dodge headed back East to continue his survey in eastern Iowa. Farnam had also gotten Polk County, the county in which Des Moines is located, to raise a large $300,000 bond issue and he was working on Jasper County for a $200,000 bond. Dodge and the other executives of the M&M Railroad were busy buying up land they thought the railroad would pass through or where rail yards would be established.

On January 12, 1857, Dodge attended the Iowa legislature and entreated them to pass a bill to raise a militia in western and northern Iowa for the purpose of protecting the citizens from possible attacks by bands of the Sioux and other tribes. The legislature did nothing on this matter. Two months later, on March 8–12, 1857, Inkpaduta committed the massacre in the Iowa lakes region. On January 22, Dodge attended the Republican State Convention in Iowa City, representing Pottawattamie County.

In March of 1857, snow fell on the ground during Dodge's survey. On the 12th of

March, bright sunlight caused all the men in Dodge's crew to have snow-blindness. By morning of the next day, no one on the crew could see. The whole crew was taken by wagon to Iowa City. For most of the crew the snow-blindness was temporary. However, to Dodge, who was looking through his survey instrument all day, the sun's brightness was magnified. He was kept in a dark room for a month before he recovered.[89]

Iowa became a state in 1846. At that time Iowa City was the capitol, as it had been in the last years of the Iowa Territory. It was noted many times by politicians that as Iowa expanded to the west, the state capital should be moved farther west. The area where Fort Des Moines and later Des Moines were located was sometimes mentioned as a possible new location for the state capital.

Lawyer James A. Williamson, who would later become an officer in the 4th Iowa Volunteer Infantry, was deeply involved in the fight to move the state capitol. When asked by an investigating committee what influences had been used to move the capital from Iowa City to Des Moines, Williamson replied he had employed "all lawful and legal means ... including Chesapeake and Sardinian appliances, and any quantity of whiskey." To placate the citizens of Iowa City it was decided to locate the University of Iowa in that city.[90]

The governor of Iowa, James W. Grimes, appointed a commission of five members to determine the exact location of the capitol building in Des Moines. One of the five commissioners was Benjamin R. Pegram, who was one of the associates in Baldwin, Dodge and Co.[91] The citizens of Des Moines were to donate to the State of Iowa the land where the capitol and other state buildings were to be located. The "Eastsiders" of Des Moines wished the capitol and other state buildings to be located on that side of Des Moines. Another group, the "Westsiders," wished the buildings to be located on that side of the city. Each group was willing to put up land and money for the capitol grounds, and each side accused the other side of using bribery and other methods of skullduggery to get the location on their side of the city. When the Eastsiders won out, the Westsiders claimed they had offered more land and incentives to locate the capitol on their side of town and that the fix was in. The Westsiders hired John Kasson to be their attorney, and Kasson demanded from the legislature a special investigation of the matter. The special investigation was hampered somewhat by their lack of power to bring out all the testimony. In all probability, both sides were guilty of some improper and illegal methods.[92]

It came out that some of the five commissioners had taken bribes, including Benjamin Pegram, who some said was the worst offender. John Baldwin's name was also mentioned in connection with this affair. Grenville Dodge was in Des Moines when all this broke out, and Dodge launched a public relations effort to save the reputations of his business associates. Dodge was largely successful, although other events helped push the capitol relocation scandal off the front pages. By October 1, 1857, even though the capitol buildings were not completed, the packing and moving of the State of Iowa offices from Iowa City to Des Moines began.[93]

As often happens when scandal breaks out, a larger and more important scandal broke out. The capitol location scandal was moved to the back burner, and when the state began moving into its new location on the east side of Des Moines the capitol location scandal was somewhat forgotten. The new scandal was that the State of Iowa was missing a large amount of money. The State of Iowa was confronted with the fact that declining revenues and increasing expenses indicated a problem. A look at the finances of the state showed extremely sloppy bookkeeping and collection procedures, and outright theft of public funds that caused revenues to plummet. Perhaps the worst offender was the state superintendent of public instruction, who had been dismissed for misappropriation of funds.[94]

All of the wheeling and dealing of Harry Farnam and the other executives of the M&M Railroad—the buying of land and securing of bond issues—came to naught. The Panic of 1857 late in that year dried up all investment funds as banks all over the United States went bankrupt. All the bank depositors were left holding the bag, as there was no insurance for depositors. On Wall Street, the stock market had been in a steep decline since the early 1850s and insurance companies were going broke. Even in Europe and Great Britain this financial panic was felt. The directors of the M&M Railroad were forced to end all survey and railroad building work in Iowa at this time. Land values in Iowa fell, and most of the land bought for railroad speculation was now worth only a fraction of what had been paid for it.

In October of 1857 Dodge's survey work for the M&M Railroad ended due to the bad financial conditions. He went to St. Louis, bought a prefabricated house for $400 and had it shipped to a lot he owned in Council Bluffs. It cost Dodge $500 to have the house erected, plastered and painted. It made a pleasant cottage for the Grenville Dodge family on Pierce Street.

Since the land business of Baldwin, Dodge and Co. had suffered greatly due to the Panic of 1857, the partners opened up a mercantile business called Baldwin, Pegram and Co. in 1858. The mercantile business prospered, as emigrants to the West were passing through Council Bluffs in great numbers and they needed supplies for their journey. The company also freighted supplies out West and sent the first wagon train full of flour to Denver, Colorado. They also set up a trading post at Fort Cottonwood, later known as Fort McPherson, near the present-day city of North Platte, Nebraska, to trade with the large numbers of pioneers going out to the Western regions and with the Native American tribes in the area. They sent Grenville Dodge's father Sylvanus to look after their store at the Fort.

During the summer of 1858, the M&M Railroad executives decided to keep their promise to the citizens of Pottawattamie County and begin grading land for the purpose of laying railroad tracks. Dodge graded twelve miles of the road out of Council Bluffs; however, as the bonds issued were not selling and the money dried up for this project, the work had to be suspended in November of 1858. Dodge then, off and on, would do survey work for the M&M Railroad until 1861. Most of it was done west of the Missouri River.[95]

In 1859, Dodge had his serendipitous meeting with Abraham Lincoln in Council Bluffs, Iowa. Dodge became a delegate who helped nominate Lincoln, and Lincoln was elected president. In a letter to his mother and sister written on December 16, 1860, Grenville Dodge outlined some of his thoughts on the political situation. Dodge in the letter stated that in the election of Lincoln, "We have won a great victory which has placed us in the true light of the constitution and for one I never will agree to have it frittered away by compromise or the knuckling to the hue and cry of the south." Dodge said he had written to James Grimes, who was the third governor of Iowa and in 1860 was a United States senator from Iowa, and Samuel Curtis, who was one of the first Republicans elected to the United States House of Representatives from Iowa. Curtis was also a rival railroad man to Dodge who said the North ought "to be liberal to the South but not to give an inch of our just rights; to stand firm and if necessary stand to their guns. No amount of clamoring should move the North and the South never should be allowed to break up this union. As the South threatens, let the nation financially go under and let every river run with blood but never let it be dissolved because the old dominant party has had to succumb."

Dodge was afraid those in the East, such as the city of Boston, would give in to the South: "Old hypocrite Boston I see trembles…. She had better pattern after a western city, Chicago, which stands to her guns and defends a negro from Nebraska being taken to that territory as a slave."[96] Dodge was referring to a case that happened in Nebraska City, Nebraska Territory. A wealthy merchant, Stephen Nucholls, in that city brought five slaves to Nebraska City. All of his slaves escaped on the Underground Railroad aided by stations in Civil Bend and Tabor, Iowa. One of the female slaves, Eliza, had been forced to become the mistress of Nucholls. She and another female slave escaped from Nucholls and were aided by a black man, John Williamson, who worked and lived in the Civil Bend and Tabor areas as well as helping out on the Underground Railroad. Eliza made it to Chicago, where Nucholls with another man went to capture her. Nucholls had an arrest warrant from the Nebraska Territory for Eliza's return. A mob of black and white abolitionists in Chicago aided Eliza and refused to hand her over to Nucholls and the other man. Chicago policemen ignored the arrest warrant from the Nebraska Territory and told Nucholls and his henchman that they had better head back to Nebraska before the mob tore them apart.[97]

Henry G. Ankeny was originally from Somerset, Pennsylvania. He made his way out to Iowa, and prior to the war, resided in Quincy in Adams County. He joined the 4th Iowa Volunteer Infantry in July of 1861. He was made first lieutenant of Company H. Later he was promoted to captain of Company H (courtesy State Historical Society of Iowa, Des Moines).

In a letter of December 16, 1860, to his mother and sister, Dodge added a personal note about their father Sylvanus. He noted that his father wrote to him every week and that the store they had near Fort Cottonwood was doing great business. Native Americans camped close by the fort so they could trade with Sylvanus. Dodge also told his mother that they were going to put a post office in the store and that Sylvanus would once again be a postmaster.[98]

When Dodge made his way back to Council Bluffs after attending Lincoln's inauguration in Washington, D.C., he noticed that his companies Baldwin, Dodge and Co. and Baldwin, Pegram and

Co. had not been doing well. Nathan Dodge, the bookkeeper, had indicated that he thought John Baldwin was using company funds to increase his own personal wealth. Pegram was—as usual—not completely trustworthy. Grenville Dodge became completely dissatisfied with the business methods of John Baldwin and Benjamin Pegram. Grenville Dodge dissolved his business partnerships with these two men and these two businesses.[99]

When the Civil War started in April 1861, Dodge was made a colonel in the Union army, and he had to raise and train what would become the 4th Iowa Volunteer Infantry regiment. Dodge drilled the men and tried to turn them into soldiers. After a while, they looked good marching on the parade grounds. However, Dodge had the task of turning his regiment into a cohesive fighting machine and not much time to do it in. Most of the men in the unit had just recently moved to Iowa, and if you asked them where they were from they would not say Iowa but the state they had left, such as Indiana, Ohio or Pennsylvania. Some of the men in the unit had no idea what county they lived in, and the recruiters just made a guess as to what congressional district they resided in. Could Dodge make these strangers care about one another, care to fight for the Hawkeye state, and not bring dishonor to Iowa? Finally, the orders came for the 4th Iowa Volunteer Infantry to move out of their training grounds in Council Bluffs. They were to head south. The Civil War would now become real to them. No one knew what waited for the regiment. With only one month of training, would the men break and run at the first sound of gunfire? Would the men of the 4th Iowa distinguish themselves on the battlefield? How would their colonel and other officers react? Both fear and anticipation awaited these men.

## Chapter 2

# "Who were those black-coated devils?"

James A. Williamson wanted to keep the North and the South together as one Union. Although an Iowa Democrat, many of whom thought the Civil War unnecessary, Williamson believed the war was essential to keeping the Union solidified. He had a letter of recommendation from Caleb Baldwin of the Iowa Supreme Court to Colonel Grenville Dodge. Williamson had never met Dodge, but Baldwin spoke highly of him. Williamson was hoping to get an officer's slot in Dodge's 4th Iowa Volunteer Infantry regiment; however, if none were available he was willing to enlist as a private in any Iowa regiment.

However, after talking to Dodge, who seemed to be very influenced by Caleb Baldwin's recommendation, Dodge offered Williamson a position as the adjutant of the regiment with the rank of first lieutenant. Williamson left his home in Des Moines and joined the regiment in August of 1861.[1]

A Southerner by birth, James Alexander Williamson was born in Columbia, Adair County, Kentucky, on February 8, 1829. His father died when James was young and at three years of age, Williamson with his widowed mother and maternal grandparents moved near Indianapolis, Indiana. James was somewhat introspective in temperament, and he was a good student in school. As often happened at the time, without a father James was forced to work hard early in life. He worked mostly as a farm laborer as a young man. In 1845, at age fifteen, he and his extended family moved to the Iowa Territory to Keokuk County. They moved by prairie schooner pulled by a team of oxen. A year after their move from Indiana, Iowa became a state.

James decided to attend Knox College in Galesburg, Illinois. Knox College was founded by an anti-slavery colony with ties to the Congregational and Presbyterian churches. Knox College, and Galesburg in particular, was a hotbed of abolitionist activity. Both the town and college became important stopping points on the Underground Railroad, which sent fugitive slaves to Chicago and to Canada. James graduated from this college but apparently did not catch the abolitionist or Republican fever. Williamson would be a Democrat in politics until the Civil War was underway.

Williamson then went to the small town of Lancaster, Iowa, in Keokuk County, and as was done at the time read for the law in the office of an established attorney. He built a solid clientele in this town. The trust the people in Lancaster had in Williamson was expressed by the fact that various businessmen sent him to Boston and New York City to buy goods for their stores.

At age twenty-four in 1853, Williamson married Ann W. Gregory from nearby Birmingham, Iowa, in Van Buren County. Thinking there was more opportunity elsewhere in Iowa, Williamson decided to move to what was then called Fort Des Moines in the central part of the state.[2]

Once in Fort Des Moines, Williamson became involved in the banking and land business. He immersed himself in the state Democratic politics of the day. Williamson was instrumental in getting the Iowa state capital moved from Iowa City to Des Moines. By 1860, Williamson was the head of the Democratic Party in Iowa. He was also a delegate to the Democratic National Convention held in Baltimore, Maryland, that year. He supported the ticket of Senator Stephen A. Douglas of Illinois for president and former senator Herschel V. Johnson of Georgia for vice-president.[3]

Already by 1860, the nation was experiencing problems over the issue of secession. Originally, the Democratic Party was to meet in Charleston, South Carolina, to nominate a presidential and vice-presidential candidate in April of 1860. Charleston was probably the most pro-slavery city in the United States. The atmosphere in Charleston was so toxic that the Northern and Southern delegates could not agree on any nominations. Six weeks later the convention convened in Baltimore and nominated Stephen A. Douglas and Herschel V. Johnson.[4]

Williamson came back to Iowa to find the state divided over the question of slavery and secession. After Lincoln won the election of 1860, Williamson called for a convention in Des Moines in the winter of 1860–1861 for people who wanted to avert a war. However, despite the fact that most people understood how divided the country was over the question of slavery and the breakup of the Union, few in Iowa believed the country would go to war over these issues. The delegates at this Iowa convention were unwilling to consider these issues in a serious manner. Williamson, however, seeing the rancor of the Southern and Northern delegates at the Democratic Convention of 1860 and having been born in a slave state, understood these questions could easily lead to a civil war.

After the Civil War started in April of 1861 and Lincoln began a 75,000-man call-up for the Union Army, Williamson began to put his business affairs in order. By the summer of 1861, he had his business affairs organized and was ready to join an Iowa unit. He had interviewed with Grenville Dodge for the position of adjutant for the 4th Iowa Volunteer Regiment. By August of 1861, he had bid his wife and children goodbye and had joined the regiment.[5]

James A. Williamson was born in Columbia, Kentucky, and when he was 15 his family moved to southeastern Iowa. He came highly recommended to then-colonel Grenville Dodge and became Dodge's chief of staff. Williamson became Dodge's protégé, lifelong friend and confidant (courtesy State Historical Society of Iowa, Des Moines).

By the summer of 1861, the state of Missouri

was in chaos. Western Iowa, the Nebraska Territory and the state of Kansas all received much of their supplies, equipment and dry goods from St. Louis and St. Joseph, Missouri. If the Confederates were to gain control of the state of Missouri, these three areas would have great difficulties in getting the necessities to the citizens of these regions. An overland route through Iowa with wagons to move supplies to the western part of the Hawkeye state, the Nebraska Territory or the state of Kansas would be very expensive. It was much less expensive and faster to rail these supplies to St. Louis or St. Joseph, Missouri, and then put them on a steamboat bound for these areas. However, the state of Missouri was in a great commotion, mainly due to its governor, Claiborne Jackson. The question of whether Missouri would stay in the Union or join the Confederacy was largely in doubt as long as Jackson was governor.

Claiborne Jackson had run for the governorship in 1860 on a platform of keeping Missouri in the Union. Jackson was a slave owner and a believer in the slave-holding culture. Almost immediately after being elected governor, Jackson began working behind the scenes to have Missouri leave the Union and join the Confederate government. In his inaugural address, Jackson declared that Missouri had more in common with her slave-holding sister states and should join them in a new government. He thought that if he called for a state convention to decide whether Missouri should stay in the Union or join the Confederacy, the attendees, who were overwhelmingly born in slave states, would agree to leave the Union and join the Confederacy. This convention was called for in Missouri in February 1861. Former governor Sterling Price, a slaveholder, presided over the proceedings. However, this state convention backfired on Jackson. The members voted 98–1 to stay in the Union. The convention convened several times, and in July of 1861, they vacated Jackson's governorship and installed Hamilton R. Gamble as governor. However, between February and July of 1861 Jackson had time to initiate plenty of mischief and plunged the state of Missouri into its own civil war between Unionists and Rebel sympathizers. Jackson caused plenty of unnecessary blood to be spilled in Missouri.[6]

One of Jackson's more devious plans was to take over the huge federal arsenal in St. Louis. This arsenal, the largest federal arsenal in any slave state, held 60,000 stands of arms, powder, ammunition, field-pieces and arms-manufacturing machinery. Jackson figured he could supply the Confederate army in Missouri and much of the Confederate army in the South with these muskets, ammunition and cannons. Jackson had refused Abraham Lincoln's request for Missouri men for the Union army. In May of 1861, Jackson appointed Sterling Price to be the head of the Missouri State Guards. Sterling Price, a very popular man in Missouri, was known as "Old Pap." Price had been a governor of Missouri and a brigadier-general in the United States Army during the Mexican War. Although Jackson did not fully trust Price, he knew Price's prestige and popularity would make it easier to recruit men to the guards. Price at this time was loyal to the Union. Jackson had hoped to use the State Guards as the foundation of the Confederate army in Missouri. To recruit members to the guards, Jackson claimed they were only going to resist an invasion by an outside army, in other words the Union army.[7]

Jackson recruited men for the Missouri State Guards and placed them all over Missouri in "training camps." From one of these camps near St. Louis, called Camp Jackson, the governor was going to launch the attack on the federal arsenal in St. Louis. Jackson was in correspondence with Jefferson Davis, president of the Confederacy, and other high-ranking men in the Rebel government. The State Militia in Louisiana had taken over the federal arsenal at Baton Rouge, and they agreed to ship muskets, ammunition, cannons and other military supplies to St. Louis so Jackson could use them for his attack on the St. Louis arsenal and eventually arm his Confederate army. These military stores were shipped on the steamship *J.C. Swan*, bound for St. Louis. So as to not arouse suspicion, this freight was addressed to Greely and Gale, two well-known Union men in St. Louis. Of course, Jackson would take possession of these military stores before Greely and Gale ever knew they were in St. Louis.

Captain Nathaniel Lyon, a Union officer in charge of the federal arsenal in St. Louis, caught wind of this plot and raided Camp Jackson before the men could take possession of the military stores. Lyon did this without notifying his superior officer, General William S. Harney, commander of the Department of the West. Lyon captured the 639 men and 50 officers at Camp Jackson and had them arrested and taken back to St. Louis. In his report Lyon disparaged, "their extraordinary and unscrupulous conduct, and their evident design and the governor of this state, to take a position of hostility to the United States."[8]

Sterling Price was a very popular ex-governor of Missouri and war hero from the Mexican War. Claiborne Jackson had been elected governor of Missouri in 1860 on a platform of keeping Missouri in the Union. Almost immediately after being elected governor, he began negotiations with Jefferson Davis and other Confederates to move Missouri from the Union to the Confederacy. Jackson enlisted the aid of the popular Price and put him in charge of the Missouri State Guards, which became a pro–Confederacy army. Eventually, Price had most of the Missouri State Guard become part of the regular Confederate Army (Library of Congress).

Many in Missouri were glad Lyon had arrested these "Rebels." However, as Lyon marched these Confederate sympathizers back into St. Louis, hostile crowds appeared shouting, "Hurrah for Jefferson Davis" or "Damn the Dutch." The crowd began throwing stones and other projectiles at Lyon's Union men. Lyon had recruited 3,000 loyal Union men in St. Louis as a "reserve corps." Most of these men were newly arrived German immigrants to St. Louis who were extremely anti-slavery. Some of these reserve corps of Union men were helping Lyon with the Rebel prisoners. Someone from the hostile crowd open fired on one of the German reserve corps recruits and killed him. Lyon's men turned on the civilian crowd and fired into it, killing 28 people including one woman and her baby and injuring 75. Lyon suffered four more deaths in his ranks. This inflamed and outraged many newspaper editors and ordinary folks in Eastern Missouri. Sterling Price became so angry at this action that he turned his back on the Union and declared himself a Confederate general and the Missouri State Guards a Confederate army.[9]

Price and Jackson knew Missouri was in a weak position to join the Confederacy. Traffic on the Mississippi River had come to a standstill. Missouri had no direct rail lines to the Confederate states. Missouri was surrounded on three sides by Union states. Only Missouri's southern border was with a Confederate state—Arkansas. However, they were not sure if one Confederate state would help another or put its troops in another state. Large numbers of German immigrants who detested slavery populated Missouri's largest city, St. Louis, and its state capital, Jefferson City. They needed time. Price and Jackson would negotiate with General Harney as if they wanted peace. All the while, they would build up their army (the Missouri State Guards) and build up their military supplies. Price and Jackson were sure the Union army in Missouri would inflict more outrageous acts on her citizens, as Lyon's men had, thus making it easier for Missouri to join the Confederacy. Jackson and Price thought time was on their side. Price had talks with Harney; the Union general obviously did not want the war to come to Missouri. Harney agreed to let Price's Missouri State Guards keep law and order in the state. The Union soldiers would take no military action in the state. The newspapers in Missouri thought this agreement between Price and Harney was a good and prudent one. Would Missouri avoid the war that some did not want? However, there were others in Missouri, such as Lieutenant Governor Reynolds, who thought the agreement was hogwash. Reynolds wrote to Jefferson Davis asking him to send a Confederate army to the state to occupy Missouri so as the state could secede from the Union. In addition, many of Price's State Guards stationed in the capital of Missouri at Jefferson City wanted to fight the federals immediately.[10]

Lyon was promoted to brigadier-general and put in command of the Department of the West in St. Louis. Lyon negated the Harney-Price agreement. Lyon promised Price and Jackson free passage from Jefferson City to St. Louis if they wanted to negotiate a new agreement. After four hours of Price and Jackson trying to negotiate and giving Lyon several major concessions, Lyon began to dominate the negotiations. Lyon would concede little in the authority of the Federal government and told Jackson and Price, "Better, sir, far better that the blood of every man, woman, and child within the limits of the state should flow, than that she should defy the federal government. This means war." Lyon then left the room. Price and Jackson hurried back to Jefferson City, cutting the telegraph lines between St. Louis and the capital on their way. They also ordered the destruction of the important Gasconade Bridge. Price had moved the state armory to Boonville, Missouri. Jackson called for an enrollment of 50,000 Missouri men to repel the Union invasion of Missouri. Lyon looked on that as a proclamation of war. Lyon moved his troops quickly and occupied the state capitol at Jefferson City. He then moved his forces to Boonville and routed the Missouri State Guards at that location. Lyon captured Rolla, Missouri. Thus, Lyon and the Federals controlled almost all of the state's rail lines, river routes, population and wealth. Price moved his army to southwest Missouri, hoping to get some kind of reinforcements from Arkansas.[11]

Back in Western Iowa, the rumors of a large Confederate army in Missouri ready to pounce on the Hawkeye state were rife. A Confederate flag was supposedly flying over the post office in St. Joseph, Missouri, with the whole town turned into a Confederate stronghold. St. Joseph was only 80 miles from the southern border of Iowa.

Caleb Baldwin of Council Bluffs, a justice of the Iowa Supreme Court, had been given the duty by Iowa governor Kirkwood of keeping the border between Iowa and Missouri safe from any Rebel invasion. Baldwin told Dodge to send 200 of his men to the Iowa-Missouri border to ascertain if any of these invasion rumors were true and to guard the border. Baldwin told Dodge not to go into Missouri unless it was absolutely necessary. Baldwin did not want Dodge's men creating any incidents that would cause Missouri's Rebel elements to invade southern Iowa. Dodge with 200 of his men went to Page County, Iowa, a county on the border with Missouri, in July of 1861. He sent Frederick K. Teal from Decatur County in Iowa south into northwest Missouri to gain any intelligence. Teal had been recommended to Dodge by Hub Hoxie, the United States marshal in Iowa and a Republican friend. Hoxie told Dodge that Teal would be excellent for any special assignment that Dodge might have.

Teal came back and said that there were as many false war rumors in Missouri as there were in southwest Iowa. He said every Missourian had his own tale of what was happening in Iowa. Teal said there was one rumor that should be investigated, however. There was a Colonel Poindexter near Gentryville, Missouri, who had a number of men and three cannons and might be up to mischief. Dodge sent Teal back into Missouri to Gentryville to check this out. Colonel John A. Poindexter was an officer in the Missouri State Guard of the 1st Cavalry Regiment, 3rd Missouri Division. Poindexter in the early part of the war operated in the northern part of the state and was accused of using guerrilla war tactics. Teal came back from Gentryville and reported that Colonel Poindexter and his men, hearing of Dodge's movement to the Iowa–Missouri border, had scattered in great excitement and had dumped their three cannons into the river.[12]

In eastern Iowa, the rumors of war were just as prevalent as in western Iowa. Three regiments were raised there in Keokuk: the 1st Iowa Infantry, the 2nd Iowa Infantry and the 3rd Iowa Infantry. It was rumored that they would never leave Iowa, as there was imminent danger of an invasion of Rebel troops from Missouri. These rumors all proved to be false, and these three regiments, armed with the Springfield muskets that Dodge had procured from the Allegheny Arsenal, eventually moved out.[13]

Dodge and his men headed back to Council Bluffs, but their time there was brief. The regiment was ordered in early August to head out to Jefferson Barracks in St. Louis, Missouri. They would become part of Iowa General Samuel Curtis' brigade. By the steamboat *Emile*, part of the regiment headed down the Missouri River to St. Joseph. At St. Joe these companies boarded the Hannibal–St. Joseph Railroad. From Hannibal, Missouri, Dodge's men took the steamboat with the interesting name of *Sucker State* from Hannibal to the Jefferson Barracks in St. Louis. Dodge and the rest of the regiment soon followed.[14]

Less than a month after the 4th Iowa Infantry Regiment railed on the Hannibal–St. Joseph Railway, disaster struck. On September 3, 1861, Missouri Confederate guerrillas, known as bushwhackers, had burned the wooden tresses of the Little Platte River railroad bridge, which was about nine miles east of St. Joseph. The bridge, a 100' span about 35' above the river, looked to be intact, but when the weight of the train went on it, the bridge collapsed. The bushwhackers had hoped a Union troop train would be passing on it, but it was a passenger train filled with about 100 civilians that went crashing into the river. Seventeen civilians including women and children were immediately killed, while most of the other passengers and crew were injured. Some of those injured would die of their injuries after the train wreck.[15]

The Hannibal–St. Joseph Railroad had a very interesting history. It was the first railroad to cross the state of Missouri. The first plans for the railroad were made in 1846 in the office of John Marshall Clemens, the father of Samuel Clemens—better known as Mark Twain. The line was finished in 1859. Most of the letters sent on the Pony Express were railed on this line to St. Joseph, the beginning of the Pony Express route. At this time, St. Joseph was the second largest city in Missouri and Hannibal was the third largest city in the state. St. Louis was by far the largest city in the state. Abraham Lincoln in 1859 took this line on his way to Council Bluffs, Iowa, where he met Grenville Dodge and talked of a transcontinental rail line. In 1864 John Wilkes Booth, Lincoln's assassin, took the line, although it was somewhat blocked by a snowstorm, on his way to an engagement in St. Louis.[16]

First Lieutenant and Regimental Adjutant Williamson noted when they were in St. Louis that few of the men in the 4th Iowa Volunteer Infantry had uniforms. Most of the men in the regiment, including Williamson, had only the clothes they wore on their backs when they joined the unit. They only had a few Prussian muskets, and when practicing with these weapons 13 of them burst. They had no pretense of being a fully equipped regiment. They only had enough working muskets to post guards. They were an army regiment in name only.[17]

The 4th Iowa was only at the Jefferson Barracks in St. Louis for a short time. By the end of August, they were ordered to Rolla, Missouri, and were railed to that point. Captain W. L. Elliot of the regular United States Army inspected the weapons of the 4th Iowa and said their arms were unfit for use. He reported to his superior officers, "I consider that this regiment as now armed is unfit for active service, although composed of men raised on the frontier and accustomed to the use of fire arms."[18]

While at Rolla, even though he was woefully short of equipment, Dodge began drilling his men in the fall of 1861. Other regiments came into Rolla: the 36th Illinois Volunteer Infantry, the 24th and 26th Missouri Volunteer Infantry, and some independent companies of artillery. As Dodge was the ranking officer, he became acting commander of the post.[19]

Governor Kirkwood wrote to Dodge almost sheepishly and apologized for his lack of arms, uniforms and equipment. Kirkwood addresses the matter of the 6,000 Springfield muskets Dodge had found, which had been hijacked by other Iowa regiments. Kirkwood gave a lame excuse, saying that a situation had developed in eastern Iowa, requiring the muskets; when the danger passed they had tried to get the arms to Dodge, but by then his men had moved out to Missouri and they were unable to get them to him. Kirkwood said that by now the muskets were so scattered it would be impossible to get them to Dodge. Kirkwood said he was trying through Washington and General Frémont to get the required equipment Dodge and the 4th Iowa Infantry needed. Kirkwood told Dodge he would like to help, but the state had no money, the Iowa war bonds were not selling, and Dodge's only hope of getting supplies was through the federal government.[20]

Dodge sent Williamson into St. Louis to try to get supplies by seeing Major General John Frémont. Williamson got the runaround from Frémont's staff. Williamson noted that he was at a great disadvantage in that he still did not have a proper uniform himself. Frémont's staff would give Williamson some ungodly meeting time such as 6:23 in the morning. Williamson would be there at the proper time and be told by the guards that Frémont never saw anyone before noon.[21]

Finally, Williamson was able to procure, but not through regular army channels. By going to a stationary store he obtained some canteens for the men. He got clothing from a hardware store and cooking utensils from a dry goods store. Later Dodge went to St. Louis and through General Curtis was able to procure uniforms, arms, underwear, shoes and black overcoats for his regiment. The enlisted men were very appreciative of Dodge's efforts. One of the enlisted man wrote to the Council Bluffs *Nonpareil*,

> Through the exertions of Col. Dodge—who has been in St. Louis for some time, the Forth has been provided with a full outfit, from head to foot of winter clothing, of excellent material, well made up. Also extra heavy overcoats for wintry days; extra covers to tents—and new equipment of arms, knapsacks, haversacks, canteens, etc. so that the Forth now, after three months hard service, is better outfitted and equipped than nine-tenths of other regiments.
>
> Col. Dodge also procured pay for us from the time we were enrolled in the State, up to the first of September—and it speaks well for the morale of the regiment that out of their wages, the boys have sent home to their friends, some $7,000 dollars.

This soldier went on to mention the difficulties in fighting an enemy who sometimes used guerrilla or bushwhacker hit-and-run tactics. The soldier overestimated the numbers in Price's army as 45,000 men. Dodge did not know it at the time, but the black overcoats he procured for the 4th Iowa gave them a very distinctive look.[22]

When Williamson got back from St. Louis, all of the other officers in the regiment presented Dodge with a petition asking Williamson to resign because of his inexperience. It was obvious that some of the other officers in the ranks did not like Williamson. It is hard to say why. Perhaps it was the fact that Williamson had been so deeply involved in Democratic politics. Many of the officers had been Republicans.[23] Back in Iowa, the Democratic Party was being associated with the Copperhead movement. The Copperhead movement was opposed to the war. Some in Iowa, and elsewhere in the North, thought slavery acceptable and wanted, to let the Confederacy alone and not to conduct a war against them. Some did not think the United States should engage in a civil war over slavery or states' rights. Most of those associated with the Copperhead movement were members of the Democratic Party in Iowa. By the end of 1861 to end of the war, United States Marshall Hubert Hoxie would go to war against the Copperhead movement and the Knights of the Golden Circle, an organization that opposed the war with the South.

Hoxie was extremely aggressive and conducted something of a reign of terror. Many times he did not have warrants to arrest those he felt were Copperheads, and many times these people were jailed with no charges brought against them and no trial date given. They would just be released months later. Marshall Hoxie told Governor Kirkwood that he would smash the Knights of the Golden Circle by arresting their leaders. However, far from being harmless, the Copperheads did try to interfere with the recruiting of Union soldiers and the sale of war bonds, and they spread many false rumors about the Lincoln administration and the Union war effort. Hoxie kept his old friend Grenville Dodge advised of what he was doing with the Copperheads and Knights of the Golden Circle.

Hoxie even went so far as to arrest former Iowa United States Senator George Wallace Jones. He also arrested well-known Dubuque newspaper editors D.A. Mahoney and Gideon S. Bailey. Also arrested was Henry Dean Clay, one of the most vocal opponents of the war and a man causing great mischief in the state of Iowa. At a rally where Copperheads and supporters of the Civil War clashed, a Copperhead speaker was killed; but witnesses said the Copperhead speaker had begun firing into the crowd.[24]

The reasons behind the petition for the removal of Williamson are hard to ascertain. In all his other endeavors, he was quite capable. In the petition, the reason given for his removal was his inexperience. Some of the men in the regiment had been in the army before and realized some of Williamson's methods were not by the book. However, it would be hard to describe most of the officers and men in this raw regiment as experienced. Was it Williamson's ties to the Democratic Party and the suspicion that he might be a secret Copperhead that motivated the petition by the other officers? Needless to say, Williamson was greatly annoyed by the petition. Dodge had never heard any complaints about Williamson until he received the petition. The leader of the group against Williamson was a Lieutenant S.D. Nichols of Guthrie County. Dodge noted that Nichols was a very bright and capable young man.

Dodge began to give some of the other officers some of Williamson's duties as adjutant to give them an idea of how difficult a job Williamson had. However, Dodge remained steadfast in his support for Williamson, who Dodge thought was a bright, hard-working and loyal officer. After a while, Nichols and the other officers withdrew their petition against Williamson and issued a statement that they had the utmost confidence in Williamson and his competency. Dodge noted that in time, Nichols and Williamson became fast friends.[25]

During the fall of 1861, Frémont or his officers in St. Louis were ordering Dodge's command to go out and scout for supposed enemy troop movements. Invariably Dodge's men would go lickity split through the heavy underbrush and round about the countryside and find nothing. This was wearing out the men and the cavalry horses sent on these missions. Commander Sterling Price of the Missouri State Guards knew it would be hard for him to get replacements for his Confederate army, so he was judicious in how he used his army. He did not want them to engage the enemy unless he had overwhelming numbers or there was no other choice. He often used hit-and-run tactics.

One of the problems Dodge's men were running into, as were other Union regiments, was the abundance of militia in Missouri. Some of these militias were organized and supported by the Federal government; they were sometimes called the Home Guards or Enrolled Militia. The State Guards were organized by Jackson. Some militias were organized in sympathy with the Confederate government; some were organized only for mischief, vandalism and robbery. Some had mixed motives; some were well meaning, and some had unclear motives that could change from week to week. Most of these militias had no uniforms, and their weapons were what they brought from home. Some of the leaders of these militias had their own agendas. The militias would appear and then melt into countryside, where the next day they would appear as civilians.

Not all of Dodge's patrols turned up empty-handed. In a dispatch dated October 15, 1861, Dodge told of one of his patrols meeting up with Confederates at Dutch Mill or about 20 miles east of Lebanon, Missouri. Dodge tells of killing 16 Confederates and wounding 38. Captured prisoners numbered 32, and 37 horses were taken.[26]

Dodge was summoned to Frémont's headquarters in St. Louis. Dodge spent two days at Frémont's headquarters and was never let in by his adjunct general. Dodge noted that Frémont's headquarters were in chaos. Dodge left St. Louis and went back to Rolla. He received a communiqué from Frémont asking why he had not come to St. Louis. Dodge went back to St. Louis to Frémont's headquarters and was kept waiting. Finally, after seeing Frémont and even having a long conversation with him, Dodge had no idea what this leader of the Department of the West wanted him to do with his command in Rolla.[27]

Price and his Confederate army were busy during this time, heading towards Springfield, Missouri, in the southwestern part of the state. Some question Lyon's generalship in following Price to Springfield. Lyon had all the important elements in the state and could have taken defensive positions protecting these assets. However, Lyon wanted to punish the secessionists in Price's army. Lyon could be ruthless. A graduate of West Point and a veteran of the Mexican War while stationed in California, Lyon had wiped out two small groups of peaceful Native American tribes numbering 400 human beings, including women and children, after they were wrongly accused of killing three whites. Lyon was sometimes chastised by his superior officers for excessive punishment of his enlisted men. Lyon was stationed in Kansas during the "Bleeding Kansas" days and grew to hate slavers and those who called for the breakup of the Union.[28]

John C. Frémont captured the imagination of the nation with his four expeditions to the Western territories. Handsome and dashing, Frémont became a darling of the new Republican Party, and he became their first presidential candidate in the election of 1856, which he lost. When the Civil War broke out, Frémont was made a major-general and put in command of the Department of the West with headquarters in St. Louis (Library of Congress).

At Carthage, Missouri, part of Lyon's forces commanded by Colonel Fritz Sigel engaged Price's State Guards, who outnumbered them four to one. They were routed but made an organized retreat. Brigadier Ben McCulloch's Arkansas soldiers made an appearance in Missouri even after he was told not to go to the neutral state. McCulloch and his men quickly left the state. McCulloch was in command of Confederate troops in Northern Arkansas. He was a former colonel in the Texas Rangers and a veteran of the Mexican War. At this time, McCulloch was the only Confederate general who had not graduated from West Point. He never wore a uniform, preferring a black velvet suit. McCulloch had grave concerns about the fighting ability of Price's State Guards and the fact that almost 2,000 of them had no weapons.

After Boonville, Lyon had received two Kansas regiments, a Kansas cavalry unit, and the 1st Iowa Volunteer Infantry into his ranks. The 1st Iowa men were only enlisted for 90 days. The 2nd Iowa, 3rd Iowa and 4th Iowa regiments were enlisted for longer terms, usually three years. The 1st Iowa Volunteer Infantry, as well as the 2nd and 3rd Iowa, had been organized in Keokuk, Iowa. Keokuk was close to the Missouri border and there were some in that part of the state that supported the Confederacy. E.F. Ware, a private in the 1st Iowa, reported that before he shipped out of Keokuk for Missouri he was at a party with a number of the 1st Iowa lads. A pretty girl was playing the piano; when she finished she turned to Ware and said, "You are not going to go and fight for old Ape Lincoln." This was the first time Ware had heard Abe Lincoln being referred to as Ape Lincoln, and he thought it terribly witty. He heard the saying many time afterwards. Ware stated that the girl, a Southerner by birth, after the war married a man who had been a Union soldier and received a Union pension. Ware noted the lady was now a widower and living off her husband's Union pension.[29]

After a trying forced march, Lyon advanced his army into Springfield, Missouri. The largest town in the Ozarks at 2,000 inhabitants, it was supportive of the Union. Sigel's troops from Carthage and Sweeny's troops came into Springfield, giving Lyon a little under 6,000 troops and leaving him very short of supplies. Lyon was outnumbered by the Confederate troops. Lyon wrote that some of his Missouri troops and the 1st Iowa had only signed up for 90 days, putting him in danger of having his troop numbers drop to only 3,500 men. Lyon also wrote that he was seriously overextended on his supply lines and that he might have to fall back to St. Louis via Rolla.[30]

Discipline was a problem with many of these units. In Lyon's 4th Brigade, made up of the 1st and 2nd Kansas Infantry regiments and the 1st Iowa Infantry regiment, one of the soldiers killed another. The killer was immediately court-martialed and sentenced to be executed. The culprit was made to dig his own grave on the morning of the execution. In the afternoon all the men in the brigade were called out to view the execution. The killer was sitting on a box in front of the grave he had been made to dig. Twenty-eight men were drawn to be part of the execution squad. Half of them received guns that were not loaded and the other half received loaded guns. The order was given, "Make ready—take aim—fire." A volley of gunfire went off; the killer rolled over and struggled for a short time and then pitched into the grave he had dug. The killer was quickly covered over in his grave and the men were dismissed. There was no chaplin at this time in the 4th Brigade, so no religious words were spoken. The whole execution ceremony was over in a few minutes.

The men had noticed that Lyon seemed to be in a foul mood all the time. He always seemed nervous and irritable. He never had a good word to say to anyone. When Lyon did talk to his men, he addressed them in a way that made it clear he regarded them as incompetent. About all the men had to eat at this time was beef and some corn meal.

Temperatures in August were reaching over 100 degrees. Some of the men in the 4th Brigade decided they did not much care for Lyon.[31]

A 20-foot-wide road ran parallel to the telegraph line from St. Louis to Springfield, Missouri, to Pea Ridge, Arkansas, and down to Fort Smith, Arkansas. The road was at times called the telegraph road or wire road. Ben McCulloch's Arkansas troops and another brigade of Arkansas troops had been convinced to come into Missouri. The two Arkansas brigades hooked up with Price's State Guards on the telegraph road and headed for Springfield. They had a combined number of 12,700 men with 3,400 cavalry.

McCulloch's troops on August 6 camped on Wilson's Creek, a small stream that ran into the James River. Wilson's Creek offered fresh water, cornfields, good forage and a good camping ground. Price wanted to attack right away. Three days later McCulloch, whose relationship with Price was deteriorating, finally agreed to attack Springfield. Much to the dismay of McCulloch, Price's cavalry had met a force of Federal soldiers on August 2 and had been routed.

Men whose enlistments had ended were leaving Lyon's camp daily. When asked to reenlist for three years, most of them said no. Lyon knew he would have to attack before his troops dissolved away. Sigel came up with a plan that was approved by Lyon. Even though outnumbered they would split the command; Lyon would attack the front of the Confederates and Sigel and his German troops would use a flanking maneuver and attack from the rear. Sigel's German troops had an almost blind admiration of him. Many of them spoke little or no English, and Lyon knew he would have trouble countermanding any of Sigel's orders to his men. Lyon knew he had to trust in Sigel, his men and his plan. Lyon now had 3,800 infantrymen, 350 cavalrymen and 150 artillerymen with ten cannon.[32]

Many of the civilians in Springfield sensed that a big battle was shaping up, and they were leaving town. Even some of the shopkeepers were moving their stores to safer grounds. The first major battle in the Western Theater of the Civil War was about to begin. The Battle of Bull Run in Virginia had occurred only a few weeks before the Battle at Wilson's Creek. Lyon's men approached the Confederate army at one in the morning of August 10. They could see the glow of their campfires. To their surprise, they met no Southern pickets. They would wait until Sigel's men were in position. Sigel's men marched during the night of the August 9 and 10 and took a position on a hill where they could see the Confederate cavalry. After a gloomy and uninspired speech by Lyon, the men of the 1st Iowa Infantry began telling each other what they wanted their coffins to be made out of and how they were to be decorated. The enlisted men of the 1st Iowa stated they had little confidence in their commanding officers and that only the lieutenants and sergeants performed admirably.

Lyon moved his men forward, and they ran into foraging troops of the Missouri State Guards at four in the morning. They alerted the rest of the Confederate army. Lyon and his Missouri regiments, Kansas regiments and the 1st Iowa reached the crest of what was known as "Bloody Hill." They cleared the Missouri State Guards cavalry of Brigadier General James S. Rains from the hill. Confederate artillery then slowed Lyon's advance. The 1st Iowa fought members of the 3rd Louisiana Infantry Regiment, some of which were called the Pelican Rangers. Many of the 3rd Louisiana had weapons taken from the Federal Arsenal in Baton Rouge. Private Ware of the 1st Iowa had an usual gun he had brought from home. He was glad when he found one of the dead Pelican Rangers used the same ammunition as he did, and he took the dead man's ammunition box. Ware noted that the Louisiana boys had grit, but the 1st Iowa dislodged them from the Bloody Hill anyway. Ware told of a friend in the 1st Iowa who received a Minnie ball on the crest of his forehead; the ball tore his scalp and made a dent of an eighth of an inch on his skull. The man bled profusely and wandered around semi-conscious, oblivious to the battle raging around him. According to Ware, the man was a great athlete, but after the wound, he wasted away to a skeleton and died soon after he was mustered out of the service.[33]

Sigel's attack was successful at first. Many of the unarmed Missouri State Guards surrendered to Sigel's men. The German was convinced his plan was working. He thought he saw members of Lyon's troops and was worried about killing Federals with friendly fire. He saw some gray-clad troops. The battlefield was a chaotic mess of different uniforms. At one time Federal and Confederate troops aligned in the same battle line, thinking they were on the same side. Some of the companies of the 1st Iowa Infantry wore gray uniforms, and Sigel thought he was seeing them breaking through the mist and smoke of the battlefield. Unfortunately for Sigel, these gray-clad men were from the 3rd Louisiana Infantry, and they opened fired on Sigel's men at almost point-blank range. Many of Sigel's men did not return fire, believing they were being fired upon by mistake by members of the Federal army. The Louisiana troops captured some of Sigel's artillery.[34]

Sigel had scattered his command thinking victory was close at hand, and he could not form a line of fire. Confederate cavalry began to chase Sigel's brigade, and they began to break and run. A full-scale rout of Sigel's command was at hand. Sigel and about 250 of his men headed back to Springfield. After the rout of Sigel's men the Confederates could pay full attention to Lyon's men, who were the aggressors; but soon they were forced to take defensive positions. The 1st Kansas and 2nd Kansas regiments broke one of the Confederate advances on Bloody Hill with a "buck and ball" charge. This was a cartridge with one large musket ball and three buck shots. This gave the Kansans overwhelming firepower.

Lyon was wounded in the leg; then a bullet grazed his head and he was bleeding profusely from his leg and head. Lyon retired to the rear and then came forward again. Lyon pulled the 1st Missouri Infantry and the 2nd Kansas Infantry out of the line and attempted to make another charge. He was killed immediately when a ball entered his chest, hitting his heart and lungs. Lyon was the first Union general killed in battle during the Civil War. Captain Samuel J. Crawford of the 2nd Kansas Infantry noted that the men in his unit were firing over Lyon's body. Few knew that Lyon had been killed, and the 2nd Kansas drove the Southerners from the hill. Crawford went on to have an interesting career. He became a brevet major general during the Civil War. He also became a commanding officer in the 2nd Kansas Colored Infantry, which later became the 83rd U.S. Colored Infantry. During 1864, while still on active duty in the Civil War, Crawford was elected the third governor of Kansas. He became the first governor of Kansas to be elected to two terms. When tribes of Plains Native Americans started killing white settlers in Western Kansas in 1868, Crawford resigned the governorship to become the commanding officer in the 19th Kansas Volunteer Regiment to fight these Plains uprisings.[35]

On Bloody Hill, Captain James Totten's artillery had helped break up the Confederate advances on several occasions. After Lyon's death, Major Samuel Sturgis took over command of the Union army at Wilson's Creek. The Confederates launched their third assault, but Sturgis and the Federals, aided by Totten's artillery, turned it back. It was 11:30 in the morning. Sturgis knew his men were low on ammunition and outnumbered. He decided to head the Army of the West back to Springfield. The Confederates never followed them. The Federals got back to Springfield at sunset of that day.

As Civil War battles go, the number of men involved cannot compete with some of those battles in the Eastern Theater. However, compared to Bull Run and many of the other battles in the Civil War, Wilson's Creek had a high percentage of casualties. The Union soldiers in the battle had an almost 25 percent casualty rate. Doctors on both sides took care of each other's wounded.[36]

Once in Springfield, Sturgis relinquished his command to Colonel Sigel. All the officers held a war council, deciding that their position in Springfield was untenable and they should head back to Dodge's command at Rolla. The storekeepers in Springfield told the Federals to take what they wanted of meat, tobacco and groceries. They moved out the next day, August 11, with a baggage train of 370 wagons. Many Unionists in Springfield followed the Federals back to Rolla. Price's Confederate State Guards occupied Springfield the afternoon of the same day but made no effort to harass the retreating Federals. McCulloch and the Arkansas brigades headed back to their home state. The breach in the relationship with the Missouri State Guards was growing even wider. It took the Federals until August 17 to get back to Rolla.[37]

After Price's men reached Springfield, James McIntosh, a captain in the Confederate States Army and adjutant to the general of the brigade, wrote, "The flag of the Confederacy now floats over Springfield the stronghold of the enemy. The friends of our cause who have been imprisoned there are released.... The private property of citizens of either party must be respected. Soldiers who fought as you did day before yesterday cannot rob or plunder."[38]

In a letter, Dodge, the eternal optimist, told of the grand sight of the retreating Federal army, camping near Rolla with the white tents of their encampment spread out over the valley. He also told of the need to feed the residents of the Springfield area and their families who retreated to Rolla with the Union army. Dodge wrote of sending out a thousand men to try to discover where McCulloch and his Texas Rangers were, obviously not aware that McCulloch and his men had headed back into Arkansas. Dodge also was concerned that Price's men were on their way to Rolla. Interestingly, Dodge wrote in a letter that the men of the 4th Iowa Infantry didn't care for Lieutenant-Colonel Galligan admitted that it had been a mistake to appoint Galligan to his post. However, he would not listen to the men complain about Galligan.[39]

Price and his Missouri State Guards were busy. In September, about a month after the Battle at Wilson's Creek, the Missouri State Guards headed to Lexington, Missouri. This was the county seat of Lafayette County, a very rich county on the Missouri River about 45 miles east of Kansas City. In 1860 Lafayette County contained more slaves than any other county in Missouri. (The main crop in Missouri that used slave labor was hemp. The fibers of the hemp plant were used to make rope. Rope was a product in high demand. The American South supplied 7/8 of the world's cotton. All those cotton bales had to be tied on the ends with rope. All ocean vessels and steamboats had a need for rope, as did farmers and ranchers. Missouri and Kentucky usually vied for which would be the state to produce the most hemp. Lafayette County was right in the middle of one of the best hemp-growing areas in Missouri.) When Price's Rebel army moved northward, they received little resistance. Originally, Price had thought about invading southeast Kansas at Fort Scott. However, Kansas regiments rallied in a show of force and after a brief skirmish, he thought it to chancy to try to invade Jayhawker territory.

Price also got information that the Union quartermaster had stores at Lexington and had artillery and mortars in the garrison in town. This looked like a good prize for the always-supply-strapped Confederates. Union Colonel Jeff Davis was ordered out of Jefferson City by Frémont to help reinforce the garrison at Lexington, but Davis frittered away a week before he got moving. General Pope had 4,000 Union soldiers, but he also took his time and was late getting to Lexington. That left the Federals in the Lexington garrison with about 3,500 soldiers up against Price's more than 10,000 State Guards. Because of the Confederate victories at Wilson's Creek and Bull Run, many Rebel-leaning Missouri citizens were eager to join Price's State Guards.

A battle line was created close to the city of Lexington. The Federals were dug in well, and Price despite his much larger force could not dislodge them. Price, who was running low on supplies, put off an all-out attack until his supply wagons could get to him from southern Missouri. Price put the Federals under a siege, and the Rebels had gained control of the Unionists' water supply. The Federals held the high ground, and Price knew it would cost him dearly to make a frontal charge. When Price's supply train got to town "Old Pap" knew it was time to strike. General Thomas Harris of the 2nd Division of the Missouri State Guards came up with a plan. He had found some bales of hemp in a warehouse, and he soaked them in water for a day so they would not catch on fire. The Confederates slowly climbed the hill where the Federals had dug in, using the bales of hemp as a moveable breastwork. The Unionists turned their artillery on the advancing Rebels and checked their advance briefly. However, the State Guards continued to move up the hill, supported by heavy artillery fire. The Federal command knew they were in an untenable position, so they flew the white flag and agreed to lay down their arms at Lexington. General Frémont had an advance warning of ten days and could have put 25,000 troops in Lexington, but because individual Union commanders did not care about their fellow troopers, this valuable town was now in Rebel hands.[40]

Probably the most humiliating thing the 3,000 captured Federals had to do was listen to a rant from Claiborne Jackson about how they had invaded his state. Soon after the battle, Price paroled the Federal prisoners. This would be the high-water mark of the Confederacy in Missouri. Many Unionists in Missouri began to wonder if the Federal government could hold the show-me state. Many wondered if Price would sweep through the Missouri Valley in the area known as "Little Dixie," which encompassed counties along the Missouri River from Kansas City to Jefferson City. These counties were prosperous and held many slaves; the region was the major hemp-growing area in Missouri. To add to the displeasure, many Missourians were chafing under the treatment of Union General James Lane and General John Pope, who robbed and mistreated all Missourians regardless of whether they were Union men or not. Lane had destroyed the town of Osceola, Missouri. A small detachment of Rebels held the town, but Lane quickly dispersed them and then shelled the town and burned it down—but not before Lane and his men robbed the town's bank and other stores. Osceola was a prosperous riverboat town on the Osage River before Lane laid waste to it.[41]

All during the fall of 1861, Dodge was probing to find out where Price's men were located. In mid-October, he reported that over 1,500 men of the Missouri State Guard were in Lebanon, Missouri, about 50 miles from Springfield and about 60 miles from Rolla. He also stated that two months after Wilson's Creek, the wounded were still coming into Rolla. Thirty-three men had come at one time in ambulances. Presumably, they had been kept in Springfield until they were well enough to make the over-100-mile trip on bad roads to Rolla.[42]

In October 28, 1861, Claiborne Jackson, protected by Price's army, declared Neosho, Missouri, to be the provisional capital of Missouri. Neosho was the county seat of Newton County, the county in the far southwestern part of the state that bordered Arkansas. Seven miles to the northeast of Neosho lay the Granby lead mines. These mines could produce 200,000 pounds of lead a month for the Confederacy, which was a good percentage of what the Rebels needed every month to supply their army. Whichever side controlled the lead mines in Missouri had control of very valuable assets. Jackson met with Missouri legislators who were in sympathy with the Confederacy. Over the next few days, Jackson and the assembly declared that Missouri would secede from the Union and be part of the Confederate States. They would also send representatives to the Confederate Congress. Jackson had nowhere near the quorum of the Missouri legislature needed to declare this legally. The Confederacy accepted Jackson's declaration, Missouri became the 12th state to join the Confederacy, and authorities in Richmond added a 12th star to the Confederate flag. However, Jackson's declaration had little basis in reality, and the real Missouri governor and government, dominated by Union men, still met in Jefferson City.[43]

In late October, Frémont took a force of some 38,000 men to march on Springfield. However, after he took back Springfield he was relieved of his command, on November 2, after clashing with Lincoln and following an unflattering report on his command by the War Department. Price quickly moved his men south of Springfield and no great battle was fought. Major-General David Hunter, an Illinois friend of Lincoln whose career in the U.S. Army was mostly as a paymaster, was the head of a division under Frémont. He took over command of the Western Department from Frémont. Instead of following Price and then attacking McCulloch in Arkansas, some think Hunter could easily have driven these two Confederate commands south of the Arkansas River. Hunter then mysteriously wired Washington that there was no enemy in the area. Washington then told Hunter to march his men back to Rolla and Sedalia, Missouri. Hunter then sent 18,000 of his men to U.S. Grant so he could use them in Tennessee. Hunter had command of the Department of the West for only a week; then General Henry W. Halleck took over command. Halleck was a good administrator but not a good field commander. Price over the next couple of months would move his Missouri State Guard out of the Lexington area and consolidate his forces to meet Frémont in southern Missouri. Price's dream of rolling his army up through the Missouri Valley from Kansas City to Jefferson City was over.⁴⁴

After the Frémont-Hunter debacle at Springfield, Price quickly moved the Missouri State Guard back into Springfield and up the road to Lebanon. By late November, Dodge reported that Missouri State Guard pickets were still operating ten miles east of Lebanon. Dodge reported that some of his scouting party had been taken prisoner between Springfield and Lebanon. Dodge also reported that Price's men were scattered over a large area because they were living off the land "for subsistence." In November, Dodge sent out a reinforced patrol of 1,500 men to Texas County, Missouri, to catch the Missouri State Guard cavalry regiment of Colonel Thomas R. Freeman. Dodge had received several reports from Union people that Freeman and his men had been robbing and murdering Unionists in that region. Freeman never filed any reports with his superiors and apparently lived off the land, foraging for his troops and horses. He mostly operated on his own in Missouri and Arkansas. Dodge reported they had captured several prominent Rebel prisoners because of this raid. Dodge told Colonel Greusel of the 36th Illinois Volunteer Infantry Regiment, who was in charge of the patrol, to punish all Rebel sympathizers who were aiding and abetting Colonel Freeman. Dodge said, "Be sure they are aiding the enemy and then take all they got." The Federals seized $70,000 in property from Rebel sympathizers, including slaves. Dodge was criticized for taking the slaves away from their masters. Shortly before December, Dodge reported that his scouts had picked up a slave escaping from the Cherokees in the Indian Nations of what is now Oklahoma. The slave reported that the Cherokees, whose richer members owned slaves, and the Cherokee Nation, who supported the Confederacy, were afraid of an attack by the Federal garrison in Fort Scott, Kansas. On December 5, Dodge learned through intelligence that Confederate general McCulloch was building barracks at Pea Ridge in Arkansas and that Price's Missouri State Guards were low on supplies. Later that month, a patrol Dodge sent of 22 men to Wright County, Missouri, killed nine Rebels, wounded four, and brought in 17 prisoners. Dodge had his men build log-type cabins for the winter. He noted his men had the best accommodations of any unit, yet the sickness and illness seemed to be as great in the 4th Iowa Infantry as in other units. Dodge surmised that it must be due to improper sanitation practices.⁴⁵

By December 18, 1861, Dodge reported that Price's men had abandoned Lebanon and that there were no enemy soldiers between Springfield and Rolla. In late December, Dodge's scouts found Freeman's bushwhackers again robbing and creating havoc, and they were chased back into Springfield. Dodge reported that there were several Confederate guerrilla outfits stealing and robbing to supply Price's Missouri Guard units.⁴⁶

Since Dodge had several Missouri Union units in his command, he found good men who knew southern Missouri and northern Arkansas like the backs of their hands. Often Dodge would send these men into these areas to gather intelligence. He found, as he had done with Frederick Teal, that an individual who knew the people and area could sometimes come back with much better military intelligence than a large scouting party could. This was the beginning of Dodge's creating the best spy network in the Western Theater of the Civil War. Dodge called his group of spies his "Corps of Scouts." Dodge called in his provost marshal, who had a small cash account made up of fines and other miscellaneous monies. Dodge used this fund to pay the travel expenses of these spies.[47]

Most of the colonels in the Union army were doing the work of a much higher officer, such as commanding a brigade or division. Most of these colonels had friends in high places at their state capitals or in Washington, D.C. Most of them thought they should be promoted to be a brigadier-general or major general. Dodge was no different. His friends Caleb Baldwin, Herbert Hoxie, Francis W. Palmer (editor in Des Moines of the *Iowa State Register*) and John Kasson in Washington, D.C., were all campaigning for Dodge to be promoted. However, Lincoln and the secretary of war decided that promotions to generalships would be made by success on the battlefield.[48]

In late December 1861, a pistol Dodge was carrying went off while he was riding a horse and wounded him in the thigh. Although not a serious wound, it was very bothersome, and it did prove to become irritated when Dodge rode his horse. Dodge rested for two weeks but hobbled around for several months. In late December, General Samuel Curtis took over the command of the district of the southwest.[49]

In early December, Captain Phillip Sheridan reported to Dodge as he was made quartermaster and chief commissary of subsistence for the Army of the Southwest. Sheridan had spent some time in General Henry Halleck's office in St. Louis straightening out the accounts of John C. Frémont. By this time, Frémont had been relieved of his command, much to the delight of many of the Union soldiers and citizens of Missouri. These accounts for quartermaster supplies were a mess. Sheridan dove into this accounting quagmire with the vigor he did everything and got the accounts straightened out. Frémont's lavish expenditures on the behalf of the Western Department and his inability to account for where the money had gone were two of the major reasons for his being sacked. Sheridan then was posted to Rolla and made some changes in how many wagons a regiment could have. Sheridan noted that some of the regiments had 40 to 50 wagons, while others had three or four wagons. Sheridan went about trying to standardize how many wagons a regiment could have in order to downsize the wagon train the Army of the Southwest would need over the horrible roads found in the Ozarks at this time. This angered many of the commanders in the Army of the Southwest. Dodge com-

Philip Sheridan was a West Point graduate and career army officer who had reached the rank of captain at the start of the Civil War. He was eventually given a field command in the U.S. Cavalry and became the best-known cavalry officer in the Union army during the Civil War. When Sheridan wrote his memoirs, he gave much praise and thanks to Grenville Dodge and the 4th Iowa Volunteer Infantry for their help to him while serving as quartermaster of the Army of the Southwest (Library of Congress).

plied and grew to like Sheridan. Sheridan was a can-do type of man that Dodge was drawn to. Sheridan was regular army and a graduate of West Point.[50]

In late January 1862, Dodge was assigned to the command of the 1st Brigade, 4th Division of the Army of the Southwest. The brigade consisted of the 4th Iowa Volunteer Infantry, 35th Illinois Volunteer Infantry, 24th Missouri Volunteer Infantry and the 1st Iowa Independent Light Artillery Battery. Colonel Carr commanded the division. Carr was a regular army officer and West Point graduate. Most people thought that the career army officers were better able to command than officers who had been civilians only a few months before. However, Captain Sheridan told Dodge that he could accept this or protest it, because Dodge had been made a colonel before Carr and thus Dodge technically outranked Carr. Dodge brought the matter up before General Curtis, but Curtis ruled that the regular army officers outranked the civilian volunteer officers no matter what date the commission was made. The matter was kicked upstairs to General Halleck, who reversed Curtis' decision and decided the date the ranking was made would be the determining factor. Thus Halleck decided Dodge should have command of the division. However, his ruling was made several months after Dodge made his protest, and the point was moot. Dodge was proud of the fact that he had helped a precedent to be made as far as the ranking of officers.[51]

General Samuel Curtis decided to attack Price's and McCulloch's armies regardless of where they were. Curtis had an army of around 12,000 Federal troops. Samuel Ryan Curtis had been a graduate of West Point. He served three terms as a Republican congressman from the Iowa 1st District. At the beginning of the Civil War, Iowa had one slot for a brigadier-general, and that position was given to Samuel Curtis. Curtis and his army were heading down south to recapture Springfield. The Army of the Southwest had received information that Price was going to make a stand there.

Rain and then freezing temperatures turned everything into an icy and muddy mess along the dirt telegraph road on the way to Springfield. Soldiers' clothing was often stiff with ice. Wagons got stuck in the mud up to their axles. Price was supposedly fortifying Springfield. After the Confederacy had accepted the mostly symbolic transfer of Missouri to the Confederate States of America, Price tried to get a commission in the regular Confederate army. Jefferson Davis told Price that he could become a major general if he raised a division. Price thought it would be an easy matter of transferring his Missouri State Guard into a division of the Confederate army. However, many of the men in the Missouri State Guard would not transfer, and some of them said they would not go out of state to fight. Even though Price had not raised a division, Davis gave Price his general stars in the Confederate army. Price was now in charge of a split command of Confederate States soldiers and Missouri State Guardsmen. Because Price and McCulloch did not get along, Jefferson Davis appointed Major-General Earl Van Dorn to be commander of the District of the Trans-Mississippi. Even though Ben McCulloch was by far the most able general of the three, Jefferson Davis felt that since McCulloch had not graduated from West Point he was not capable of a large command. Davis liked to appoint men he knew, or friends, to high command posts regardless of how much ability they had. This was one of his leadership flaws. Van Dorn was a very vain man, and he thought he was quite the dandy and a ladies' man. In about 14 months, after taking command of the District of the Trans-Mississippi,

Van Dorn would be dead shot by a physician whose wife Van Dorn had been giving too much attention.[52]

After the Federals were close to Springfield they were harassed slightly by Rebel cavalry. Dodge's 4th Iowa Volunteer Infantry were to make the first assault on Springfield. At midnight, Dodge lined up the 4th Iowa in a skirmish line for a daylight attack. The men of the 4th Iowa could hear the heavy Federal artillery fire of Sigel's Germans on their right flank. However, as his skirmish line moved forward Dodge lost sight of it. He sent Williamson to look for it, but Williamson could not find it. Dodge and Williamson expected the worst, that their skirmish line had been captured by Price's Rebels. Company E of the 4th Iowa Infantry regiment was the first to enter Springfield. These were men from Polk, Dallas and Warren counties in Iowa. Much to Dodge and Williamson's surprise, when daylight came they saw their men coming down the road, some of them riding horses and in a festive mood. They had entered Springfield and only found token resistance; now the town was empty of Rebel soldiers. On February 12, General Curtis wrote to his superiors that the flag of the Stars and Stripes once again flew over Springfield and that the enemy had only given light resistance with a rear guard.[53]

Price's Missouri State Guards was an undisciplined outfit; the men could come and go as they pleased. These men usually brought their own guns, ammunition, and uniforms from home, but they had some real fighters in the unit. While in Springfield, the Federals captured a raw-boned youth who was known to be an excellent shot and very brave to the point of recklessness. This Missouri State guardsman had fought at Wilson's Creek near Bloody Hill but had been left behind because he had the measles. Childhood diseases were very dangerous to the Confederate and Union armies, as most of the rural soldiers had not built up immunity to them. Chicken pox, measles, mumps and whooping cough spread through regiments in epidemic proportions. Of these childhood diseases, the measles was the most deadly. The name of this Missouri State guardsman who had the measles was Frank James; he liked to read and quote Shakespeare. The Federals let him go home to Kearney, Missouri. Once in Kearney the Federal garrison learned of his Rebel participation at Wilson's Creek, and they arrested him. He had to give an oath of allegiance to the United States and post a bond of $1,000. This was a hefty sum for the day, but the James family had money, so the bond was posted and Frank was let go and paroled. At the time Frank was 19 and his brother Jesse James was 14. Frank violated his parole, took up arms against the United States and fought with the guerrilla bands of William Quantrill and Bloody Bill Anderson. His brother Jesse joined Bloody Bill Anderson's guerrilla band at age 17. These guerrilla bands proved to be very troublesome in Missouri. They attacked small Federal outposts, robbing and murdering Union men in the state. By 1862, the Congress of the Confederate States passed the Partisan Ranger Act, which acknowledged the value of these guerrilla bands in supplying the regular Confederate army and in tying up regular Federal army units. The Federal army sometimes had trouble keeping track of the Confederates violating their parole from the Confederate army. However, they certainly felt they had the right to shoot on site any member of these guerrilla bands. Another of these Missouri State Guards was Cole Younger, who fought with Price at the Battle of Carthage. Cole Younger was from one of the richest families in Missouri. Even though they owned slaves, they supported the Union cause. Cole Younger's father Henry had gotten rich with U.S. government contracts to haul the U.S. mail. However, members of the Federal Missouri Home Guards murdered Henry Younger. Cole was branded a spy, and he was on the run until he joined Price's men. Younger joined some of these guerrilla bands and later became a member of the notorious James-Younger gang. Many of those who would after the war become members of the James-Younger gang also rode with Price's State Guards and the guerrilla bands in Missouri. Jo Shelby was another member of Price's State Guard. Shelby became the best cavalry officer west of the Mississippi River. He fought in Price's State Guard at Carthage and Wilson's Creek. Shelby's men also fought at Pea Ridge. He then transferred to the regular Confederate army and became a general in it. It was said Shelby's cavalry could "ride between the raindrops."[54]

General Henry W. Halleck on March 13, 1862, seeing the danger these guerrilla bands posed, issued General Order Number 2. This order went as follows:

> Evidence has been received at these headquarters that Maj. General Sterling Price has issued commissions or licenses to certain bandits in this State, authorizing them to raise "guerrilla forces" for the purpose of plunder and marauding. General Price ought to know that such a course is contrary to the rules of civilized warfare, and that every man who enlists in such an organization forfeits his life and becomes an outlaw. All persons are hereby warned that if they join any guerrilla band they will not, if captured, be treated as ordinary prisoners of war, but will be hung as robbers and murders. Their lives shall atone for the barbarity of their general.[55]

Later in the war, Confederate general Sterling Price received guerrilla leader Bloody Bill Anderson. From the reins of his horse, Anderson had hung scalps of Union men and soldiers he had killed and scalped. Price made him remove the scalps from his reins before he would see him.[56]

After Dodge's troops and the rest of Curtis' army had taken Springfield, Price retreated along the telegraph road to the Missouri-Arkansas border. Price's rear guard tried to slow the advance of Curtis' Army of the Southwest. This Union general did not rest his army during the middle of the winter in Springfield as many Union generals would have done, but committed to a sustained offensive. Dodge noted that Price's rear guard mostly made stands at the crossing points of streams. Some said Price would try to make a stand at Wilson's Creek, site of their victory six months earlier. However, after a stop for breakfast, Price's Missourians headed south from Wilson's Creek in retreat. Even at this point Curtis was not convinced that Price's army was in full retreat. It was an organized retreat, but Curtis was expecting Price to make a defensive stand any day with all his army and maybe troops from Arkansas.[57]

General Earl Van Dorn, C.S.A., assumed command of the Trans-Mississippi District on January 29, 1862. He made it to Arkansas and set his headquarters up in the Arkansas town of Pocahontas. Van Dorn had big plans for his department and hoped to cover himself in glory. He wanted not only to hold Arkansas and the Indian Nations of what is now Oklahoma but also to retake all of Missouri, including the grand prize of St. Louis. Van Dorn's strategy was to initiate his plan at the first signs of spring. His communications with Price's army were poor, and he had no idea that Curtis and the Federals were advancing towards the Missouri-Arkansas border with a highly unusual winter campaign. Van Dorn did not learn that the Federals were even on the move until after they had taken Springfield, the most important town in southwestern Missouri. Pocahontas was in the northeast part of Arkansas, while Curtis and eventually Price and McCulloch's armies were in northwest Arkansas. Van Dorn at Pocahontas was way out of position in relationship to the rest of his army. At Pocahontas, Van Dorn was some 225 miles from the main body of his army. The reason he settled in Pocahontas was that he thought he was in a better position to strike at St. Louis, his ultimate goal.[58]

Curtis actually had a split command. He commanded half the troops and General Sigel the other half. Sigel gave many of his commands in German, as the Army of the Southwest had more foreign-born soldiers from a single ethnic group than any other Union or Confederate army during the Civil War. General Franz Sigel commanded the 1st Division in the Army of the Southwest. When Curtis was named overall commander of the Army of the Southwest in December of 1861, Sigel in protest resigned his commission. Sigel thought he should have had that command post. Halleck talked him into coming back to the army. Born in the Grand Duchy of Baden near the present border of Germany and France, Sigel received some military training in Baden. He served in the duke's army as a lieutenant. Sigel became a revolutionary and was forced to leave Europe. He came to New York and then St. Louis. At the outbreak of the Civil War, Sigel volunteered his services. He was made a colonel in the 3rd Missouri Infantry Regiment, made up mostly of Germans from St. Louis. His troops attached an almost cult-like status to Sigel. He was an outstanding recruiter and considered a hero in the German immigrant community. Some of the other non–German officers in Curtis' command, including Dodge, thought Sigel a prima donna and thought the Germans were given preferential treatment by the Union high command. However, the truth of the matter was that the Union cause west of the Mississippi desperately needed these German immigrants in their army, and they were very important in keeping border state Missouri in the Union.[59]

It often looked as if Price was ready to make a fight. Dodge would get the 4th Iowa Regiment ready in a skirmish line, as well as the rest of his brigade, mostly at creeks with a wide-open valley. Price would open with his artillery and cavalry and give every indication that he was ready to make a heroic defensive stand. The Union cavalry out in front would fall back and let the infantry catch up. Then Price's men would slip away. Only at Crane Creek, Flat Creek and Sugar Creek were there sharp skirmishes. Some were surprised Price did not make more of a fight of it at Flat Creek. Sometimes Price's men would line the road, fire off two volleys and then slip off the road into the woods. Finally, Curtis' army crossed the state line into Arkansas. Curtis' men then came to a broad plateau known as Pea Ridge. There his men found a strong contingent of Confederates with infantry, artillery and cavalry blocking the Telegraph Road, ready to make a stand at Little Sugar Creek. Thinking these were Price's men finally not retreating anymore, Curtis made a cavalry charge and was surprised the Confederates did not run as they had before. However, in front of Curtis were the fresh Arkansas and Louisiana troops of Confederate general Ben McCulloch. Curtis called up reinforcements of Dodge's 4th Iowa Infantry and the rest of the 1st Brigade. After an artillery duel, the Confederates withdrew under the cover of darkness. By the time Dodge's troops got into line, the fighting was over. McCulloch decided that their main encampment at

Cross Hollow was not a good defensive position. His men abandoned it and went to Fayetteville. Fayetteville had plenty of food, ammunition and other military stores, and McCulloch, not wanting Curtis to get his hands on them, set the town ablaze. McCulloch and Price then headed their armies south to the Boston Mountains along the Telegraph Road. Price's army had been retreating for 120 miles from Springfield. Hungarian-born Union general Asboth went down to Bentonville, Arkansas, and found the town deserted. However, they found 32 Rebel soldiers hiding in the underbrush. They then went to Fayetteville and found little resistance. The Rebels had left poisoned food and drink, and 42 Union men became violently ill while one Union soldier died. At Bentonville and Fayetteville, the Rebel flags were taken down, and now the flag of the United States of America flew over these two Arkansas towns. Lieutenant Henry G. Ankeny of the 4th Iowa Infantry Regiment wrote to his wife of the rugged terrain around Springfield, Missouri, and as they drove into Arkansas he penned, "We must rid Arkansas of all the Rebel bands and restore the 'old flag' to these people."[60]

During this campaign, Dodge tented with Sheridan. Dodge marveled at Sheridan's efficiency in feeding the army and his horses. In the Eastern Theater of the Civil War, the armies could be supplied by steamboats or railroads. However, in the Pea Ridge campaign, Curtis and Sigel's armies were sometimes 300 miles away from the nearest railhead or steamboat landing. The food had to be foraged for or hauled by wagons over some of the roughest terrain in the United States. This area of southern Missouri and northern Arkansas was sparsely settled, with few roads; and what roads existed were usually dirt ones of poor construction. Many times the farm fields were little patches on the side of a mountain, not like the acres of good farmland in Iowa where the crops could be seen to the horizon for miles and miles. Foraging could at times show very slim pickings in this region.

However, Sheridan attacked these problems with the zeal he was to show for the rest of his career. Sheridan relied on Dodge's 4th Iowa and the 36th Illinois Volunteer Infantry to help him forage for livestock for the troops to eat. These men found chickens, beef cattle and the famed razorbacks; many of these pigs ran wild in the Arkansas and Missouri outback. Sheridan found all the millwrights, machinists and millers in the 4th Iowa and 36th Illinois to run the mills in southern Missouri and northern Arkansas. There was not a lot of wheat in this region, but corn for corn meal was more common. Sheridan and these mills kept the Army of the Southwest in flour and cornmeal. Sheridan was somewhat miffed because Sigel's troops would not help forage or supply food for his army. Sheridan was forever grateful to Dodge and the 4th Iowa for their help. In his memoirs Sheridan stated, "I was several times on the verge of personal conflict with irate regimental commanders, but Colonel G.M. Dodge so greatly sustained me with General Curtis by strong moral support, and by such efficient detail from his regiment-the Forth Iowa Volunteer Infantry—that I still bear him and it great affection and lasting gratitude."[61]

Sheridan confided in Dodge that he would like to get a field command and get out of the quartermaster corps. Sheridan was of the mind that with a field command he could make a name for himself. However, Sheridan had no friends in high places that could make this happen. Sheridan had discovered that certain members of the Army of the Southwest were stealing horses from the army and attempting to sell them back to Sheridan. After he had proof this was happening, Sheridan refused to pay the thieves for the stolen horses. The matter was kicked upstairs to Curtis, and Curtis told Sheridan to pay for these stolen horses. Sheridan refused. Curtis and Sheridan came to loggerheads over the matter, and Curtis made it clear he would have Sheridan's commission if he did not comply with Curtis' wishes. Sheridan knew he would lose this argument and resigned his position as quartermaster. Sheridan was reassigned to the telegraph office in Springfield. Dodge and some of the other officers in the Army of the Southwest went to Curtis about reinstating Sheridan. Dodge and the other officers had been impressed with Sheridan's efficiency. Curtis got very angry and adamantly told Dodge and the others that he would not reinstate Sheridan. Curtis' adjutant general, Captain T.J. McKinney, told Dodge and the officers that if they pressed the matter they would lose their commissions.[62]

The Boston Mountains were to the south of Curtis, and after Curtis took Fayetteville, he decided the town left his army too exposed. He knew an offensive into these mountains would likely not be successful. Therefore, he moved his "American" division to Cross Hollow and Sigel's "German" division to McKissick's Creek, not far from Bentonville. It took Van Dorn nine days to reach the armies of McCulloch and Price in the Boston Mountains. Van Dorn, during his trip, had fallen into an icy stream and was ill with a fever. He arrived in the Boston Mountains in an ambulance. Van Dorn's plan was to attack Sigel's forces with his much larger army, later attack Curtis' smaller army, and then take his armies north to St. Louis. Van Dorn ordered General Albert Pike and his Texans and Native Americans from the Indian Nations to join him in his attack. Van Dorn wanted the men to take just three days of rations, as he figured that after their victory they could live off the Federal stores. By now, Curtis' united command of his and Sigel's divisions equaled 10,000 men, while Van Dorn had 16,000 men. Van Dorn called his new Confederate outfit the Army of the West. Van Dorn, supremely confident and impulsive, did not get adequate scouting reports or reports on the terrain ahead. The rugged topography of northwest Arkansas slowed his army down and the slogging up and down this terrain wore his men out. All Van Dorn could think about was destroying Curtis' army and heading for what would be his fountain of glory: the capture of St. Louis.

Each side committed to raids on the other's camps. Curtis' cavalry raided their way back into Fayetteville but left after three days. A Texas cavalry unit raided in Curtis' rear at Keetsville in Missouri. Dodge's men were on the extreme eastern flank of Curtis' army, and when the Texas cavalry came back to their base in the Boston Mountains, Dodge became very alarmed that such a large force had come so near to him. He moved his troops closer to the main body of Curtis' army at Cross Hollow so he would not become cut off from the main body of the Federal army.[63]

Van Dorn moved out his army to the north. Price's men were in great spirits to be on the offensive again and with the strong hope of getting back to their beloved Missouri. However, their mood soon changed. Van Dorn marched his men at an unreasonable pace, and when they came to Fayetteville, a winter storm blew into northwest Arkansas, and the cold wind brought snow and sleet. When the Army of the West stopped for the night, they had no tents, as Van Dorn had them traveling light. They almost froze to death. Because of the bad weather, Curtis had no pickets out. When

Curtis heard that the Confederate Army of the West was on the move, he decided to abandon Cross Hollow for defensive positions along Little Sugar Creek. This withdrawal was hard because of the snow and cold and miserable conditions. Captain Henry J.B. Cummings of Company F of the 4th Iowa Infantry wrote to his wife, "It was snowing and most intensely cold.... I never suffered so much in my life." Cummings had been the prosecuting attorney for Madison County in Iowa prior to the Civil War. He helped raise Company F and was made captain by the men in that company. By September of 1862, Cummings was made regimental colonel of the 39th Iowa Infantry. After the war Cummings was elected to the United States Congress from 1877 to 1879. Cummings lived the rest of his life in Winterset in Madison County, Iowa, and passed away in 1909.[64]

The steep limestone bluffs of Little Sugar Creek and the redoubts built for artillery and rifle pits that Curtis had constructed after the men made it from Cross Hollow looked formidable. Curtis tried to impress upon Sigel the importance of moving his troops quickly. As usual, Sigel took his time, but he managed to get the main body of his troops close to Curtis before Van Dorn could cut them off around Bentonville. Only Sigel's rear guard did not make it in, and to no one's surprise, Sigel was in personal command of his rear guard. Curtis set his defenses facing south, convinced that Van Dorn's Confederates would attack from the south to the north on the Telegraph Road. Sigel and his rear guard finally made it into camp, having been harassed by General James McIntosh's Confederate cavalry brigade. Another Union outpost in Huntsville was abandoned as it was in danger of being surrounded, but they made it to the defensive position of Little Sugar Creek.[65]

When Dodge was in Rolla he had organized scouts and spies from the 24th and 25th Missouri Volunteer infantries. These men knew northern Arkansas very well, and on March 6 they came to Dodge with the information that Van Dorn with a large contingent of troops was planning to attack the Army of the Southwest from the north. They would achieve this by going up the Bentonville Detour Road; where it made a junction with the Telegraph Road, Van Dorn would head south on the Telegraph Road to reach Curtis' rear. The Bentonville Detour was on the extreme right flank of the Army of the Southwest. Dodge notified Curtis of this, but Curtis seamed peeved and dismissive of Dodge's report. Dodge suggested they go on the Bentonville Detour and fell trees to slow the Confederates' advance. If Dodge was right, then Curtis had fronted his defensive structures all wrong. Curtis, probably still smarting from Dodge's support of Sheridan, barked out, "You take a portion of your command and go there and blockade the road." Even though there were other commands much closer to the Bentonville Detour Road, Dodge took six companies from the 4th Iowa Infantry and one company of the 3rd Illinois Cavalry and headed for the Bentonville Detour. There was a gorge along the Bentonville Detour called the Cross Timber Hollows that Dodge noted was perfect for obstructing the road. For three hours, Dodge's men felled trees across the road and created a formidable blockade of the way. Putting these timbers on the road to obstruct the Confederate army's progress had a profound impact on the outcome of the battle. Captain S.D. Nichols of Company C of the 4th Iowa got lost, but Dodge was glad when they finally showed up, as they had encountered Van Dorn's army. Dodge reported to Curtis that Van Dorn's men were coming down the Bentonville Detour road to the rear of the Army of the Southwest and that he thought they would also strike the right flank of Union lines. Curtis had no pickets set up on the right flank. Again, Curtis dismissed Dodge's report and told him he was mistaken. Van Dorn had completely fooled Curtis with a ruse. The Confederate general had a small group of men stationed to the south of Curtis' defensive works on the Telegraph Road. He had these men create a large group of campfires, giving Curtis the impression of a large force in front of him, all the while Van Dorn was moving the Army of the West to the right and rear of Curtis' army.

Curtis called Dodge along with other division and brigade commanders to a Union war council. During this meeting, Curtis heard heavy fire coming from their rear around the area of the Elkhorn Tavern. Dodge had disobeyed orders and pulled his men out of the Little Sugar Creek fortifications, as he was certain that Van Dorn was attacking from the rear. He had his men moving towards the area of the Elkhorn Tavern. Curtis heard firing from that direction and wanted to know whose men those were. Dodge said, "Mine." Dodge's men were near the Elkhorn Tavern and Colonel Carr dispatched the 9th Iowa Regiment from his division to that area. A bomb fell among Dodge's fifers and drummers, and for the rest of the day they were quiet. Dodge had trained a company of skirmishers and sent them to meet the Confederate troops. The 4th Iowa Infantry were right in the middle of the fighting with Price's army. General Van Dorn had attached himself to Price's army.[66]

Dodge's brigade, anchored by the 4th Iowa Regiment and the 9th Iowa Regiment, imposed a standoff with the larger forces of Price's army. Dodge estimated they had 3,000 men holding off nearly 5,000 Confederates. The musket fire and artillery fire were most intense. The 4th Iowa Infantry in their black overcoats that Dodge had procured in St. Louis were most notable on the battlefield. Dodge's brigade held firm, but the 9th Iowa Infantry had to fall back. Dodge sent Williamson to go to Colonel Carr, the division commander, and inform him of what was going on. Dodge also noticed a new line of Union artillery was sending half of its shells into the rear of his brigade. The enemy at almost point-blank range discovered Williamson but could not hit him. Williamson got back and told Dodge they were surrounded. Dodge then fell back, his brigade coming into the view of the enemy, but due to the smoke, haze, artillery and gunfire the enemy were unable to ascertain that they were Union soldiers. All the while, Curtis still had most of his command stationed behind his defensive position at Little Sugar Creek. Curtis rode up to Dodge, who told him they were out of ammunition. Curtis said they would have to make a bayonet charge. Before Dodge could give the command, the 4th Iowa Regiment had their bayonets in place and were charging across the field. Fortunately, the enemy had moved out, or Dodge's casualty rates would have been even higher than they were. The 4th Iowa and the 9th Iowa regiments suffered the highest regimental casualty rates at Pea Ridge. Carr's 4th Division of which both the 4th Iowa and 9th Iowa were a part, suffered the highest casualty rates of all four of the Union divisions. In his official report Curtis said, "These two regiments [the 4th and 9th] won imperishable honors."[67]

Captain William H. Kinsman of Company B, 4th Iowa Infantry, was from Council Bluffs and had at one time been a reporter for the local newspaper. He gave this account of the Battle at Pea Ridge:

**The M1841 Mountain Howitzer was a small 12-pounder smoothbore that worked well in the western mountainous regions such as in Arkansas. It did not have the range of the bigger guns, but it was easy to disassemble and carry into remote areas where there were no roads. Some of these howitzers made their way to the battlefield at Pea Ridge. Eventually, these howitzers were used out West to fight the Plains warriors (author's collection).**

Colonel Dodge opened the ball and the battle was soon raging all along the line with a fierceness and obstinacy which omened a terrific struggle.... The thunder of the artillery was terrific and the shot and shell hissed and screamed through the air like flying devils, while the infantry of both armies with their rifles, shotguns and muskets, kept a perfect hurricane of death howling through the woods. The rebels fought well, but generally fired too high, and their batteries, although getting our range accurately, missed the elevation much of the time. Their poor shooting was our salvation. Had they done as well as our men with the tremendous odds against us they must have annihilated us. The enemy was clear around our right flank, enveloping us, and it looked as though they would capture Dodge's brigade, when Colonel Dodge took a battalion of Colonel Carr's regiment, the Third Illinois cavalry, and charged the forces that were turning our right flank like a whirlwind. Everything gave way before them. Every man in that battalion seemed to ride for his life, and they swept way around our front, routing and demoralizing that flank of the enemy, and effectually freeing our rear and flank. Price told some of our boys of the Fourth Iowa who were captured on the day of the fight and have since escaped, that we fought more like devils than human beings. The Rebel Colonels (several of them) inquired of our boys who those black-coated fellows were and who led them. They said there must have been at least 3,000 of them. When the boys told them there were less than 600 of them, the Colonels said they needn't tell them any such stuff as that; that they knew it was a damned lie. But they sent their compliments to Colonel Dodge for the bravery of himself and his command, and well they might ... many of these Confederate troops did the hard fighting at the

**Elkhorn Tavern, Pea Ridge, Arkansas. Although the surrounding terrain at Pea Ridge is extremely rugged and almost impassable in places, Pea Ridge sits on a broad plateau right over the Missouri-Arkansas state line, and this was where the majority of the battle took place (author's collection).**

> Wilson Creek battle. All day, from 8:30 in the morning until 5:30 at night Dodge's Brigade held its ground, dealing death into the Rebel ranks, and when dark came with ammunition expended the Fourth Iowa walked away from the field in good order, with the sullen savage tread of men who might be driven by main strength, but could not be conquered.

A log cabin close to the Elkhorn Tavern area, which the Federals were using as a field hospital, was overrun by the Confederates. The hospital steward, Baker, reported that when General Price came up he asked him who those black-coated devils were, and when Baker told him there were only 600 men he did not believe him. He said no 600 men could stand such attacks, and paid the brigade a very high compliment for those fighting, and told Baker to give them his compliments. Captain William H. Kinsman was a good example of the hardscrabble frontiersman that were common in the 4th Iowa Infantry. Born poor in Nova Scotia, Canada, Kinsmen went to sea for three years as a youngster. He managed to save up enough money to take some law and college courses in the United States. He made his way from Cleveland to Davenport, Iowa. He ran out of money at Davenport and had to walk roughly 300 miles across the state of Iowa to reach Council Bluffs. While in Council Bluffs, Kinsman taught school, wrote for the local newspaper, and passed the local bar association to become a lawyer. In 1859, he caught the gold fever and walked the 600 miles out to the gold fields of Colorado. He had to pass through hostile territory of some Native American tribes. He walked back to Council Bluffs from Colorado, and when the Civil War broke out he enlisted and was made a lieutenant in the 4th Iowa Infantry. He rose up to the rank of captain. Kinsman was made a lt. colonel and then colonel of the 23rd Iowa Infantry. At the Battle of Champion's Hill in May of 1863, his luck ran out and he was killed on the field of battle.[68]

Fortunately for Curtis, the Confederates' advantage in manpower slowly began to evaporate. Because of the long marches from the Boston Mountains in bad weather that Van Dorn had forced on his men and the lack of food for the men in Price's and McCulloch's forces, men began to drop off in significant numbers on the Bentonville Detour. Finally, Curtis started to bring men out of the defenses at Little Sugar Creek to the main battlefield by Elkhorn Tavern and the Pea Ridge Plateau and relieved Carr's 4th Division. Van Dorn became alarmed at how strung out his army had become and by the fact that his cavalry was boxed in behind the slow-moving infantry. He originally had planned an early morning attack, but there were parts of his command that would not get there until the afternoon. Dodge's felled trees had greatly helped in delaying the commands of Price and McCulloch. Both Price and Van Dorn mention the trees as a great impediment to their advance. Van Dorn had no engineer corps that could have cleared this blockade faster. Van Dorn heard about a shortcut from the Bentonville Detour called Ford Road, which he had McCulloch's men take. Van Dorn also sent Pike's Native Americans and his Texans to follow McCulloch's men.[69]

Curtis moved some of his men up by Leetown, where they clashed with McCulloch's men in a firefight. Leetown was close to Curtis' defense position along Little Sugar Creek. Union artillery fire startled McCulloch and McIntosh's cavalry. They had heard the gunfire and artillery fire near Elkhorn Tavern, and they thought that was going to be where they fought. The Union's 1st Missouri Flying Artillery opened up, as did a charge of Bussey's Union cavalrymen. But they were both badly outnumbered and were defeated by the overwhelming forces of the Confederates. Pike's Native American units were composed of Cherokees, Choctaws, Creeks, Seminoles, Chickasaw and a few other Native Americans from different tribes, plus some Texans. These Native American troops did capture a couple of Federal artillery batteries. Stand Waite's Cherokee Mounted Rifles were there. Waite would become the only Native American in the Confederate army to obtain the rank of general. Clement V. Rogers was a hard-charging slave owner, father of famed American humorist and author Will Rogers. Clement V. Rogers was an officer in Waite's Mounted Confederate Cherokees. Instead of immediately following up, McCulloch's men milled around the battlefield admiring their work. In sworn affidavits, Federals said they saw Pike's Native Americans scalping and mutilating members of the 3rd Iowa Cavalry.[70]

As McCulloch's men reorganized Osterhaus, the Union division commander had Colonel Greusel's infantry of Sigel's 2nd Brigade form a line. Bussey's scattered command started to reorganize. Curtis had bypassed Sigel and dealt directly with his division commanders. McCulloch, seeing the Federals reorganizing, decided to gather intelligence as he often did. General Ben McCulloch, with his black velvet suit on, rode with two companies of cavalry as bodyguards and was gathering intelligence on the enemy in front of him. McCulloch was spotted on a slight hill between some bushes and trees, a lone rider with a Maynard rifle slung over his shoulder. Sharpshooters from Company

B of the 36th Illinois Infantry saw him; shots rang out and the Confederate commander pitched off his horse, dead. Command of McCulloch's men now fell to cavalry leader McIntosh. However, McIntosh did not have the temperament for such a large command, and before he could see if his orders were being carried out, he went with his old unit, the 2nd Mounted Arkansas Rifles. He was charging Greusel's troops when they opened fire, and he fell dead off his horse. Ironically, there were few casualties on either side at Leetown, but two of the highest Confederate commanders had been killed. That left Colonel Hébert and his Louisiana and Arkansas troops in command. Hébert did not know McCulloch and McIntosh had both been killed. Hébert advanced as planned on Osterhaus' division, covering the left flank but not realizing he had no support on the right flank. McCulloch's subordinates decided to pull back, leaving the right Confederate flank exposed.

Curtis ordered reinforcements to both the Elkhorn Tavern area and Leetown. The general in six hours had changed the facing of the Union Army of the Southwest from south to north. Asboth was able to reinforce Carr and Dodge, who were fighting near the Elkhorn Tavern, but Asboth and his men arrived late in the day. Dodge had been struck by a large branch of a tree and knocked off his horse. He did not think much of it at the time. Union colonel Davis reached the Leetown area with reinforcements and waited for Hébert's charge.[71]

Hébert's men and the Union soldiers came to quick blows in the dense overgrowth of trees and bushes in what was known as Morgan's Woods. Hébert made some advances but kept waiting for reinforcements or word from McCulloch, but that never came. Thousands of men and artillery stood frozen, leaderless, none of McCulloch's subordinate commanders coming to Hébert's aid. Hébert pressed forward, but his men lost track of him and no word came from the Louisianan. His command faltered, and without the exhortations of their leader, their advance collapsed. Confederate general Pike briefly took command, but no one took his orders seriously and eventually the Arkansas politician and his Native Americans retired from the field. The Confederate army was in a general retreat from the Leetown area, and some were trying to make their way to Price's army near the Elkhorn Tavern. Many of the others were heading back to Ford Road and the Bentonville Detour. A Texas cavalryman, Colonel Elkanah Greer, learned he was ranking officer, but he could not rally the frightened and retreating Confederates. The fight at Leetown was concluded. The order from Van Dorn to hold their positions went unheeded, and the retreat to the Bentonville Detour was now in full force. It later would be discovered that Hébert had been taken prisoner.[72]

On the night of the 7th of March, Dodge's troops stayed put with no camp fires to warm them or food to eat. General Van Dorn stayed in a nice bed in the Elkhorn Tavern that night. He had moved his artillery by the tavern, and they were keeping the Federals at bay. Van Dorn was proud of the way Price's Missourians had fought. They looked like experienced troopers. However, as Van Dorn looked at his overall situation, things did not look good. He was about out of ammunition and his chief ordinance officer could not find his ammunition wagons. McCulloch and McIntosh had been killed, and Hebert was missing. Van Dorn's right flank was in full retreat. Only a few of McCulloch's command had reached Van Dorn at Elkhorn Tavern. At seven in the morning, Van Dorn opened up with an artillery barrage that drove Jeff Davis' Union men backwards. Curtis and Dodge waited for Sigel to get his men in line at a slow pace. Sigel's men had a good night's sleep and ate a leisurely breakfast before finally getting in line. Dodge drove his troops to the east, hoping to get to Van Dorn's rear. By 10:00 o'clock Van Dorn knew the situation was hopeless, and he prepared to retreat south on the Huntsville Road. Dodge did not know it at the time, but his advance was merely a fight with Price's rear guard heading down the Huntsville road. Dodge had three horses shot out from beneath him. One time he and another officer were riding side by side, and one Confederate bullet went through both horses, killing them instantly. Dodge managed to jump free of his dead horse. Dodge was so intent on the battle that he forgot about the other officer, who was pinned under his dead horse. The officer said, "Colonel, you are not going to leave me this way, are you?" Dodge hurried back and freed the officer from underneath his dead horse. Dodge was ordered back in line at the Elkhorn Tavern. It seems that Sigel had withdrawn his troops and was heading back to Missouri. After Dodge moved his men back into line he pitched forward off his horse and collapsed. He had to be carried to his tent. The wound he had received the previous day was more serious than he had thought. He obviously had been running on adrenaline, and that had worn off. The doctors did not think the wound was due to a tree branch but to a shell that had exploded near his side.[73]

The 4th Iowa Infantry lost almost one half of the regiment at Pea Ridge due being killed, wounded or missing in action. The day after the Battle at Pea Ridge was over, Dodge received a note from a widow in Illinois. She said she had three sons fighting for the Union and her youngest son, who was not in good health, was in Dodge's brigade. She pleaded with Dodge to send her youngest son home because her heart was heavy with loneliness. Dodge investigated and found that her son was Preston Green, who had died valiantly on March 7 at Pea Ridge. When Dodge was forming the 4th Iowa Infantry in Council Bluffs, a father and his two sons from Madison County, Iowa, all joined together. They were Isaac Debusk, age 48, his son William S. Dubusk, age 20, and youngest son Elihu Debusk, age 18. When the 4th Iowa was stationed in Rolla, Missouri, the youngest son, Elihu, died of typhoid fever. On March 7 during the Battle at Pea Ridge, William S. Debusk was wounded and died the next day. The father Isaac had been on the sick list, and he died eight days after his son William died. The cause of Isaac's death was listed as unknown, but most of the men in the 4th Iowa thought Isaac had died of a broken heart. The newspaper in Winterset wrote this, and it was reprinted in the Davenport (Iowa) *Daily Gazette*, "[Isaac] had been on the sick list for some time, whose death lay at the door of the traitors who are seeking to destroy the Government."[74]

The battle at Pea Ridge had cleared the Confederate army out of Missouri. If Missouri had been a Confederate State, it would have had the second largest white population of any of the Confederate States. St. Louis's wealth would have been a key addition to the coffers of the Confederate treasury. Missouri's lead mines and other treasures would have been a major factor in the Confederacy's continuing to fight. Van Dorn and Price took their armies many miles away from the Federal lines to Van Buren, Arkansas. Then Van Dorn was told to move his Army of the West to the east side of the Mississippi River. It looked like there was a big fight brewing around the Shiloh Church in Tennessee.[75]

2. "Who were those black-coated devils?" 73

**Four artillery pieces remain silent at the Pea Ridge National Military Park in Arkansas. The Union army had an advantage in artillery pieces during the battle. Bronzed rifled artillery pieces were common in the Union army, while the Confederates had only four rifled artillery pieces at Pea Ridge (author's collection).**

The wound on Dodge's side would not heal. In a letter to his father Sylvanus, Grenville told how weak he was. It is unknown whether his wound became infected. He was taken by ambulance along with the other wounded on a rugged journey to the better-equipped Federal hospital in St. Louis. When Dodge's ambulance got to Lebanon, Missouri, he received word that he had been promoted to brigadier-general for his actions at Pea Ridge. At Rolla, Dodge was able to travel by rail, which was a little better than the jarring ride of a wagon. Lt. Colonel John Galligan of the 4th Iowa Infantry had been wounded at Pea Ridge, and he resigned his commission. The men of the 4th Iowa voted that they wanted Adjutant Lieutenant James A. Williamson to be the next regimental colonel of the 4th Iowa and S.D. Nichols to be lt. colonel. Governor Kirkwood would not appoint S.D. Nichols as lt. colonel. Dodge was not certain why Nichols was not appointed. Dodge noted that Nichols was very bright and had studied military tactics but could be at times troublesome. Williamson was promoted to lt. colonel and then colonel and took over command of the 4th Iowa Volunteer Infantry. Captain George Burton of Company D, who was born in Ireland, was elevated to lt. colonel. Burton was wounded and had to be taken to the hospital in St. Louis. He had a terrible wound in his arm and thought he would lose it. However, the doctors managed to save it. Dodge noted that Burton under fire was a cool as a cucumber and that he had nearly bled to death. One of the captains in the 4th Iowa was angry that Lt. Williamson was made colonel and jumped over all the ranking captains. This officer then joined another Iowa unit.[76]

Van Dorn's adjutant wrote to Curtis thanking him for allowing a Confederate burial squad to come back to Pea Ridge and bury the Confederate dead. Curtis wrote back that he was very disappointed in Pike's Indian division for their scalping and mutilation of the Union dead. The Confederates countered by saying that when their men surrendered to become prisoners of war they were "murdered" by the Union German troops. It was noted by Curtis that a Captain Clark, a Confederate officer, was killed in the battle; he was the son of renowned explorer Meriwether Clark of Lewis and Clark fame.[77]

CHAPTER 3

# Battle Tested

Alonzo Gaston was coming home for summer break at Oberlin College. He could see his home town of Tabor, Iowa. He would be glad to see his father George, his mother Maria, and his brothers and sisters. However, his heart was heavy. He wanted to join the Union army, but his mother and father refused to give him their blessing and let him enlist. His mother was especially adamant against his joining the Union army. His brother Alex also wanted to enroll in the Union army. However, when Alex got married he gave up the idea of becoming a soldier. At 22 Alonzo certainly thought he was old enough to make his own decisions. Already his friends Ed Hill, Ben Sheldon, Sturgis Williams and George Weavers had joined the 4th Iowa Volunteer Infantry Regiment, and they had just won a huge battle at Pea Ridge in Arkansas.[1]

His parents certainly believed in the Union cause. It was not as if his parents and family had never faced danger. When Alonzo was in his pregnant mother's womb, they crossed the unpredictable Missouri River in a hollowed-out log that served as a ferry. His brother Alex, then two years old, went across with them along with a barrel of flour in the front of the log to act as ballast. When they crossed the Missouri River and went from Iowa to the Nebraska Territory, they spent five weeks so his mother could recover from giving birth to Alonzo. They proceeded to the Pawnee Indian Reservation 125 miles west of the Missouri River. The Gastons were missionaries and government farmers on the reservation. The Pawnee Reservation was under constant attack by the powerful Sioux tribe. Alonzo and his brother Alex learned to spread out on the floor along with the Pawnee children when they heard the Sioux's war whistles, made of turkey bones.[2] The Gastons spent five years at the Pawnee Reservation. When the Sioux started attacking and killing more on the Pawnee Reservation, the reservation was moved closer to the Missouri River. After Maria became sick with the ague (a kind of fever), the family decided to move back to their home in Oberlin, Ohio. After they moved back, George could not get the Missouri Valley out of his head, and he pondered the idea of establishing an Oberlin-like college in southwest Iowa.[3]

Oberlin College supported the equality of the races and genders and was adamantly against slavery. The Gastons moved to southwest Iowa and established the town of Tabor, Iowa. Because of financial considerations, they were not able to start the college until after the Civil War. However, the Gastons' house became a stop on the Underground Railroad for slaves escaping from Missouri, Arkansas, the Indian Nations of what is now Oklahoma, and Kansas. Kansas was known in the 1850s as "Bleeding Kansas" due to the ongoing battle for control of the state between the anti-slavery abolitionists and proponents of slavery. The Gastons helped collect guns, ammunition, clothing and other items for the anti-slavery settlers in Kansas to fight against the pro-slavery settlers. Loren, Alonzo's adopted younger brother, once found a large trunk full of Bowie knives in the house. There were Sharps rifles hidden under the bed. Out in the barn were long muskets, and ammunition was all over the place. Mother Maria called this "Kansas furniture."[4] John Brown, the famous abolitionist and fighter against slavery, stayed often in the Gaston house. One day Brown brought two fugitive slaves with him. Brown, the fugitive slaves and the Gastons, along with Alonzo, were eating dinner. A slave hunter came to the door, asking father George if he had seen the two runaway bondsmen. Brown and the bondsmen hid away in the house. George answered that he would not tell the slaver anything. The slaver then left. The Gaston family helped dozens of fugitive slaves to escape bondage. Alonzo had known John Brown and his men John Kagi and Aaron Stevens. Alonzo knew John Brown's sons, who were killed at Harper's Ferry: Oliver Brown and Watson Brown. Kagi was killed at Harper's Ferry during their raid on the federal arsenal there to arm black slaves in the South. Stevens and Brown were hung for the Harper's Ferry raid.[5]

Samuel Curtis was an Iowa congressman and West Point graduate. He resigned from Congress and was quickly promoted to brigadier-general in the Union army. Curtis was commander of the Army of the Southwest and was credited with the victory at the Battle of Pea Ridge, where he was outnumbered by Rebel forces (Library of Congress).

On August 27 of 1862, Alonzo went to Council Bluffs and joined the 4th Iowa Volunteer Infantry Regiment. He was put in Company A so he could be with his friends Hill, Sheldon, Williams and Weavers. Alonzo was listed as being 5'9" and of dark complexion with black hair. He received a $25 bonus (standard for the time for signing up in the Union army), and his term of enlistment was for three years. Although he had been a student, his occupation was listed as farmer. On September 5, 1862, Alonzo married fellow Tabor resident Hannah Maria Cummings. He was only with his bride for a week before he shipped out in mid–September.[6]

A few weeks after the Battle at Pea Ridge, the 4th Iowa was sent to Forsyth, Missouri. The men were short of rations and clothing. Lieutenant Ankeny of Company H of the 4th Iowa wrote to his wife of this time, "One will never get used to short rations." Nobody could supply an army like Phillip Sheridan. From Forsyth the men of the 4th slogged their way to Batesville, Arkansas, during a period of intense rain. The men described Batesville as being a beautiful place along the White River. The regiment could be resupplied by steamship from the river. From Batesville the men marched to

Helena, Arkansas, on the Mississippi River. The 4th Iowa got to Helena on July 3, 1862, and were in need of new clothing and equipment, as the rain and heat had taken their toll. Captain Taylor of the 4th Iowa Infantry wrote to Dodge of their march to Helena. He said, "We arrived here day before yesterday, worn down by a long and wearisome march, made on half rations with scarcely any water, men naked almost and covered with vermin." Taylor was convinced that if Dodge had still been in command, these hardships would not have befallen the 4th Iowa. Alonzo Gaston caught up with the 4th Iowa while they were in Helena.[7]

In November, Alonzo started writing terse entries in his diary that give a clue to the life of an enlisted man. On November 27, 1862, he wrote, "Left camp at daybreak and boarded the steamer *Nebraska*. Fleet started about 2 p.m. Sailed to Delta, landed and camped." On November 28, Gaston wrote, "Marched about 22 miles. Camped away from water and ate." The next day, "Reached the mouth of the Coldwater [River]." The Coldwater River is in northwest Mississippi. The November 30 entry reads, "Moved camp and rested." On December 1 Alonzo and the 4th Iowa "lay till 4 p.m. then marched six miles farther and back nearly to the same camp." On December 2 Alonzo stood picket as it rained more or less all day. Two days later, it rained all afternoon and into the night. The men stayed in camp.[8]

At some point in November of 1862, discipline broke down in the 4th Iowa. Twenty soldiers from the 4th Iowa went on a foray into Mississippi and got into serious trouble. Colonel Williamson wrote to Dodge in desperation of "acts by soldiers which would disgrace any army of half civilized men on earth. Theft and rape were the chief results of the expedition." John A. Miller, the 1st sergeant of Company G of the 4th Iowa, wrote to a friend it was believed that 2nd Lt. Frederick Teal would be charged—Teal, who had so ably served as a spy for the 4th Iowa in Missouri at the start of the Civil War. It is not clear what punishment Teal or any of the others in the 4th Iowa received. It is known that at a later date Teal was promoted to the rank of captain and eventually was severely wounded. After the war Teal became deeply involved in the Union reunions of the Army of the Tennessee.[9]

On the 5th of December, the 4th Iowa was on the move again. Alonzo wrote, "Started at daybreak on the way to Helena. Road very muddy, snowed a little in the a.m. Cleared off about noon. Camped about 3 miles west of the Hill Plantation." The next day, "Marched about 20 miles, camped about 7 miles from the river." On the 7th of December the diary entry reads, "Sabbath morn; marched to the river, took a boat and arrived about 2 p.m. and was detained and did not reach camp until about 5 o'clock."[10]

Grenville Dodge, now Brigadier-General Dodge, was receiving congratulations from all over the country for the stand he and the 4th Iowa had made at Pea Ridge. He was still in St Louis recovering from his wound, which would never quite heal. His wife Anne had joined him in St. Louis to nurse him back to health. They were staying with Charles Pegram and his wife in St. Louis. Although Dodge did not always see eye to eye with Pegram, the Dodges appreciated Pegram's hospitality. Pegram was supplying the Union army with provisions and goods and making money hand over fist. Pegram wanted Nathan Dodge to join him in his money-making army supply business, but Nathan stayed in Council Bluffs. Although Dodge's military life was going well, his personal life was not. His brother Nathan Dodge was sending him reports that John Baldwin was dissolving the business of Baldwin and Dodge and also Baldwin and Pegram and Co. Baldwin was selling off the assets of these companies at bargain-basement prices, and instead of paying off the considerable debts of these two companies, Baldwin was converting the cash into his own accounts and building up his herd of sheep. Grenville had been sending a good portion of his colonel's salary to retire the debt of these two companies and was naturally upset with Baldwin. Also, the House of Representatives had passed a bill authorizing a transcontinental railroad, and Dodge's railroad-business associates such as Peter Dey were pleading with him to resign his commission in the Union army and get ready to start building this new railroad line. However, Dodge was steadfast in his belief that the Union cause must be seen to its conclusion. In May, Dodge told his superiors that he had recovered. He reported to General Henry Halleck at Corinth in Mississippi. He met up with Phillip Sheridan again. Sheridan was still a captain and Halleck's quartermaster. However, much to the delight of Dodge, Sheridan was to receive a field command of a cavalry unit and the rank of colonel. Within days, he was given the command of a brigade, and he soon distinguished himself on the field of battle and was promoted to brigadier-general.[11]

Dodge received his orders to report to General Quimby in Columbus, Kentucky. Dodge was to rebuild the Mobile and Ohio Railroad from Columbus, Kentucky, to Corinth, Mississippi, a distance of some 150 miles. Dodge had 8,000 men in his pioneer corps, but he used two regiments of Wisconsin lumberjacks as the heart of his corps. Dodge wrote to his wife Anne that he was back in the railroad building business, and he seemed very happy to be so.[12]

However, Dodge became very frustrated that as soon as he repaired the track, the regular Confederate cavalry of Nathan Bedford Forrest and William H. Jackson tore up the track and shot at his pickets. In addition, Confederate guerrilla bands were doing the same thing. Dodge initiated the building of two-story log blockhouses. Each story faced a different direction so those inside could see attackers coming on any route. These blockhouses were placed near bridges or other valuable assets, and a company of Union soldiers in these blockhouses could stand off a regiment of Confederates. The only serious vulnerability of these blockhouses was to artillery, but very few of these railroad-raiding Confederates had artillery with them. Once these blockhouses were erected, successful attacks against Dodge's rebuilt railroad diminished dramatically. Dodge also issued a general order telling civilians that if they aided and abetted these Confederate guerrilla bands or if they knew they were in the area of Federal forces and did not notify the Federals, they could be subject to the forfeiture of their property. In addition, Dodge said that anyone—white or black, male or female—who provided reliable information as to the whereabouts of these guerrilla bands would be eligible for a liberal reward.[13]

Dodge's reputation as a railroad-builder extraordinaire was spreading among the high Union command. His blockhouse idea had caught on and was being used in other Union commands. When Dodge was headquartered in Trenton, Tennessee, his troops met a company of Faulkner's Rebels who were part of Jackson's cavalry at Dyersville, Tennessee. They killed some 30 Rebels and took 53 horses, and most of Faulkner's command were left without clothes, arms or horses. Dodge said two black men took his men through the Rebel pickets when no whites would help. They were able to completely surprise the Confederates. Dodge reported that many Rebel men from Missouri and Kentucky were in Tennessee, and well-armed. In September of 1862, Lincoln issued the Emancipation Proclamation, which would take effect in January of 1863. However, slaves were already arriving in Dodge's camp daily, and problems arose about how to feed and protect them. At Island #10 on the Tennessee River, Dodge with 100 men, defeated a larger Confederate force and captured their colonel and several officers plus 1,400 state militiamen.[14]

The 4th Iowa Infantry was ready to ship out from Helena, Arkansas, down the Mississippi. A large armada of steamboats was ready to take the 4th Iowa and other units down to Vicksburg, Mississippi. If the Federals could control the Mississippi River, they could stab a dagger into the heart of the Confederacy. Vicksburg was the key. One half of the world's cotton floated down the Mississippi River, destined to be sold and shipped to textile mills in New England in the United States, and to mills in England and France. The Mississippi River also greatly contributed to other commercial activity that would cripple the economy of the Confederacy. In addition, complete control of the Mississippi would cut off Texas, Arkansas and parts of Louisiana from the rest of the Confederacy.

The 4th Iowa Infantry was assigned to General J.M. Thayer's brigade of General Frederick Steele's division. Steele's division was part of William T. Sherman's 15th Corps. Thayer was from the Nebraska Territory and raised the 1st Nebraska Volunteer Infantry Regiment. He was made a colonel at the beginning of the Civil War. After serving with honor at the battles of Fort Donelson and Shiloh, Thayer was promoted to brigadier-general. After the war was over Thayer managed to become one of the first United States senators from Nebraska and eventually he became governor of the state of Nebraska and the Wyoming Territory.[15]

Alonzo Gaston wrote in his diary, "December 21st, 1862: Left camp in pursuance of order about noon and marched to the wharf, where we were obliged to be until about 10 o'clock before going aboard the boat. Finally when the boat came we went aboard the *John J. Roe*." His next entry read, "December 22nd: Stay at Helena till about 4 p.m. when the fleet start down the river; went 12 or 15 miles and tied up." On December 23 Gaston wrote, "Started about 4 or 5 o'clock a.m.; a man fell off this boat before we started but gained the shore and was saved. Passed the mouth of White and Arkansas Rivers. The Arkansas presents a reddish appearance. Day cloudy, threatening rain. Tied up at Gains landing."

A Missouri newspaperman gave an account of the situation aboard the steamships. He said they were grossly overloaded. The steamboats did not have enough facilities to accommodate this many passengers, so the sanitation was poor and a stench grew about these ships. In addition, it was so crowded the men were almost compelled to sleep standing up. To make matters worse, the men had each been issued a canteen full of whiskey, so chaos prevailed. The officers, rather than setting an example for the men, were engaged in gambling and drinking all day and night. Alonzo was a teetotaler. The communities of Tabor and Oberlin, where they were heading, were almost as opposed to drinking as they were slavery.[16]

When they got to Gaines Landing, the banks of the river were lined with slaves. They were cheering and hurrahing. Some of them thought the boats had been sent to help them escape from slavery. The blacks pointed out houses whose owners had left to join the Rebel army. These houses were burnt to the ground. On December 24 Alonzo wrote, "Stay at the landing till about noon, when we started and did not stop until about 4 o'clock next morning at Milliken's Bend, Louisiana, where the whole fleet was tied up. In both divisions said to be 68 steamers. They presented a very beautiful appearance as we passed them in the evening. It being Christmas Eve, 4 or 5 of us told of the scenes in which we had been engaged on previous Christmas anniversaries." Alonzo's Christmas entry read, "Christmas morning beautiful. Said to be 20 or 25 miles of Vicksburg by water and 12 miles by land. Rebel Pickets seem but a short distance back. But retired when approached by our men. There are rumors afloat that a planter this morning shot his slaves to prevent them from coming to us. Fleet lay till about noon when between that and 2 p.m. it got under way. Had hardtack, cheese and coffee for Christmas dinner!!!! Ha Ha. Town burned just below the landing at the mouth of the Yazoo River." On the 26th of December Alonzo wrote, "Went up the Yazoo as far as the old riverbed. Landed and spent a dark rainy night on shore."[17]

The Battle at Chickasaw Bayou was the opening conflict for the purpose of taking Vicksburg. Sherman's troops landed on the Yazoo River to the northeast of Vicksburg. Grant was to take his corps and march south down the Mississippi Central Railroad. Grant had hoped to lure Confederate general John C. Pemberton's army out of Vicksburg and met him at Grenada, Mississippi, where there was a garrison of Confederates. Grant planned to then defeat Confederate Pemberton's army. However, unbeknownst to Sherman, Van Dorn and Nathan Bedford Forrest had attacked Grant's supply lines, including his main supply depot at Holly Springs, Mississippi, and destroyed most of his supplies. Ironically, Julia Grant, Ulysses Grant's wife, was residing in Holly Springs when Van Dorn raided the town. Mrs. Grant and her children often followed Ulysses to be near her husband at his command centers. Fortunately, Mrs. Grant was out of town when the Van Dorn raid occurred. Several of Van Dorn's Confederate officers knew where Mrs. Grant was residing, and it was obvious that they wished to capture her. Mrs. Grant was the daughter of a Missouri slave-owner and planter and had owned slaves herself. She had one slave named Julia who had been with her a long time and served as a nurse and maid to Mrs.

After the Battle at Pea Ridge, Grenville Dodge was promoted and was given the star of a brigadier-general (courtesy State Historical Society of Iowa, Des Moines).

Grant. This slave, Julia, was with Mrs. Grant when she resided in Holly Springs, Mississippi. Eventually Julia was freed and left the employ of the Grants.

Without supplies or his supply depot at Holly Springs, Grant made the decision to head back to Memphis, Tennessee, in hopes of keeping his army intact. Pemberton was able to transfer three infantry brigades to fight Sherman instead of keeping them to fight Grant's corps. Sherman did not find out for eight days that Grant's corps would not be able to support him. Now all Confederate commands were alerted to Sherman's intentions. Every spare artillery battery and infantryman was rushed to the area of the Chickasaw Bayou.[18]

The place where the 4th Iowa disembarked was a haze of dense undergrowth. The dense, bushy undergrowth had to have a path hacked through it. The men of the 4th Iowa were ordered back onto the steamboats. On December 27 Alonzo wrote, "Had orders to go aboard the boat again, which we did and went 2 or 3 miles further up the river and disembarked again. Were put in line of battle. Batteries were planted, an indication of an impending battle. Finally moved about 2 miles towards Vicksburg and camp." On the 28th the 4th Iowa Infantry was on the right flank of the brigade, acting as skirmishers and pioneers, and were not generally engaged with the enemy. For the 28th of December, Alonzo's entry into his diary read, "Moved on about one mile and halted. And a battery having been planted proceeded to silence the [enemy's] batteries on the hill in front. The enemy responded little but to good effect, killing 2 and wounding more. It being found that the charge on the batteries must be made over a narrow causeway over which but a platoon of eight could pass, the project was abandoned and a retreat was ordered, which was made and we reached the landing about dark. Got aboard the boat about midnight. The day's loss was 4 or 5 killed (1 or 2 from our regiment) and several wounded."[19]

The area around Chickasaw Bayou was full of natural defensive positions. Manmade rifle pits and felled trees gave the Confederates protection from Union bullets. The thick underbrush choked the land around a series of small streams, bayous and swampland, making movement by the Union army very difficult. The Chickasaw Bayou was about chest deep and about 50 yards wide. There was an area known as the Walnut Hills or Chickasaw Bluffs that was a natural spot for Confederate artillery to rain down shells on the Union forces.

On December 29 Brigadier John M. Thayer took command of five Iowa infantry regiments and the 1st Iowa artillery battery. He told all officers who were riding horses to dismount so Confederate sharpshooters could not single them out. The 4th Iowa Infantry with Colonel James A. Williamson as regimental commander acted as skirmishers for General Thayer. They were crossing a bayou, advancing towards a hill. The underbrush and rifle pits were acting as natural protection for the Confederates. They crossed a high fence and were moving up a hill when General Thayer looked around and discovered that his other regiments and artillery battery had disappeared in the heavy underbrush and only the 4th Iowa regiment was advancing. The 4th Iowa was taking the brunt of the enemy's rifle and artillery fire. Thayer saw a Union regiment, not one of his, that was cowering in a ditch, completely protected against Rebel fire. Thayer ordered, then begged the regiment to move forward in support of the 4th Iowa, but the Union regiment stayed in the protected ditch.[20]

General Thayer told Williamson and the 4th Iowa to stand their ground and he would come back with reinforcements. In his official report on the Battle of Chickasaw Bayou, General Thayer wrote, "The Fourth Iowa was then drawing the concentrated fire of all the enemy's batteries and rifle pits." When Thayer was unable to find any reinforcements, Williamson and the regiment retired. Thayer wrote in his official report of the battle, "The conduct of Colonel Williamson, his officers, and men through this trying ordeal is worthy of the highest praise." At some point, Williamson was wounded but refused to leave the field of battle. The 4th Iowa regiment going into the battle had only 480 men. Out of that number 112 were killed or wounded at the Battle of Chickasaw Bayou. Because of their bravery a board of officers allowed the 4th Iowa Infantry to put on their banners, "First at Chickasaw Bayou."[21]

On December 29 Alonzo Gaston describe the battle this way: "Landed about 7 o'clock the other side of a bayou and went to reinforce Sherman's [?] division. In the afternoon, the 4th Iowa made a charge on the enemy's batteries and rifle pits but being under a galling crossfire and not being supported, we were obliged to fall back with great loss in wounded mostly, few being killed. Toward night rain set in and being fully obliged to pass the night without fires, it was long and dismal." On December 30, Alonzo wrote, "Fell back a little ways and rested. Cleaned guns, etc." On the last day of 1862 Alonzo wrote, "Stay in camp till dark when we marched under orders with 2 day's rations in our haversacks and 60 rounds of cartridges. Went aboard the *South Wester*. Were ordered as soon as on board to lie down and keep perfectly still. About 3 o'clock Captain Nichols of Co. C came and woke his men up, lots of them. They were to pass under a Rebel battery of 13 guns. They must keep still and that God would be with them. Night very frosty." The Missouri newspaperman reported that Sherman sent out parties under a flag of truce to bury the dead and bring the wounded back with them. However, the Union burial party found that the Confederates had carried off the slightly wounded as prisoners of war and only left those who were too badly wounded to walk. All the dead had been stripped of their valuables, haversacks and clothing. During the day the Rebels came down under a flag of truce and were very friendly, bringing newspapers from Vicksburg with glowing accounts of how the Yankees had been defeated. The Rebel soldiers even helped bury the Union dead.[22]

On the first day of 1863, things were not getting any better for the 4th Iowa. Alonzo Gaston wrote in his diary, "In the morning found that there was a malignant case of small pox on board; hence, were ordered on shore. Found that the order under which we had marched the night before was countermanded about midnight. Stay on our arms all day and night. Day beautiful. Wrote home to my wife for the first time after leaving Helena. Went aboard the *John J. Roe*. Found the whole army was embarking about noon. Started, sailed out of the Yazoo and turned up the Mississippi. Rain set in, making it very severe for the soldiers. George, Ben and I slept in the hold." On the 3rd of January Alonzo's terse entry in his diary was, "Raining still continued all day. Stay along the shore all day as well as night. Received a letter and paper from home. Slept again in the hold."[23]

Grant and Sherman had let their combined armies of 70,000 men be defeated by a Confederate force about half their size. The papers in the North were having a field day. Charges were renewed that Sherman was crazy and Grant was a drunkard. Union general John A. McClernand was sent down to take command of the operation at Chickasaw Bayou but arrived too late. McClernand was a windbag political appointment who was a thorn in the side of Grant and Sherman. His main attributes were that he was a friend of Lincoln and was a great recruiter. The newspapers in the North incorrectly stated that McClernand relieved Sherman of his command. In fact, McClernand outranked Sherman and took overall command from him. Sherman talked McClernand into attacking Fort Hindman, or as it was sometimes known, Arkansas Post. Fort Hindman stood on the Arkansas River. It protected gunboats from approaching with a moat and drawbridge. In addition, the fort raided and harassed Union supply and troop ships going up and down the Mississippi River. The fort had about 5,000 Rebel troops in it that Sherman could pit his 30,000-plus army against. The fort was a large four-sided earthen fortification.[24]

On January 7 Alonzo wrote, "Moved occasionally and stopped to wood semi-occasionally. Sick in the p.m. Night sailed up the opposite to the mouth of the White River." On the 9th the diary entry read, "About 9 o'clock started up the White River. Ran through the cutoff into the Arkansas, the banks of which are reddish clay soil. Stopped within 3 or 4 miles of Ark. Post and lay overnight." The 4th Iowa disembarked from the steamboat, and on January 10 Alonzo wrote, "Landed and marched out through swamp and back. Halted for supper, after which we marched through awful mud to surround the Post after losing the way once or twice and waiting to find it again. We reached the desired point about 5 o'clock of the morning of the 11." Ben Sheldon, in an article that appeared years later in the local paper the *Tabor Beacon* said, "the night of January 10th 1863, [he] remembered the assault on the Arkansas Post as the nastiest battle of his enlistment…. The 4th Iowa Infantry marched 10 miles through snow, slush and mud to get into position to attack Arkansas Post." The Confederates scrambled to get into their well-fortified fort. Admiral David Porter agreed to escort the troop steamboats with three ironclads, but only if Sherman led the ground troops. Porter disliked the glory-seeking politician McClernand with a passion.[25]

Colonel Williamson, in command of the 4th Iowa Infantry, reported that they were under fire all day. They were ordered to make a charge. However, the white flags went up in the fort and the charge was countermanded. Williamson said that if the charge had been made it would have wiped out his command, as the enemy's entrenchments and rifle pits were well formed, and the 4th Iowa

Julia Dent Grant was the daughter of a very wealthy Missouri slaveholder. She fell head over heels in love with West Point graduate Ulysses S. Grant. Her father did not approve of the marriage because Grant's prospects as a career army officer looked bleak. Grant's father and grandparents did not approve of the marriage because Julia's parents were slave owners (Library of Congress).

would have been compelled to pass over a very level, open piece of ground to reach them. Admiral Porter put his large ironclads so close to the fort that their bows were actually on shore. His guns at point-blank range blasted bricks, guns, timbers and Confederates into the air. The Rebel gunners abandoned their posts, and the white flags went up. Alonzo wrote on the 11th, "Lay down. Still after daylight when we got breakfast. Were soon marched forward within sight of the enemy breastworks. Firing commenced about 1 o'clock when the enemy surrendered and the front was ours. Took eight regiments prisoners and in the night two more were taken coming in as reinforcements." These prisoners were sent to a P.O.W. camp in Alton, Illinois. In total almost 4,800 of the fort's 5,000 Confederate troops became P.O.W.s.[26]

On January 12, 1863, Alonzo Gaston made his last entry in his diary. After that, he was too sick to record any entries. Like many of those who became ill due to disease during the Civil War, the cause of the illness is hard to pinpoint. It was said Alonzo caught a severe cold during the battle that caused his death. Grenville Dodge in writing his book on Regimental Commander James A. Williamson noted that at the Battle of Chickasaw Bayou, Rebel bullets felled many Union soldiers in the 4th Iowa Infantry. However, Dodge wrote that the water from the Yazoo River caused more deaths in the 4th Iowa regiment than did Rebel bullets. Was Alonzo Gaston made sick by drinking the water from the Yazoo River? Did this contaminated water contribute to his death? On Wednesday, January 21, Alonzo was admitted to the General Hospital in St. Louis, Missouri. Later Alonzo was admitted to the Jackson Hospital in Memphis, Tennessee. Alonzo died late in March of 1863. Chronic diarrhea was listed as the cause of death, which could have been from any number of afflictions. Alonzo wrote from his deathbed how homesick he was and that he wanted his father to visit him before he passed. Apparently, George Gaston tried to make it to Memphis but was too late. Alonzo's emaciated body was sent back to Tabor, Iowa, for burial. As can be imagined, the family grieved very much.[27]

In late January, the 4th Iowa and Colonel Williamson, along with other units in the Union army and over 1,000 former slaves, worked on a canal above Vicksburg that Grant had decided to build. The idea was that the canal would change the course of the Mississippi River so that the large artillery guns that the Confederates had placed on the high ground around Vicksburg would become useless. In addition, traffic on the Mississippi River could bypass Vicksburg, leaving it high and dry. However, Williamson had little confidence in the canal. Williamson wrote to Grenville Dodge, "The canal which we are working on will never amount to anything for the reason that if a sufficient rise should take place to wash it out, it would wash the whole army away, as there is not a spot within fifty miles that does not overflow, except Vicksburg." Williamson's concern proved to be prophetic. Finally on March 8 after days of rain, the Mississippi River broke through the dam at the head of the canal and all hell broke loose. Men scrambled to keep from drowning. The canal project was abandoned in late March.[28]

The 4th Iowa Infantry had landed at Young's Point opposite of Vicksburg. The 4th Iowa along with the rest of the brigade had to camp on top of a Mississippi River levee. The river was very high and the men had thrown down brush, trees and debris to lie on upon the levee so they wouldn't get wet. The 4th Iowa was a regiment in name only. Those killed, wounded, disabled, and dead by disease and missing had taken their toll, and the regiment could now only muster in about 300 able-bodied men total. Many of these men were hardly in great shape. The 4th Iowa regimental commander, Colonel James A. Williamson, noted that his health was deteriorating and he had lost 30 pounds. One of the mistakes the Union army made in recruiting new soldiers early in the war was that they kept raising new regiments and let their battle-hardened, experienced regiments dwindle in numbers. The Confederates on the other hand mixed new recruits in with the experienced regiments, keeping these experienced regiments at full strength. This way the new recruits could learn from the experienced soldiers. In the Union army, a whole regiment might be made up of mostly new, raw recruits, making them less effective, while battle-hardened units fell in numbers, making them a shell of a regiment and less successful. Some military historians would blame some of the early Northern defeats to this method of recruitment.[29]

The 4th Iowa Volunteer Infantry in the spring of 1863 joined General Frederick Steele's division in fighting regular Confederate forces and Confederate guerrillas. The area where Steele's troops found themselves was a rich agricultural area, and the 4th Iowa and the rest of the division spent a lot of time destroying the abundant cotton, corn and forage crops in the region. Cotton gins were destroyed as well as buildings. Colonel Williamson wrote of this time, "Slaves by the thousands joined the columns, bringing all their belongings with them, expressing great joy and offering prayers for Mr. Lincoln. The fervent shouting of 'Glory to God' was impressed upon my mind and formed scenes never to be forgotten."[30]

Many of the Iowa soldiers in the Union army might have been indifferent to the plight of the slaves in the South at the start of the war. As the Union army drove further south and encountered more slaves and more scenes like this played out, many of the rank-and-file soldiers of the Union army became convinced that they were on a mission to free the slaves from their inhuman bondage.

General Lorenzo Thomas held the position of adjutant general of the army. Secretary of War Edwin M. Stanton and President Abraham Lincoln had told Thomas to go to the Mississippi Valley and recruit black soldiers, mostly ex-slaves, into the Union army. Thomas threw himself into this project with great vigor, recruiting numerous regiments of black soldiers with white officers. At times Thomas tried to educate various white regiments on the value of these black units. He asked some white regimental commanders their opinion of recruiting black soldiers. Thomas made his way to the 4th Iowa Infantry and other Union regiments. Thomas wanted to know the officer's feelings about arming the black soldiers and incorporating them into the Federal army. Thomas asked the 4th Iowa regimental colonel, James A. Williamson, to be the first officer to speak on this idea. Williamson got up to speak and said he "favored the organization of the negroes, saying [he] believed they would make good soldiers, as I had seen many cases of bravery and devotion on their part, and had no doubt they would become efficient under proper officers." Much to Williamson's surprise, because he had no idea how the other soldiers felt on this matter, he received a lot of applause after his short speech. General Thomas spoke to the command and said he would detail officers to form regiments out of the thousands of blacks who were now following division commander Steele's army. Williamson said, "This was one of the most decisive and notable incidents I witnessed during the war."[31]

General Thomas started to recruit black soldiers into their regiments from the blacks who were following Steele's division. He also appointed their white officers. Black men flocked to be recruited into the Union army even though they were discriminated against. The black soldiers only received $10 a month pay and one ration a day, while the white soldiers received $13 a month and full rations. Thomas exhorted the white soldiers to welcome the black troops into the Union Army and to share any extra uniforms, firearms, or rations with their newly enlisted black brothers. Thomas could commission white soldiers regardless of rank to become officers for the black units. Thomas also had the power to dismiss any white soldier who mistreated any black soldier. Thomas issued General Order #43, which established recruiting stations for black soldiers in Maryland, Missouri and Tennessee. It didn't take long for the black soldiers to prove their worth. One naval officer wrote this account of a Confederate attack: At the end of May around Vicksburg, 5,000 Confederate soldiers attacked two black regiments and one partial white regiment. The black soldiers performed brilliantly by holding off the overwhelming numbers of Rebels. The white officers in these black regiments ran away. A gunboat, the *Choctaw*, was sent to help relieve these soldiers. It opened up with its big guns and chased the Rebels away. Other reports of the positive fighting abilities of these black regiments began to filter into Grant's and Halleck's headquarters.[32]

**Alonzo Gaston died as did a majority of the Union soldiers: not in a hail of bullets in the glory of battle, but of disease. The Gaston family lived the danger-filled life of pioneers, including being missionaries to the Pawnee tribe, who were attacked regularly by the powerful Sioux, and being conductors on the Underground Railroad, helping dozens of fugitive slaves to freedom. He fought in the battles at Chickasaw Bayou and at the Arkansas Post (also known as Fort Hindman) before becoming ill. His cause of death was listed as chronic diarrhea (author's collection).**

In April the 4th Iowa Infantry participated in the Deer Creek Valley Expedition with General Frederick Steele's division. Steele and Grant, along with Rear Admiral David Porter, were trying to attack the right flank of the Vicksburg line by sailing down the rivers and bayous. However, Porter's boats got stuck and had to be rescued. The Deer Creek Valley Expedition proved to be a flop, and the men and boats ended up where they started with no gain in cracking the Vicksburg defenses. Grant and Sherman seemingly could not conduct a positive action against Vicksburg. However, their luck was about to come back.[33]

The 4th Iowa was marched down to the Grand Gulf. They then moved towards Jackson, Mississippi, the capital of the state, and then marched to Vicksburg. By May 18, Grant's army, including the 4th Iowa Infantry, had chased Pemberton's mauled Confederate forces into the fortifications at Vicksburg. Before Pemberton went into Vicksburg, he sent in Major Samuel Lockett. Lockett was an engineer and devised a brilliant defensive structure for Vicksburg. Before getting into this important town, the Rebels had set many houses and bridges on fire in the surrounding countryside so the Yankees could not use them.

All this time Colonel Williamson was very ill. On May 19, the 4th Iowa took part in some heavy fighting. The land they were on was impassable. Colonel Milo Smith of the 29th Iowa Infantry, while consulting with Colonel Williamson, was shot dead as they talked. Soon Williamson became ill. His wife was also deathly ill, so he had to take a 30-day leave of absence. The 4th Iowa Infantry soldiered on and was involved in the action against Vicksburg. However, Vicksburg would still prove to be a tough nut to crack.[34]

Supplies for the Union army were coming through with little trouble. The 4th Iowa Infantry, along with the rest of the Federals, were learning to live off the land. This Union army was feasting on local hams, cornmeal, dried apples, dried peaches, honey, butter, molasses, roasted fowl and of course the local cattle they shot and butchered. As usual, slaves were flocking to the Union lines, and they brought some of their masters' goods including pigs and sheep.[35]

The Confederate commander of Vicksburg, John C. Pemberton, was from Philadelphia and a graduate of West Point. He married into a Virginia family, and when the Civil War broke out joined the Confederate army to be loyal to his wife's people. Pemberton wanted to hold out for as long as he could in Vicksburg so the people of the Confederacy would not accuse him of giving up on this strategic river town because of his Northern birthplace.

On May 22, 1863, Grant decided to open up a direct assault on the fortifications around Vicksburg. All the field artillery and gunboats opened fire on the defenses. Then an assault by the blue-coated Federals ensued. Grant became convinced that Pemberton's troop moral had to be low. However, the Rebels performed magnificently, and the bodies of the Bluecoats began to pile up before the defenses of Vicksburg. The 4th Iowa Infantry was part of General Frederick Steele's division on the right flank in Sherman's XV Corps. To make matters worse, the old feud between Grant and General McClernand ignited again. McClernand said he had captured two of three forts in the Vicksburg defenses. Grant did not believe a word of it, but Sherman told him he had to take it seriously. Grant sent reinforcement to McClernand, and the political general misused them. Grant and Sherman later found out that McClernand had not captured anything. Grant was furious. Grant called off the attack and decided he would have to invest in a siege of Vicksburg. It was obvious a direct assault of the Vicksburg defenses was not going to work.[36]

Brigadier-General Grenville Dodge and Colonel James A. Williamson corresponded often after Williamson took over command of the 4th Iowa Infantry. Williamson constantly asked Dodge's advice in handling the problems of the 4th that inevitably surfaced. Dodge approved of the way Williamson handled the 4th Iowa. Williamson wished that Dodge could take direct command of the 4th Iowa. However, Dodge was rebuffed in his efforts to do that. Usually Dodge's division and the 4th Iowa regiment were not close enough for Dodge to have any practical way to take command of the 4th in his division.[37]

Dodge's corps were kept busy building and guarding the rail lines and protecting Grant's flank. An incident occurred during this time that gave insight into Dodge's success as a military commander. Dodge was in a warehouse near a steamship landing. A steamship pulled up to the dock. Dodge was interested in this ship because its cargo included railway equipment and ammunition. The steamship caught on fire, but the troops around the area were reluctant to go aboard and put out the fire because they were afraid the ammunition would explode due to the fire. The fire was in the rear of the steamship, and the ammunition in the front of the steamship in cases. Dodge reasoned they could get the ammunition off the steamship, thus avoiding a large explosion in the area. Dodge ordered the men aboard but they hesitated, and then he went on board and started to unload the ammunition himself. A large crowd of soldiers followed him on board and in no time, they got the ammunition off. One of the soldiers said, "If you are willing to risk your life at it, we can risk ours." Dodge never gave a soldier an order that he would not follow himself.[38]

A regiment of loyal Tennessee Union men was organized. These men were put under the overall command of Dodge. Dodge and others commented that they had never seen such a hard-looking group of soldiers who were so poorly clothed. As he had done before, Dodge found several of the men to be good spies in that part of the country. These men and their loyal relatives provided Dodge with good, reliable intelligence. Dodge said they became very valuable to him. As he had done in Missouri and Arkansas, Dodge used spies to gather intelligence. Dodge produced the largest and most important spy ring in the Western Theater of operation.

He used soldiers, civilians and former slaves for his spy ring, and he paid their expenses and gave them cash. Many times Dodge would go through $5,000 a month to supply his spies with cash, which was about what a major-general in the Union army made in a year. Even when questioned by a congressional committee about war expenses, Grant trusted Dodge with these large amounts of cash. Some of the soldiers and civilians took no money, figuring they were doing their patriotic duty for the United States of America. To get the funds, Dodge used monies collected for trade permits with people selling confiscated cotton and other goods from disloyal planters. Dodge also retained copies of all pay vouchers for his spies instead of sending them to the War Department. Dodge did not want the names of his spies to ever be known by anyone but himself, lest they be harmed or ostracized by the Confederates. Unlike Allen Pinkerton's wildly inaccurate intelligence to General George B. McClellan in the Eastern theater of operation, Dodge's intelligence was usually right on the money.[39]

Dodge trained his spies, some of whom were illiterate, to determine the number of units they came across. Dodge cautioned his spies to avoid the exaggerations that Pinkerton and other spies were often guilty of presenting. One way he taught his spies to determine the size of an enemy unit was to measure the length of its column along a road. Dodge taught his spies to count companies, regiments, brigades and divisions. Dodge told them to notice what units were moving by trains and taught his spies how many men could fit into a boxcar. Some of Dodge's spies dressed in Confederate uniforms. Dodge was a good judge of character and noted that his spies were extremely loyal to him and the Union cause. Most of Dodge's intelligence went to General Grant and General Sherman while he was a member of the Union's Army of the Tennessee.[40]

Dodge's command center at Corinth looked like a war room with maps covering the walls. As intelligence reports came in, Dodge updated his maps. Dodge knew telegraph lines were vulnerable to being tapped, so he liked to use messengers to inform his spies and to get reports. He usually sent messengers with his spies so they could get reports back to him faster. Dodge refused to give out the names of his spies even to his own staff members. When his direct commanding officer, General Stephen A. Hulbert, wanted the names of Dodge's spies and their reports, Dodge refused to give them to him for fear their names would get out and put them in danger. Hulbert denounced Dodge and cut off his funds for his spying. Dodge went over Hulbert's head to Grant, and Grant backed Dodge. Dodge employed as many as 120 spies, and even today, we do not know the names of most of them. Two of Dodge's favorite spies were Jane Featherstone in Jackson, Mississippi, and Mary Malone. Mary Malone was illiterate but very effective as a spy. She did spy work in Meridian, Columbus and Jackson, Mississippi, and Selma, Alabama. At one time Malone received $750 for her work, a very large amount of money for the time. Dodge was very protective of his female spies. When Mary Mainard was captured, Dodge was going to abduct the wife of a high-ranking Confederate officer to create an exchange for Mainard. However, Dodge realized that this action could cause more problems than it would solve and decided against it. Mainard spent the rest of the war in a Confederate jail. Dodge knew the importance of keeping the names of his spies confidential even long after the war was over. A good example of this was Miss Elizabeth Van Lew of Richmond, Virginia. When Grant went east to fight Robert E. Lee's army, one of his most important spies was Miss Van Lew. Van Lew was from one of the most prominent families in Richmond. After the war was over it became known that Van Lew had been a Yankee spy. Grant had to send troops to guard her house in Richmond from the many threats she was receiving. After the troops left, Van Lew was shunned by the people of Richmond. When Grant became president, he made her postmistress of Richmond. After Grant left office she lost this post, and she lived in her mansion, shunned by the people of her own home town. Even when she died in 1900, 35 years after the war was over, Van Lew was still ignored by everyone in Richmond.[41]

Dodge recruited a regiment of Alabama and Mississippi men who were loyal to the Union; it became known as the 1st Alabama Cavalry. Dodge found many of these new recruits to be excellent spies. Dodge placed spies in Chattanooga, Atlanta, Selma,

Montgomery, Mobile, Meridian, Jackson and Vicksburg. Dodge was proud of the accuracy of his spies. They never put the number of Johnston Confederates as over 30,000 men, which was accurate. His spies never left their stations but communicated often with their wives or other relatives who came to Corinth to pass their information to Dodge. It is estimated that one-half of Dodge's spies were captured, court-martialed or in some cases executed. Dodge's spies lost their lives but never gave up the ring, and there were always others to take their places. In some cases, prominent Southern army officers and politicians vouched for Dodge's spies when they were captured. One of Dodge's most colorful spies was Philip Henson. Henson went on a long and successful spy mission gathering intelligence all through the South. He was captured and gave the Confederates enough information that they thought he was confessing. Henson seemed so sincere that the Confederates hired him as a spy to gather information about the Northern army. Henson then left the Confederates and returned to Dodge for his next assignment. Dodge ran into trouble with the red tape of the army. A quartermaster gave Dodge a large amount of money, $22,000, and wanted signed vouchers for receipts. Of course, none of his spies would sign anything that would incriminate them. General Grant always backed Dodge and made the quartermaster sign all monies over to Dodge that he needed for his spy ring. In addition, to help fund his spy network Dodge had

**Levee and steamboats at Vicksburg, Mississippi. Vicksburg was the prize the Union army was trying to take and the Confederates trying to hold. Complete control of the Mississippi River was essential to the Union victory over the Confederacy. The 4th Iowa did some of the dangerous work of building "trenches" close to Confederate lines. The capture of Vicksburg would prove to be one of the turning points of the Civil War (Library of Congress).**

seized a large amount of cotton, which was sold at a public sale. Grant wanted Dodge to keep daily contact with him about information his spy network would bring to Dodge.[42]

Another of Dodge's most important spies was Levi Holloway Naron of Chickasaw County, Mississippi. Naron, who was born in Newton County, Georgia, had served in the Mexican War. He was with the Mississippi Rifles, commanded by future Confederate president Jefferson Davis. Naron was involved in several battles in Mexico and also did some spy work during that war. After the Mexican War Naron, due to the sweat of his brow, bought and owned 1,100 acres of land in Mississippi. His wife had inherited six slaves. He had six children and was well thought of by his Mississippi neighbors. When Mississippi seceded from the Union and the Civil War started, Naron became an outspoken critic of the Confederacy and remained loyal to the Union. Naron was repeatedly threatened by his fellow Mississippians and moved from the area. Naron tried to organize loyal Union men in Mississippi for a Union regiment but was rebuffed. Naron became a spy and was known by the code name of "Chickasaw."[43]

All this time Dodge kept a hand in the goings-on back in Iowa. He backed his friend John Kasson for the congressional seat in Dodge's district. Kasson was grateful for Dodge's support, as the soldiers in the Union army voted overwhelmingly for Kasson. Peter Dey also kept Dodge abreast of the bill for a transcontinental railroad. Also, Dodge wanted Captain W.H. Kinsman of the 4th Iowa to be his assistant adjunct general. Kinsman was from Council Bluffs, but at this time Kinsman was promoted to be the lt. colonel of the newly formed 23rd Iowa Infantry.[44]

Secretary of War Stanton used the anti-slavery editor of the New York *Tribune*, Charles A. Dana, as a troubleshooter in the field to detect fraud and misappropriation of funds by quartermasters or suppliers to the Union army. Dana was also sent to Grant's command to see if his drinking problem was as bad as the press made it out to be. Dodge reports that Dana and George W. Boutwell, a future United States senator, U.S. congressman and governor of Massachusetts and later secretary of the treasury under Grant, tested the sentiment of the soldiers about freeing the slaves. Their mission was much like that of General Lorenzo Thomas.

When called upon to offer his sentiments about freeing the slaves, Dodge said,

> I had already, in two or three orders, taken a position to the rights of the freedom of the negroes and of their use in the army. I was then employing nearly 1000 of them on the railroad and in the camps and I remember I stated to the commission that I was sent into the army by Iowa for the purpose of putting down the rebellion and that I was anxious to do it and ready to utilize any policy or plan that would accomplish it; that I believe in using the negroes as much as possible for teamsters, in the Pioneer Corps for cooks, servants, & etc. [the question of arming them had not yet come up] but I believe that they should be freed, as they were the mainstay then of the south, as they were raising the crops while all the citizens were in the army.

Dodge saw that his speech pleased both Dana and Boutwell.[45]

Dodge received a letter from Williamson about how poorly the 4th Iowa was being treated. Williamson also expressed concern about the fact that as the Union army drove further south into Confederate territory and was required to live off the land, general looting had become a daily and common thing for the Union army. Williamson also expressed concern about how much food and manpower it took to feed the thousands of slaves that were following the Union army. As he did in most of his letters to Dodge, Williamson asked if Dodge could get the 4th Iowa put under his direct command. Dodge also wrote to his brother Nathan about the concern of the many resources the Union army must expend to feed and care for the thousands of ex-slaves who followed the army. He also told his brother that the North needed to institute the draft to get more soldiers in the army. He also expressed his concern about how newly recruited soldiers were put into new regiments instead of mixing the new recruits with the old veteran regiments. In a letter to Iowa governor Kirkwood, Dodge also expressed his belief in instituting a draft and in the practice of sending new recruits into newly formed regiments. Dodge also wrote to Kirkwood, "All here are anxious to go forward again. When new regiments are raised take old experienced officers for them, and for God's sake don't put in the sulkers and hang-backs that have gone home from sore toes, and a few bullets, but reward the men who, sick or well, have stood to their post, and returned to their duty as soon as they were able. These men need rewarded, and there it is due. Most of our poor officers have left; our good ones are in the field—let us keep them there."[46]

Kirkwood immediately wrote back to Dodge that the War Department had issued an order prohibiting old experienced officers from commanding new regiments. Dodge and other officers in the field made many protests over this order. Dodge also noted at another time how Iowa had met and greatly surpassed her quotas for men. Iowa's quota for men was 10,570, while she had more than doubled that number by sending 21,219 men to the Union army. In a letter, another Iowa senior army officer noted to Dodge that he had communicated with Colonel Williamson and Williamson had expressed his disgust with General Samuel Curtis.[47]

Dodge was given the command of the District of Columbus, Mississippi, in the fall of 1862. He had command of the 4th Division and was rebuilding the railroad from Columbus to Corinth. Grant requested Dodge send as much of his command as he could spare to help in the Battle of Corinth, with which Dodge complied. After the Battle of Corinth was over, Dodge was told to go and meet with Grant. When meeting with Grant, Dodge was complimented for his railroad work. Grant wanted Dodge to command the 2nd Division at Corinth, Mississippi, in the Army of the Tennessee. General Rosecrans had said the 2nd Division was made up of cowards, something Grant took exception to, since the 2nd Division was made up of a lot of Illinois men. Grant took Rosecrans' comments on the cowardice of the 2nd Division personally, and he wanted a competent general such as Dodge to prove Rosecrans did not know what he was talking about. This comment by Rosecrans made his relationship with Grant icy, to say the least. After taking this command, Dodge was in constant contact with Confederate forces. Most of these contacts were firefights. Through the fall of 1862 Dodge's railroad instillations were attacked by General Earl Van Dorn or General Sterling Price's Confederate cavalry, including an attack of 2,000 of Van Dorn Rebels near the Hatchie River. When Dodge's railroads were not being attacked he was on the offensive against various units of the Confederate army, mostly in Tennessee and Mississippi. Dodge also reports a firefight at Burnt Bridge near Humboldt, Tennessee, and the capture of steamboats at Walker's Landing. Firefights at Meriwether's Ferry in Tennessee and Popular

Corners near Humboldt, Tennessee, occurred during this time. Also, an expedition was conducted against Rebel camps in Covington, Durhamville, and Fort Randolph, Tennessee. By December of 1862, Dodge reported that his scouting parties had penetrated 100 miles into Alabama, and they had skirmishes near Tuscumbia, Alabama, with Confederate troops of General Braxton Bragg. The day after Christmas in 1862, Dodge reported a successful rout of Rebel troops and supplies in a series of towns along the Mobile and Ohio Railroad from Corinth to Tupelo, Mississippi. Early January of 1863, Dodge managed to capture 600 Confederate prisoners and four cannons. Any movement beyond Dodge's picket lines produced firefights with the Confederates. Van Dorn attacked Corinth, but Dodge managed to chase his force over 100 miles to the north.[48]

In December of 1862 and January of 1863, Dodge engaged in a campaign against Confederate general Nathan Bedford Forrest's cavalry. Forrest grew up poor and only had a few months of formal education and no military training. He became a successful riverboat captain, slave trader, and real estate mogul and plantation owner, and was one of the richest men in Memphis, Tennessee by 1860. When the Civil War broke out Forrest enlisted as a private but was soon made an officer and later became a general. His cavalry tactics were surprisingly innovative for one with no military training, and his cavalry became much feared by the Union soldiers. Unfortunately, Forrest's reputation took major hits after he massacred black Union troopers and Southern men who stayed loyal to the Union at Fort Pillow. He also, after the Civil War, became closely associated with the Ku Klux Klan and its reign of terror. Later in life, Forrest tried to distance himself from these two events. The *New York Times* said that in his later years, his chief occupation seemed to be trying to explain away the Fort Pillow affair.

Forrest's cavalry was threatening Jackson, Tennessee, and Dodge went to attack him. Dodge's troops intercepted a Confederate messenger of Forrest's; they put their own spy on the messenger's horse with the Confederate gear and gave the messenger false information to pass on to the Rebels to keep Forrest's cavalry from being reinforced. Dodge had studied Forrest's tactics. He was always very aggressive and usually began his attacks by hitting the flanks and rear of the enemy. When the enemy became fully engaged with these attacks, Forrest would pound their main body and was usually successful. Dodge told his men to be sure to hold the middle no matter what—which they did, repulsing Forrest's cavalry. Dodge had also slowed Forrest's retreat by destroying all the bridges and ferries across the Tennessee River. Forrest's men had to get rafts to get across the river, while their horses swam. It was estimated that Forrest lost 1,500 men, who were either killed, wounded, captured or missing. Three hundred and fifty horses were captured, along with ammunition and cargo wagons and a cache of small arms. Several of Forrest's top officers were killed, wounded or captured. Forrest's command was scattered all over the Tennessee River Valley and would take some time to recover. Eventually Dodge managed to put one of his spies under Forrest's command. Before Dodge defeated Forrest's cavalry, they had destroyed much of the track of the Mobile and Ohio Railroad. Dodge had to bring his railroad repair equipment by gunboats to repair the damaged railroad tracks.[49]

Grant moved against Vicksburg. Dodge was to protect his left flank and keep Bragg's army out of the battle. Unfortunately, Grant's supply base in Holly Springs, Mississippi, was successfully attacked, causing him to retreat to Memphis. Sherman was defeated at Chickasaw Bayou near Vicksburg and headed to Fort Hindman in Arkansas. The Union army needed to regroup and again attack Vicksburg. That left Dodge virtually alone, facing the Confederates in Corinth, Mississippi.

Sherman, after Fort Hindman, was able to move his army near Vicksburg. Grant asked Dodge to do as much damage as possible to Colonel Roddey's Confederate cavalry. Colonel Philip Roddey, later General Roddey, was a former Alabama sheriff who had raised a regiment of cavalry. He operated more or less independently in his native North Alabama and also in Tennessee and Mississippi. Dodge got the extra cavalry reinforcements he needed and conducted a campaign against Roddey, pushing him east of the Tennessee River. Dodge's men captured all of Roddey's cargo train of 20 mule teams, 300 head of cattle, 600 head of sheep and 100 horses and mules. Also destroyed were factories and mills that were supplying the Rebel army. Dodge's spy network told him that Earl Van Dorn's cavalry had been ordered to General Bragg's army. Dodge sent his cavalry after Van Dorn's cavalry in Alabama, attacked his rear columns, and captured 200 prisoners, supplies, firearms and an artillery piece. From the wife of one of Dodge's spies in the 1st Alabama Union Cavalry he learned enemy troop strengths in Mobile, Meridian and Jackson, which Dodge passed on to Grant. Dodge also reported to Grant that Confederate deserters and conscripts were flocking to his lines daily. Admiral Porter and Union gunboats were busy up and down the Mississippi trying to keep river traffic open for the Federals.[50]

In the spring of 1863, Grant agreed to a plan that sent Dodge's troops on a campaign through the Tennessee River Valley to clear the Rebel army and deprive the enemy by destroying everything in the valley that could be of value to them. That included cotton, grain and livestock. However, other private property was to be protected. At this time, Dodge had in his ranks 8,000 infantry and 2,000 cavalry. It was determined that generals Van Dorn, Forrest and Roddey were collecting supplies in the valley and storing them along the line of the Memphis and Charleston Railroad to give them to General Braxton Bragg's army. General Roddey had reorganized his command and recruited new cavalrymen after his previous disastrous engagement with Dodge's Corps. Grant also wanted Dodge to screen Bragg's army away from Vicksburg so he wouldn't need to worry about Bragg attacking his flanks or rear areas.[51]

Of course, Dodge wanted to get intelligence on the present state of these three cavalry units. Dodge sent his chief of staff, George Spencer, on a mission. Dodge noted that Spencer was a genius at getting behind enemy lines; Dodge would make it easier for Spencer to get there. Under a flag of truce Spencer was to approach Roddey's pickets and tell them he had information about a prisoner exchange. Spencer did this, and he told the picket's officer that he had to go directly to Roddey's headquarters. The picket officer had a friend who would be involved in the prisoner exchange, and he wanted to expedite the process. Roddey's headquarters were some 50 miles from the picket lines, and Spencer was able to ascertain troop strengths and buy newspapers from Jackson and Chattanooga that contained much information. Roddey was furious that the picket officer had allowed this Union army officer so deep into Confederate territory. Standard procedure was to hold the person who flew the flag of truce at the picket lines; any officer who needed to see him would come there. Spencer gathered much military intelligence on this mission. Ironically, after the war, Union officer George Spencer and

Confederate general Philip Roddey became fast friends and even went into business together.[52]

Dodge—in charge at this time of what was known as the left wing of the XVI Corps, made up mostly of the 2nd and 4th divisions—went on the offensive and attacked the Rebel positions at Tuscumbia, Alabama, and at Little Bear Creek. Dodge had his soldiers travel lightly so they could move quickly. Dodge defeated the enemy at these places and destroyed much cotton, fodder grain and other stores meant for Bragg's army. Unfortunately, some of Dodge's enlisted men, as did many in the Union army, took to looting private houses and then burning them to the ground. Dodge became furious over this. He wanted the looting and burning of houses stopped immediately, so he took quick action and issued a general order that stated in part that any soldier found to have burned a house, whether it be occupied or not, would be shot on site. Any soldier must have permission from the brigade commander to visit a house, and if found not to have permission would be immediately arrested. Dodge's men had destroyed seven cotton factories. One of these factories had 300 looms and employed 2,000 people. They burned 200,000 bushels of corn, captured 60 prisoners, many officers and 200 horses. Dodge's men also burned down railroad depots and tore up track; these facilities were not rebuilt until after the war. Telegraph lines were cut, and dozens of ferries and flatboats were destroyed. Dodge's Tennessee River Valley assault was deemed a success. Dodge deprived Bragg's army of much needed foodstuff and stores except for one notable exception. Colonel A. D. Streight of the 51st Indiana Infantry Regiment was to join Dodge's troops at the steamboat landing in Eastport, Mississippi. Colonel Streight was delayed coming out of Nashville. His regiment of infantry was mounted on horses and mostly mules. Some of these mules were not broken, and others were under two years of age and not ready to be ridden or to carry loads. Streight lost a number of mules while unloading them at Eastport. In addition, heavy rains slowed Streight's advance. His ammunition got wet and most of it was useless. Forrest's cavalry engaged Streight's regiment, and because most of his ammunition was useless, the Indiana colonel was forced to surrender. Streight's raid into the Tennessee River Valley was a dismal failure. Streight was sent to Libby Prison in Richmond, Virginia, but managed to escape a year later.[53]

The local authorities in the Tennessee River Valley, through the press, threatened Grenville Dodge with immediate hanging if he were ever captured. On his way back to his headquarters in Corinth, a couple of thousand former slaves followed Dodge's army. Dodge had to feed, clothe and find shelter not only for his own army but also for the legion of slaves that followed him back to headquarters. Dodge posted guards to keep these former slaves safe. Some of the white soldiers in Dodge's Corps objected to this duty. Dodge then formed from these former slaves, under no one's authorization, two companies of armed black troopers to guard the former slaves. These two companies later became the core of the 1st Alabama Colored Infantry.

Grant and Sherman were trying to deliver a knockout punch to Vicksburg for control of all the Mississippi River. They needed much intelligence on the defenses at Vicksburg. One of Dodge's best spies was Philip Henson. At six foot two with a wiry, muscular build, Henson had a friendly countenance. He talked and moved slowly and to the average person seemed to pose no threat. However, Henson had an almost photographic memory. He did not need to make notes that could later incriminate him. Henson, who was Southern by birth, had spent time in the West before the outbreak of the Civil War. At the outbreak of the war, he was clerking in a store in Mississippi. To avoid service in the Confederate cause, which he did not believe in, he had a neighboring plantation owner hire him as a slave overseer. These slave overseers were exempt for service in the Confederate army. At first, Henson came to the notice of the Union army for the shrewdness with which he bought Southern cotton for the Federals. He came to the attention of Ulysses S. Grant and became a spy for the Union army. Grant then introduced Henson to Dodge, and Dodge became his handler. Henson went on a spy mission to gather information on General Roddey's cavalry. Roddey's cavalrymen arrested Henson. Roddey did not care for Henson, and could not understand why Henson was not in the Confederate army. Roddey jailed Henson. Henson learned that some of the people he knew in Alabama and Mississippi were in Roddey's cavalry, including a colonel and captain who would vouch for Henson. Roddey reluctantly let Henson go, with the provision that Henson would join the Confederate army. Henson made his way to Dodge's headquarters with all the information about Roddey's cavalry movements. When Dodge's headquarters were in Corinth, Mississippi, he wanted to know what was going on in the Confederate army in Columbus. He sent Henson, who was captured within Confederate lines and taken to Confederate general Ruggles. Henson knew some people in Ruggles' command who would vouch for him, including Henson's brother. Henson maintained his hatred for the Yankees. He gave Ruggles some unimportant information about Dodge's command, and Ruggles became interested in Henson's becoming a spy for him, to which Henson agreed. Ruggles paid Henson to become a spy for him. Three other Confederates in command position would "hire" and pay Henson to be a spy. Henson always followed Dodge's rule: Give out as much information as needed to extract yourself from a situation, but do not to give out important information.[54]

Dodge dispatched spy Philip Henson to go to Vicksburg to see what defenses Confederate general Pemberton had employed. This would be one of Dodge's and Henson's most important spy missions. Henson had a friend, Jesse Johnsey, who had seven sons in the Confederate army, several of them around Vicksburg. Henson offered Johnsey a horse to take him to Vicksburg to visit his sons. When Johnsey and Henson were stopped by Confederate pickets, Henson told them they were on their way to see Johnsey's sons. Henson and Johnsey were arrested and taken before General Pemberton, but Henson convinced the Confederate general that he was a loyal Southerner. Henson denounced the Yankees as being a cruel army of occupation. Pemberton was so impressed with Henson's hatred of the Yankees that he had Henson go tell his tale of Yankee hatred to the troops all over Vicksburg. Pemberton hoped this would improve the moral of his troops. This of course gave Henson full access to all the fortifications of Vicksburg. Pemberton wrote Henson and Johnsey a pass to come and go as they pleased in Vicksburg. Henson made his way back to Dodge's lines. So good was the information Henson obtained that Dodge presented him with a fine horse named Black Hawk.

Joseph E. Johnston claimed to have an army of 60,000 men and intended to attack Grant's rear around Vicksburg. A Dodge spy put the number closer to 30,000 men. This information gave Grant some relief, as he had Sherman meet Johnston's army with the correct amount of troops, and Grant did not have to pull additional troops away from Vicksburg. Dodge sent spy Levi Naron to go deep into Mississippi with some other spies to gather intelligence. Naron sent one man to Atlanta and another to Mobile to get newspapers and be on the lookout for Confederate troop movements. He also had the *Augusta Chronicle* sent to him for six months and had subscriptions to other Southern newspapers (delivered to his spies with the proper Southern addresses) that yielded much information. Naron would have his spies report to the gunboats at Pittsburg Landing to receive these newspapers. Naron gathered much information on Confederate defenses and troop strengths, for which Dodge paid him handsomely. Dodge put 15 spies under Naron's control and told Naron to increase this to 25 spies. Another incident shows how Dodge built trust with his spies. Naron's farm and property were confiscated in Mississippi by the Confederate government. His wife and children were forced to flee the county, and she made her way to Dodge's headquarters in Corinth. Dodge found Naron's wife and family a fine house to live in, gave them food to eat, and loaned them money. Naron said he would never forget Dodge's kindness to his family.[55]

Grant then told Dodge he was requested to go to Washington to see the adjutant general. No reason for this request was given, and with much trepidation, Dodge went to Washington. He could think of no other reason than that he was to be sacked for arming black soldiers without permission from higher-ups. However, when Dodge got to Washington, he found out it was Lincoln who wanted to see him. When he met Lincoln, Dodge was still anxious about the reason for the meeting. The president was cordial in his meeting with Dodge, and much to Grenville's relief Lincoln wanted to talk to him about railroading. Lincoln was trying to figure out the best place for the eastern terminus of what would become the Union Pacific Railroad. Lincoln had never forgotten Dodge and his meeting with Lincoln in Council Bluffs. Every city on the western edge of the Missouri River from Sioux City, Iowa, to the north and Kansas City, Missouri, to the south wanted the terminus located in its municipality. Dodge said that from an engineering point of view, the line should begin in Omaha (in what was then the Nebraska Territory) as this was where the Missouri River narrowed, making it easier to build a railroad bridge across this major river. Several months after his meeting with Dodge, Lincoln would issue an order that the eastern terminus of the Union Pacific Railroad would be in Omaha. Lincoln would later fix the terminus of the Union Pacific as Council Bluffs, across the river from Omaha.

Lincoln went on to discuss his disappointment that his transcontinental railroad project was moving so slowly. The bonds for the railroad were not selling. Dodge countered that no private railroad would want to take on such a large project with the war going on, and financing was difficult to obtain. Dodge said the government would have to become directly involved in the building of the railroad. Dodge also pointed out that the bonds were not selling because they were in essence a second mortgage with the government holding the first lien on the bonds, and nobody was satisfied with that arrangement. Dodge hurried to New York and informed Harry Farnam, the Durants and others of his meeting with Lincoln. This caused great excitement; however, nothing much was done on the Union Pacific until the Civil War was over.[56]

Dodge's brother Nathan, back in Council Bluffs, told Dodge that Lincoln's designation of these points as terminuses set off a land-buying frenzy, and land prices reaching new heights for the area of Council Bluffs and Omaha. Unfortunately, Grenville was unable to participate in this land buying, as his general's salary was being used to pay off the debts of Baldwin and Dodge.

When Dodge got back from Washington, D.C., and New York City to the Army of the Tennessee in Corinth, he threw himself back into the task of war. Grant was getting ready for his siege of Vicksburg. Grant had heard of reports of a large number of railroad cars and locomotives concentrated around Meridian, Mississippi. Grant was afraid of a large movement of troops to reinforce Vicksburg from Meridian. Grant wanted Dodge to send one of his spies to check the veracity of these reports.

Dodge selected an enlisted man name E.D. Coe for the job. Coe set out on his journey on a mule. He threw away all his papers in case he was detained as a spy, except for a map of Mississippi and Alabama. Once Coe got behind Confederate lines, he sold the mules for 50 dollars in Confederate money. The mule had proved to be unfit for travel. Coe met up with a family who fed and housed him for a few days. He made up a story that he was a deserter from the Union army and had to keep on the lookout for them. Coe said he was trying to make it to his uncle's place in Georgia. He said he wanted someone from the Confederate army to parole him so he could go to Georgia. The next day a Confederate captain and four men questioned Coe. They thought his story was plausible, so they paroled him. The Confederate captain even wrote out a note giving Coe a free pass through Rebel lines to go to Georgia to live with his uncle. Coe bought a horse for 200 dollars. The horse was poor, as a good horse would run 400–600 Confederate dollars. Coe's Confederate pass worked well; he was stopped often, but his pass seemed to satisfy all. He next stayed with a hard-line rebel, Doctor Owens, who was glad to hear Coe's story of being a Yankee deserter. Coe made his way to Meridian. He found out the cars and locomotives were from the Mobile and Ohio line and other rail lines that were not running. The cars and locomotives were just being stored there, as there was no tracks to run them on, because the Union army had destroyed so many railroad tracks in the Confederacy.[57]

Coe had to make his way back north by a different route. He made his way through Alabama and he changed his story, saying that he was going to his uncle's in North Carolina. On his way back, Coe stayed with a man who was a great reader. This man told Coe that an order had been passed by the Confederate general in that area that any Yankee deserter who remained in the South for over 30 days could be conscripted into the Confederate army. Coe got a copy of the order from the Macon newspaper and changed his story to say he was a deserter who was heading back to his home in Illinois. Coe told people who stopped him that if he headed back to his unit in the Union army he would be hung as a deserter. Coe made it to around Tuscumbia, Alabama, where he was detained as a Union spy. This was close to the Union lines. Coe pleaded his innocence. When Confederate soldiers searched Coe they found 300 dollars in Confederate money and 120 dollars in gold. Dodge had given Coe 1,000 dollars in Confederate money and 120 dollars in gold. The gold was to bribe guards if he got into trouble. Coe was put on trial, but they could prove nothing about Coe being a spy. Coe restated his remark that he could not go back to his Union unit as he would be court-martialed and then hung as a deserter. The Confederates were going to send him to Braxton Bragg's army. Since Coe was only 30 miles from Dr. Owens' place, he said Owens would vouch for him. Dr. Owens was sent for, and Owens' travel expenses were taken out of Coe's money. Owens stated that he did not know Coe well enough to vouch for him. Coe managed to get into Owens' good graces, and the doctor said that if Coe would give him his word that he would not leave his place, he would allow Coe to come home with him provided he paid for his room and board. Coe agreed, and for two days Owens watched him like a hawk. On Coe's second night at the Owens place there grew an alarm that Yankee cavalry was coming down the road. Coe acted scared enough, and Coe and one of Owens' slaves went to hide in the bushes. Coe was hoping they would be found by the Union scouts, but it all proved to be a false alarm. The slave told Dr. Owens that Coe had acted scared when he thought the Yankee cavalry were coming. Thereafter, Owens thought it was safe to keep Coe there and let Coe come and go as he pleased. Some days Coe was gone all day fishing. There was a woman in the neighborhood who said she and her husband were Union sympathizers and that her husband had already left for the Union lines. She had a five-year-old girl. She was trying to leave the area with her household goods, but her neighbors threatened to burn her stuff if she tried to leave. Coe told her to leave her goods, as the Yankees would take care of her. He offered to meet her at a creek crossing in the morning. Coe told her to tell her neighbors she was going on a 10-mile trip. Coe estimated they were within 50 miles of the Union pickets. Coe had to swim across the creek to get a skiff to carry the woman and her child across the stream. They travelled in the woods during the day so as to not be seen. They then rested at dusk and resumed travel during the night. Around ten o'clock they lost site of the road. The little girl fell asleep, and Coe carried her. They found the road again and walked till daylight, but Coe recognized they must have been walking in a circle, as they were only about 10 miles closer to the Union pickets. They kept walking until one o'clock in the afternoon, when Coe spotted Union pickets. Coe knew he could not let the woman know he was a Union spy, so he gave her 20 dollars in gold money and 20 dollars in paper money. Coe then gave himself up to the Union pickets and was taken to Dodge's headquarters. Dodge was very glad to see Coe and shook his hand heartily; then Coe was debriefed. Dodge gave Coe a month off and a free pass on all the railroads. Coe went home to Illinois. When he came back he would go on his next spying assignment.[58]

Dodge's spies in Jackson, Meridian, Mobile, Selma and Montgomery kept information current on Confederate general Johnston's forces. At the Battle of Champion Hill, Dodge's intelligence on the number in Johnston's army was very helpful to Grant. Champion Hill proved to be a bloody mess. Fellow Council Bluffs officer William Kinsman was killed in action at this battle. As a colonel in the 23rd Iowa Infantry, he was leading his infantry regiment in a charge. Dodge kept enlisting black men into infantry units and putting experienced officers in charge of these regiments. White, loyal Southerners kept pouring into Dodge's headquarters at Corinth. He enlisted the men in the various Southern Union regiments, but he was unable to feed and clothe the great number of women and children who accompanied the men into Corinth. Dodge sent about 500 women and children north to be resettled in Illinois.[59]

With Pemberton's army firmly installed behind the defenses around Vicksburg, Grant decided on a siege strategy. To be successful, a siege must keep the defenders from being reinforced or resupplied. Grant had ten divisions facing Vicksburg along the seven-mile front. Eventually Grant would have 79,000 troops, including the 4th

Iowa Infantry Regiment, and 248 pieces of artillery around Vicksburg, compared to Pemberton's 29,500 rebels. The 4th Iowa Infantry was attached to Sherman's XV Corps, Steele's division and General Thayer's brigade on the northern flank of Vicksburg. Grant had to study up on siege tactics while at Vicksburg. Sieges were common military tactics on the Continent and in Asia but were rather unfamiliar to the American armies at this point in the Civil War. Grant kept his artillery booming and snipers plying their trade from sunrise to sunset, even on the Sabbath. Grant had miners and sappers, including members of the 4th Iowa Infantry, getting as close as possible to the Rebel defenses with what they called "ditches." The 4th Iowa Infantry along with other sappers created a maze of trenches with parapets and firing steps from which snipers could fire. Even though members of the 4th Iowa had to crawl in the muck of these trenches, they understood the importance of their work. Captain Henry G. Ankeny penned to his wife, "Everything depends on Vicksburg." These sappers got so close to Rebel lines that they could lob hand grenades into Confederate trenches. In some cases, the sappers set off explosives as close as possible to the defenses.[60]

The Confederate strategy was somewhat muddled. The president of the Confederacy, Mississippian Jefferson Davis, wanted Vicksburg held at all costs. General Joseph Johnston, who was technically in charge of all the troops in the West, implored Pemberton not to be trapped in Vicksburg but to save his army to fight another day. However, Johnston was ill and Pemberton routinely did not obey Johnston's orders. In addition, Pemberton's and Johnston's intelligence about the Union army before them was woefully inadequate, unlike Grant with Dodge's spy network.

Vicksburg was a city of 4,500 residents and now had to make room for 29,500 troops. Water and food were already in short supply and became increasingly problematic. Pemberton thought he had 60 days' provisions for his troops and was short on ammunition. The cemetery for Vicksburg was outside Confederate lines, so hundreds of bodies had to be buried in improvised locations. Even the newspapers in the North, which were often critical of Grant, were impressed with the speed Grant had moved his army. In 18 days, Grant had moved his army 200 miles, won five battles and kept Pemberton's army from joining with Johnston's army, forcing the rebels into a siege situation in Vicksburg. Lincoln was ecstatic over Grant's victories.[61]

Admiral Porter's gunboats and mortar boats lobbed shells that weighed 250 pounds while Grant's mortars and artillery poured shells into the Vicksburg defenses. Porter's gunboats and mortar boats fired throughout the day and night. The Rebels built trenches, and many local citizens started to live in the caves around Vicksburg or dug caves into the sides of hills. Food for the locals and Pemberton's army became half rations and then a biscuit a day with a little piece of pork. Mule meat—some even say rat meat—became protein to survive another day. A camel was even slaughtered for food. The Confederates were gaunt and shell-shocked. As the weeks dragged by, the Rebel position became more desperate. Jefferson Davis employed Johnston to mount some kind of a relief effort for Vicksburg, but Johnston's efforts proved to be too timid.

On July 3, 1863, Grant and Pemberton met, with two other generals present. Terms of surrender were discussed and argued; then at ten o'clock at night Grant sent his final terms. Confederate officers could keep their sidearms and one horse. The whole of the Vicksburg garrison would be paroled. The next day, July 4, 1863, at 10 o'clock in the morning as prescribed in Grant's surrender terms—according to Confederate commander Pemberton—Union general Frederick Steele's hard-nosed division marched into Vicksburg, bayonets and sabers glittering in the Mississippi sun. This would have included the 4th Iowa Infantry. However, according to Grant's memoirs, "Black Jack" Logan's 3rd Division were the first Union troops into Vicksburg. We do know, from the Official Record of the War of the Rebellion, that the 45th Illinois Infantry was given the honor of putting the Stars and Stripes above the courthouse in Vicksburg, and we know the 45th Illinois was part of Logan's 3rd Division. The 45th guarded important junctures and raised the U.S. flag above the Vicksburg Post Office and other principal buildings. General James McPherson's XVII Corps occupied Vicksburg, and Logan's 3rd Division was part of the XVII Corps. The Confederate flags were driven down. Union bands played patriotic music and the gunboats let go salvo after salvo. Grant and Pemberton climbed the courthouse steps and watched the proceedings. The 4th Iowa Infantry had lost 80 men during the siege.[62]

Along the Confederate lines, in organized fashion, the Rebels came out of their trenches and stacked their arms in silent dejection. Lucy McRae, a resident of Vicksburg, wrote of this day, "How sad was this spectacle that met our gaze; arms stacked in the center of the street, men with tearful eyes and downcast faces walking here and there; men sitting in groups feeling that they would gladly given their life-blood on the battlefield rather than hand over the guns and sabers so dear to them."[63]

Halleck thought Grant's terms to be too generous. However, Grant would later write to General Marcus J. Wright, "I was very glad to give the garrison of Vicksburg the terms I did. There was a cartel in existence at that time which required either party to exchange or parole all prisoners either at Vicksburg or at points on the James River within ten days after capture, or as soon thereafter as practical. This would have used all the transportation we had for a month. The men behaved so well that I did not want to humiliate them. I believed that consideration for their feelings would make them less dangerous during the continuance of hostilities, and better citizens after the war was over."[64]

The Union soldiers, seeing the sickly and emaciated condition of the Rebel defense forces, reached into their backpacks and shared their rations with their new Confederate comrades-in-arms. Both sides milled around and talked to each other with respect well into the night. Grant, of course, was right; the transformation of 30,000 Confederate soldiers into P.O.W.s would have been a logistic nightmare. Grant already had to feed, clothe, shelter and supply medical care for his 79,000-man army and provide for thousands of ex-slaves who were pouring into Union lines and hundreds of white Southern Union sympathizers. Along with the victory at Gettysburg, the North in July of 1863 finally had feelings of jubilation to cheer about and a feeling that there might be an end to this infernal war.

However, the Confederate government contested the paroles of Pemberton's men on technical grounds, and most of them made it back into the Confederate army in August of 1863 at Mobile Harbor, Alabama. Many of Pemberton's troops took part in the Battle at Chattanooga in September of 1863. Many of these men also fought against Sherman's troops in Georgia in May of 1864. This dispute over parole was brought up with Grant in April of 1864 when he was general-in-chief of the Union army. Because of this incident of the paroled Vicksburg Confederates and their repatriation back into the Rebel army, Grant stopped almost all prisoner exchanges.

Grant sought to keep the pressure on the Confederate army. He wanted to go after Joseph Johnston's army immediately after Vicksburg fell. Grant ordered Sherman's XV Corps, reinforced by Major-General Edward Ord's XIII Corps, to engage Johnston's army. Major-General Frederick Steele's division in Sherman's XV Corps also included the 4th Iowa Infantry. Grant wanted these units to be ready to go and ordered each man to carry 150 rounds of ammunitions and at least five days' rations with them. Sherman would have 13 divisions go after Johnston's four divisions. Johnston, who was normally cautious, had no intention to engage Sherman's reinforced corps. Johnston retreated to Clinton and then to Jackson. Johnston's Confederate army stopped in Jackson and tried to fortify the town, but it became obvious that Sherman could destroy his army. Johnston felt his main objective was to keep his army intact and when the opportunity seemed right, for him to attack. Now was not that time. Johnston quickly left Jackson, Mississippi, and on July 16, 1863, Sherman's Corps again occupied Jackson. Captain Ankeny of Company H of the 4th Iowa wrote of Jackson, "Our regiment was on picket close to the Rebels works last night. This morning at daybreak a great cheer greeted us along our lines. It was discovered that the Rebels had evacuated Jackson leaving some of their heavy artillery." Johnston was headed to Alabama, and Sherman decided to end the chase there. Sherman determined Johnston was far enough away to prove no danger to the Mississippi Valley. In his first occupation of Jackson, Sherman had burned anything that would prove to be helpful to the Confederate army. This time he set the whole town on fire. Sherman's men in XV Corps were desperately in need of rest. They marched back to the Black River and stayed there almost two months.[65]

All through the summer of 1863, Brigadier-General Grenville Dodge was kept busy with his spy network and other considerations. General Oglesby, who had been severely wounded at the Battle of Corinth, tried to resign from the Union army because of physical limitations. However, his resignation was not accepted, and he was reassigned and put on light duty in the North. Dodge was given command of Oglesby's three divisions and of the left wing of the XVI Corps. Dodge also learned from news in Iowa that the Republican Party wanted to nominate war heroes for important positions. Dodge's name came up, but some were not sure if he would give up his generalship in the Union army, so others were chosen. In addition, after Vicksburg, Dodge had been assured by those close to Grant that his name was at the top of the list to be made a major-general. However, only one name on Grant's list was given a promotion. Dodge noted that as a brigadier-general he had command of many more troops than some with of the rank of major-general.

A Confederate force tried to capture Jackson, Tennessee, but Dodge's troops moved north and pushed the Rebels back across the Tennessee River. Phil Henson was sent south again on a spy mission to try and ascertain the troop movements in the area. He found a Confederate general's wife who had a yearning for fancy hats, gloves and other luxuries, only found in the North or in Paris. With a generous expense account provided by Dodge, Henson was able to provide her with these luxuries—of course provided she gave him equally valuable information on the movements of the Confederate army. After this successful mission, Henson headed to General Ruggles' headquarters again, but Ruggles had moved on and even with all of Henson's impressive Confederate passes, a cocky Rebel provost marshal had Henson arrested and jailed. Henson found one of his guards was corruptible, and he paid him 100 Confederate dollars. Henson then rode off to Dodge's headquarters on Black Hawk.[66]

General William Rosecrans was given orders to march into east Tennessee before Confederate general Braxton Bragg could be reinforced. However, Rosecrans delayed any action. All through the spring and summer, when Bragg had sent a large part of his army to fight against Grant at Vicksburg, Rosecrans had been ordered to attack Bragg's weakened army, but Rosecrans did nothing for six months. Even the *New York Times* wondered about Rosecrans' inaction in Tennessee. General Halleck gave Rosecrans intelligence that Bragg was sending elements of his army east to Richmond. For some reason Rosecrans believed this before all other intelligence. Rosecrans was a man of great ability, but he was quarrelsome with his superiors and arrogantly believed he was the best general in the Union army. Dodge had a very trusted spy who was actually assigned to Longstreet's Confederate army in the east. When Longstreet's Corps set out to reinforce Bragg's army in Tennessee, Dodge's spy was able to telegraph Dodge of this movement. Dodge sent dispatches to Grant and Rosecrans with this information. Rosecrans sent Dodge a very sharp reply stating that he had different information and that Dodge was incorrect in stating that Longstreet was going to reinforce Bragg. Dodge told Grant of Rosecrans' reply. Grant told Dodge in the future to send all intelligence to him only. Rosecrans did not care for Grant, and the feeling was mutual.

Dodge instructed Lt. Colonel Phillips in his command to go on a raid and destroy as much Confederate railroad equipment as possible. The usual practice was to break off the side bar pistons, but engines could be put back into service after this was done. Instead, Dodge told Phillips to completely decommission the engine by lighting the fuse of a shell and bursting it inside the firebox. The firebox on a steam engine was where the fuel was burned to power the locomotive. Dodge told Phillips the Confederates had the equipment to replace the side bar pistons but not the firebox. Phillips went to Grenada, Mississippi, on the Mississippi Central Railroad and destroyed many Rebel locomotives and rail cars. It was said that when Dodge's men were sent to destroy railroad tracks or rail equipment, it stayed destroyed forever.[67]

There were two sad incidents in Dodge's command during the summer of 1863. Colonel F.M. Cornyn of the 10th Missouri Union Volunteer Cavalry was one of Dodge's most trusted officers. Cornyn and Lt. Colonel William D. Bowen did not get along, and Cornyn had Bowen court-martialed for not following orders. During a recess in Bowen's court-martial Bowen took a pistol and shot and killed Cornyn. Although, incredibly, Bowen was acquitted of this killing, he was made to resign from the Federal army. It is interesting to note that Frederick W. Benteen had been a major under Cornyn and then became the lt. colonel of the 10th Missouri Union Volunteer Cavalry. He led that unit from February 1864 to the end of the Civil War. Benteen would be part of Custer's 7th Cavalry at the Little Big Horn in 1876, and Benteen would be criticized for not coming to Custer's aid in a timely fashion.[68]

The other distressing incident that occurred in Dodge's command was the desertion of one A.J. Johnson of the 1st Alabama Union Cavalry. Dodge had very few desertions in his command; this one was even more egregious because the deserter, Johnson, then joined the Confederate guerrillas. One of Dodge's scouting parties, the 5th Ohio Cavalry, found Johnson and had him arrested and brought back to Corinth. Johnson was with a Confederate guerrilla band of Captain Carpenter. Dodge polled the men of the 1st Alabama Union Cavalry, and almost to a man they told Dodge that Johnson needed to be made an example of. Johnson was tried and found guilty, and the penalty was execution. With full military convention with the fifes and drums playing, Johnson was taken out into a field and surrounded on three sides by Union soldiers. Johnson and a chaplain of the 21st Ohio rode in a wagon with a coffin. The prisoner and chaplain dismounted from the wagon, and the chaplain said a final prayer for the condemned man and for his mother, his wife and child. Johnson was asked if he had a final request, and he said he would like to see the picture of himself that had been taken in the morning. Enough time had not passed to get the picture of Johnson developed, so the request was denied. The coffin was placed on the ground and the condemned man sat on the coffin in obvious distress. The line of rifleman who were to be his executioners were put in place. A white handkerchief was put over the condemned man's eyes. Everyone was in a somber mood, and a reporter said even some of the executioners had tears in their eyes. Finally, the provost marshal said "Ready" and then "Aim," and everyone held their breath for the last word, "Fire." Johnson pitched backward over the coffin and no death struggle was observed. Every member of the whole command filed by the dead deserter and his coffin, and the first military execution of the Union Army of the Tennessee was over.[69]

In the last part of August of 1863, Grenville Dodge took ill. Dodge had what he called a congestive chill and was losing weight. He was sent north to Council Bluffs to recuperate. Dodge kept in touch with his army while convalescing.

Colonel James A. Williamson came back to the 4th Iowa Infantry Regiment from sick leave. Lt. Colonel George Burton had taken command of the 4th Iowa while Williamson was gone. Burton, a tough man born in Ireland, had received a severe wound at Pea Ridge from grapeshot and almost bled to death. Dodge had noticed Burton's stoic manner while wounded. Burton was from the eastern part of Iowa at Lyon. He was 43 when he entered the Union army. Lt. Colonel George Burton took over command of the 4th Iowa Infantry, while Williamson was given command of the 3rd Brigade, 1st Division, and Sherman's XV Corps. Williamson took over command of General John M. Thayer's old brigade, of which the 4th Iowa was a part. Thayer then went to Fort Smith, Arkansas, and took over command of a cavalry unit.

General Ulysses S. Grant proved to be one of the few Union generals who could win battles. Grant depended on Dodge's military intelligence, the result of Dodge's spy network and scouts. Grant also began to look at Dodge as the best and most efficient railroad builder he had. After the war was over, Grant and Dodge remained close friends (Library of Congress).

A panel of Union officers decided that the 4th Iowa could put on their colors and guidions, "Pea Ridge, First at Chickasaw Bayou, Arkansas Post, Vicksburg, siege and assault, 19th and 22nd, Jackson." On September 22, 1863, the 4th Iowa took steamers to Memphis. Colonel Williamson took over a different command of the 2nd Brigade, known as the Iowa Brigade, which included the 4th Iowa Infantry Regiment, 1st Division, with General Peter J. Osterhaus commanding. They were part of Sherman's XV Corps.[70]

In late September disaster struck the Union army. General Rosecrans' Army of the Cumberland had occupied the important rail and manufacturing center of Chattanooga, Tennessee. Rosecrans had visions of marching from Chattanooga into the heart of Dixie at Atlanta. He continued to underestimate the size of Braxton Bragg's Rebel army before him. Unfortunately, Rosecrans' continued delays had allowed Bragg to significantly increase the number of troops in his army. As Dodge had tried to tell him, parts of Longstreet's Corps from the Eastern Theater had joined Bragg. In addition, elements of Pemberton's paroled Confederate army from Vicksburg were streaming into Bragg's lines. General Phillip Sheridan and General Wilder, a few days before the Battle at Chickamauga, had captured soldiers from Longstreet's Corps and taken the prisoners to Rosecrans. The Union general emphatically denied that Longstreet was in front of him and had called one of the captured Confederates a liar for insisting he was with Longstreet. At a small creek in Georgia, the Chickamauga, Rosecrans' Army of the Cumberland and Bragg's Army of Tennessee met for a bloody battle. Longstreet's men found a gap in Rosecrans' lines and exploited it to the hilt. Rosecrans and a large part of his army were sent running back to Chattanooga in a disorganized rout. General James A. Garfield, future president of the United States and Rosecrans' chief aide, told of Rosecrans' meltdown during the battle. Only Union general George Thomas stood firm and became known as the "Rock of Chickamauga."

Sherman ordered Dodge to move his troops up the Tennessee River Valley while Sherman moved his XV Corps to eastern Tennessee. Sherman became somewhat concerned about Dodge's health and asked if he was up to the rigors of troop movement. Dodge assured him he was up to the task. Dodge thought that going into the field might be the quickest way to bring back his health. Dodge turned to spy Levi Naron to get information about troop movements in the Tennessee River Valley and the fording opportunities at Eastport. Before Dodge left Corinth, he mustered in the 1st Alabama Cavalry and the Battery D 1st Alabama Colored Artillery. These units he left in Corinth to help garrison this Union stronghold. After a few days, Naron reported to Dodge of the fording places near Eastport. After victories at Vicksburg and Gettysburg, it looked as though the Union army had finally turned the corner, and now Rosecrans had blundered badly at Chickamauga. The copperheads in the North were calling for an end to the war. Bragg, as a Confederate commander, was hardly a visionary and was mediocre at best. Rosecrans was dismissed from command of the Army of the Cumberland and never would be given an important assignment again in the Union army. Jefferson Davis, president of the Confederacy, was extremely excited over the triumph and proclaimed, "A grateful country recognizes ... your glorious victory on the field of Chickamauga."[71]

The 4th Iowa was on the move from Memphis, Tennessee. They were obviously being sent east to reconsolidate the situation in Chattanooga and northern Georgia.

They marched towards Decatur, Alabama. At Dalton Station in Alabama on October 20, the 4th Iowa had a skirmish with Confederates. The next day at Cherokee Station in Alabama, the 4th Iowa and Williamson's Brigade had a larger skirmish with Confederate forces. Williamson's 2nd Brigade along with the 4th Iowa were put on either side of the road, where they were attacked by mounted Rebels. The 2nd Brigade repulsed the attack, and General Osterhaus reported, "The brave men of the 2nd Brigade drove them back across the open field." Later in his report Osterhaus said Williamson and the 2nd Brigade "all did their whole duty." Dr. Mynn W. Robbins of Council Bluffs, Iowa, was the chief surgeon of the 4th Iowa Infantry Regiment and had been promoted to be the chief surgeon of the 1st Division. Robbins reported that while the number of wounded was not great at Cherokee Station, there were a number of serious wounds and medical operations that occurred. On November 26 at Barton Station, another firefight occurred; however, the 4th Iowa was kept in reserve during that engagement. At Tuscumbia, Alabama, on October 27, the 4th Iowa Infantry with the 2nd Brigade and other Union elements took the town and occupied it. Along the way, the 4th Iowa had fought against Nathan Bedford Forrest's cavalry, as well as Wheeler's, Lee's and Walker's Confederate cavalry units. On the October 30, Williamson's Brigade, with the 4th Iowa included, crossed the Tennessee River at Chickasaw Landing and marched with the rest of the Army of the Tennessee to Chattanooga. On November 16, the Chattanooga road via Alabama was cut up by large locomotives and blocked by dead mules; this considerably slowed down their advance to Chattanooga. During their march, they noticed Rebel cavalry was close by, but they never attacked their column. On November 23, the 4th Iowa and the Iowa Brigade were at Lookout Creek. The 4th Iowa Infantry had little time to rest or resupply, as the next day they would be involved in the Battle of Lookout Mountain.[72]

After Rosecrans' disaster at Chickamauga, Bragg's army had pinned the Federals up in Chattanooga. A siege was put upon the Federals at Chattanooga, and things looked dire for the Union soldiers. By the third week of the siege, Union soldiers were hungry and everyone was put on quarter rations. Grant, Sherman, and their armies went on a relief expedition into Chattanooga. Lookout Mountain dominated the scene around Chattanooga, close to the Tennessee River. Rather than a mountain, it was more of long ridge with a rocky, thickly wooded wall. Lookout Mountain left the state of Tennessee and wound its way across the upper corner of Georgia, ending far into Alabama. One soldier described the terrain on Lookout Mountain as untouched forest growth, seamed with deep ravines and obstructed with rocks of all sizes. The Confederates were dug in on Lookout Mountain. What would be called the "Battle Above the Clouds" was about to begin.

The 4th Iowa and the Iowa Brigade were put under General Joe Hooker's command. They were to dislodge the Confederates from Lookout Mountain. A narrow plateau belted Lookout Mountain, and the Rebels had built breastworks and rifle pits as defensive positions along this plateau. As the day went on the mist settled lower and lower and it became darker and darker on the battlefield. At this time the regiment of the 4th Iowa was depleted to the point that they had only 293 men active for the battle. The 4th Iowa Infantry, led by Lt. Colonel George Burton, moved across an open field to Lookout Creek and came under heavy fire. They crossed the creek with heavy artillery fire all around them. The 4th Iowa was ordered to protect a Union battery in front of Lookout Mountain. Later in the day the 4th Iowa Infantry and Williamson's Iowa Brigade moved up on the mountain and advanced on the Rebel lines until they were above the foggy clouds. The 4th Iowa had moved farther up on the mountain than Williamson and his other three regiments. Williamson could not see the position of the 4th Iowa Infantry because of the thick clouds. Finally, Williamson found the 4th Iowa and ordered them to help relieve an Ohio regiment that had run out of ammunition. Williamson brought ammunition to the forward regiments. His brigade became the point and was the first unit to break through the Rebel lines. The Confederates made several counterattacks, but all were repulsed. The 4th Iowa Infantry held their ground throughout the night on Lookout Mountain, and on the morning of the 25th of November they discovered the Confederates had retreated off of Lookout Mountain onto Missionary Ridge.[73]

The next day the Rebels crossed Chattanooga Creek and burned all the bridges across it. At three a.m., the 4th Iowa Infantry pushed up onto Missionary Ridge. The Rebels held a gap on the ridge but soon were overwhelmed. The 4th Iowa Infantry was ordered into the gap to hold the blue line. The 4th Iowa then advanced to the crest of Missionary Ridge, as Rebel reinforcements were on their way to dislodge the Federals. The 4th Iowa Infantry went double-time until they came within 50 yards of the Rebel lines and the 4th Iowa opened fire. The Rebels, terrified, then fell back. Williamson reported that the 4th Iowa Infantry was the first to reach the crest of Missionary Ridge. Many Confederate prisoners were taken during this time. On the 26th of November, the 4th Iowa Infantry took care of their wounded and buried their dead. The Rebels had burned bridges so the Union could not advance its artillery. The Confederates were pushed towards the town of Rossville, Georgia, and another steep ridge called Taylor's Ridge. The 4th Iowa Infantry was ordered to help support the 76th Ohio Infantry, which was pinned down. They made their way under fire up Taylor's Ridge. Colonel Williamson of the 2nd Brigade, of which the 4th Iowa was part, said of Taylor's Ridge,

> [It] is a bold rocky faced ridge, and very difficult to ascent. Bragg's Army had all the time they wanted to get there, and to form in line on this crest almost out of any danger from an attacking force.... I was ordered by General Osterhaus to go forward, keeping my right well toward the gap. I endeavored to go up, and did go up, under a killing fire in which I saw more valuable lives thrown away, absolutely sacrificed, without any apparent purpose or reason (as it afterward developed) than I have ever seen out of so small a number before, but except what General Osterhaus says in his report, this whole battle seems to have been lost sight of in history, so far as I can learn. In the attack my brigade lost over eight hundred men.

The 4th Iowa Infantry made their way to the crest of Taylor's Ridge, and a sustained attacked by a superior Rebel unit could not dislodge them. Williamson and the 2nd Brigade and the 4th Iowa saw the enemy trying to burn two bridges across East Chickamauga Creek and were able to save them. General Osterhaus mentioned in his report of this campaign the excellent work done by Colonel James A. Williamson and Major Samuel D. Nichols of Panora, Iowa, and the 4th Iowa Infantry. Also mentioned for their bravery were First Lieutenant Charles W. Baker of Washington County, Iowa, who was killed. In addition, noted for bravery in this campaign were Captain George E. Ford of Council Bluffs and Lieutenant Lemuel Shields of Glenwood, Iowa. 2nd Lieutenant Thomas H. Cramer of Page County, Iowa, was mentioned for his valor and was only 23 years old when he died. He joined the 4th Iowa Infantry about the same time as his father Joseph Cramer had enlisted. Joseph Cramer was a veteran of the Mexican War, having obtained the rank of first sergeant. When he joined the 4th Iowa in August of 1861, Joseph was given the rank of captain of Company K. Joseph rose to the rank of major but resigned in August of 1863 when he was 49 years old.[74]

Captain Henry G. Ankeny of Company H of the 4th Iowa wrote of this time, "The 4th Iowa is covered all over with glory Bragg is on the retreat and we are after them." At one point Ankeny took inventory of the men wounded and killed recently under his command: "Young severely [wounded] in the thigh, A.D. Thomas a slight bayonet wound in the hip. Sergt. J.B. Chaney slight wound in the head and was taken prisoner. This makes two killed and five wounded yesterday. J.A. Smith was killed and J.D. Baker was wounded" (Baker later had his leg amputated). Earlier Ankeny had penned, "We were in the slaughter pen yesterday for thirty minutes but it was fearful. I had three men killed." Probably the hardest death for Ankeny to take was that of his friend Rufus Campbell. Campbell was also from Adams County in Iowa, well liked, and he and Ankeny had joined the 4th Iowa on the same day in July of 1861. Ankeny wrote, "Rufus E. Campbell shot through the head and killed instantly." Ankeny noted that Adams County would mourn his death. Campbell had $12 on him, which the captain took and immediately sent to Campbell's mother in Iowa. The 4th Iowa Infantry then went to Woodville, Alabama, for their winter quarters. On January 1, 1864, the men of the 4th Iowa reenlisted. A panel of Union officers said the 4th Iowa could add to their battle flag "Chattanooga." On the 25th of February the men of the 4th Iowa Infantry were granted a well-earned furlough to rest and recruit more members to their depleted regiment. They arrived in Des Moines on March 9, 1864. Captain Ankeny had written to his wife, hoping she could meet him while he was in Des Moines. The 4th Iowa Infantry were greeted in the capital city of Iowa as war heroes. The Iowa legislature was in session but adjourned to give the 4th Iowa a royal reception. Resolutions were passed praising the 4th Iowa Infantry for reenlisting: "The citizens of Des Moines are preparing to give them a proper reception; and deeming it our duty as their representatives, to express our appreciation of their gallantry and their services in the suppression of the rebellion." The Iowa General Assembly resolved "That we have watched with pride and admiration the Fourth Iowa Infantry, as step by step they have borne the ensign of the free … and in their long and weary marches, enduring all the privations and hardships of a soldier's life, they have toiled on and fought for home, kindred and country, until the mute graves of their comrades in arm point in sadness to the remnants of brave men, who have honored their state and added to the glory of the nation." The city of Des Moines gave the men of the 4th Iowa a magnificent reception. The ladies of the city along with the Iowa General Assembly gave the men of the 4th Iowa a large banquet and gave honors to individual soldiers. Addison A. Stuart in *Iowa Colonels and Regiments* states, "To no Iowa regiment is the state more largely indebted for its military renown that to the noble 4th Iowa."[75]

While Grenville Dodge was in Council Bluffs recuperating, he was being tempted and tugged in several directions. His wife Anne had never really wanted him to serve in the army. She would have much preferred that Grenville give up the army and railroading and just stay with her and their small family in Council Bluffs. Dodge's railroad friends were putting pressure on him to resign his army commission and join them in the venture to start a transcontinental railroad. Local Iowa political dignitaries also wanted Dodge to shine his light on them. A politician with a war hero as a friend could go a long way during these Civil War days. Hub Hoxie asked Dodge's favor to curry the vote of the Iowa soldiers so they would elect his slate of Republican candidates. Dodge made his way to New York City, where Thomas Durant offered Dodge the position of chief engineer of the Union Pacific Railroad at a gaudy salary. Dodge turned Durant down, but Durant said he would keep the position open until spring. Dodge still tried to keep in Durant's good graces. However, others of Dodge's Iowa friends, such as John Kasson and Iowa senator James Grimes, who were trying to get Dodge a major-general promotion, were perplexed that although they were trying hard for his promotion, he might throw it away and go back into railroading.[76]

When Dodge returned to his command post in Corinth, he still was not completely healthy. He suffered from neuralgia and weighted only 126 pounds. Dodge found when he returned to his post that his spy network had been scattered. General Sherman was especially anxious to get intelligence from Dodge's spies. However, one of Dodge's most important spies, Levi Naron, had been very active. He had increased his spy network under Dodge's direction from 15 to 25 spies. About half were citizens of the South, while the other half were Union soldiers who were from the southland. None of these spies made less than 100 dollars a month. As the war dragged on the value of Confederate money became less and less. In 1862, it took $120 in Confederate currency to equal $100 in gold. By 1863, it took $300 in Confederate money to equal $100 in gold. In 1864, it took $1,800 in Confederate money to equal $100 in gold. By the end of the war in April of 1865, it took $5,500 Confederate currency to equal $100 gold. Dodge and his spies had to adjust their payments, when using Confederate money, as the war went on. Dodge sent Philip Henson to see if the Rebels were going to attack him in Corinth. Then he sent him on a mission to ascertain the Confederate defenses around Columbus, Mississippi.[77]

Twice a week Naron sent his scouts to Pittsburg Landing in Tennessee to hook up with others of Dodge's scouts to relay information to them. Naron received a lot of his information from Southern newspapers. Naron sometimes gathered a few of his spies as scouts and captured small groups of Confederate guerrilla fighters who were plaguing Tennessee and Mississippi.[78]

Other spies came up with intelligence that General Joe Johnston was not aware of Sherman's troop movements to eastern Tennessee. On November 8 Dodge's troops crossed the Tennessee River by steamboats.[79]

Naron and a few of his other spies were out in front of Dodge's column in Confederate uniforms looking for serviceable horses and mules that could be used by the Union army. Dodge passed on information gleaned from Southern newspapers and other military intelligence from his scouts and spies to other Union generals. Dodge received an order from Sherman that came from Grant, instructing Dodge to quit moving his troops forward but to repair the over 100 miles of railroad tracks from Nashville to Decatur and guard it. Grant needed that rail line open to supply his troops. Dodge's spies told him there were about 1,000 Rebel and guerrilla cavalry who would tear up the tracks if they were left unguarded. Dodge was deeply disappointed with this order, as he wanted to be with Grant, Sherman, and their campaign against Chattanooga, Lookout Mountain, Missionary Ridge, Taylor's Ridge and Rossville.[80]

This railroad repair by Dodge and his pioneer corps was particularly important for Grant to supply his and Sherman's armies. Grant also noted that Burnside's army of 25,000 men would have to be supplied over this track. In addition, the rugged landscape of this part of Tennessee made repairs over breathtaking ravines very difficult. Since Dodge and his troops had not started out to repair rail track, they did not have readily available the proper equipment to make repairs. Some of the repairs to be done had to go on bridges 600 feet long and 72 feet high; a couple were 600 feet long and 40 feet high. Grant was impressed with Dodge's repair work and mentioned it in his memoirs. He wrote, "He [Dodge] had no tools to work with except those of the pioneers-axes, picks and spades…. General Dodge had the work assigned him finished within forty days after receiving his orders. The number of bridges to rebuild was one hundred and eighty-two, many of them over deep and wide chasms; the length of the road repaired was over one hundred and two miles." To add to the difficulties of Dodge, some of the track was the responsibility of the Army of the Cumberland, and there could be some jealousies regarding who was responsible for the repair of this track. However, Grant knew Dodge was the best man for this important job.[81]

For the repair work on the Nashville and Decatur Railroad Dodge made his headquarters in Pulaski, Tennessee. Dodge recruited a large number of blacksmiths and carpenter shops in the area to make the tools and equipment needed to repair the railroad track. Dodge's 8,000-man army needed to get much of their supplies from the Elk River Valley. Dodge knew many of the residents of this valley were staunchly supportive of the Confederate government. Again Dodge used his great ability for common sense and wrote a circular to the residents of the Elk River Valley that he would pay for all foodstuffs for his men and forage for his animals that they brought into his camp. When they came into his camp, if they were supporters of the Confederacy he would not make them take an oath of allegiance to the Union but would let them go their way. Dodge wrote that if his men had to come get the foodstuffs and forage from the residents of the Elk River Valley, they would be given certificates for their produce, which meant they would have to wait a long time to be paid, or they might not be paid for their products at all. Dodge also staffed several mills in the area with soldiers who had been mechanics or had worked in mills to run them so he had plenty of corn meal and wheat for his troops. The citizens of the valley brought in their produce for Dodge's army. His army was well fed and Dodge's animals were taken care of properly. Sherman wrote to Dodge of all the dead mules and livestock in terrible condition as his army got closer to Chattanooga. Grant approved of Dodge's common-sense approach to solving problems and described Dodge as "being a most capable soldier."[82]

In addition to running his spy network, General Dodge had to be aware of counterintelligence work. Confederate spies were continuously trying to find Dodge's whereabouts and the disposition of his army. The chief of Dodge's scouts was James Hensal of the 7th Kansas Cavalry. The 7th Kansas Cavalry, a unit in Dodge's XVI Corps, had a very interesting history. Organized by Colonel Charles R. Jennison in Leavenworth,

Kansas, the unit became known as "Jennison's Jayhawkers." Jennison was one of the most radical and violent abolitionists in Kansas prior to the Civil War, when it was known as "Bleeding Kansas." Jennison had a terrible reputation in the 1850s as an abolitionist who seemed more interested in how much he could steal or how many slavers he could kill. During the late 1850s there were many fine-blooded horses, obviously stolen from Missouri, that had no pedigree papers, showing up in Iowa horse-sale barns. Certain witty auctioneers would say that these fine-blooded horses had a pedigree of "out of Missouri by Jennison." During the Civil War Jennison's 7th Cavalry became known as a unit that would accept slaves into its lines regardless of the changing official policies of the Lincoln administration or the Union army. Jennison and the 7th Cavalry continued with their Jayhawker ways of stealing, destruction and murder; sometimes they were known as "Redlegs." However, in April of 1862 Jennison resigned his commission due to jealousy over the promotion of another officer. After Jennison's resignation, the 7th Kansas Cavalry became a more professional and reliable fighting unit. When the 7th Cavalry was serving in Tennessee in 1862, Lt. Colonel Daniel R. Anthony, brother to leading women's-rights advocate Susan B. Anthony, was arrested and relieved of his command in the Union army for issuing an order forbidding slave catchers to enter his regimental camp who were looking for runaway slaves. Other notable members of the 7th Kansas Cavalry were William Frederick "Buffalo Bill" Cody, who entered as a private and served in the cavalry for one year, seven months and ten days. After the Civil War during what became known as the Indian Wars, Cody became a civilian scout for the United States Army and one of the few U.S. private citizens to win the Congressional Medal of Honor. Cody became a famous showman and proprietor of "Buffalo Bill Cody's Wild West and Congress of Roughriders of the World." Another member of the 7th Kansas Cavalry was Major Edmund Needham Morrill, who later became governor of Kansas.[83]

General William Tecumseh Sherman was probably Grant's most trusted general. As did Grant, Sherman depended heavily on Dodge's spy network and scouts for military intelligence (Library of Congress).

Dodge told Hensal to be on the lookout for Confederate spies and scouts who Dodge believed were operating within his lines. Hensal's first capture of Confederate spies was a good one. He captured Samuel Davis, who was wearing an odd Confederate uniform and a dyed Union army overcoat plus a Union army cap. Colonel Henry Shaw, Joshua Brown and others in Confederate uniforms were also arrested. When stopped by members of the 7th Kansas Cavalry, Davis was asked to take off his shoes. Hidden in his shoe were maps meant for Confederate general Braxton Bragg, newspapers clips and letters, and other information telling of the position of Dodge's troops. Most disconcerting, there were papers that had come directly from Dodge's desk. Davis was taken to Dodge and he surmised Davis was just a courier. Dodge became convinced that E. Coleman was behind this espionage. Coleman had been a thorn in Dodge's side when he was the head of Confederate general Braxton Bragg's scouts and spies. Unfortunately, the general knew Coleman only by name and not by sight. In fact, the soldier presenting himself as Colonel Shaw was actually Coleman. Dodge wrote to Sherman that he thought he would have Davis talking in a couple of days.

Pressure was put on Davis; he was told he would be tried as a spy and hanged if found guilty unless he gave up the identity of Coleman. Dodge and the others in his command were impressed with Davis' manner and his obvious intelligence. Looking much younger than his 21 years, Davis had come from a wealthy family and gone to a military academy in Tennessee. Davis persisted and would not give up Coleman's identity. Nobody knew how those papers had gotten from Dodge's desk to Davis the courier. Some theorized a Tennessee beauty had mesmerized a junior Union officer in Dodge's XVI Corps to take papers off his desk. Many people in nearby Tennessee towns pleaded for Davis' life. Davis was tried, found guilty of being a spy by a Union military tribunal and sentenced to be hanged. Levi Naron, one of Dodge's top spies, asked to speak to Davis to see if he could make him change his mind. Naron was unable, as were others who tried to appeal to the youthful Davis to save his life. Davis was hanged on November 27, 1863. Levi Naron said what many Union officers believed, including Dodge: "I have often regretted the fate of this young man, who could brave such a death when his life rested in his own hands. His mind was one of principle, though engaged in a wrong cause." Throughout the South, Davis became a martyr and legend. Poems, novels and plays were written about this young Tennessean, and schoolchildren all over Dixie knew his name years after his death. A statue of Davis was erected in Nashville, and after the war Dodge sent some money for the monument. Colonel Henry Shaw, aka Captain Coleman, and the other captured were sent north to prisoner-of-war camps and eventually exchanged for Union prisoners. It was not until years after the end of the Civil War that Dodge learned Shaw/Coleman's true identity. Joshua Brown, one of the men captured with Davis, later became a businessman who told Dodge how close he had come to capturing the elusive Coleman.[84]

Dodge was asked by Grant to build the railroad to Columbia, Mississippi. Dodge ran into command jealousies when his men went foraging in territory of the Army of the Cumberland. However, Grant stepped in, realizing Dodge was the best man to rebuild the railroad. The Army of the Cumberland had even taken to arresting Dodge's men when they went foraging in Cumberland territory. Grant issued a blistering attack on the officers of the Cumberland who were arresting Dodge's men and left no one in any doubt of whose side Grant would take in a territorial dispute. If these Cumberland Union officers continued to harass Dodge's men, they risked jeopardizing their army careers.[85]

Dodge wrote to Sherman that he wished to reorganize his 12,000-man corps into two divisions. He told Sherman that a lot of his infantry was mounted, so he could react quickly to Confederate aggression. He also told Sherman that the Tennessee River was so shallow that Roddey's Cavalry could ford at almost any point on the river. Dodge reported that all of his teamsters were black men, and according to Grant's wishes, all available black men who were able to work on railroad repair did so. Recruiters for the black Union regiments tried to conscript Dodge's black workers, but they had become so valuable, especially those with knowledge of building bridges, that Dodge wrote to Grant to get an exemption for his black men who had skilled labor abilities. Grant approved Dodge's exemptions. In another section, General Roseau was trying to rebuild the railroad and especially was having trouble with the bridges. Dodge tried to consult with him on what to do, but Dodge came to the conclusion if it were to be done, Dodge's corps of soldiers and workers would have to do it, which they did. To make matters worse Dodge had contracted with a bridge maker in Chicago to make permanent bridges, but they were behind on their orders. Temporary bridges would have to be put in until the permanent ones were sent south. Telegraph lines were being cut with regularity. Dodge had Colonel Phillips' cavalry repair the telegraph lines and had Phillips notify rich and influential Rebel supporters near the cut line that they would have to pay for the repairs. Dodge noted that the telegraph lines after this were rarely cut. All through the fall and early winter of 1863, Dodge and the XVI Corps fought a number of firefights and skirmishes with the Confederate cavalry of Roddey, Forrest and others. In addition, Confederate guerrillas did their best to harass and tear up Dodge's tracks. However, in almost every case the XVI Corps triumphed.[86]

In December of 1863, Grant moved his headquarters to Nashville. While in Nashville, he called for all his corps and army commanders of the Army of the Tennessee to discuss strategy. They called upon Tennessee military governor Andrew Johnson, who would become Lincoln's vice president and eventually president after Lincoln's assassination. They all decided to go to the Shakespearean play *Hamlet*. Sherman was a great lover of the works of the bard. However, this production was second rate, and Sherman loudly criticized the play as it went on. Dodge told Sherman "not to talk so loud, some of the boys will discover us, and there will be a scene." When the gravedigger's scene came and Hamlet soliloquized on Yorick's skull, a Union soldier stood up in the audience and said, "Say pard what is it, Yank or Re?" The whole house came down in laughter and Grant said, "We had better get out of here." Nobody in Nashville knew what Grant and Sherman looked like, and when they went to eat they were treated poorly. The next day this information hit the Nashville newspapers, and prominent citizens came to apologize to Grant. He and the Union generals were offered all sorts of accommodations in Nashville.[87]

Grant had a grand plan to strip Tennessee and New Orleans of a large number of troops and attack Mobile, Alabama. The idea was that the Alabama River out of Mobile and the Coosa River could be used to supply his troops for the expected Battle at Atlanta. However, Lincoln objected to the plan, thinking that once the Confederates figured out what Grant was doing, Longstreet and others would reoccupy Tennessee and all their gains in the Volunteer State would be lost.

Most of the veterans in Dodge's Corps reenlisted, which was good news. However, the Federal government had promised these veterans that if they reenlisted, they would receive a month's furlough. So from January into February, Dodge's Corps was very much under-staffed. Throughout the winter, a game of cat and mouse was played, with

Dodge looking for any sign of cavalry movements on his rail lines and especially the bridges.

Dodge heard from his brother Nathan and from Peter Dey and Hub Hoxie about the progress of the Union Pacific Railroad. Thomas Durant was in charge. Durant was a con man at heart. Dey was frustrated because Durant would not make up his mind as to where the terminus of the railroad would be. What Durant was really doing was manipulating the value of the stock of the different rail companies he had an interest in. Durant would tell everyone the terminus was going to be in Omaha, and the stock of the M&M Railroad would skyrocket. Then Durant would sell his M&M Railroad stock and claim that the new terminus would be to the north of Omaha and the line would hookup with the Galena and Chicago Railroad. Of course, when the price of the Galena and Chicago Railroad was cheap, Durant had loaded up on it, and he would watch that stock rise in price while the M&M stock took a nosedive. Then when the M&M stock was cheap Durant would load up on it and claim the terminus was going to be in Omaha. Durant and his friends were making millions on these stock manipulations. Previously, Dodge—not knowing the game Durant was playing—had written to Durant telling him the best terminus was Omaha because the Missouri River narrowed there. Peter Dey, as chief engineer for the rail line, was going crazy with Durant's game. Dey did not know whether to do a new survey or not. He knew, like Dodge, that the Platte River Valley would be by far the best route to the West.[88]

In January Dodge had a spy attached to Johnston's Confederate army who estimated that at that time, Johnston had only 25,000 men. This spy reported that desertions were a real problem for the Rebel army, especially with northern Alabama and Mississippi troops leaving in droves. In February, Dodge sent Philip Henson on a spy mission to Mississippi. Sherman was marching his army out of Vicksburg, headed straight east to Meridian, Mississippi, with the idea of going into Alabama. Sherman captured the large supply depot at Meridian. Henson rode hard and got to the tent of Confederate general Gholson. Gholson offered Henson a cot in the back of his tent to sleep on. Henson pretended to be asleep, snoring loudly. Gholson's tent became a beehive of activity, with couriers coming and going. It was obvious something important was about to happen. Even Forrest sent a messenger. Several Confederate units were to meet at West Point, Mississippi. When morning came, Henson could not get out of there fast enough. However, Gholson wanted to talk to Henson about a spy mission for him in the North. Henson agreed to the spy mission just to get away. Henson headed north and had to cross a raging river that almost cost him his life. He got to Dodge's headquarters and told Dodge of the Rebel units that were to converge on West Point. Dodge passed this intelligence on to Sherman. Unfortunately, Sherman was to receive cavalry support from General William Sooy Smith. Even though Smith had the numbers, he blundered badly when attacked by Forrest's horsemen. Smith and his cavalry unit were defeated and retreated to Memphis. This engagement only added to the legend of Nathan Bedford Forrest, and the Southern newspapers hailed it as a great Confederate victory. While there was not a great loss of life on either side, Sherman was forced to head back to Vicksburg.[89]

Most of Dodge's spy missions going into Confederate lines involved a few days. However, Dodge had a mission that would take a month or more: he wanted someone to map out the exact locations of the Rebel armies and where these units were located. He knew Phil Henson was the best man for the job. Dodge and Henson picked timetables of military projects and other items that looked impressive but actually were of little value to show Confederate General Gholson and other high-ranking Rebel commanders that Henson was spying for the Confederacy. Henson was arrested near General Nathan Bedford Forrest's headquarters near Tupelo. Henson did not want to be quizzed by Forrest, a tough old bird if there ever was one. Henson told Forrest he was a spy for Gholson. Gholson's unit was nearby and the general was called for and made his way to Forrest's headquarters. Gholson vouched for Henson. Much to Henson's delight, both Forrest and Gholson were impressed with his military projects timetable. Henson also gave them new information. One was the location of Dodge's army but it would be impossible for Forrest in that short of time to move on Dodge's Corps. Henson then said Dodge had sent a completely new group of spies into Georgia, which was true. What Henson did not say was that all of them had returned to Dodge's headquarters, failing in their mission. Forrest then wanted Henson to track down every one of Dodge's Yankee spies and turn them over to him. Henson agreed. This would be a perfect cover for his real mission. Forrest gave Henson a sixty-day pass and a letter to Confederate general Polk. Forrest sent one of his best scouts along with Henson. Unknown to Henson, Forrest also had one of his spies trailing Henson.

Henson rode to General Polk's headquarters and they discussed the methods Henson was going to use to track down these "spies." Polk gave Henson 500 dollars for expenses. Polk also gave Henson a captain to aid him on his mission. Henson crept through alleys, looked at hotel registers and visited prisons. Forrest's scout and Polk's captain were impressed with his diligence. Henson persuaded the captain to let him go off alone. Henson was then able to pursue his real mission to map out the location of Confederate armies. Henson made his way back to Polk's headquarters. Polk then asked Henson to spy for him against the Yankees, to which Henson agreed. Henson made his way back to Federal lines with a pass provided by Polk. When Henson reached Dodge's headquarters and showed him the information he had, Dodge was ecstatic. Henson had done far better than even Dodge had expected. Dodge then asked Henson if he would go on one more spy mission for him.[90]

Dodge wrote to Adjunct General Thomas telling him that many of the planters in Tennessee were coming to the realization that their former slaves were free. The planters were willing to pay wages to the former slaves to get their work done. In March of 1864, Grant was given command of all the Union armies. He would be headquartered in the East. Grant named Sherman commander of all the Union armies in the West. Grant wanted to take a number of the Western officers, including Dodge, with him to the East. However, Sherman objected and in the end, the only officer Grant took was General Philip Sheridan. Grant talked strategy with Sherman, and they agreed to put continuous pressure on the armies of Lee and Johnston. That way they could not switch corps or divisions back and forth between the Eastern front and Western front, depending on where the greater was risk was located. During this time, Dodge had requested from Grant that in the next big offensive, which obviously would be in Atlanta, Dodge be given a battlefield command. Would Sherman honor Grant's promise to him?[91]

Dodge received information from his spies about the location of Confederate troops in Atlanta and northern Georgia and passed it onto Grant and Sherman. During the spring of 1864, Dodge and his XVI Corps were engaged in various firefights and skirmishes; of course in trying to protect the rail lines; and in rebuilding the ones that were destroyed. They battled against the usual suspects; Roddey and Forrest's Cavalry. In addition, Confederate guerrillas were also engaged in this activity.[92]

In April, Dodge received orders to move to the East, and he marched his men towards Chattanooga. Then in early May, General McPherson, to whom Dodge's Corps was attached, sent him a message to quickly transport his men on rail cars and bring ammunition with them. Dodge's Corps' baggage trains and artillery would follow on the road. Dodge and the men of the XVI Corps were in good spirits. It was obvious that the big offensive was on into the heart of Dixie.[93]

# Chapter 4

# "The last full measure"

After their heroes' welcome in Des Moines and the rest of Iowa, the 4th Iowa Volunteer Infantry were back in their winter quarters in Woodville, Alabama. On March 14 near Claysville, Alabama, a small contingent of the 4th Iowa was involved in a skirmish with the Rebels. They were badly outnumbered, and while casualties were light a number of the 4th Iowa were captured by the Confederates. These men ended up in various Confederate P.O.W. camps, including Andersonville. Most of the regiment and brigade moved out to Chattanooga to begin the campaign against Atlanta. Colonel James A. Williamson took command of the 2nd Brigade, 1st Division, of the XV Army Corps. The 4th Iowa was part of Williamson's Brigade. Lt. Colonel Samuel D. Nichols had taken over the direct command of the 4th Iowa Volunteer Infantry. Nichols was smart and brave. He was from Panora, Iowa, in Guthrie County. He was 29 years old and had been born in New Jersey. He received his lt. colonel promotion on April 5, 1864. Lt. Colonel George Burton, the tough, stoic Irishman who had formally led the 4th Iowa after Williamson became a brigade commander, had resigned his commission on April 4, 1864. The 4th Iowa would be part of General Peter Osterhaus's division. Osterhaus was sick from July 15, 1864, to August 15, 1864, and General Charles Woods took over command of the 1st Division. Major General John Logan was in command of Sherman's old XV Corps. Major General James McPherson was commander of the Army of the Tennessee. General William T. Sherman became overall commander of the armies in the West. Dodge had reports of a build-up in Forrest's Cavalry, but he surmised Forrest had just come north to feed his troops and animals. Forrest quickly left for safer environments in the south. Dodge's brother Nathan came out for a brief visit. Brigadier-General Grenville Dodge, commanding the left wing of the XVI Corps, also moved out to the south. In front of the Union army was Joseph Johnston's Confederate army. Johnston became convinced that the Union army would follow the rail line down from Chattanooga to Atlanta. The rail line ran through the Georgia towns of Ringgold, Dalton, Resaca, Kingston, Marietta and then Atlanta. Johnston now had an army of 70,000 men, and at Dalton he had constructed fortifications 13 feet thick. There was a formidable ridge called Rocky Face making a frontal attack impractical. Sherman thought that Dodge's XVI Corps would go around the Confederate left flank to a place called Ship's Gap, a passage on a range of mountains near the Georgia border. General James McPherson noted that this was a 30-mile journey and wondered if Dodge's troops would be able to cover that much ground in that short period of time. Sherman said, "Let him try."[1]

Dodge was successful in reaching a place called Snake Creek Gap. He found only a handful of Rebels there, and they were quickly rounded up. Dodge's Corps, which was undermanned, and parts of Logan's XV Corps emerged from the mountains on May 8, 1864. They were a day ahead of schedule. Dodge and elements of the XV Corps found themselves almost to the rear of Johnston's army. On May 9, Dodge proceeded to Resaca with his 2nd Division, commanded by General Thomas W. Sweeny. Dodge found that only one brigade of Rebel infantry was in the area, and he quickly pushed them back into the city of Resaca. The 1st Alabama Union Cavalry also was ready to charge into Resaca with Dodge's troops. However, Major-General James McPherson, head of the Army of the Tennessee, rode up and asked what was going on. Colonel Spencer, leading the 1st Alabama Union Cavalry, said he could capture Resaca in fifteen minutes. Dodge pointed out to McPherson that they could cut Johnston's rail and supply lines to Atlanta.

Johnston was hemmed in on the west by the mountains, and he would have to retreat to the east off his line of defense. McPherson argued that they were not following Sherman's orders. Some believed that the Battle of Atlanta could have been over by then if McPherson had listened to Dodge and Colonel Spencer of the 1st Alabama Union Cavalry. However, McPherson would not let the town be attacked. Sherman declared, "Such an opportunity does not occur twice in a single lifetime." Dodge later claimed that Sherman said the troops available at that time could have broken up Johnston's army. McPherson was a very popular general, and he later admitted he was wrong. McPherson was killed at the Battle of Atlanta, and some were reluctant to criticize him at a later date. In his official report on the campaign, Sherman said, "General McPherson was thereby enabled to march within a mile of Resaca almost unopposed." Sherman went on to say that he was "disappointed at the result" of McPherson not attacking at that time.[2]

Johnson, hearing of the Union movement to his rear, began moving troops from the Dalton area to the hills around Resaca. The combined Union armies Johnston had to face in Georgia included the Army of the Tennessee, the Army of the Cumberland, the Army of the Ohio and Blair's XVII Corps. The Union total was 98,797 men and 254 pieces of artillery. The 4th Iowa was soon put in battle position. They were attached to the XV Corps, now headed by Major-General John A. Logan. Logan was a political general who had been a Douglas Democratic congressman from Illinois prior to the war. After the war, he became a force in the G.A.R. and Republican Party. Although he was loud and opinionated, Logan was considered to be an above-average civilian general even though he had no formal military training except as an officer in the Mexican War.[3]

Dodge sent skirmishers from the XVI Corps to test the Confederate Cavalry, but the Rebels continued to retreat to fortifications around Resaca. On May 13, the Union army probed the Confederate lines. On the 14th the fighting became more intense, but the Federals were repulsed. On the 15th Dodge sent Sweeny's division across the Oostanaula River on the newly developed Cumberland pontoon bridges. Dodge's 2nd Division headed to capture Johnston's rail supply lines. At one point Walker's Confederate Division, considered one of its best, was in front of a small force of Dodge's. Dodge had the 64th Illinois Regiment, which was equipped with Henry magazine rifles. The 64th Illinois fired rapidly, and Walker thought a much larger force was in front of him. This bought Dodge enough time to send another brigade to reinforce the 64th Illinois. The

4th Iowa Infantry of the 2nd brigade was put in line with Osterhaus' 1st Brigade of the 1st Division. The 4th Iowa's Colonel Nichols and Williamson's 2nd Brigade were ordered to move forward. They were under heavy fire from the Confederates and took a hill in front of the Rebel fortifications. The 4th Iowa was ordered to support elements of the 1st Brigade and then were ordered into the town of Resaca. The Rebels had retreated out of Resaca, and Johnson had his entire army in retreat. The 4th Iowa occupied the town of Resaca along with Williamson's Brigade and elements of the XV Corps.[4]

Dodge's XVI Corps, along with other units, chased Johnston's army to Adairsville, Georgia, to the south of Resaca. Major Arthur MacArthur, Jr., father of World War II and Korean War general Douglas MacArthur, commanded two regiments that suffered heavy casualties at Adairsville. Arthur MacArthur, Jr., at 17 became a first lieutenant and was promoted to brevet colonel at nineteen years of age, becoming known in the North as the "Boy Colonel." Dodge was talking to a man when the man was killed by a sniper, while another soldier was killed while holding Dodge's horse. Dodge's command was taking a number of prisoners and his casualties were mounting. Dodge and the XVI Corps marched to Adairsville and then camped at Kingston for three days. Johnston continued his retreat out of Adairsville. There were two roads going south out of Adairsville, and Johnston correctly guessed that Sherman would divide his army, so Johnston planned to attack one-half of Sherman's army.[5]

Dodge had complained to Sherman that some of the generals in the Army of the Cumberland wondered why a brigadier-general such as Dodge was commanding a corps while there were major-generals commanding lesser-sized units in the Army of the Cumberland. Sherman wrote to Dodge not to worry about it but just keep doing his job. Major-General Oglesby was severely wounded; the Union army refused to accept his resignation but put him on light duty. Oglesby wanted to resign his generalship so he could run for governor of Illinois. Oglesby said he would only resign if Dodge got his major-general slot. John A. Kasson, now in Congress, hurriedly worked Dodge's name through the United States Senate. He worked to get Dodge the promotion to major-general and secured a brigadier-general slot in the regular army for Dodge and a brigadier-general slot for Colonel James A. Williamson in the volunteer army. In June of 1864, Dodge was finally able to put the two stars of a major-general on his uniform. Dodge had been able to begin investing again to build up his personal fortune. He wrote to his brother Nathan that he had to be careful not to invest in anything related to the army lest it be considered a conflict of interest. During the Civil War, a Union brigadier-general's pay was $3,700 a year. A Union major-general's pay was an increase of almost a third, to $5,484 dollars a year. A general in the Union army could also expect an officer's allowance for food and forage of over $1,200 a year. Dodge had been offered a generous salary by Thomas Durant to be chief surveyor for the Union Pacific Railroad at $5,000 a year. His decision to stay in the army, if he could survive the war, looked like a good one. However, Williamson's star would take a while longer. In December of 1864, he was made a brevet brigadier-general in the volunteers. In the spring of 1865, he received the rank of brigadier-general in the volunteers.[6]

Sherman divided his army as Johnston thought he would, some going down the Kingston Road and the rest going down the Cassville Road. Johnston wanted Sherman to believe the bulk of his army was on the Kingston Road, and he sent General Hardee's

Corps to hold that position. Sherman sent McPherson's Army of the Tennessee and most of Thomas's Army of the Cumberland to the Kingston Road. Along the Cassville Road, Sherman sent a smaller force, Schofield's 11,000 men and one corps of Thomas' Army of the Cumberland. Johnston sent his much larger Army of Hood Corps and Polk's 20,000 men to the Cassville Road. The plan had a good chance of working. However, when Hood lined up for battle, he noticed the Federals were on his flank and to the rear of his corps. It took him time to realign his troops, and he eventually thought he had taken too much time and retreated to Polk's lines. Hardee's men had been pushed to the south. Johnston, thinking too much time had been lost, again put his men in a retreat mode. Dodge was then ordered to send his 3rd Brigade, 2nd Division, to garrison in Rome, Georgia. On May 22, Dodge's forces rested. Sherman put his army on one-half rations; the rest they would have to gather from the countryside. He did this because his army was going on the offensive and he needed to conserve supplies. Sherman's much larger army kept flanking the Confederates, usually to the west of the railroad lines, while Johnston kept retreating.[7]

Dodge had Spartan ways and the direct manner of a plainsman; he lived much like a common soldier. He and Major-General James McPherson were two of the favorite generals in Sherman's army. Some of the generals, such as Francis Blair, lived in almost palatial splendor, with huge baggage trains for their personal comfort. Some of the generals also had a large contingent of reporters making sure people back home knew how important they were. McPherson, who was first in his class at West Point, always had a smile on his face and was courteous and respectful to those with lower ranks. He genuinely cared about his troops.

Dodge figured spy Philip Henson had one good spy mission left in him. Henson's continued double-crossing of Confederate generals was sure not to escape their attention. Henson's mission was to find the location of the Confederate cavalry of Nathan Bedford Forrest and other Confederate cavalry forces. Dodge gave $6,000 in Confederate money to Henson to help him on his mission. At first, Henson sent back very detailed reports of the whereabouts of the Confederates and what their numbers were. Unfortunately, Henson rode into territory controlled by General Roddey's cavalry. The last time Henson had seen Roddey, the general told him he wanted to see him in a Confederate uniform in 60 days. The former Alabama sheriff did not trust Henson and yelled at him, "Where have you been." Before Henson could answer, Roddey had him thrown in a stockade. Henson was then transferred to General S.D. Lee's headquarters in Tuscaloosa, Alabama, for a trial. Roddey had sent a note to Lee that Henson was "the worst man in the Confederacy." Roddey also said that if Lee didn't have Henson shot, Roddey would kill Henson the next time he came through his lines. Lee had a number of his West Point officers quiz Henson, and they thought him a spy. General S. D. Lee had a young Confederate lawyer who was familiar with military trials question Henson. The young lawyer thought Henson was innocent and should be released. General S.D. Lee quizzed Henson and asked him, if he were a true spy for the South where the Union army would attack next. Henson gave him an answer. In a day's time, Lee got a telegraph message that the Federals had attacked exactly where Henson had said they would. Now Lee was convinced that Henson was a true Southern patriot. Henson knew it was too late for the Rebels to act on his information.[8]

General S.D. Lee and the young Confederate lawyer felt it would be a miscarriage of justice if they hanged Henson. Lee sent Henson to General Leonidas Polk for his decision. Polk at one time had paid Henson to spy for the Confederacy. Henson felt he might have a chance to get out of this mess if he could talk to Polk. General Leonidas Polk had a broad background. He had graduated from West Point but became a large planter with hundreds of slaves. He also graduated from seminary and became Episcopal bishop of the Diocese of Louisiana. He was known as the "Fighting Bishop." During the Atlanta campaign, Polk was the second-highest-ranking Confederate general, behind Joseph Johnston. Polk had just hanged a Yankee spy, Sam Gebbins, and the gallows was still in place when Henson was put in Polk's custody. Polk greeted Henson as an old friend and wanted him to get back to Union lines so he could spy for the Confederacy. Henson told Polk of Roddey's and Forrest's desire to see him dead. Polk wrote a pass for Henson and sent along a Captain Burton to make sure Roddey and Forrest did not molest Henson.

However, at Tupelo, Mississippi, troops of General Forrest arrested Henson. Henson was manacled about his wrists and feet. A 64-pound ball and chain were added to the manacles. Henson was sent to a prison in Mobile, Alabama. On the way to Mobile at the stops, men were told a famous Yankee spy was on board the train, and on several occasions, they tried to lynch Henson. Henson was put in prison at Mobile, and on the 4th of July, he was paraded shackled before the townspeople, who yelled, "Hang him." He was put in a sweatbox for weeks at a time. Henson's wife came to Dodge, and he gave her money to hire a Confederate lawyer, Benjamin Davis, who was a cousin to Confederate president Jefferson Davis, to try to secure his release. Lawyer Davis told Henson they had no proof he was a spy—no notes, no signed papers—so no trial was held. The Rebels knew they could not prove Henson was a spy, so they simply held him with no chance of a court date. Henson began to lose a dangerous amount of weight. Dodge did not learn of Henson's fate for several months.[9]

On May 23, 1864, Dodge moved most of the left wing of the XVI Corps across the Etowah River and camped on the Pumpkin Vine Creek. On May 26 Dodge realized that most of Hardee's Corps was entrenched in front of him. Dodge's men built their own defensive positions and repulsed a couple of fierce Rebel attacks. On May 29 Dodge's men skirmished all day long with the Confederates, and at night the Rebels made five charges into his lines. Dodge's men were out of ammunition and were pinned down. Dodge and his staff under the cover of darkness resupplied his men with ammunition. Dodge captured a number of Rebels. They had been told that the Union army in front of them was made up of green 100-day volunteers who would run when fired upon. The Confederates were angry when they found out the army in front of them was made up of veterans of the Union Army of the Tennessee and the Army of the Cumberland. On June 1, 1864, the XVI Corps made their way to new entrenchments. They were able to cover their movements because two of Dodge's skirmish units, the 66th Indiana Infantry and 64th Illinois Infantry, both had repeating Henry rifles, and they were able to put down a barrage of fire. The enemy thought they were still in their old entrenchments, hearing the volume of fire coming from the XVI Corps.[10]

Johnston's army kept retreating to the south. When they left an area, they were sure to take all the livestock with them. Also forage, wheat and oat fields were left bare. This made it difficult for the Union army to live off the land.

After Dodge had moved out on the Atlanta campaign, he received an interesting letter from a citizen in Pulaski, Tennessee. The letter was from Mrs. Elizabeth Brown, whose husband, John C. Brown, was a general in the Confederate army. Mrs. Brown had gone to Dodge when he moved his headquarters to Pulaski. She was afraid that when his Union troops found out a Confederate general's wife lived in town they would destroy her property or abuse her family. Dodge assured her she would be fine and said he would post guards by her house. She said that would not be necessary; that if Dodge just had one of his officers live at her house, that would be enough. Therefore, Dodge sent two of his staff officers to room and board at her house, and she was not bothered during his time there. Mrs. Brown said in her letter that she never felt safer during the war than when Dodge and his men garrisoned Pulaski. Dodge reported that Mrs. Brown gave him much information about the people living in the area and who might cause trouble. One of Dodge's lieutenants was captured by Brown's Confederate troops, and Brown wrote Dodge a note that he would take care of the young man and would send him back to Dodge as soon as he could. He told Dodge that he appreciated his looking out for his wife and family. Soon after the Civil War was over, Brown would become governor of Tennessee; and later he and Dodge would work on the Texas and Pacific Railroad together.[11]

After garrisoning at Resaca, the 4th Iowa was relieved of this duty and rejoined the rest of the XV Corps. At the Battle of Dallas they held the extreme right flank of the line held by the Army of the Tennessee. The Confederates had occupied a line about one mile southeast of the Georgia town of Dallas. The 4th Iowa was ordered to build rifle pits and hold the line. Williamson's brigade was supposed to hook up with the XVI Corps. During the night the Confederates repeatedly attacked the 4th Iowa and the rest of Williamson's brigade, but they were repulsed. At first Osterhaus refused to reinforce Williamson and the 4th Iowa, but when he saw with his own eyes the build-up of Confederates, General Osterhaus had his 1st Brigade relieve the 4th Iowa and the rest of Williamson's 2nd Brigade, as Williamson and his men had been under fire continuously for several days. When the 4th Division was pinned down by extreme pressure from the Rebels, Osterhaus sent Williamson's 2nd Brigade, which included the 4th Iowa, to help relieve the 4th Division. The 2nd Brigade had to move at double time, and according to the official report of the battle, Osterhaus said they moved "just in time to assist our comrade of the 4th Division, in repelling a fierce assault deploying on the extreme right of the Army Corps. Colonel Williamson, commanding brigade, and the officers commanding regiments, deserve praise for the prompt and energetic manner in which they executed the maneuver and enabled us to gain and hold a position forbidding any further attempts on the part of the rebels." Around this time, Captain Ankeny of Company H of the 4th Iowa wrote, "No one has any idea of the situation on the front." Osterhaus' 1st Division was engaged until June 1 around Dallas, when they went to the area by the New Hope Church that was held by the Army of the Cumberland and relieved them. The 1st Division stayed around the New Hope Church while the Union and Rebels exchanged gun fire until June 5, when the 1st Division realized the Confederates had abandoned their lines and had retreated again.[12]

On June 15 Dodge moved the left wing of the XVI Corps so that his line faced Kennesaw Mountain. He was keeping in the line established by the much larger Army of the Cumberland. He charged a peach orchard that had several log cabins occupied by the enemy as blockhouses. A charge by the XVI Corps drove the Confederates from their positions and captured several Rebel prisoners. During this campaign, Sherman ordered all the sick, wounded and those unable to perform their duties as soldiers to the rear of the Union lines so they would not tax his dwindling supplies.

Colonel James A. Williamson and his Iowa Brigade were gaining a reputation as fighters of the first order. In addition to the 4th Iowa, the 9th Iowa Volunteer Infantry was in Williamson's brigade. The 9th Iowa Infantry was organized in Dubuque, Iowa, by their then-congressman William Vandever. Vandever was made regimental colonel. By the time of the Vicksburg and Atlanta campaigns, David Carskaddon of Marion, Iowa, was regimental colonel. The 9th Iowa had fought in almost all the battles the 4th Iowa did, including Pea Ridge, Vicksburg, Lookout Mountain and now Atlanta. At Vicksburg one of the men, Sergeant James M. Elson, later lieutenant, was awarded the Medal of Honor. The 25th Iowa Infantry, which was organized in Mount Pleasant, Iowa, in September of 1862, was also in Williamson's Iowa Brigade and was led by Colonel George C. Stone. The 30th Iowa Volunteer Infantry was organized in Keokuk in September of 1862. The original regimental colonel was Charles Abbott, who was shot in the face by Confederates at Vicksburg and died. Colonel William M.G. Torrence became the regimental leader. When the 30th Iowa was sent east with Sherman's army to relieve Chattanooga, the 30th Iowa was ambushed by Rebels near Cherokee Station. Their regimental colonel, William M.G. Torrence, was killed during this ambush. The 31st Iowa Infantry was organized in Davenport in October of 1862. Its regimental colonel, William Smyth, was an immigrant from Ireland.[13]

In June the Union high command was shaken by Confederate cavalry officer Nathan Bedford Forrest. Sherman's plan to keep Forrest bottled up in Mississippi so he could not bother Sherman's Georgia campaign was good strategy. Forrest had struck fear into the Union command with a raid into Kentucky and Tennessee. At Fort Pillow, Forrest massacred black soldiers and white Southern Union loyalists when they tried to surrender. Sherman became concerned that Forrest's cavalry would disrupt his supply lines in Tennessee. Sherman had General Sturgis' 8,000-man cavalry unit attack Forrest's smaller 5,000-man cavalry at Brice's Crossroads in Mississippi. Forrest's cavalry routed Sturgis' command back into Memphis. Forrest had 492 casualties while the Union had 2,240 casualties, including 1,500 prisoners. Most criticized Sturgis' generalship for the loss and his possible over-use of alcohol. After this defeat, Sturgis was exiled to the frontier. He did somewhat rehabilitate his reputation while taking command posts on the plains after the Civil War. He was the Colonel of the 7th Cavalry, and his Lt. Colonel was George Armstrong Custer. The town of Sturgis, South Dakota, where the big motorcycle rally is held every year, was named after General Sturgis. Grenville Dodge was told that the only Union unit that did not embarrass itself at Brice's Crossroads was Bouton's brigade of black soldiers. Dodge had recruited some of Bouton's black soldiers into the Union army.[14]

Dodge's wing of the XVI Corp stormed the Confederates' left flank while Logan, Thomas, and their armies hit the Rebels' right flank at Kennesaw Mountain. The 4th Iowa, along with Williamson's Iowa Brigade, were on the left flank of the Union lines. The 4th Iowa, along with Osterhaus' 1st Division, was held in reserve. However, on

June 27 150 men of the 4th Iowa were attached to the 2nd Division for an attack. They were under the command of Captain Daniel E. Cooper of Winterset, Iowa, who was the brigade officer of the day. They were to clear out rifle pits on the right flank of the Confederates. The official report states, "Though exposed to terrible fire, Captain Cooper and his men performed their part in the most gallant manner, carrying the pits by assault, use of the bayonet freely." Sherman had vowed not to use a frontal assault on Johnston's army, but he did precisely that at Kennesaw Mountain. Union army commanders McPherson, Logan and Thomas doubted that Sherman's assault would work. Repeatedly, a frontal assault on an enemy behind good fortifications proved to be fruitless. The Union army charged on a broad front but was repulsed by the Rebels and their 12-foot-thick fortifications. Two of Dodge's regiments, the 64th Illinois and the 66th Indiana, outfitted with their Henry repeating rifles, made it within 300 feet of the top of Kennesaw, and two members made it within 100 feet of the Rebel lines. In less than an hour of the attack, the Union army had lost 3,000 men while the Confederate losses were less than 700 men. McPherson's Corps managed to turn Johnston's left flank, making Kennesaw Mountain an untenable position. Johnston retreated southward through Marietta and to his defensive positions on Nickajack Creek. On July 3 Dodge's men were in the Confederate entrenchments on top of Kennesaw Mountain. They were led by the 64th Illinois, equipped with their Henry rifles.

On July 4, Dodge's men charged by the order of General McPherson. McPherson wrote that Dodge's Corps "gallantly executed" his order and ended up one-and-a-fourth mile east of Nickajack Creek. Johnston's troops then dug in at the Chattahoochee River. Sherman's army could see Atlanta. Dodge noted the hustle and bustle of Johnston's troops building the fortifications in Atlanta. He had to admit that Johnston was doing a splendid job of erecting the defensive positions around Atlanta. The defenses looked as formidable as or better than those around Vicksburg.[15]

The city of Atlanta had come into being as a railroad city. In 1840, there was no Atlanta. Three rail lines converged in Atlanta, making it a railroad hub. The Georgia Railroad extended from the east to Augusta, while the Macon and Western Railroad came up from the south. The Western and Atlanta Railroad came out of Chattanooga, Tennessee. By 1860, Atlanta had 10,000 residents, and during the war, the population had grown to 20,000 people. Atlanta became a manufacturing city with factories, machine shops, mills and foundries in addition to its railroads.[16]

General James B. McPherson was one of the most beloved men in the Union army, among both fellow officers and enlisted men. He seemed to have a genuine concern for the well-being of his troops. As a major-general, he became head of the Army of the Tennessee (Library of Congress).

Sherman had noticed some Confederates atop a small hill misnamed Pine Mountain. He thought they were very cheeky in exposing themselves in this way. He had Captain Peter Simonson open up canon fire on these Rebels, and his first shot caused them to scatter. The Confederates on Pine Mountain were none other than the brain trust of Joe Johnston's army, including Johnston himself, General William J. Hardee and General Leonidas Polk. Simonson's second canon shot ripped into Polk's chest, eviscerating him. Polk, known as the Fighting Bishop, was second in command to Johnston, and his intelligence and calm would be missed when Jefferson Davis sacked Johnston at the gates of Atlanta.[17]

After vowing to never make a frontal assault on a fortified position, why did Sherman go against his own and other Union generals' better judgment? There were a number of theories. Grants orders to Sherman and the Atlanta Campaign were thus: "Move against Johnston's Army, to break it up, and get into the interior of the enemy's country as far as you can, inflicting all the damage you can against their war resources." The fact is that Johnston's army had about the same numbers when they started the Atlanta Campaign as they did on Kennesaw Mountain. Sherman had done little to "break up Johnston's Army." The main thing Sherman feared was that Johnston would send part of his army to Lee to fight against Grant. General George Thomas was a much better tactician, but Grant trusted Sherman to get the job done. Sherman thought Thomas' Corps moved too slowly. Grant had also problems with Thomas. Sherman's battle plans sometimes were not very good, and he blamed others for his plans not working. During a battle, Sherman was not able to make proper adjustments that might bring victory from what would become a defeat. Sherman at times could be brilliant, and he understood perfectly Grant's dictum to constantly keep the pressure on the enemy. One of the best descriptions of Sherman was by General George W. Morgan, who said, "He is a man of immense intellectuality, but his brain is like a splendid piece of machinery with all the screws a little loose."[18]

General Grenville Dodge noted that experienced Union regiments when faced against an experienced Confederate regiment would sometimes make their own truces. This was done between the 52nd Illinois Infantry and the Rebel 49th Tennessee Infantry when their lines were only 30 yards apart at Kennesaw Mountain. Perhaps they remembered each other from the time when the 49th Tennessee Infantry was captured after the Confederate loss at Fort Donelson. The 52nd Illinois had guarded the 49th Tennessee Infantry to their P.O.W. prison in Chicago at Camp Douglas. The exchange went, "Hello Yank!" The 52nd answered "Hello Reb!" "The Rebels asked, "What regiment is that?" The Yanks shouted, "52nd Illinois." "Bully for the 52nd," hollered the Rebels. "Yank you won't fire, will you?" The 52nd, "No, if you don't." It was understood that if one side tried to assault the other's lines, the firing would begin. Confederates: "All right." The 52nd shouted, "Where is old Polk?" The Tennesseans answered, "Gone to Hell." The 52nd said, "How would you like to exchange Lieutenant Generals for solid shot?" There was no reply from the Rebels. The 52nd shouted, "Hello Johnny!" The Confederates answered, "Hello Yank!" The 52nd, "Where's old Pemberton?" The 49th Tennessee said, "Played out." Then they said, "Where's McClellan." They keep up the conversation until another regiment came to relieve the 49th Tennessee Infantry and the firing commenced again. Another exchange went, "Hello Johnny! Hello Yank!" The Union boys shouted, "Is there a good camping ground at Atlanta?" The Confederates answered, "Yes but you can't see it." The Yanks said, "Is there plenty of chickens over there?" The Rebels answered, "Yes, but not for you." The talking stopped and both sides begin shooting at each other again.[19]

Sherman came to Dodge's headquarters and asked him to go Roswell, Georgia, to build a bridge that the Army of the Tennessee could cross. Sherman wanted a double-track trestle bridge and asked Dodge how long it would take him to build it. Dodge said he would have to cut the timbers there locally; he thought the bridge would have to be 600 or 700 feet long and it would take him a week to build. This seemed to please Sherman.[20]

Dodge went to Roswell to assess the situation. Roswell had cotton and woolen factories that had been running at full blast during the war making, among other things, Confederate uniforms. A Union cavalry unit under the command of General Kenner Garrard had burned many of Roswell's factories, which were located near the spot where Dodge wanted to build his bridge. Dodge thought he had better ask for Sherman's permission to destroy these buildings. One of the buildings had a French flag flying above it. Dodge had several lawyers in his corps who advised him that by destroying this building he might cause an international incident. Sherman answered back in typical Sherman fashion. He wrote to Dodge, "I know you have a big job but that is nothing new for you.... I know the bridge at Roswell is important and you may destroy all of Georgia to make it good and strong." Dodge destroyed all the buildings. The area where the bridge was to be built was rock bottom and without shoals. It only took Dodge three days to construct the 710-foot bridge that was 14 feet high. Dodge also restored telegraph service. Dodge established a bridgehead on the southern side of the bridge. Sherman was elated when he found Dodge had built the bridge so quickly. Soon Logan's XV Corps and the Union Army of the Tennessee would be marching across the bridge on the Chattahoochee River on their way to Atlanta. Dodge also told Sherman of a good bridge some eight miles up the Chattahoochee that had not been destroyed by the Rebels. Sherman immediately wired General Garrard and his cavalry to save that bridge. About 600 women who worked in these Roswell factories were out of employment. Dodge hired many to become nurses to the Union army. Sherman had the rest sent north. Oliver O. Howard, a general in Thomas' Army of the Cumberland, commented, "Who could build a trestle bridge like General G.M. Dodge, who was not only a superb commander of men in battle, but was already an eminent practical engineer."[21]

Around this time, Dodge was having trouble with the commander of his 2nd division, Brigadier-General Thomas Sweeny. Born in Ireland, Sweeny joined the New York militia and was called up to active duty during the Mexican War. He transferred into the regular army and during the Mexican War, he lost an arm. During the Civil War Sweeny rose through the ranks and was made a brigadier-general. He commanded the 2nd Division in Dodge's XVI Corps. Sweeny grew to have a strong dislike of Dodge. Sweeny was in the regular army, and he detested what he considered political appointments to the officers' ranks of men like Dodge. What is ironic is that Sweeny never had any training for the military, while Dodge had taken all the courses on the military at Norwich University. The college was headed by a man who had been superintendent at West Point. Sweeny was also extremely jealous that Dodge was ten years his junior, held the higher rank of major-general and was Sweeny's commanding officer. Dodge had noticed that sometimes his orders or the object of his orders went over Sweeny's head. Sweeny could be hotheaded and at one time challenged his corps surgeon to a duel; he also told an orderly to horsewhip the surgeon. Sweeny's officers restrained him, and he threatened to kill the surgeon the next time he saw him. Sweeny was a stickler for regulations, and he resented what he considered the lax attitude of the army volunteers. The officers of Sweeny's 2nd Division wrote Dodge a letter saying they did not like Sweeny's command style and that on occasion he recklessly exposed the men of his division to unnecessary dangers of the war. Dodge wrote to Sweeny telling him of these complaints. The general resented it and wrote back to Dodge in the most unsatisfactory way.[22]

When General McPherson, commander of the Army of the Tennessee, heard the complaints by the surgeon who had been spoken to by Sweeny in a most vile manner and of Sweeny's threats to horsewhip and kill the surgeon, McPherson felt he had had enough of Sweeny. McPherson knew the men in Sweeny's division had little confidence or respect for him, and Sweeny was responsible for several other ugly incidents. McPherson wrote to Dodge to have Sweeny arrested and to conduct a trial for the purpose of a general court-martial. Dodge called Sweeny in and told him of the charges against him. Sweeny did not seem to grasp the seriousness of the situation against him and made excuses for his behavior. Dodge told Sweeny he would rather get along with him than court-martial him. Sweeny then admitted that he had trouble with alcohol and that when these incidents occurred, Sweeny was drunk. Sweeny promised to curtail his drinking and change his ways. Dodge told him that if there was one more incident, he would relieve Sweeny from his command and that would probably ruin his career. Dodge took no action against Sweeny at this time.[23]

Lincoln and General Henry Halleck, the Union army's staff head, had thought Grant would knock out Lee before the November presidential elections in 1864. The anti-war Copperhead movement was gaining steam, and the Democrats had won the governors' races in important states such as New York and New Jersey. Lincoln and Halleck knew they needed a big Union victory to give the people in the North the confidence that the war was being won. However, Grant was taking extremely heavy losses, 60,000 men in a few months' time, and yet he had not defeated Lee. During the summer of 1864, Grant was stalled in front of Richmond, the capital of the Confederacy. Grant's men and officers were doubting his abilities and were tired of his offensive assaults that saw the Union army being slaughtered. At Cold Harbor on June 3, 1864, 7,000 Union soldiers lost their lives in less than ten minutes in a vain effort to breach Lee's lines. Lincoln and Halleck became convinced that Grant would not be victorious before the November elections. In August, the Democrats would have their convention and there would be a steady drumbeat to discontinue the war. Halleck turned to Sherman and told him he would have to do what Grant had failed to do against Lee: deliver. Sherman needed to deliver a knockout punch or produce a big Union victory before November. Now all eyes in the Union were on Sherman.[24]

Dodge had two spies working overtime in Atlanta. They were bringing in accurate information daily on troop movements and artillery placements. One of them gained access to Johnston's headquarters and gave up-to-date intelligence on the number of men in Johnston's army and the names of all the division, brigade, and regimental officers. Dodge had sent out a very bright young man from the 2nd Iowa Infantry to the South to gain military intelligence. Dodge had not heard from him for some time. Then on July 20 the young man appeared in the Union lines. The soldier had the morning papers; the article that caught everyone's attention was that Joe Johnston was out as commander of the Confederate Army of Tennessee and in his place was General John Bell Hood. Dodge took the papers over to Sherman. Sherman was with General Schofield's column. Schofield, who had graduated from the same class as Hood at West Point, said Hood would fight. Hood had suffered much during the Civil War; his left arm was rendered useless and his right leg had to be amputated. Even with an expensive artificial leg, Hood could not walk without crutches. When he rode a horse, he had to be strapped in with his artificial leg dangling from his saddle and an orderly riding behind him with his crutches. Despite these impediments, Hood had a reputation for bravery that bordered on recklessness. Sherman, Dodge and Schofield talked about what changes would come from Hood's aggressiveness as compared to Joe Johnston's cautious approach to military tactics. Sherman decided to use Hood's lack of prudence to the Union's advantage. The Union Army of the Tennessee had captured Decatur, Georgia, thus cutting off Atlanta from Richmond, Virginia, the capital of the Confederacy. It would now be very difficult for Lee and Johnston to transfer any soldiers from their respective fronts to the other. The only Confederate trains coming into Atlanta now would have to come from the south on the Macon and Western line. The young spy from the 2nd Iowa had been in the South for six months, and people began to get suspicious of him, so he joined the Rebel army. When he saw the paper with the change of leadership in the Rebel Army of Tennessee, he knew this was important. He made his way through Confederate lines to Dodge's headquarters. He did not want to stay with the Union army in Georgia for fear he would be captured and hanged if found out. Dodge sent the young spy to Nashville with a note to the commander that he was to post the young soldier somewhere where he would be safe.[25]

On July 17, 1864, Jefferson Davis had enough of Joe Johnston and named John Bell Hood head of the Confederate Army of Tennessee. Hood moved quickly and on July 20 attacked General Thomas' Army of the Cumberland. Hood's cavalry had noticed a large gap in the Union lines between Thomas' army and McPherson's Army of the Tennessee and Schofield's smaller Army of the Ohio. Hood's cavalry thought McPherson and Schofield were moving towards Decatur, Georgia, when in fact they were moving from Decatur to Atlanta. There was a gap, but Hood's attack was a dismal failure on Thomas' army on Peachtree Creek. The next day Sherman's army was within two miles of Atlanta in full range of his Union artillery. The next day the Army of the Tennessee occupied Rebel entrenchments. Dodge was ordered by General McPherson to send a brigade to the flank of the XVII Corps. Dodge sent a brigade from Fuller's 4th Division. The other brigade of the 4th Division was left in Decatur, Georgia, to protect the parked wagon trains. Dodge was to move his men (except those guarding the wagon trains in Decatur) from the right flank of the Rebels to their left flank. Fuller, who was born in Great Britain, picked a very good position for the rest of his division to fight. Dodge ordered General Sweeney's 2nd Division onto the east bank of Sugar Creek, where it forks. However, a heavily wooded area to the rear of the left wing of the XVI Corps gave

Rebels the ability to move close to Dodge's men. Dodge's men were to destroy the railroad tracks. Dodge taught his men to pull the rails out, pile them onto the rail ties, and burn them. When the rail tracks were white-hot, they were to be twisted so they could not be used again.[26]

Schofield was right: it would only take a few days before Hood decided to fight in a most aggressive way. Hood had decided to attack the wagon trains at Decatur that Dodge's Brigade was guarding, but as the day of the 22nd appeared, it became obvious that Hardee could not get there in time. Therefore, he had Wheeler's cavalry proceed to Decatur. This overwhelming Confederate force attacked Dodge's 2nd Brigade of his 4th Division, led by then-colonel John Sprague. Wheeler captured Decatur, but Sprague managed to move almost all of the supply and baggage train and kept them under Union control. Sprague later was promoted to brigadier-general and in 1894 was posthumously awarded the Medal of Honor for his superb action at Decatur.[27]

Hood ordered Hardee's corps to go to the flank of the Army of the Tennessee, circle around back and hit the rear of the Union's XVII Corps, commanded by General Francis P. Blair. He also planned simultaneously to hit McPherson's front with two corps. He thought he could crush the Army of the Tennessee. Dodge's XVI Corps had been pushed out of line when the Union lines were reorganized and moved to the left of Blair's corps, facing away from Atlanta. There was a half-mile gap between Blair's and Dodge's corps lines, and Rebels were pouring through the gap. Dodge repulsed two of Hardee's corps' assaults and then charged the Confederate lines, driving them back into the woods even though Dodge's corps was on open ground. Dodge's corps was able to take prisoners from 49 Confederate regiments, eight brigades, and three divisions and captured eight Rebel battle flags. Sherman later said in his official report, "Dodge had caught and held well in check the enemies right and punished severely, capturing many prisoners." General Blair said, "The Lord placed Dodge in the right place that day."[28]

On July 22, 1864, disaster struck the Army of the Tennessee. Its well-liked leader, Major-General James B. McPherson, was killed close to Dodge's lines. Dodge's flanks were overrun and he requested help. Knowing McPherson was close by, he sent a messenger to McPherson. Dodge's messenger met McPherson and told him of Dodge's position. The messenger warned McPherson of the dangerous area where he was located. McPherson had only one aide with him and kept on going until he met Rebel skirmishers, who ordered him to halt. When McPherson and the aide refused to comply with the Confederate orders and wheeled their horses, a volley rang out from the Rebel skirmishers, and McPherson pitched forward off his horse, dead. Later men from Dodge's 4th Division found some of McPherson's personal items on one of the Confederate soldiers. Even Sherman, who was occasionally critical of McPherson's generalship, was grief-stricken at the loss of this popular general. Sherman said in his official report of McPherson's death, "The suddenness of this terrible calamity would have overwhelmed me with grief, but the living demanded my whole thought." Sherman also stated that McPherson acted in the "highest professional capacity and with a heart abounding in kindness." In another dispatch Sherman wrote, "Not his loss, but the country's, and the army will mourn his death and cherish his memory.... History tells of few who blended the grace and gentleness of the friend with the dignity, courage, faith and manliness of the soldier." Confederate commander John Bell Hood, who was a classmate at West Point and boyhood friend of McPherson, felt sincere sorrow at his death. Sherman had McPherson's body sent north.[29]

As usual, the 4th Iowa Regiment was in the middle of the fighting for the Battle for Atlanta on July 22. They were attached to Colonel James A. Williamson's Iowa Brigade under the direct command of Lt. Colonel Nichols. The 4th Iowa was on the extreme right of the Army of the Tennessee. Confederate general John C. Brown's division of Stewart's Rebel corps broke through the Union army's Morgan L. Smith's division of the XV Corps on the road to Augusta. The Rebels threatened to cut the Union army in half. The Confederates poured lead into Captain F. DeGrasse's artillery battery. All his horses had been killed, and his 20-pound Parrott guns were captured by the Rebels. DeGrasse, who was described as a mere beardless boy, had spiked the artillery. The 4th Iowa, along with Williamson's Iowa Brigade, moved down the flank of Brown's division. The situation was so fluid and dangerous to the Union command that Sherman was watching this situation and personally ordered Williamson's brigade to Brown's flank. Williamson later wrote for the official record, "I left the 9th Iowa Infantry in the works and sent the 4th Iowa to the right to occupy a rebel battery which commanded the head of a ravine which led to our line in the only place where there were no entrenchments. The regiment had not more than formed before it was assaulted by a brigade of rebel infantry under Colonel Baker, and a very stubborn fight ensued. The regiment nobly held the position and finally repulsed the assault, inflicting great loss upon the rebels in killed, wounded and prisoners." Williamson's brigade also recaptured DeGrasse's Parrott artillery. In the official report, it said Williamson's brigade inflicted a "great slaughter" on the Rebels. Lt. Colonel Nichols was wounded. A reporter for the *New York Tribune* wrote of Williamson's Iowa Brigade in the Battle for Atlanta on July 22, "It was one of the bravest, truest most fighting brigades that has marched to the rescue of our Nation's liberties the 4th had fought bravely at Resaca, New Hope Church, Kennesaw Mountain ... until loss had reduced its numbers below two hundred.." Dodge had also sent the 2nd Brigade from his 2nd Division from his XVI Corps to help Williamson's brigade in the recapture of the DeGrasse battery. Sherman reported the Union losses were 3,722 killed on July 22 in front of Atlanta.[30]

The 4th Iowa moved into Decatur, Georgia, for a short time and then was ordered to destroy the rail lines between Decatur and Atlanta. They moved out with the rest of the XV Corps, marching from the left to the right of the Union battle line, a distance of about ten miles. After the different Union corps got into line, the 4th Iowa found themselves near Ezra Church. The 4th Iowa then erected breastworks made out of railroad ties and rail tracks.[31]

After McPherson's death, the command of the Army of the Tennessee was a difficult decision. General John Logan received temporary command and was the logical choice to succeed McPherson. Soon after the Battle of Atlanta was over, General Thomas told Sherman that he could not work with Logan. Logan was considered loud and an inept political appointment by some West Pointers such as Thomas. However, Logan had a fine war record. When General Joe Hooker, Sherman's senior officer, did not receive the command of the Army of the Tennessee, he resigned as commander of the XX Corps. As a compromise, Sherman appointed General Oliver O. Howard as the head of the

Army of the Tennessee. Dodge reported that after the appointment of Howard, he saw Logan, and that the big, tough general had tears in his eyes. Thereafter, Logan disliked Sherman for most of his life, even though he put forth his best face when asked about the situation. As Logan aged, his opinion of Sherman was modified. In his diary Dodge stated that the Army of the Tennessee had thought Logan should be named its commander, and that the soldiers were disappointed that Sherman named an outsider to the post. Dodge, always the optimist, in a letter to wife Anne gushed about Howard's good qualities; he did not drink or swear, he was a Christian and a good example to the men. Sherman also called Howard "a polished and Christian gentleman." After Howard took over as commander of the Army of the Tennessee, he conducted religious services for all the senior officers in his headquarters on Sunday mornings. It was his request that all senior officers attend, but most of them took it as an order. The Rebels learned of this and on Sunday August 14 began shelling the XVI and XV corps. Prisoners said the Confederates were just doing a false attack to break up the religious services.[32]

On the day of the battle for Atlanta, Dodge was surprised to see that General Sweeny was not with his troops. Sweeny's 2nd Division was in line and fighting for their lives. When Dodge finally saw Sweeny, he was on foot and had obviously been drinking. In the absence of Sweeny, Dodge had to take personal command of the 2nd Division. On July 25 Dodge and Fuller were in his tent talking about the battle. Sweeny joined them and said his right flank was unprotected on account of Fuller's 4th Division running. Fuller claimed the 4th did not run. Sweeny, then again drunk, called Fuller "a God-damn liar" and struck Fuller in the face. Although Sweeny was a large man, Fuller would not strike Sweeny back because of his missing arm. Then Dodge and Sweeny got into an argument. Sweeny yelled at Dodge, "You are a God-damn liar. You are a God-Damned cowardly son of a bitch." Sweeny also added, "Go you God-damned inefficient political General." Sweeny challenged Dodge to a duel. By then Dodge had had enough of Sweeny and struck him. Sweeny struck Dodge, who was slightly built and had lost a lot of weight in the past year due to illness. General Fuller jumped on Sweeny and almost choked him to death. Dodge had the drunken Sweeny arrested for a court-martial. The officers of Sweeny's 2nd Division had often complained to Dodge about Sweeny's drunken behavior. Sherman had reservations about relieving Sweeny of his command in the midst of the Atlanta campaign. General Logan was in complete agreement with Dodge; and Colonel Clark, who was now Logan's aide and had been McPherson's aide, knew what a drunkard Sweeny was, the trouble he had caused and how many in his command did not respect him. Sweeny was court-martialed in Louisville, Kentucky, on December 3, 1864, but was found not guilty. Dodge did not testify against Sweeny, as Dodge did not care if Sweeny were court-martialed or not. Dodge just wanted Sweeny out of his command. Most in the War Department and General Oliver Howard, commander of the Army of the Tennessee, agreed with Dodge's assessment of Sweeny, as he did not receive another field command throughout the remainder of the war. After the Civil War, Sweeny became involved in a hair-brained scheme to invade Canada and hold it for ransom until Ireland was set free by England. Of course, this set off an international incident, and Sweeny was arrested again. Incredibly, Sweeny was allowed back into the military and retired in 1870.[33]

After the Battle of Atlanta on July 22, 1864, both sides were like tired heavyweight boxers in the last round of a long fight. Both sides were punched out and moved slowly. Sherman had Howard's Army of the Tennessee move to the west side of Atlanta for the purpose of cutting off the city's last supply rail line from Macon, Georgia. General Oliver O. Howard, commander of the Army of the Tennessee, put Dodge's wing of the XVI Corps on the left, Blair in the middle, and Logan's XV Corps to the right with Williamson's Iowa Brigade, including the 4th Iowa Infantry. Hood saw what Sherman was attempting to do. Again he tried his major military tactic. He would try to separate parts of Sherman's army and then smash each part by pouring his whole army against the divided parts. Although he was commander of the Army of the Tennessee for only a few days before the battle at Ezra Church, Howard understood the predicament he and his army were in and had the XV Corps build trenches to fortify their lines. Confederate General Stephen D. Lee, who was even more reckless than Hood, kept attacking Howard's reinforced positions. General Logan, head of the XV Corps, feared Williamson's brigade would become the vocal point of the Rebel attack and asked him if he could hold his point at all costs. Williamson answered, "I will do my best; that he knew my command and knew that they were not accustomed to giving way, and that we would hold that point as long as there was a man left." Williamson then said of the battle, "They came in double lines, and kept coming." Williamson noted the ground was such that "if our fire was too high for the front line it was sure to catch the next or the next, and later, when I looked over the battle-field it had the appearance of a whole line of battle that had fallen with the front line only a few yards away from us. This was the most sickening sight that I had ever witnessed. It looked more like a slaughter than a battle." The governor of Iowa, William W. Stone, who himself was a Union army veteran of Shiloh and Vicksburg, was visiting the Army of the Tennessee on the day of this battle. Sherman told him that Colonel Williamson was "at the front with his brigade, pitching in, as he always does." The Confederate losses were pegged at 3,000 men while the Union dead were fewer than 700. Dodge's corps was attacked and he had, among other regiments, the 64th Illinois and 66th Indiana equipped with their Henry repeating rifles. General Oliver Howard saw how effectively they worked and seemed impressed. After the Battle at Ezra Church in August, Sherman sent to Dodge some 32-pounder cannons and told him to fire them 50 rounds per day per artillery piece.

Few men suffered as much as General John Bell Hood, CSA, during the Civil War. His wounded left arm was useless and his right leg had to be amputated. Even with an expensive artificial leg, he had to walk with crutches. When he rode his horse, he had to be strapped in with his artificial leg dangling from the saddle and an orderly riding behind him with his crutches (Library of Congress).

Dodge pushed his line forward, captured some Confederate skirmishers and got possession of their rifle pits and entrenchments. Dodge moved his men forward into these areas. Dodge's artillery could shell Atlanta, and Sherman had over 100 artillery pieces firing into Atlanta as they pleased. By mid–August, Dodge was told to hurl shells into Atlanta every ten minutes during the day. As Dodge got closer to Atlanta, he could see the railroad depot in Atlanta from his headquarters.[34]

Sherman ordered a cavalry raid to the rear of Hood's command to cut off lines of communication, but it proved to be a failure. McCook and Stoneman each had a cavalry division and were to hit the Macon Railroad to cut off Hood's supply line. Stoneman presented a plan that would have his men—after they helped McCook and his cavalry division destroy the Macon Rail Road line—proceed to Macon, Georgia, and free the some–1,500 Union officers from prison there and then head down to Andersonville, the notorious Confederate prison camp in Georgia, and liberate the some–30,000 Union P.O.W.s there. McCook and his men followed orders and tore up the railroad tracks on the Macon line. Stoneman bypassed this important step and proceeded to Macon prison. Stoneman was always on the lookout for military actions that would bring him personal glory. He thought the liberation of the Macon and Andersonville prisoners would be just the ticket. Stoneman took his time, thinking he was in no danger. A mixed bag of Georgia home guards, militia and wounded Confederate soldiers repulsed Stoneman's feeble attack on Macon, Georgia. McCook, angered that Stoneman had not followed orders and joined him, headed back north towards the Chattahoochee River, where his cavalry division was destroyed by elements of General Wheeler and General "Red" Jackson's Confederate cavalry. After Macon, Stoneman's cavalry division was pursued and defeated by Confederate cavalry, and Stoneman was forced to surrender. Instead of freeing the men in Macon and Andersonville prisons, Stoneman and his cavalrymen became prisoners in those two P.O.W. camps. Stoneman became the highest-ranking Union general to be taken prisoner during the Civil War. Due to the Stoneman debacle, Sherman lost two of his four cavalry divisions. Later in the fall, Sherman arranged for a prisoner exchange that freed Stoneman. In all reality, Stoneman—even if he had freed the over 30,000 Union P.O.W.s, would have had little chance to get these half-starved men to the Union lines.[35]

Hood's normal aggressiveness was put in check by the fact that the Confederate Army of Tennessee, under his command for only a few weeks, had already lost 11,000 men. It could ill afford to lose more. Hood's army and local militias had built a ring of forts and fortified positions around Atlanta. The Rebels decided that their best strategy would be to stalemate Sherman in Atlanta. Lee's superior generalship could keep Richmond out of Grant's hand. Possibly the war-weary North would oust Abraham Lincoln as president in November of 1864, and hopefully the Confederacy could achieve some sort of an agreement with the newly elected Democratic president. A Richmond paper stated that if the Rebels could hold out just six weeks more before the armies of Grant and Sherman, they might be able to sue the new Union government for peace. Sherman tried his best to lure Hood out of Atlanta, but Hood stayed behind his fortified positions. Sherman knew it would be reckless and possibly suicidal to attack Hood's fortified positions in Atlanta. Sherman thought about another flanking maneuver, but that would put him ever farther away from his rail supply lines, deep in enemy territory. Sherman once again tried to send General Schofield to capture the Macon Railroad line, which was Hood's last supply line into Atlanta. Sherman then began a regular artillery shelling inside Atlanta, but unlike at Vicksburg, his artillery barrage seemed to have little effect on the Rebel army or citizens inside Atlanta.

In early August of 1864, General Dodge had a brief moment of happiness. His old friend from Norwich University and the man who helped him find employment in the railroad industry, Thomas E.G. Ransom, reported to Dodge's XVI Corps. Ransom had achieved the rank of brigadier-general and had been a veteran of Shiloh and Vicksburg. However, Ransom had suffered three serious wounds. Dodge's time with Ransom was very short. Ransom took over the command of Dodge's 4th Division from General Fuller. Brigadier-General J. M. Corse took over command of Dodge's 2nd Division, Sweeny's old unit. It was apparent that Dodge, like the rest of his command, was getting war-weary. Dodge wrote to his father, "Military honor and glory looks well upon paper but when won by such hard blows, by such continual exertion ... it all gives way to a matter of fact duty and becomes stern reality. How many, many of my friends have fallen! How many lie now bleeding in unwelcomed towns I dare not estimate!"[36]

Hood sent Wheeler's reinforced cavalry of about 6,000 riders to disrupt Sherman's supply line on the Western and Atlantic Railroad. Wheeler captured a small Union garrison and tore up some track, but the track was quickly repaired and the damage Wheeler did was insignificant. Wheeler rode on up into eastern Tennessee, which took him and his cavalry out of action for a while.

It became obvious to all that to take Atlanta, another flanking movement would have to take place and cut off Hood's supply line on the Macon Railroad. So far, none of the attempts to cut the Macon Railroad had been successful for any amount of time. Since Dodge's troops were closest to Atlanta, Sherman asked him on August 18 if he could not break through Hood's lines. Dodge sent out Colonel Phillips and General Ransom on this task but their report was unsatisfactory in Dodge's opinion. Dodge then went to look for himself. Dodge's line was so close to the Rebels that any part of a man's body seen above the entrenchments would be hit by Confederate sharpshooters. The men in the 7th Iowa Infantry told Dodge the only safe way to view the enemy was through a peephole they had. As soon as Dodge put his eye to the peephole, a Confederate sharpshooter hit Dodge in the head. Dodge was knocked unconscious and carried to the rear area in a blanket. The second day after the wound, Dodge was still unconscious. Grenville finally heard General Sherman's voice say to his medical director, Dr. Kittoe, "Kittoe, Dodge isn't going to die; he is coming to." Fortunately for Dodge, the sharpshooter's bullet had hit Dodge with a glancing blow, but even at that, it had hit him in the forehead and knocked him unconscious. It gave him a concussion, tore a ribbon of scalp off his head, and almost exposed a portion of his brain. Dodge bled profusely and for several days, his eyes felt as though they were full of sand and he could not see. His slouch hat had a bullet hole in it. Sherman put a blackout on news of Dodge's wound, but that only made matters worse. The rumor mill churned out the story that Dodge had been killed. Even two New York papers, the *Herald* and the *Tribune*, reported that Dodge had been mortally wounded. Dodge's brother Nathan his father and old friend Hub Hoxie at first read that Grenville was dead, but then the correct news that he had been severely wounded reached his relatives and friends.[37]

Sherman gave Dodge 30 days to recover from his wound. He was shipped north to Nashville, where his wife Anne met him. Then they went on to Greenville, Indiana, home of Grenville's brother-in-law, to convalesce. While in Greenville Dodge was surprised to hear how strongly the Copperhead movement had entrenched itself in the North. Ransom took over leadership of Dodge's left wing of the XVI Corps.

A crude wooden sign marks the spot where Union general James B. McPherson was killed on July 22, 1864, during the Battle of Atlanta. McPherson was the second-highest-ranking Union general to die in battle. McPherson was near Dodge's XVI Corps when Dodge informed him his flanks were in danger of being overrun. McPherson, with only a staff person with him, was warned by Dodge's men that he was riding into a dangerous area, but he kept going and was killed by Confederate skirmishers. When Dodge was on his Western campaign, he renamed Fort Cottonwood in the Nebraska territory Fort McPherson in honor of the fallen general (Library of Congress).

Sherman tried another cavalry raid with General Judson Kilpatrick in charge of a little under 5,000 riders to halt the trains on the Macon Railroad line. He was not successful. Sherman knew it would take a full-scale flanking attack by most of his army to accomplish the abandonment of Atlanta. During the nights of August 25 and 26, most of the Union army in front of Atlanta pulled out of its trenches, leaving only the XX Corps in front of Atlanta. Soon Rebel pickets told Hood that most of Sherman's army had pulled out of the front of Atlanta. Confederate cavalry told Hood that the Union Army of the Tennessee was to the south of Atlanta. Hood sent Hardee and S.D. Lee's corps to block and push the Army of the Tennessee into the Flint River.

The Army of the Tennessee was sweeping to the south of Atlanta near Jonesboro, Georgia. Williamson's Iowa Brigade, along with the 4th Iowa Infantry, was with the Army of the Tennessee. For about the last year and a half, the 4th Iowa Infantry had never been close to being a full regiment. They were lucky if they could muster up 200 or 300 able-bodied men to fight at any one time. The Army of the Tennessee got to Jonesboro first. They were able to put their army between Hardee's Rebel Corps and Atlanta. The Union army was able to start building trenches and breastworks. Hardee's Confederates arrived but waited for Lee's Corps before attacking on the afternoon of August 31. This of course allowed the Army of the Tennessee even more time to build up its fortifications. However, the Iowa Brigade and the 4th Iowa were ordered by divisional general Osterhaus to occupy a place in the Union line where there was no cover or breastworks, and the 4th Iowa was completely exposed to Rebel fire. Osterhaus said the 4th Iowa Infantry held its ground "most gallantly" and poured fire into the Confederate positions. The Rebel line broke and scattered in all directions. The Confederates took cover in a forest, regrouped and tried more attacks but were not able to break the 4th Iowa's line or the Union line. Colonel Williamson was wounded in the hand on September 1. Osterhaus commended the 4th Iowa Infantry and Williamson and mentioned the "promptness, zeal and bravery which they exhibited on so many occasions during this past month." The 4th Iowa also helped save a battery of artillery from Confederate hands. They also were involved at a skirmish at Lovejoy Station. On September 5 they headed back towards Atlanta to chase Hood's army. During the Atlanta campaign, Williamson was nominated chairman of the Republican delegation from Iowa to go to the Republican National Convention in Baltimore to nominate Abraham Lincoln for a second term. However, Williamson refused to leave his men and the field of combat.[38]

News came to Hood that the Macon Railroad and telegraph lines were in the hands of the Union army. He felt that to save his army he had to abandon Atlanta and Jonesboro. Major General Henry R. Slocum, who had taken over the Union's XX Corps from Hooker, now occupied Atlanta. Slocum reported on September 3, 1864, that there were just a few remaining Rebel cavalry in Atlanta, which would be easily disposed of, and that the Rebels had blown up 80 boxcars full of ammunition. Even as the Army of the Tennessee was fighting Hardee for control of Jonesboro on August 31, the Democrats gleefully nominated George B. McClellan for president, sure that with no big victories the Union would vote the Democratic candidate for president in the November election. However, the fall of Atlanta would put the momentum behind Lincoln, Sherman and Grant for complete Republican victory. Hood moved his army toward the Alabama state line. After Hood left Atlanta, deserters, thieves, stragglers, runaway slaves and refuges began looting the stores of Atlanta. When the Union army entered the city, Atlanta mayor James Calhoun symbolically surrendered the city and asked the Union army to protect the lives and property there. The Union army agreed, but this agreement lasted only a few days. On September 8, 1864, in one of his most controversial moves in a very controversial career, General Sherman issued Order Number 67. This order stated that all of the citizens of Atlanta except those connected to the Union army must vacate the city. After many protests, in about ten days Atlanta was cleared of all its citizens not connected to the Federal army.[39]

Even though the Battle at Jonesboro was an overwhelming Union victory and the loss of life was much greater on the Confederate side, some Union soldiers paid the price. One of these was Amos W. Ames, a corporal in the 4th Iowa Infantry. Ames was born in Era, Pennsylvania, on February 22, 1840. Amos Ames was 15 years old when his parents moved and started farming near Afton, Iowa, on Three Mile Creek. Ames enlisted in 1861 in the 4th Iowa Infantry Regiment and reenlisted in 1864, obtaining the rank of corporal. Ames was in Company H of the 4th Iowa Infantry. On August 31, 1864, he took part in the Battle of Jonesboro against Confederate General Hardee's corps. Hardee's men were entrenched along the rail line. Company H was supporting a section of artillery that was shelling Jonesboro about 200 yards in front of the Union lines. In the afternoon, the Rebels charged Company H's position but were repulsed. After the Rebel attack, Ames was sent out with 11 other men to act as skirmishers. Ames halted his men and then went forward to reconnoiter and was captured by Confederate soldiers. Ames was taken to Jonesboro under guard with other Union prisoners. Ames was one of the 49 men who during the war were captured from the 4th Iowa Infantry. On September 1, 1864, Amos and the rest of the Union prisoners in Jonesboro were fed a little cornbread and musty beans. Confederate soldiers contributed the food that Ames and his fellow prisoners ate. Amos and the other Union prisoners were closely guarded and in the afternoon, they were sent to Griffin, Georgia.[40]

On September 2, 1864, Ames and 22 other prisoners were loaded onto the top of freightcars. They were headed for the infamous Confederate prison camp at Andersonville, Georgia. About 25 miles south of Griffin, Georgia, their train hit a northbound freighter. Ames was thrown from his car and tried to make an escape. He traveled hard all day and waited until dark to sleep in a swamp. He bent down a bush to sleep upon. He noted that when the trains collided, one prisoner broke his leg and another received a sprained ankle, but 44 Confederate soldiers were either killed or injured during the train wreck. Ames traveled through forests, swamps and mud, making sure he kept off all the roads. While trying to escape Ames felt very tired and worn out. When he was within 15 miles of Lovejoy Station, Georgia, he could hear cannon fire. Half an hour later, a scout from the 3rd Arkansas Rebel Cavalry spotted him and recaptured the Iowan. Ames was put under guard and traveled in a Confederate wagon train back to Griffin. He was put in his former place and noted that other prisoners had been recaptured with the use of hounds. Ames was sent to Macon, Georgia, very hungry and while in Macon, he drew one day's rations, a pint of unsifted meal and four ounces of bacon. On September 9, 1864, Ames received two days' rations, meal and bacon, and it was very warm. More Union prisoners were brought in. By the 10th the weather had cooled. Ames helped remove Union soldiers from a hospital and load them onto box cars. The

11th was a Sunday, and in the afternoon a Confederate preacher provided a sermon for the prisoners. The sermon was about Daniel in the lion's den, which Ames thought was very appropriate. He drew a day's rations and molasses. Some captured Union soldiers from General Hugh J. Kilpatrick's unit were brought in. Kilpatrick was known for his rough handling of his men and horses and earned the nickname Kil-Cavalry. Kilpatrick was involved in an embarrassing incident late in the war when Rebel cavalry raided his camp and he had to leave his quarters without his pants, accompanied by his lady friend.[41]

On Monday, September 12, a deserter from the 78th New York was brought in bucked and gagged for having stolen a bottle of molasses from Rebel prisoners. Ames noted that there was a number of Rebel prisoners mixed in with the Union P.O.W.'s. These Confederate prisoners were mostly deserters. Some had committed some sort of crime, and others were awaiting being sent to the front. That night it was very cold and Ames had no blanket. Some more of Kilpatrick's cavalrymen were brought in to be transferred to East Point, Georgia. Rumors began to circulate around the camp that Sherman and Hood were setting up some sort of prisoner exchange. Some Union escapees were recaptured and brought back to prison. The Confederates found a tunnel the Union men were making to escape, and two of the men found tunneling were shackled with ball and chain. Ames noted that prisoners were constantly being brought in. The Union prisoners were on one side of the stockade, while the Rebel prisoners occupied the other side. On September 16 two drunken Rebel officers were brought in. The Rebel prisoners robbed one of $360 and the other of $4,700. Prison officials looked for the money but could not find it. Any Confederate prisoners brought in were usually robbed of any valuables by the Rebel prisoners. After three days of bad rain there was a fight among Federal prisoners. On September 21 a rumor went around that Ames and others would be taken to Macon, Georgia. Ames wrote that if he were to be taken to Macon he would try to escape. At night, a Rebel prisoner was shot trying to escape. On September 8 General Hood proposed to Sherman a prisoner exchange, and the Union general agreed. One hundred of the Union prisoners were taken out for a prisoner exchange, but they were brought back because Hood had acted in bad faith and only chose men whose terms of enlistments was up or who were so wounded that they were not able to rejoin the Union army. Ames could not believe these men's bad luck, since many would die in Confederate prisons. The hundred that were refused were sent to Savannah, Georgia, and 260 more that had been rejected by Union officials were brought into the Macon prison. The 260 who had been rejected were moved out, and another 278 prisoners from the front were brought into Macon. On September 26, 90 prisoners were brought in from the front. A total of 190 Union officers were brought in from Charleston, South Carolina; out of those, 140 were exchanged for Confederate P.O.W.'s.[42]

A black barber was brought into the stockade to give much-needed haircuts. More Rebel deserters and drunks were brought in. One day one of the Rebels to be taken to the front chopped off his hand so he would not be sent to the battlefield. Seventy-seven Confederates were taken to the front on September 30. A partition was put up to separate the Union and Rebel prisoners. Some of the prisoners were released on parole of honor; most of them were officers. On October 2 six or seven prisoners were brought in, and two Federal prisoners tried to escape and were fired on. Word came down that anyone attempting to escape would be shot. At early roll call the next day, everyone was present and accounted for. The next four nights were cold and Ames, without a blanket, had a hard time sleeping. Another tunnel was found, and some of the Federals were shackled for this "crime." Seven of the paroled officers were brought in for refusing

The Ponder House (at one time known as Potter House) in Atlanta after experiencing Union artillery bombardment. After the Battle of Atlanta, Hood retreated into Atlanta and built formidable defenses. Dodge's XVI Corps was one of the closest Union units to Atlanta; Dodge could see the Atlanta Railroad depot from his headquarters (Library of Congress).

to sign a paper that was a condition of their parole. On October 17 at four in the morning, Ames and other prisoners were taken out to be transferred to Camp Lawton near Millen, Georgia. On the way to Millen about a dozen Union soldiers cut a hole in the box car and jumped out. Ames figured that at the high rate of speed they were going, most of them probably died. However, Ames noted that they had taken the motto of "give me liberty or give me death." When taken to the stockade, several of the Union soldiers who had been given Rebel clothing because their clothes were in tatters slipped away. Ames found in the new stockade some of his fellow soldiers from the 4th Iowa Infantry. Corporal Charles Nelson of Bedford, Iowa, had been captured over a year earlier at Black River, Mississippi. Nelson would survive till the end of the war. Sergeant John Chaney of Quincy, Iowa, who was from Indiana originally, was captured near Ringgold, Georgia, in November of 1863. Chaney had been wounded but managed to survive to the end of the war. Samuel Hutton from Page County, Iowa, had been wounded while on picket duty in Rolla, Missouri. Later he was captured at Black River, Mississippi in August of 1863 and managed to survive till the end of the war. They all asked Ames to quarter with them. Ames drew one day's rations, a little meal, beans and fresh meat. On October 21 Rebel guards searched the quarters for axes, spades and the like belonging to prisoners, but the Union prisoners managed to bury them underground before they could be found. Camp was organized into a division of 500 men with a sergeant in charge, and this was divided into 100-man units with a non-commissioned officer in charge. They had no tents or shelter of any kind. The night of October 22 was extremely cold and frosty. On the morning of the 23rd, the camp looked like a battlefield, with dead and dying prisoners lying all around. Rumors floated around. One of them was that the Rebels had recaptured Atlanta. Another was that they were all to be sent to Savannah. The names of all the foreign-born Union prisoners were taken, causing a stir in the camp. Three days later all the foreign-born prisoners were given a chance to serve in the Confederate army. About 300 joined, and the rest came back to the stockade. Ames was surprised, as he thought most were loyal to the Union. A day later, two of the foreign-born prisoners were back in camp for trying to escape from the Confederate army. Ames later learned that about 60 or 70 or more of the foreign-born Union prisoners had run off from the Rebel army. It became obvious to Ames that a lot of them had joined the Rebel army as a ruse to escape back to Union lines. The Rebels asked for carpenters to work outside on a parole of honor. Ames joined the wood squad to hunt for wood outside the camp.[43]

Hood planned to attack Sherman's rear areas and disrupt his supplies and communication. Jefferson Davis met Hood's army at Palmetto Station to give a speech, in hopes of giving Hood's army and the people of the Confederacy a morale boost. Davis told Hood's troops that they would compel Sherman's army to make a retreat from Georgia just like Napoleon's disastrous retreat with the French army from Moscow. Davis in these speeches also denounced Georgia governor Joseph E. Brown and General Joseph Johnston. Sherman heard about the speech and was appreciative that Jefferson Davis had forewarned him of their battle plans. What if Sherman instead of retreating moved forward? Sherman kept the XX Corps in Atlanta and sent a division to Rome, Georgia, and another division back to Chattanooga. He sent General Thomas and the Army of the Cumberland to Nashville, and General Schofield's Army of the Ohio to

Knoxville to hold onto Tennessee and northern Georgia. All commanders were instructed to guard the railway lines and keep them open.⁴⁴

Hood had wired Jefferson Davis that he needed more soldiers. His men needed rest, and morale was bad because of the retreats and defeats. Many of his men had uniforms that were no more than rags, and many of them were shoeless. At any one time during the Civil War, it was estimated that a third of the Confederate army was shoeless. Worse yet, many of his men had not been paid in ten months and they needed money to send home. Jefferson Davis told General Hood that he had done all he could to give him manpower and supplies. Hood's army was now at about 40,000 men. Davis also told Hood that it was imperative for Hood to bring back all the Confederate "absentees." General Forrest and his cavalry were supposed to stir up as much trouble in Tennessee as possible. The Union army was building up supplies in Allatoona, Georgia, so Hood dispatched Rebel general French to attack this supply depot with a division. However, Dodge's old 2nd Division was guarding the supply depot, and French met stiff resistance and broke off the attack. On September 11 Hood was marching his men towards Dalton, Georgia. On September 13, General Logan, commanding the XV Corps, recommended that Colonel James A. Williamson be promoted to the rank of brigadier-general. Sherman also wrote to General Halleck in Washington, D.C., that Williamson should be one of only three colonels in his command that should be promoted to the rank of general.⁴⁵

In October, Williamson and the 4th Iowa Infantry were chasing Hood's Army of Tennessee back to the Volunteer State. Towards the end of the month, Williamson's unit was called back into Atlanta. It was obvious something big was up. While Dodge was convalescing, he had gotten news that one of his spies and scouts, James Hensal of the 7th Kansas Cavalry, had been sentenced in Nashville to five years in prison for smuggling and other things. Dodge did some investigating and found out Hensal was merely carrying out orders for a spy mission. Dodge had Sherman write a letter to get the charges dismissed against Hensal. In September, Dodge was able to take his first steps since his wound, and in the middle of the month he made trips to Davenport and Des Moines and saw his old friend John Kasson. Dodge went from Davenport to St. Louis and then onto Council Bluffs, where this local hero was given a public reception. By October, Dodge still had not recovered fully from his Atlanta wound. General John A. Rawlins, an aide to General Grant, suggested that if Dodge was up to it to make a trip out to see Grant and the Army of the Potomac. This Dodge did, and he had many frank discussions with his friend Grant at City Point, Virginia. Grant stated that the desertion rate was getting out of hand and as many as 1,400 troops had deserted from the Army of the Potomac in one week. Dodge could see the tension around Grant and the negativity of some of his high-ranking officers, even though the Eastern Army was better equipped than the Western Army. When Dodge got up to leave, Grant suggested Dodge go to Washington, D.C., to see Lincoln. Dodge was somewhat stunned, as he was given no particular reason to see Lincoln, but like a good soldier, Dodge went to see the president. Grant's top aide, General Rawlins, wrote to his wife and said, "General Dodge of the Western Army is here. It does one's heart good to meet one from the army that has made such a bright record for its country's honor and its fame." When Dodge got to Washington, he met Iowa senator Harlan, who went with Dodge to see

Lincoln. Lincoln had a number of visitors and he obviously wanted to talk to Dodge. Lincoln dismissed the other visitors, and Harlan left. Lincoln then took Dodge to a cabinet room and began reading from a very funny book called *Gospel of Peace*. While Lincoln read from the book to Dodge, both laughed heartily at the humorous passages. This put Dodge at ease, and Lincoln invited Dodge to have lunch with him. Lincoln asked Dodge about everything he had seen at Grant's headquarters. To sum things up Dodge told Lincoln, "You know out West we believe in General Grant. We have no doubts. Give him time and he will succeed; in what way or how, I don't know, but you may depend upon it he will succeed." After Dodge said this Lincoln jumped to his feet and said, "I am thankful to you for saying so." Later after the war, Dodge asked Rawlins about these meetings with Grant and Lincoln. Rawlins said that the pressure on Grant and Lincoln at that time was great, and many people in Washington did not think they were up to the task. However, both men knew Dodge was a straight shooter and an optimist by nature. Apparently, his support of Grant and his belief in the ultimate outcome of the war bolstered their confidence. Dodge said he learned later that Lincoln's desk was full of letters telling him that Grant was a failure and to replace him.[46]

When Dodge left Washington, D.C., he went to New York City to see the Union Pacific people. They assured him that when he left the army they would need his services. Dodge would later learn from his old friend Peter Dey that he had resigned from the Union Pacific because of Durant's duplicity. Dey felt Durant's Credit Mobiler of America was nothing more than a way to defraud the United States government out of money. Dey did not want his name attached to the project. Dodge then went to Massachusetts to see his boyhood home and meet old friends. Dodge had become a war hero in this part of the country as well as the Midwest. Dodge went to a function in Boston at Faneuil Hall in which the most famous orator in the United States was to speak—Edward Everett. Everett made a point to acknowledge Dodge and his war exploits in the West and called him to the speaker's platform. The crowd cheered, "Dodge, Dodge, Dodge." Grenville was given a torchlight parade over a mile long in Peabody, Massachusetts, and more receptions at North Danvers, Rowley and at Salem. At Salem, an enthusiastic crowd greeted Dodge. As he was giving a speech, a well-meaning lady threw a bouquet of flowers at Dodge that hit the wound on his scalp, and blood flowed freely from the still-not-healed wound. Dodge headed back to Greenfield, Indiana, and he received news of the death of his old friend General T.E.G. Ransom. Dodge was given orders to go to Vicksburg and take command of the so-called right wing of the XVI Corps. Sherman and others, though, were concerned about Dodge's health and were unsure he could stand the rigors of the march to the sea. This order was countermanded, and Dodge was to report to St. Louis and take over the Department of Missouri from General Rosecrans.[47]

By November, Sherman had formulated his plans. He would use about half his army to defend Tennessee and northern Georgia. The other half he would use to march through Georgia, living off the land and not needing the lines of communications to the North. Lincoln and Grant had reservations about his plan. Sherman issued Special Field Order #120. This order stated that Sherman's army of 60,000 infantry, 2,000 artillery men and 5,000 cavalry would forage liberally while marching through the South. Sherman wanted his wagons to have ten days' rations for his men and three days' forage for his livestock. Soldiers were to respect private property, but if Sherman's men were attacked by guerrillas or bushwhackers or bridges being burned, then the corps commanders were to use their own judgment in these cases and to "order and enforce a devastation more or less relentless accordingly to the measure of such hostility." In addition, it was at the discretion of the corps commanders whether to destroy mills, cotton-gins or houses. Worn-out horses and mules could be traded at will with the locals. Of course, this order left enough room for total destruction of a 30-mile strip roughly from Atlanta to Savannah. Sherman had maps and crop production and livestock reports from the 1860 census. He would march through some of the richest agricultural areas. From the rear he would need to bring up only ammunition. However, resistance would be for the most part light. Sherman had reorganized his army for the march to the sea. The 4th Iowa was still in Williamson's Iowa Bridge, which consisted of the 4th Iowa, 9th Iowa, 25th Iowa, 30th Iowa and 31st Iowa infantry regiments. Lt. Colonel Samuel D. Nichols was in charge of the 4th Iowa regiment. Williamson's brigade was the 3rd Brigade of Brigadier-General Woods' 1st Division. The 1st Division was part of Major-General Peter Osterhaus' XV Corp and part of Major-General Oliver O. Howard's right wing. The right wing consisted of two corps, the XV and XVII corps. Major-General Henry W. Slocum commanded the left wing of Sherman's army. The left wing had two corps, the XIV Corps and XX Corps Judson Kilpatrick commanded a division of Kil-Cavalry. On November 15, Sherman's army started their march across Georgia.[48]

General Woods ordered Williamson's brigade to destroy track on the Macon Railway. At Griswoldville, Woods' 1st Division met three brigades of Georgia militia and some of Confederate Wheeler's cavalry. The 4th Iowa participated in this skirmish in which the Georgia militia was swept from the field with heavy losses, mostly of captured militiamen on November 22. The Union losses were minimal. The area Williamson's men marched through until December consisted of desolate pine forests and swampland. On December 3, Williamson's brigade secured a bridgehead over the Ogeechee River while the Rebels were attempting to burn the bridge down. The 3rd Brigade cleared out the resistance. Sherman's army began to invest in taking the city of Savannah. Williamson's Iowa Brigade was to cross the Ogeechee River at the Jenks Bridge at 5 a.m. on the 9th of December 1864, and clear the area for the trains of the 1st and 2nd divisions.[49]

As the Union army gained control of the Ogeechee River and Fort McAllister fell to General Hazen's Division, the noose around Savannah was being tightened. Confederate general Hardee's troops were in Savannah. All the rice fields around Savannah were flooded by the Confederates, making entrance into that city more difficult. On December 17, 1864, Sherman sent a note to Hardee that he had guns that could easily reach the interior of Savannah and that he was willing to unleash a barrage on the city. In addition, he had all routes of supply into the city covered. Hardee evacuated his troops on December 20. His men made makeshift pontoon bridges and escaped. The next day the mayor of Savannah and a delegation came out to surrender. Sherman in a famous telegraph to Lincoln stated that he was giving him a Christmas present of the city of Savannah.[50]

Amos Ames had been a prisoner of war for two months. One thousand prisoners came in from Andersonville, and 600 prisoners from Alabama to the prison in Macon, Georgia. On November 2, 1864, the Confederacy held a day of fasting and prayer, another excuse not to feed the prisoners. The Confederates were constantly appealing to the prisoners to join the Rebel army. As early as August of 1864, General Robert E. Lee appealed to Confederate secretary of war Seddon: "Unless some measure can be devised to replace our losses the consequences may be disastrous. Without some increase in of strength, I cannot see how we are to escape the natural military consequences of the enemy's numerical superiority." On November 8, 1864, the Rebel prison commander held a bizarre mock presidential election. The prisoners were given a blank piece of paper and asked whom would they vote for in the election, Lincoln or McClellan. The Rebels were hoping the majority of men would vote for McClellan. The prisoners were told they would get extra rations if they voted for McClellan. However, even these half-starved men voted overwhelmingly for Lincoln.[51]

Rumors swirled around that a prisoner exchange would be set up for the sick and wounded. On November 9 Ames came down with a bad cold. The next day he said he felt better. In answer to Confederate appeals, 150–200 prisoners answered the call to join the Rebel army. Some Union prisoners were paying Confederate guards 50 dollars and up to get their names on the exchange list. A couple more prisoners that were captured around Claysville, Alabama, in March of 1864 from Company H of the 4th Iowa were brought in. They were Sergeant Jacob Fees from Quincy, Iowa, and Joseph Z. Darwin, who was born in France and resided in Ross Grove, Iowa. Sergeant Chaney was on one of the exchange lists but was brought back. On November 19, 1,000 sick and wounded were taken out for exchange. Ames was examined but was not sick enough to make it onto the exchange list. About 1,500 prisoners including Ames were taken down to the rail depot and put in hog cars on November 22. The engine on the train broke down, and the prisoners waited in the hog cars until a new freight engine could be brought from Savannah. The men camped out in a forest. They were reloaded onto cars. Arriving at a new site late at night, they did not get any wood for the cold night, and prisoners who had gotten there earlier would not share theirs. Three men escaped and were fired on, but they were brought back the next day (November 26). One thousand were men taken out to be paroled; however, a short while later they were brought back. Ames was at a prison at Blackshear. There was no gate to the stockade, just two stakes driven into the ground. A young boy mistakenly walked over the line where the two stakes were driven and was shot and killed by Rebel guards. Prisoners tried to make escapes; some were successful, others were not. On December 3, 1864, the U.S. Sanitary Commission sent in new clothing for the prisoners, and they were issued to those in the most need. Ames flanked a Rebel guard and got his name down for double rations. One thousand were taken away, rumored to be going to Andersonville. On December 7 Rebel guards took seven men out to get wood, and only three came back. Prisoners made continued attempts to escape. Ames and the other prisoners were taken out and marched to Albany, Georgia. Two thousand men were sent to Andersonville. Ames got to Albany, and the P.O.W.s were crowded into box cars. On Christmas day they started off for Andersonville. Put in a stockade at Andersonville, some men burrow into the ground for shelter against a storm. The ground collapsed and they were killed. Rumors that Jefferson Davis had died proved to be false.[52]

Andersonville was the worst of the Confederate prisons. Its commandant, Major Henry Wirz, would be hung for murder late in 1865. The prison was opened in February of 1864. It was estimated that it contained 45,000 P.O.W.s throughout the war. It was estimated that approximately 13,000 men died there. It was said the prisoners looked like walking skeletons and were covered with filth and vermin. On January 15, 1865, the prison police were disbanded. These were Union prisoners who were to preserve order both day and night at Andersonville. These "police" received more rations than did the average prisoner. The prisoners who were sergeants were to take over the police duties in Andersonville. Through January and February of 1865, Ames heard of possible prisoner exchanges, and the Rebels tried actively to recruit men for the Rebel army. As the Confederacy kept shrinking, prisoners came in from Richmond, Virginia; Florence, South Carolina; Florida; and Meridian, Mississippi. On February 8, 1864, Commandant Wirz walked through the stockade and one Union P.O.W. yelled out, "More cornbread." Wirz threatened to cut everyone's rations until the prisoner who yelled this was brought out. By the end of February, Ames had been a Confederate prisoner for six months. Ames saw some newspapers and thought the war seemed to be going the Union's way.[53]

It was obvious that the western armies had ripped the guts out of the Confederacy. Grant wanted Sherman to bring his army and put it up against Lee's Army of Northern Virginia. Sherman, however, wanted to take his troops up through the Carolinas to strike at the Confederacy's ability to wage war. On January 13, 1865, Colonel James A. Williamson was appointed a brigadier-general. In late January of 1865, Sherman marched his troops at about 10–12 miles a day north from Savannah, Georgia, into South Carolina. Sherman's army was headed toward Columbia, the cradle of the Confederacy and the capital of South Carolina, cutting a swath about 60 miles wide. The 4th Iowa Infantry was headed by Lt. Colonel Samuel D. Nichols and was part of the 3rd Brigade, commanded by Colonel George Stone. The men of the 4th Iowa Infantry, led by Lt. Colonel Nichols, waded waist-deep across a swamp with their guns and ammunition held above their heads. Columbia was about two miles away, and there were Rebel soldiers 500 yards away from where the 4th and 9th Iowa made their crossing. When they got to the other side, they were fired upon by the Confederates. Major Albert Anderson of the 4th Iowa led skirmishers and broke up all Rebel opposition. As they were headed for Columbia, Colonel Stone met Columbia mayor Goodwin, who wished to surrender. Stone told him the terms were unconditional surrender, to which the mayor agreed. Stone and Major Albert H. Anderson of Clarinda, Iowa, who had entered the army as an enlisted man but by war's end was a lt. colonel, got in Goodwin's carriage and headed for the heart of the city. However, Stone saw some Confederate skirmishers still fighting. He told a soldier that if one Union man was killed to shoot the mayor. Stone and some men chased the Rebel skirmishers off. Stone said of the 4th Iowa that they "supported the assault in a handsome manner." Stone went to plant the Stars and Stripes above the capitol building. The Iowa Brigade had captured 43 pieces of artillery and 5,000 rifles; 40 Union officers were liberated from being P.O.W.s, and stores of ammunition and supplies were secured. When Stone came back, the streets of Columbia were full of drunken Union soldiers, P.O.W.s from Castle Sorghum, Confederate deserters and freed slaves. Supplies of liquor were plentiful in Columbia, and looting occurred. There had been a notorious Confederate prison camp in Columbia,

Castle Sorghum. The Union P.O.W.s were ill fed and mistreated, and when they were liberated, they wanted to take vengeance on the city of Columbia. Anything in the city of military value was burned to the ground. Unfortunately, many in Sherman's army wanted to punish Columbia and South Carolina for their part in leading the breakup of the Union. Things got completely out of hand in the South Carolina capital. Some have noted that a contingent of people in Columbia wanted to surrender to Sherman when his army was miles away, hoping for favorable terms and a decent occupation. However, General Wade Hampton said he would fight for Columbia house by house; of course, he fled after giving token resistance when Sherman's army approached the city.[54]

Sherman had written to Confederate cavalry officer Joe Wheeler, "I hope you will burn all the cotton and save me the trouble.... All that you don't burn I will." The day after the Union army occupied Columbia, it was estimated that two thirds of the city of 20,000 was destroyed. Sherman had written to General Halleck, "The whole army is burning to wreck vengeance upon South Carolina. I almost tremble at her fate, but feel that she deserves all that seems in store for her. Many and many a person in Georgia asked me why we did not go to South Carolina and when I answered that I was enroute for that state the invariable reply was well if you will make those people feel the severities of war, we will pardon you for your desolation of Georgia." Not that Sherman's superiors cared much if South Carolina suffered. General Halleck in Washington wrote to Sherman: "Should you capture Charleston. I hope by some accident the place may be destroyed and if a little salt should be sown upon its site it may prevent the growth of future crops of nullification and secession." The men in the 4th Iowa wondered where they would go next, to Charleston or to North Carolina. They received orders to move northward into North Carolina. However, without a doubt, of the three states Sherman marched across—Georgia, South Carolina and North Carolina—South Carolina was put under the torch and destroyed to a much greater degree than the other states. It was not all under Sherman's orders, as the average Union soldier wanted to punish and burn down South Carolina for what they felt was her part in starting the Civil War. General Lee, seeing the desperate situation of Sherman's army, told Confederate secretary of war Breckinridge that he thought General Joseph Johnston should replace Beauregard as commander of the Confederate army in front of Sherman.[55]

Dodge reported to St. Louis to head the Department of Missouri. While this department was known as the "graveyard of generals," Dodge saw only opportunities. Grenville knew how important it was to keep the Missouri River and the Hannibal to St. Joseph Railroad open to keep supplying the people of western Iowa, the Nebraska Territory and the state of Kansas. Missouri had been wracked by guerrilla warfare from William Quantrill, Bloody Bill Anderson, Archie Clement and George Todd, among others. These guerrilla bands had been ruthless in terrorizing Union targets and Union men and women in Missouri. Anderson carried scalps of his victims on his horse bridle. These were tough men who rode in these Missouri guerrilla bands. They included Jesse James, Frank James, Cole Younger, Dave Pool, Archie Clement and others who would eventually ride with the infamous outlaw James-Younger gang. In one disgusting action, Bloody Bill Anderson in Centralia, Missouri, had pulled 24 mostly unarmed Union soldiers off a train bound home to Iowa and Missouri for furlough from the Atlanta campaign. The soldiers stood in a line with their hands in the air. Confederate guerrilla Archie Clement, when asked what to do with the men, was told by Anderson, "Parole them, of course." Of these soldiers, 23 were shot down after they had surrendered, only one being spared to be used in a prisoner exchange. Major A.V.E. Johnson, upon hearing of trouble at Centralia, brought 155 Union soldiers from the 38th Federal Missouri Mounted Infantry, some of them riding plow horses, to fight the guerrillas. Bloody Bill Anderson's men killed 123 of these Union soldiers, many of them schoolboys who were following their schoolmaster, Johnson. The bodies of these boys were scalped and mutilated. The guerrillas severed the heads of these Union soldiers and put them on someone else's body. Most of the families of the 38th Missouri lived close by, and when they went to claim the bodies of their loved ones, they found their heads on others' bodies. Dave Pool, to see how many Union soldiers they had killed, jumped from body to body to get the count. It was said 17-year-old Jesse James put the bullet into Major Johnson's head that killed him.

Also in the fall of 1864, Confederate general Sterling Price tried one more time to bring Missouri back into the Confederacy with a raid, and the Union had to expend a lot of valuable resources to put down Price's foray. Grant and Halleck were not happy with General Rosecrans' inability to keep order in Missouri. In a letter, Dodge's friend and Iowa congressman John Kasson, who had lived in St. Louis for a number of years, wrote of Rosecrans, "[He] loved pleasure and society more than he loved work, and he loved flattery more than either." Even with all this activity going on in Missouri, the first thing Dodge was told to do upon arriving in St. Louis was to send all available troops to Nashville to aid General Thomas and the large Army of the Cumberland. Even though he had many assets to guard in Missouri, Dodge dutifully sent Thomas all the regiments he could from Missouri. Dodge was still stinging a little from the dissolution of his old unit, the left wing of the XVI Corps, but he did as ordered. When Dodge got to St. Louis he found the military prisons filled with prisoners who had been jailed but never had charges brought against them. He released these people from the jails. General Sherman's wife lived at their family home in St. Louis, and she told Dodge of people who were accused of being Rebel sympathizers and had been wrongly jailed. Dodge had these people released from prison, thinking it was cheaper to free these people than continue to feed

The famous picture of Abraham Lincoln, today seen on the five-dollar bill (Library of Congress).

them. Sherman, when hearing of this, told Dodge to use his own judgment in releasing prisoners and not to depend on Mrs. Sherman's advice.[56]

In mid–December Dodge got word that General Thomas' army had mauled John Bell Hood's Confederates in the Battles of Nashville-Franklin. Dodge was told that his Missouri troops had performed magnificently. Hood went into the battle with about 38,000 men. After the battle, because of those killed, wounded, and captured and desertions, his army was down to less than 15,000 troops. While in St. Louis, Dodge received correspondence from his friends and other war acquaintances. Finally, one of his best spies, Phillip Henson, showed up in St. Louis, much to the surprise of Dodge. Henson had been a prisoner in Mobile, Alabama, when the Union armed forces captured the city. Henson was moved to a prison in Meridian, Mississippi. At Meridian, Henson kept losing weight. Because of the lack of food and medical attention, he knew he had to do something or he would die. Henson told his jailors that he was ready to join the Rebel army. His only wish was that he be allowed to join the 26th Mississippi Infantry. Henson had no special attachment to the unit, but he had heard the 26th was in Virginia and he was sure he could escape somewhere along the rail line between Meridian and Virginia. Put on a train, Henson escaped around Selma, Alabama. He walked 20 miles to an old friend of his, stayed there, and recuperated. His friend had a wounded nephew who was in the Confederate army. Henson bought the wounded soldier's identification papers for $1,000 in Confederate money. Now he could continue on his journey, so he went to his sister's place in Blount, Alabama. He still needed to recuperate, as he was in bad physical condition. One day his sister told him the Confederates were on to him and he would have to go. Henson dragged himself out of bed and down to the river, where Federal gunboats were patrolling. Henson made himself known to these gunboats and was picked up and made his way to Dodge's headquarters in St. Louis. Dodge said to Henson, "The rope hasn't been made yet to hang you!" Dodge had tried to find Henson and wrote to General Dana to look for Henson on one of his cavalry raids, but apparently the Union cavalry had been unable to find him. Dodge then arranged for Henson's wife to be reunited with him.[57]

Missouri had already suffered under a number of draconian Union orders. Almost all Union commanders felt that most Missourians were disloyal with their allegiance to the Confederacy. Most famous was Ewing's Orders #10 and #11. Order #10 basically said that anyone who had aided the guerrilla bands or acted in a disloyal manner would be removed—including women and children—to another district or out of the state of Missouri to the south. Order #11 said that in certain counties and locations around Kansas City, Missouri, everyone would be removed from their homes whether they were disloyal or loyal. Those that were loyal to the Union could move to any Union military station or to the state of Kansas. The counties around Kansas City were empty of citizens. Many of Missouri's slaveholders remained loyal to the Union, but often they were the targets of robbery and even murder. Dodge chose to rule Missouri with a rather heavy hand. He wished to punish all those who were not loyal to the Union. Dodge's Order #7 said that anyone who knew of the whereabouts of guerrilla bands and did not notify the Union army could lose their property and be executed. Anyone disloyal to the Union would be removed from the state. Dodge was aggressive in carrying out this order. Dodge thought the state was 50 percent Rebel and 50 percent Union.

Lincoln received 10 percent of Missouri's votes in the 1860 election, but by the 1864 presidential election, Missouri gave Lincoln almost 70 percent of her vote. Lincoln objected to Dodge's harsh treatment of Missouri. Even when Rosecrans was head of the Department of Missouri, and also with Dodge, Lincoln tried to see if they would repeal executions or prison sentences. Most in Missouri realized that the Confederacy and slavery were outdated. By the time Dodge got to Missouri there was a lot of mistrust among Missourians of the Union army, even among those who were loyal to the United States.[58]

The family of Solomon Young were good examples of slaveholding Union-backers in Missouri who suffered under the iron glove of the Union army. Young, who was an excellent judge of livestock, made a fortune taking wagon trains and supplies out West. Granted, one of his sons joined the Confederate army, and a daughter, despite his opposition, married a Rebel bushwhacker. However, Solomon Young signed a loyalty oath and never did anything disloyal to the Union. His large farm in Jackson County, Missouri, was a target of Union soldiers and Kansas Jayhawkers during the Civil War. Jim Lane, the Kansas senator and brigadier-general in the Union army, stole almost $5,000 in livestock from his farm. General Sturgis, the failed Union cavalry officer, stole 150 head of cattle from his farm. Three other Union army raids on his place took 1,200 pounds of bacon, 65 tons of hay, 44 hogs, 13,000 fence rails, 1,000 bushels of corn and other food stuffs. It was estimated later that the Union army took $21,442 worth of goods from Young's farm, the equivalent of about a half million dollars in today's currency. The Union army threatened Young's wife and treated his family in a most barbaric way. When Ewing's order #11 was issued, the family had to leave their farm like refugees. The family had to vacate and move to a military station in Kansas City. One of Solomon Young's daughters, little Martha Ellen Young, remembers leaving their comfortable home and prosperous farm and trudging north on a dusty road in "bitter exile." The Young family was only allowed to take one wagonload of possessions, and the Union cavalry helped themselves to the rest of their property. Little Martha Ellen Young grew up and married John Anderson Truman, and they had a son, Harry S. Truman, who became president of the United States. Harry's favorite uncle, Harrison Young, the man Harry Truman was named after, was 15 years old when Union soldiers from Kansas came onto their farm and wanted to know where Solomon was. They got out a rope, threw it over a tree branch, and hanged young Harrison in the air until he told them where his father was. Harrison told the truth and said Solomon Young was out West. For good measure, they stretched his neck out and let him down. Luckily, Harrison survived. This method of Union interrogation sometimes led to death. In the case of Dr. Reuben Samuel, the Union army wanted to know where his stepson Frank James, the known guerrilla fighter, was located. They hanged Dr. Samuel and although he was not killed, he was not the same after the hanging. They chased young 15-year-old Jesse James through a cornfield and whipped him when they caught the lad. What happened to the Young and Samuel-James families was played out hundreds of times over in Missouri. Most Union people in Missouri had some relation, business associates or friends who believed in the Confederate cause, but that did not mean the Union people were disloyal.[59]

Dodge claimed that in two months he had pacified Missouri. However, he came into Missouri during the wintertime, when a lot of the guerrilla activity was at a low ebb. In addition, guerrilla leaders Bloody Bill Anderson and George Todd had been killed. Other guerrilla leaders such as George Shepherd, Jim Anderson (Bloody Bill's brother), Archie Clement and Dave Pool were all in Texas during the winter of 1864–1865. William Quantrill was killed in Kentucky, never making it back to Missouri. Dodge wanted to have the military keep law and order to help civilian authorities. He later wanted to replace Federal troops with Missouri State Militiamen, which was a good idea. The local militia might be more in tune with what their fellow Missourians were thinking than out-of-state Union soldiers. Although some of the Missouri State Militiamen were extremely lax in discipline and were as proficient in plunder and murder as were the Confederate guerrillas, Dodge thought it was worth a try. Lincoln, in a letter to Dodge and Missouri governor Fletcher, asked why, since there was no organized Confederate Army in Missouri, there were still so many robberies and murders taking place. Lincoln suggested to Dodge that, given that there was so much mistrust among the citizens of Missouri, perhaps community meetings could be held to bring people of good will together for a unified purpose. General Dodge and Missouri governor Fletcher thought Lincoln was terribly "naïve" and did not know the situation in Missouri. They ignored his suggestion. Dodge kept getting letters from Missouri Union men congratulating him on his iron-fisted rule of Missouri. However, during the spring when these guerrilla bands came back from the south, it was obvious that Missouri had not been pacified. Even several years after the war was over, Missouri was wracked by multiple outlaw bands, mostly made up of unreconstructed Rebels. However, Dodge was given even more problems when he took over the Department of Kansas along with the Department of Missouri. He moved his headquarters from St. Louis to Fort Leavenworth in Kansas.[60]

When Dodge took over the Department of Kansas, he had control of much of the West, including parts of the Nebraska Territory, the state of Colorado, the present state of Wyoming, the Indian Nations of what is now Oklahoma, and the Utah Territory. Later in March, Arkansas would be under his command. In November of 1864, Union army colonel John Chivington in a cowardly manner attacked and killed 163 unarmed Cheyenne and Arapaho Native Americans in what was called the Sand Creek Massacre. Chivington's drunken soldiers scalped and mutilated these people, including cutting fetuses out of their mother's bellies and cutting off female genitalia. The different tribes in this region—Cheyenne, Comanche, Kiowa, Apache and Arapaho—began to retaliate from the Arkansas River to the North Platte River. They tore up the telegraph lines between Omaha and Denver, attacked stagecoaches and wagon trains, and killed whites in settlements or wherever they found them. Mail routes were also blocked. The railroad people at the Kansas Pacific and Union Pacific knew the Native American tribes would have to be pacified or the chances of building rail lines to the West were nil.

General Curtis was in charge of the Department of Kansas, but he was 61 years old and because of his health, he would be dead within two years. It was decided that Dodge, at 34, would be the better man to conduct a winter campaign against these tribesmen. In addition, many considered Dodge to be a plainsman who knew how to deal with Native Americas. The Native Americans now occupied the Santa Fe Trail, the North and South Platte routes and the South Pass. Whenever troops had been sent out, the Native American warriors defeated them. Dodge, while respecting individual Native Americans, believed as did most Americans in Manifest Destiny—that those of European descent should control all of the area we now call the United States and subjugate the native tribes' people. Dodge seemed to appreciate the "friendly" Native Americans but thought those that resisted to be "savages." When Dodge found out that many friendly Native Americans were being robbed and having their cattle stolen by white bandits, Dodge issued Special Order #44. This order stated that anyone caught stealing or robbing friendly Native Americans would be arrested by the military and an investigation would follow. Dodge also believed that one of the big reasons for the "Indian troubles" Washington talked about was the violation of treaties. Some tribes had been promised annuities. One tribe received their annuity only once in ten years. Other tribes only received a portion of their annuities, the rest being taken by unscrupulous "Indian Agents" or contractors. Dodge sent out all available regiments but found that some officers were less than vigorous in fighting these Native Americans. Many located the hostile native tribesmen and went out of their way to avoid them. Very few of these soldiers would stand and fight. Dodge threatened to sack all officers who were not up to this task. Some of these officers told their men they didn't have to fight and should be mustered out of the army. Dodge butted heads with James Lane, the senator from Kansas and a general in the Union army, who controlled the politics in Kansas. Lane had many of these Union officers performing as political operatives in the state of Kansas. Dodge told him they were in the military and under his command. Lane threatened Dodge, but it came to nothing.[61]

Dodge also recruited some of the best Pawnee scouts to help him, including legendary Pawnee scout Major Frank North. Dodge also employed Native Americans, people of mixed heritage, and white men who had married Native American women to spy for him on the Plains tribesmen. In addition, wagons trains headed out West were to be armed to protect themselves, and army officers would be put in command of the trains. There was plenty of snow, in some places two feet deep on the plains in March of 1865, and it was bitterly cold. Some troops froze to death. Dodge attacked all hostile tribes from Canada to the Arkansas River. Dodge managed to get the 600 miles of telegraph lines between Omaha and Denver put back into order in 13 days of sub-zero temperatures and kept the hostiles 100 miles away from these lines. Whenever a troop stood and fought against the Native Americans, Dodge (regardless if the troops were commanded by an officer or non-commissioned officer) wired the man personally to thank him for his service. He also wired the soldiers' Regimental commanders and recommended them for the next promotion. The soldiers on the Plains had been very discouraged in fighting these Native tribesmen and mostly ran away when attacked by these warriors. Dodge said the Native Americans were the best skirmishers in the world and their horsemanship was unparalleled. Their ability to fight on open ground and their astounding ability to hide behind any obstacle was masterful. Their ability to disappear was uncanny, and they were proficient sharpshooters. Dodge noted that in some skirmishes the Native Americans could not be seen, only the puffs of smoke from their rifle barrels. Dodge had a theory about fighting the Native American tribesmen. Dodge told his men to hold their ground and never retreat, and if they did retreat, to do it very slowly all the while facing the enemy. However, as Dodge was getting his war against the Plains Native Americans organized, things back in Missouri began to explode. All the hard-nosed Confederate guerrilla bands of George Shepherd, Archie Clement, Dave Pool and Jim Anderson came back into Missouri from their winter quarters in Texas just as springtime came to Missouri and the Ozarks.[62]

The 4th Iowa headed north with the rest of Sherman's army. Sherman cut off Charleston, South Carolina, on the vine. By February 18, 1865, even the Charleston *Mercury* announced that it could not get its papers out to subscribers because the mail routes had been blocked by the military and they had not been able to get sufficient supplies of newsprint into the city to print the newspaper. With light opposition, Sherman's troops took Fort Fisher in January. In February, Sherman rolled over Braxton Bragg's troops and occupied the city of Wilmington, North Carolina. Wilmington was the last Confederate seaport on the Atlantic Ocean, and she supplied much of the material used by Lee's Army of Northern Virginia. Sherman then marched his troops towards Goldsboro, North Carolina, a major rail hub in the South. The 4th Iowa was assigned to the Iowa Brigade, whose commander at that time was Colonel George A. Stone. Even though General Joseph Johnston had gathered a small army to oppose Sherman, Stone stated that they did not meet any real Rebel opposition until they got near Bentonville, North Carolina. The battle was conducted southwest of Goldsboro. On March 20, 1865, the Iowa Brigade first met opposition on the way to Goldsboro, three miles from Bentonville. The Iowa Brigade was to clear a road to make connections with the XIV Corps, which they did, driving enemy skirmishers back to their lines through a swamp. The 4th Iowa was held in reserve. On March 21 the 4th Iowa was ordered to build defensive works. They did this under fire of the enemy while on the right wing

In June of 1864, Dodge finally was promoted to major-general and has his two stars on this uniform. Soon after, a Confederate sharpshooter hit Dodge in the head with a bullet on a ricochet; he was knocked unconscious and suffered a concussion, and when he awoke, he could not see for several days. Despite a slow recovery from the wound, he was put in charge of the Department of Missouri in December of 1864 (Library of Congress).

of the brigade's line. By that afternoon, they were to charge Rebel rifle pits and move their skirmishers to the rear. This they did, with Captain Frederick Teal, Lt. Colonel Nichols, Major Albert Anderson and Lieutenant Shields going to the skirmish line when it was wavering. Captain Teal was severely wounded in the leg. The Confederates counterattacked with ferocity and at times overran the 4th Iowa's positions. However, after three gallant charges with Union generals Howard and Logan ordering the Iowa Brigade to stand firm, the Rebels were repelled. On the 22nd of March, patrols of the Iowa Brigade found the Rebels had abandoned their positions. On the 23rd they marched to Goldsboro, meeting Rebel stragglers on the way. On the 24th the Iowa Brigade guarded the pontoon bridge to allow the corps to cross the Neuse River. Sherman's army needed to refit itself in Goldsboro. Sherman wrote that his army had been in water since Savannah about half the time, and this caused clothing and shoes to deteriorate at a fast rate. Then on April 9 came word of Lee's surrender to Grant at Appomattox Courthouse in Virginia. Sherman marched his army to Raleigh, the state capital of North Carolina, and by April 13 they occupied the city. Four days later Sherman and Johnston were in negotiations for surrender of Johnston's army. On the 26th Johnston and Sherman came to terms. On April 30 the 4th Iowa joined Sherman's army and their march to Washington for the Grand Revue of the Union army. By May 24 the 4th Iowa reached Washington, D.C., and participated in the revue. After the Grand Revue, the 4th Iowa was railed and sent by boats to Louisville, Kentucky, where it performed provost duties. They were mustered out in July of 1865 and on July 26 reached Davenport, Iowa, where they were feted and greeted as heroes.[63]

It was March of 1865 and Amos Ames was still a Union prisoner at Andersonville. All kinds of rumors swirled around the prison about proposed prisoner exchanges, yet none of them came through. On March 8, barrels were issued in which to make corn beer to counter the effects of scurvy. On March 10, Commandant Wirz sent an order that there was no foundation to the rumors of a prisoner exchange. Half an hour later, Rebel recruiting officers made their way through the prison. Ames noted that Union prisoners cut the buttons off the rear of the coat worn by their Confederate recruiter. Buttons were legal tender with Rebel soldiers, who purchased meal, beans, and other food with them. On March 20, Ames saw his cousin Henry Stoll, whom he had not seen in 17 years. Stoll was with the Company G of the 105th Ohio Infantry. Stoll had been captured near Savannah. Wilford Crandall and George B. Davis, former prisoners from the 4th Iowa, managed to get food sent to 4th Iowa prisoners Joseph Z. Darwin and Samuel Hutton.[64]

Men were coming and going at all times in Andersonville. Prisoners were paying Confederate guards to get their names on exchange lists. Ames was still not exchanged. Rumors went through Andersonville with lightning speed, but very few turned out to be true. By the end of March Ames had been a Rebel prisoner for seven months. April 1 rolled by with still no more news. On the 5th of April Ames was loaded on a car for Albany, Georgia. They lay around a camp outside of Albany and were allowed to bathe in the river. He drew three days' rations on the 9th. On the 17th the Masonic fraternity sent in boxes of clothing. Ames and the other prisoners were loaded several times onto trains but brought back for fear of being caught in Union cavalry raids. Ames and others were marched to Thomasville and then loaded on railcars. At 11 o'clock P.M. they start out for Jacksonville, Florida. The men were sent to Lake City, Florida, and then camped outside of town. While in Lake City on the 26th of April the men finally heard that Lee had surrendered on the 9th of April and that Lincoln had been assassinated on April 14. On April 28, 1865, Amos Ames reached Union lines in Jacksonville, Florida; finally he was a free man. Ames spent seven months and 28 days as a prisoner of the Confederate army. On June 26, 1865, Amos Ames was mustered out of the Union army and headed home.[65]

From January to March of 1865 there were 100 reports of guerrilla activity in Missouri, usually with a dozen or so fighters. One of the problems in identifying potential attacks was that the guerrillas wore stolen Union army uniforms. The guerrillas learned they could move about Missouri in groups of two or three men wearing Union uniforms and not be molested. These guerrillas used rendezvous points where they would all meet to form a larger force. As the guerrillas moved north in April and May of 1865, many had not heard of Lee's and Johnston's surrender and committed mayhem. Confederate soldiers coming back from the front and finding their homes in Missouri burned to the ground or, worse yet, finding their farmsteads being occupied by Yankee carpetbaggers, were also in a mood for destruction. When hardcore guerrilla fighters Dave Pool, Archie Clement and Jim Anderson showed up in May in central Missouri, Dodge restated his position that if the guerrilla fighters gave themselves up and kept out of trouble the military would not pursue them for their crimes. However, Dodge could not speak for the civilian authorities. The guerrillas, if they stayed in Missouri, would have to take an oath of loyalty and give up their arms and horses. If they wanted to go south they would be paroled. Incredibly, Dave Pool took up the offer and brought in 40 hard-nosed bushwhackers. Pool even agreed to go out and bring in 200 more bushwhackers. However, Archie Clement, Jim Anderson and others were still at large and only too willing to commit robbery and murder. In May, Confederate general Jeff Thompson surrendered in Arkansas about 10,000 of his troops to Dodge. Slowly the job of bringing law and order to the state of Missouri was being taken over by civilian authorities and not the military. However, guerrilla attacks continued.[66]

A lady presented herself to Dodge with a card from President Lincoln. Her son was to be executed in Missouri, and she had pleaded with Lincoln for a pardon. Lincoln wrote on the card, "My Dear General Dodge: Is it possible for you to do anything for this poor woman who is in so much trouble?" Dodge took it as another example of Lincoln's overly generous heart and of Dodge's need to control Missouri with an iron fist. Dodge was going to let the execution go on as planned. Then Dodge got a dispatch that Lincoln had been assassinated. There was concern that Union people might take revenge on Southerners, but St. Louis remained calm. Dodge noted that those of Southern sentiment seemed to be as upset over Lincoln's death as were the Union people. The lady called on Dodge, resigned to the fact that her son was to be executed. She wanted Lincoln's card back as a memento. Dodge said he did not have it in his heart to carry out the order; he succumbed to the great man's wishes and commuted the sentence of the mother's son to imprisonment. Dodge attended Lincoln's funeral in Springfield, Illinois, with his staff and some of his troops. Dodge took his position in the procession and commented that he had never seen anything so sad. Everywhere he heard loud sobs, and black men and women dropped to their knees and offered up earnest prayers for

Lincoln. Everyone was crying, even Dodge's troops who were battle-hardened soldiers. Grenville wrote, "As we paid the last rites to this great man the sorrow was universal, for it was one of the greatest calamities of this or any other nation."[67]

By the spring of 1865, Dodge had been successful in 30 engagements in driving the native people north of the Platte River and south of the Arkansas River. After six months of trying to get his old friend, now Brigadier-General James A. Williamson, assigned to his command, finally in June Williamson was sent to the Department of Kansas. Some of the Union soldiers balked at fighting the native people. At one point Dodge was sent 12,000 soldiers, but only 6,000 stayed to fight. Some of them deserted rather than fight the tribesmen on the Plains. Others said they had joined the army to fight in the Civil War, and now that the war was over they were released from their term of service. Some would get out to Colorado or points west and say their term of enlistment was up. Dodge had to tell Washington to stop sending him troops whose term of enlistment was almost up. Dodge began recruiting former Confederate troops to help him fight the Plains tribesmen. In March, Dodge wrote to General Pope of a group of Rebel prisoners at the Union P.O.W. camp in Alton, Illinois, called the "Galvanized Yankees." These men had been Union soldiers who were captured after the Battle of Atlanta and sent to a Confederate P.O.W. camp. Rather than die in the Rebel camp they volunteered for the Confederate army when the Rebel recruiter came by. When in the field, at the first sighting of the Union army these men all gave up. They did not want to be exchanged back into the Confederate army and were willing to fight on the Plains. Dodge also wrote of 1,000 Confederate deserters and conscripts that did not want to be exchanged back into the Rebel army but were willing to fight against the Plains tribesmen. These men were all formed into regiments for the Plains warfare. In June of 1865, Dodge conducted one of his most ambitious forays against the Plains tribes with the Powder River Expedition. Noted scout Jim Bridger acted as head guide. The Powder River Expedition was headed by Brigadier-General Patrick E. Connor. Connor sent his troops out in three columns. The tribesmen of the Sioux, Cheyenne and Arapaho had closed down and harassed settlers and wagon trains on the Bozeman trail. In July of 1865, Dodge tried to resign his commission so he could join in the construction of the Union Pacific Railroad, but Grant and Sherman would not accept his resignation and wanted him to continue with his war against the Plains tribesmen. During the Powder River Expedition, Ford and another Pawnee scout stood off a large contingent of Sioux at Crazy Woman's Fork in early August. The culminating battle of the expedition was in late August of 1865 and occurred at Tongue River where the soldiers defeated the forces of the Arapaho in hand-to-hand combat in their village. Raids stopped on the Bozeman Trail but this led to the Red Cloud War at a later date.[68]

All during the campaign against the Plains tribesmen, Dodge was criticized for money being spent. Considering the great amount of territory to be covered, his expenditures seemed reasonable, as Dodge had his men foraging whenever possible. Dodge was always incredulous at how little the president's cabinet knew about the battle against the Plains tribesmen. Secretary of the navy Gideon Wells kept a diary, and his entries told of a cabinet clueless about what was going on on the Plains. Wells wrote that Secretary of War Stanton stated there were 22,000 troops on the plains. However, Dodge said there were never anything close to that. Wells also wrote that the secretary of war was in "absolute ignorance" about the "Indian war" and "no one, it appears, has any knowledge on the question." The facts were that for three months the Plains tribesmen had shut down all the stage, wagon train, telegraph and mail routes out to California and all states and territories west of the Missouri River. Within 40 days of Dodge's taking over the Department of Kansas, all stage and wagon train routes were open, and mail and telegraph lines were restored. Dodge's point of view on the "Indian question," whether it was right or wrong, was that the United States should have followed the example of the British, who made native peoples wards of the military whom the military was to protect. Instead, Dodge said, the civilian authorities made treaties that could not be kept, and civilians made arrangements to feed and shelter the tribesmen that were rife with dishonesty and fraud. The military had ways to deal with dishonest men or those that committed fraud, while civilians would replace one dishonest "Indian agent" with another. The military were called in only to punish, and this and other questions often caused strife between civilian and military personal.[69]

Dodge was about to plan an attack on the tribesmen around the Arkansas River; however, a "peace commission" led by Senator James R. Doolittle of Wisconsin determined that Dodge's campaign was a failure and that it would cost too much to pacify the "Indians," who wanted peace as much as did the white men. An Indian agent, Colonel Jesse H. Leavenworth, sold Doolittle on his plan. Dodge noted that Leavenworth had been dishonorably discharged from the army and talked out of both sides of his mouth. Leavenworth talked of war with the "Indians" to Dodge's officers, but to Senator Doolittle he talked peace. Dodge said Leavenworth was "all things to all people." Dodge was stopped on his southern campaign. Some of his soldiers were so angered by this stoppage of the "Indian" campaign that they mutinied for a short time. Dodge thought that unless the Native American tribesmen were punished for past misdeeds they would never respect a "peace treaty." Dodge believed, rightly or wrongly, that the hostile tribes would spread their terror but when the U.S. Army closed in on them they would contact the "civilian authorities" and say they wanted peace. The native tribesmen would wait until the army pulled back and then they would start their campaign of terror again.[70]

In February of 1865, Dodge had told General Mitchell that he did not want another outrage such as Colonel Chivington had committed at Sand Creek. When Dodge sent troops out on the plains of southwestern Kansas when the weather was still winter-like, the troops had no wood to build shelters and had to create dugouts in the bluffs for shelter. Food was scarce and conditions were miserable. The men named their encampment Camp Dodge, not in honor of Dodge but because they were mad at him for sending them there at this time of the year. Supplies and more troops were sent to this point, and it became known as Fort Dodge. There was a little town that grew up by the fort so the townspeople dubbed their town after the nearby fort and called themselves Dodge City. The city later would become an important railhead for the Western cattle trade and was known as the "Queen of the Cow-towns."[71]

Many people agreed at this time with Dodge and his policies, and some thought he should deal even more harshly with the Plains tribesmen. There were many educated people such as E.F. Ware who thought only total extermination of the Indians would solve the problem. Ware was a very gifted writer who wrote of his time in the 90-day 1st Iowa regiment in Missouri during the Civil War. Ware joined the 7th Iowa Cavalry, which was sent to the Plains to fight the native people there. At one time Ware was Dodge's top aide. After the war Ware became a newspaperman, lawyer, politician, farmer and Washington bureaucrat. Ware later wrote of Dodge, "He was one of the best and bravest.... He was one of the greatest generals of the war—prompt, efficient and capable." Ware was very impressed that Dodge, only in his early thirties, was a major-general on his own merit and was a corps commander for Sherman. However, Ware was completely prejudiced against the Plains tribes. He wrote, "Those who have been in contact with him do not love him. His treachery, his cruelty, his basest kind of ingratitude, his wild, half-maniac superstitious, make those who knew him wonder where all the sentimentality about the 'noble Redman' came from." The *Omaha Daily Herald* wrote in support of Dodge's policies in January of 1866, "Embarrassed, annoyed by an imbecile half war half peace policy ... he [Dodge] has not been allowed to make a campaign upon any plan commensurate with the demands of the frontier." Cruelties abounded on both sides. In one episode the Cheyenne captured some Michigan soldiers, tied them to wagon wheels, put bacon all around them and then set the soldiers on fire. When these Cheyenne were captured by Connor's Pawnee scouts, one of the Cheyenne chiefs motioned to his mouth that he was full of the white man. The Pawnee scouts killed and scalped the Cheyenne band. Some of Dodge's policies, whether right or wrong, were the products of their time. However, Dodge time after time adamantly stated that when the whites made treaties with the native people, they needed to keep these treaties. Dodge put the blame for the Fetterman Massacre and the Custer debacle right at the feet of the white men who made a treaty with the Sioux pertaining to the Black Hills that they could not or would not keep.[72]

Unfortunately, Dodge's Powder River campaign began to flounder, mainly due to General Connor's brutality to the native people. Dodge told Connor to try to wrap up the campaign by October 15. Connor encouraged his men to kill all male native children age 12 and above. Scalping and mutilation of the native people were encouraged by Connor, especially among the Pawnee scouts. Many of Connor's over-the-top orders, such as to kill all male native children over the age of 12, were countermanded. Dodge did little to stop his out-of-control field commander and had nothing but good things to say about Connor, even recommending him for a promotion. In Connor's last communication before being mustered out of the service, Dodge and Connor were very friendly towards each other. Connor and others believed that Brigham Young, the Mormon leader, was agitating the "Indians" to attack white gentiles to keep them out of Utah. However, Mormon wagon trains were also being attacked by these Plains tribesmen. Grenville Dodge and his brother Nathan, General James Williamson and then-friend Congressman John Kasson headed out on the Plains to track the proposed line of the Union Pacific Railroad. They left Omaha via a stagecoach and were joined by two cavalry regiments at Fort Kearney. At Fort Cottonwood, where Dodge's father Sylvanus had a trading post, Grenville renamed the post Fort McPherson after the beloved general of the Army of the Tennessee. They reached Julesburg, Colorado, on August 24 only to see that the town had been burned to the ground by the native warriors. They went up north into Wyoming and into the Black Hills. In Denver, Dodge was told by citizens that they liked his hardnosed policies towards the native people. At Fort Laramie, Dodge and his group were given a large banquet with a variety of dishes, including a delicious pot of stew. Frenchman Nick Janis and his Cheyenne wife were the hosts for the feast. When Dodge dipped into the pot of stew, he thought he had pulled out a pig's foot and asked "if it was a squealer." Host Janis answered, "No it was a bow wow!" Kasson and Williamson quickly lost their appetites and regurgitated the stew they had just eaten. Later Dodge met up with the Pawnee scouts that had ridden with General Connor. These were some of the same Pawnee that had run the white settlers out of the Elkhorn Valley in Nebraska, including Dodge and Fifield. They greeted Dodge as an old friend and wanted to know how Dodge and his friend Fifield were doing. They named Dodge "Long Eye" because of his ability to see long distances with a surveyor's transom and Fifield "One Hand" because he was missing a hand from a mishap with a cannon. Then engineers under Dodge's direction found a pass through the Rockies that could be used by the Union Pacific. The Dodge party went on a buffalo hunt, and in October of 1865 back at Fort Leavenworth, Dodge got news that President Johnson wanted to deal leniently with the native people and wanted all troops off the Plains. The national government wanted to downsize the military and in November of 1865, Williamson was mustered out of the army. Dodge was to be mustered out in January of 1866, but Kasson and General Pope and Sherman made it possible for him to stay in the army as long as he wanted. Dodge saw the government make a treaty with the Sioux that included the Black Hills. Dodge told Sherman that gold had been found in the Black Hills and they would be crawling with miners in a few months, violating the treaty. Sherman replied he was just following Washington's orders. Disaster would soon follow, with miners streaming into the Black Hills as Dodge had predicted. However, Durant made Dodge an offer he could not refuse. At an enormous salary for the time of $10,000 per year, Dodge was offered the position of chief engineer of the Union Pacific Railroad. Dodge made plans to leave the army and on May 30, 1866, he became a civilian. Some of Dodge's iron-fisted methods worked in the Department of Missouri and some worked in the Department of Kansas. However, Dodge's sometimes-harsh ways sewed seeds of discontent in the future years in Missouri and on the Plains. In Missouri, past bungling by the Union army and civilian officials before Dodge got there was so great that probably no one could have brought law and order to that state. In spite of this, the Civil War was finally over for Major-General Grenville M. Dodge.[73]

CHAPTER 5

# Postbellum

After the Civil War was over, the vast majority of the members of the 4th Iowa Volunteer Infantry went back to their homes and engaged in agricultural pursuits. Many went back to the family farms they had left to fight in the Civil War, or they bought farmland or began work as hired hands, many times for relatives. This chapter will tell briefly about their lives after the war ended. Amos Ames, after surviving being a Union P.O.W. in several Confederate prisoner camps including Andersonville, came back to Iowa in June of 1865. He returned to his hometown of Afton, Iowa, and bought some farmland in the fall of 1865. In November of 1865, Amos married Sarah E. Ball. They had nine children, and Amos continued farming until his death in February 13, 1913, at age 72.[1]

Many of the soldiers coming back from the Civil War suffered mental and physical anguish, as do modern soldiers. However, due to a lack of medical knowledge, especially in the field of psychology and psychiatry, many Civil War vets "suffered in silence." In the day when agriculture was not yet mechanized, the loss of an arm or a leg could have serious consequences in endeavoring to make a living. A small pension from the federal government helped some disabled veterans, but often family members cared for and supported the disabled vets after they came home from the war. The psychologically damaged often had what at the time was called "Soldier's Heart" or "Irritable Heart Syndrome" or "De Costa Syndrome." Those with "Soldier's Heart" often suffered from what people of today would call PTSD. Hallucinations and the inability to tell real life happenings from flashbacks to the horrors of war were examples of this condition. One veteran, Albert Frank of the Eastern Theater, had offered a drink of water to his buddy sitting next to him. The buddy was hit by a shell and decapitated, his brains and blood spattering all over Frank. Frank became unable to speak or understand what fellow soldiers were saying. His barracks mates found him on the floor shaking and making bomb noises and saying, "Frank is killed." Frank was taken to the Government Hospital for the Insane in Washington, D.C. Many saw their fellow soldiers killed in a gruesome manner, often in hand-to-hand combat, and heard the horrific cries of the wounded on the battlefield. One veteran described hearing the cries of the wounded not being tended to on the battlefield and then told of a heavy rain coming down and drowning many of these wounded. P.O.W.s such as Amos Ames, because of the inhumane way they were often treated, were especially susceptible to mental illness after being released from their camps. Those soldiers suffering from depression were often referred to having a "melancholy condition." Suicides were common among the psychologically wounded soldiers during and after the Civil War. In one rare study done on the mental health of Civil War veterans, it was determined that the older the veteran, the less the effects of the psychological or physical damage. In a study published in the February 2006 issue of *Achieves of General Psychiatry* of some 15,027 Union veterans, Roxanne Cohan Silver, PhD, studied Union soldiers with mental and physical disabilities. Her findings showed that 85 percent of Union veterans showed signs of physical or mental difficulties. In the study, 40 percent had both physical and mental difficulties, and 18 percent had cardiac and gastrointestinal difficulties. Union units that suffered large rates of fatalities such as the 4th Iowa Volunteer Infantry often had as high as 51 percent of veterans suffering from cardiac, gastrointestinal and mental disease. This study found that drummer boys or young men in the service aged 9 to 17 were 93 percent more likely to suffer from physical and mental disorders than veterans aged 31 years or older.[2]

Sturgis Williams was from New York State and came out West with his uncle Reuben Williams when he was five years old. They settled in Ohio where he was educated and grew to manhood. At age 19 in May of 1856 Sturgis moved with his uncle to southwest Iowa along the Missouri River to a settlement called Civil Bend. There was a riverboat landing near Civil Bend, and the community—along with Reuben and Sturgis Williams—became active in the Underground Railroad, helping slaves escape from bondage from western Missouri, Arkansas, Kansas, the Indian Nations and even the Nebraska territories. Reuben became involved in one of the most famous escapes on the Underground Railroad in Iowa. The Nebraska territory, just across the Missouri River from Civil Bend, did not outlaw slavery until three months before the start of the Civil War. Two young ladies, one of whom was the unwilling mistress named Eliza to a rich slave owner in Nebraska City, Nebraska Territory, escaped from Nebraska City aided by a black man, John Williamson. Williamson brought the women across the Missouri River on a skiff and took them to Civil Bend. The Underground Railroad in Civil Bend forwarded the young women to Tabor, Iowa, where they were taken out on a night so dark with fog that someone had to go in front of the wagon with a lantern so the road could be seen. The young women eventually managed to make it all the way to freedom in Chicago, Illinois. Eventually Eliza went to Canada. The slaver went to Civil Bend, convinced Eliza was there. He brought 50 thugs with him, and they beat and intimidated the members of this small community, demanding information about the slave girls. A family of black people lived in Civil Bend, and the thugs almost killed their teenage boy. Reuben Williams protested to the slaver of his treatment of the citizens of Civil Bend, and the slaver hit Reuben on the side of this head, causing him to lose hearing in that ear. The slaver was arrested, and later Reuben sued the slaver and won an $8,000 judgment, which Reuben used to build a new barn. The slaver moved to Denver and several years later came back to Nebraska City to visit friends. During this time the slaver was visiting, Reuben's new barn was burned to the ground. At age 24 in July of 1861, just after the outbreak of the Civil War, Sturgis Williams joined the 4th Iowa Volunteer Infantry. Sturgis fought in all the engagements the 4th participated in, including Pea Ridge, Chickasaw Bayou, the siege of Vicksburg, Lookout Mountain, the Battle of Atlanta and Sherman's March to the Sea. At Vicksburg Sturgis was wounded in the arm. He rose through the ranks as a corporal, sergeant and finally 2nd lieutenant.

After the war was over Sturgis went back to the Civil Bend area and farmed and held different positions in the township and county governments. He also served in the Iowa legislature.[3]

Benjamin O. Sheldon enlisted in the 4th Iowa Infantry in July of 1861. Sheldon was wounded in the right shoulder near Atlanta in 1864 but stayed with the 4th Infantry until mustered out in July of 1865. He made sergeant while in the service. Sheldon had said during the Battle at Arkansas Post that it was the nastiest fight of the war as far as he was concerned. After coming home to Tabor, Iowa, eventually Sheldon became a rural-route postal carrier for the United States Post Office. Sheldon and his wife had 12 children. The adults and children around Tabor liked to hear Ben's accounts of the battles in the Civil War, as Ben was very descriptive in his recollections. Ben died in December 16, 1920, at age 81.[4]

Albert R. (A.R.) Anderson, as a major in the 4th Iowa, helped in the surrender of Columbia, South Carolina. Anderson was from Ohio, moved to Iowa in 1857 and studied law in Taylor County. In 1860 he was admitted to the bar and began his legal career in Clarinda in Page County, Iowa. In 1861 after the election of Abraham Lincoln, Anderson was named postmaster in Clarinda. On August 10, 1861, Anderson enlisted in the 4th Iowa as a sergeant. At Pea Ridge because of actions on the battlefield, Anderson was promoted to 2nd lieutenant. At Vicksburg, because of battlefield action Anderson was promoted to captain. He was later made major, and at the end of the war, he was promoted to lt. colonel. He mustered out in July of 1865. After the war Anderson moved to Sidney, Iowa, and held a couple of positions in the federal government. In 1886, Anderson wanted but didn't win the Republican nomination for the 9th Congressional District. However, he ran as an Independent Republican against the powerful Republican congressman from the 9th District, William P. Hepburn. Anderson pulled off one of the biggest political upsets in Iowa at that time. He served in Congress from 1887 to 1888. He ran again as a Democrat and was trounced. Anderson moved to South Dakota and passed away in November 17, 1890.[5]

James P. Flick was born in Pennsylvania. His family moved to Wapello County in Iowa in 1852 and then moved into Taylor County, Iowa. When he was 17, in April of 1862, Flick enlisted in the 4th Iowa Infantry as a private. He fought in most of the battles of the 4th as an infantryman and obtained the rank of corporal. Flick was mustered out of the service in September of 1864 after the battle at Atlanta. In October of 1866, he married Sarah King, and six children were born to this union. After the war Flick became the recorder for Taylor County, Iowa, and studied law. In 1870, he was admitted to the bar. Flick became the district attorney for the 3rd Judicial District in Iowa for six years. In 1888, he ran for congressman in Iowa against his old commanding officer A.R. Anderson. Flick handily defeated Anderson and served four years in the United States Congress. His first wife passed away and in 1892, Flick married Mrs. Mary Griffin. Flick returned to Bedford, Iowa, and set up a very successful law practice. He passed away in February 25, 1929.[6]

George Weavers was born in England and raised in Cambridgeshire. When he was nine years old, George with his family came to the United States and settled in Ohio. They later moved to Illinois, and just as the Civil War was beginning in 1861 they moved to Sidney in Fremont County, Iowa. George enlisted in the 4th Iowa Infantry in August of 1861. At the horrific battle at Chickasaw Bluffs at the beginning of the Vicksburg campaign, George was terribly wounded in the face. He was mustered out of service at the expiration of his enlistment in September 4, 1864. In December of 1865, he married Susanna Hall, and there were four children born to this marriage. George managed to accumulate 369 acres of some of the finest farmland in Iowa. George died in 1914 at age 74.[7]

James A. Williamson was born in Columbia, Kentucky, and at age 15 he moved with his family to the Iowa Territory in a prairie schooner pulled by oxen. A year after their arrival, Iowa became a state. He went to Knox College in Galesburg, Illinois, and graduated. Williamson came to Grenville Dodge at the start of the Civil War, highly recommended. Dodge made Williamson his adjutant. Some of the other officers became jealous of Williamson and his close friendship with Dodge. In addition, most of the officers in the 4th Iowa Infantry were Republicans. Williamson was a delegate to the Democratic National Convention from Iowa, and the fact that he was born in a Southern state caused many officers in the 4th not to trust him. Some of the officers and enlisted men had been in the regular army and noted the mistakes Williamson made. They even presented Dodge with a petition to relieve Williamson of his duties. Dodge ignored this and in time, many of these officers became fast friends with Williamson. Williamson always appreciated Dodge's loyalty towards him. Williamson was very bright and brave and made a fine officer. At Pea Ridge, Arkansas, Williamson was wounded. After Pea Ridge, Dodge was made a brigadier-general, and Williamson was recommended to be a lt. colonel and command the 4th Iowa regiment. Williamson guided the 4th Iowa through most of their battles either by being their regimental colonel or its brigade commander. For his action at Chickasaw Bayou, he was awarded the Congressional Medal of Honor. Williamson left the service as a brigadier-general and as a brevet major general in the United States Volunteers. Williamson was offered a permanent commission in the United States Army but turned it down because, in his words, "I could not accept a position in the regular army. My family is large and are of the age to need me at home."[8]

In 1866 when Dodge ran for Congress, Williamson stumped his congressional district for him. In 1868, Williamson led the Iowa delegation at the National Republican Convention in Chicago. In 1868, Williamson was put in charge of all Union Pacific lands west of Wyoming and Colorado. He then went to London and sold Western land and mining interests to investors overseas. In 1873, a slowdown in the economy in London caused Williamson to come back to the United States. In 1876, President Grant offered Williamson the position of commissioner of the general land office. In 1881, Williamson became the land commissioner for the Atlantic and Pacific Railroad, and then became its general solicitor and eventually its president. He retired in 1892 after marrying his second wife in 1891. He lived out his retirement in New York City, summering in Rhode Island and in Europe. When Dodge lived in New York City, he and Williamson were often together and spent time in Europe together. Williamson kept in touch with many of the soldiers in the 4th Iowa, and when they were in need he helped them financially. Williamson and his wife were firmly established in the society of New York City and also many service organizations such as the Society of the Army of the Tennessee and the Grand Army of the Republic. General Grant visited Des Moines and spoke of

Williamson in the highest terms as an excellent soldier who received less reward for his services and the work accomplished than any other officer of his rank in the service. In 1902, Williamson passed away, and his old friend Grenville Dodge served as one of the pallbearers.[9]

Wilford W. (Bill) Crandall was from Winterset, Iowa, and joined the 4th Iowa Infantry in July of 1861 as a wagoner. Crandall had been raised in New York State. He was wounded at Pea Ridge and obtained the rank of sergeant. He was captured by Confederate soldiers in Claysville, Alabama, in March of 1864 and sent to Andersonville Prison. At one point, Crandall escaped the prison but was recaptured after three weeks on the run. He was released from Andersonville and was mustered out of the service in May of 1865 in Davenport, Iowa. After the war, Crandall was called upon to testify against Captain Henry Wirz, the prison keeper at Andersonville. Norton P. Chipman, a lawyer by trade, was the prosecutor during the Wirz trial. Chipman had been a lt. colonel in the 2nd Iowa Infantry and eventually obtained the rank of general in the office of the Judge Advocate of the Military Court. Major General Lew Wallace would be the lead commissioner for this military trial. Wallace would later write the best-selling book *Ben Hur: A Tale of Christ*. Wallace was also the territorial governor in New Mexico when the Lincoln County War made William Henry McCarty a household name. The name he was using in the territories was William H. Bonney or Billy the Kid.[10]

Crandall testified that Wirz had dogs that worked in packs of two that would hunt down escaping prisoners and severely injure them. One such man was put in a ball and chain on each leg, and his legs had swollen up and then turned blue. Crandall said he pleaded with Wirz to take the leg irons off the man or he would die. Wirz would not. Crandall then pleaded with a surgeon to take the leg irons off the man, but he refused. Crandall said that later he buried this man's emaciated body when the man died. From June 23, 1864, to September 8, 1864, Crandall buried the dead. He noted that about 30 or 40 were shot, and it became so common that he didn't even take notice. Crandall told of a man named Austin who came into the prison and wanted to see his brother, who was also incarcerated in Andersonville. For this request, the man was put into the spread-eagle stocks, where the man was held by his neck, feet and hands. Later Crandall was called again to testify about a man named

James Williamson, after many months of promises, was promoted to brevet brigadier-general in December of 1864. By springtime, he was raised to brigadier-general of the volunteers. Dodge and his allies worked hard at getting these promotions for Williamson (courtesy State Historical Society of Iowa, Des Moines).

Armstrong who was put spread-eagle into the stocks by a guard named Duncan. Duncan then robbed the man of some greenbacks and a picture of Armstrong's sister or mother. Duncan refused to give the picture back. Crandall was again called to testify by Wirz's defense lawyer. Crandall testified that in August of 1864, a Lt. Davis was in charge of the camp. Crandall said things were about the same as when Wirz was in command, and Wirz came back in September of 1864. Another 4th Iowa Infantry soldier from Winterset, Iowa, Charles E. Tibbles, who also had been a prisoner in Andersonville at the same time as Crandall, testified. Tibbles enlisted in July of 1861 and was captured like Crandall in March of 1864 in Claysville, Alabama. He was mustered out of service in December of 1864 in Davenport. Tibbles testified that he had seen Wirz grab men by the throat, put a gun to their heads and threaten to blow their brains out. Tibbles stated, however, that he had never seen Wirz shoot anyone. Tibbles said he had to bury the dead. One day he escaped and made it 40 miles from Andersonville before being recaptured. Tibbles said there were four men in his escape group, and when they got to Andersonville, Wirz saw them and told someone to get his revolver. He asked Tibbles and his other escapees, "Where's Crandall? Where is Bill Crandall?" Wirz told the keeper of the escape hounds, that he would give $500 if they found Bill Crandall. Wirz then told Tibbles and his other escapees, "You young sons of bitches of Yankees. I'll make you smell hell before the night." Wirz put Tibbles and the other escapees in the graveyard on half rations and then put them in the stocks at night. Wirz told the guards of Tibbles and the others that if they didn't work, they were to put them on the dead pile and bury them alive. Sometime later, Tibbles was sent to South Carolina in a prisoner exchange.[11]

Crandall went back to Winterset and in 1868 married Lydia A. Chase. Eventually, Crandall made his way back to Whitesville, New York, where he manufactured proprietary medicines. Lydia and Wilford adopted a son, Wilford B. Crandall.[12]

The men detailed in this chapter were fortunate enough to live long lives after their service in the 4th Iowa Volunteer Infantry during the Civil War. Out of the total enlistment of 1,557 men, 115 enrolled soldiers were killed in battle or died of their battle wounds shortly after receiving them. There were 338 men who were wounded during battle. Those who died of disease while in the service of the 4th Iowa numbered 239 soldiers. Of the rest, 333 men were discharged because their wounds or diseases were too great for them to return to active duty. There were 49 P.O.W.s from the 4th Iowa. A number of the men died soon after their term of enlistment, such as Joseph Addington, who died in July of 1865, or Lewis Briggs, who was mustered out on October 6, 1864, and died less than a year later in May 19, 1865. Benjamin Talbot received a wound while in the 4th Iowa, but some believed he died some 17 years after the end of the Civil War due to this gunshot wound. Some lived quiet lives after the Civil War was over, and others moved away from Iowa, their life stories lost in the mists of history.[13]

Major-General Grenville M. Dodge was one of the most successful Union generals. After the war was over, he enjoyed even more success in the business world. After Dodge resigned from the military in May of 1866, he started on the project of a lifetime. He became the chief engineer for the transcontinental railroad. In two years, Hoxie and Durant had laid only 40 miles of railroad tracks west from Omaha. Dodge soon changed this. Dodge noted that a great deal of materials would be needed to build this historical railroad. However, Dodge had planned so well that the construction crews

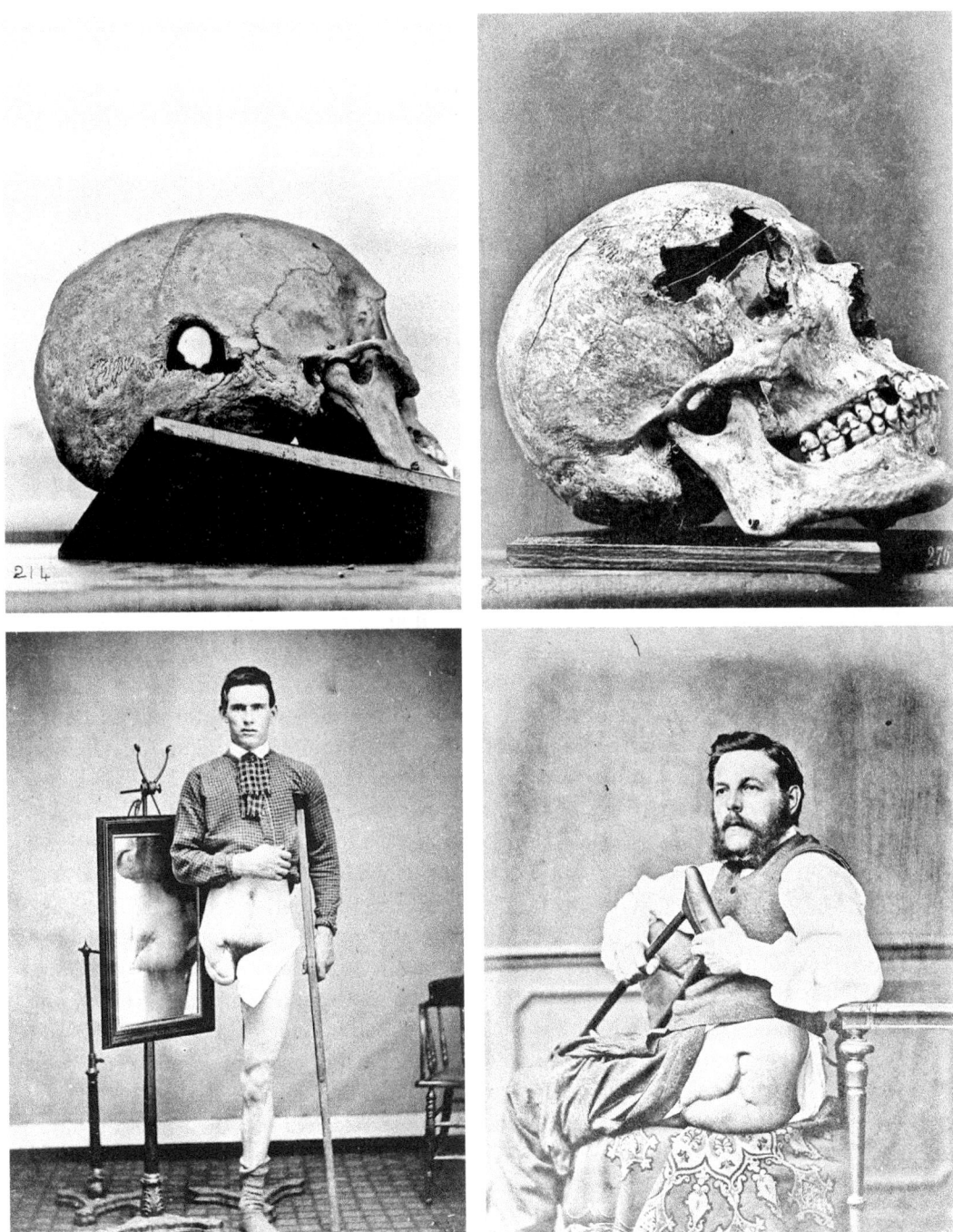

This set of surgical photographs was prepared under the supervision of the War Department, Surgeon General's Office, Army Medical Museum. The pictures show two former soldiers with amputated legs and two skulls with bullet holes in them. When these men with amputations came home from the Civil War, many had difficulty earning a living at a time when most employment opportunities depended on the ability to do manual labor (Library of Congress).

never had to wait a day for want of building materials. Dodge began laying tracks along the Platte River Valley in a rapid fashion.[14]

Incredibly, Dodge's friends urged him to run for political office even though he would have to take long absences from his railroad business. Hoxie and George C. Tichenor were especially insistent that Dodge run for Congress in the 5th Iowa Congressional District in 1866. Dodge would run as a Republican; the only trouble was that his friend John Kasson held that position and was a two-term incumbent. However, Tichenor told Dodge not to worry; they would do all the work. Tichenor, Hoxie and the publisher of the Council Bluffs *Nonpareil*, William S. Burke, all did not care for Kasson. Tichenor especially despised Kasson for promising a plum political position and then reneging on the offer. Dodge could also count on Francis Palmer, publisher of the most influential paper in Des Moines. All the soldiers coming back from the war would overwhelming support Dodge. Tichenor especially felt no qualms about destroying someone's reputation. Then Kasson handed the Dodge campaign an issue that was explosive. Kasson was going through a messy divorce for adultery, and his wife was making the divorce as public as possible. Even Kasson's wife's brother helped; he was a well-respected clergyman, the Reverend Doctor William Greenleaf Eliot, the founder of Washington University in St. Louis. Eliot would also become grandfather to well-known poet T.S. Eliot. The Reverend Eliot was only too happy to make intimate details of Kasson marriage public, including the scurrilous information that Kasson was diseased from hanging around women of ill repute.[15]

However, there were legitimate differences between Dodge and Kasson. Kasson was the lone Iowa congressman who did not believe in the voting rights of black men. Kasson also supported Andrew Johnson's policy, while the rest of the Iowa delegation believed in voting rights for blacks and did not support Johnson's policies. Dodge won the Republican nomination over Kasson. The two men never spoke to each other again. In the November general election, Dodge ran against former Union general James M. Tuttle, who was the Democratic candidate. Tuttle, while a Union general, was painted by the *Register* newspaper as being more interested in speculation on confiscated Confederate cotton than in Union victories. Dodge was out West during the fall of 1866 with his surrogates, Tichenor, Kirkwood, Williamson and Palmer campaigning for him. Dodge was in the Rockies trying to decide the best route through the area for the transcontinental railroad. Denver was the largest city in that region, but Dodge thought the route to Cheyenne and Laramie was more practical. In November, the voters back in Iowa's 5th Congressional District elected Dodge to be their congressman.[16]

Council Bluffs still did not have rail service to the town during the winter of 1866–1867. Supplies for the railroad had to be shipped by steamboats up to Omaha and then put on railcars in Omaha and transported to the work crews to the west. The Missouri River froze over during the wintertime, so building on the railroad was suspended during these months, giving Dodge the chance to go back to Washington, D.C., and attend to his congressional duties. By January 1, 1867, Dodge's crews had laid 305 miles of track. It took only a couple of months for Dodge to realize that the work of a congressman did not suit him. The constant barrage of office seekers wanting cushy government jobs and the constant streams of people wanting favors grew boring and tiresome to Dodge. As soon as he could, Dodge took leave of his congressional post and went out West to supervise the railroad construction. However, troubles with Native American warriors were threatening construction. After the Fetterman Massacre, many on the work crews wanted to go back East to safety. In addition, the town of Cheyenne was attracting gamblers, pimps, scam artists and gunfighters. Sherman refused to send out any more soldiers to protect the work crew. The cleaning up of the town of Cheyenne proved to be easier than suppressing the Native American uprisings. Sometimes Dodge organized the railroad workers who were veterans to form groups of skirmishers that went out to fight the aboriginal warriors.[17]

As if Dodge did not have enough problems on his plate, Thomas Durant began to cause even more trouble. Dodge found out that Durant was padding his requests for building materials and changing his surveys at every chance. Durant was trying to add unneeded miles to the railroad so he could overcharge the government. Dodge managed to cross the Rockies at over 8,000 feet above sea level, the highest point in the world any railroad had traversed. Durant, because Dodge was watching the company's purse strings too closely, tried to oust Dodge as head engineer. Dodge had a meeting with Grant, Sherman, and Sheridan and other notables, telling them that if Durant did not stop interfering with Dodge's work he would resign. The three generals thought the transcontinental railroad was a military necessity for the United States. They told Durant directly to leave Dodge and his work alone or the Union Pacific Railroad might lose the government's backing. Back in Washington, D.C., Dodge backed the impeachment of President Andrew Johnson. When Iowa senator James W. Grimes, one of the leading lights in the Iowa Republican Party, was one of only seven Republicans who voted not to impeach Johnson, all the Iowa newspapers and Republican newspapers condemned Grimes. Congress censured Grimes, and then he suffered from paralysis. Grimes became a *persona non grata* in Iowa and Washington politics. When Dodge and another congressman called on Grimes, the man wept at their kindness.[18]

Dodge was able to see some of the Chinese workers in action for the Central Pacific. He noted they were the "best rock workers I have seen ... very quiet, handy ... and good at almost everything they are put at." Finally, the Union Pacific met the Central Pacific at Promontory Summit, Utah, in a huge celebration. However, Durant was not finished yet with his usual skullduggery. He had not paid his workers for the last two weeks of work, so the Irish workers "captured" Durant and held him for ransom until they were paid. Dodge had to pay the poor fellows before they would let Durant go.[19]

Dodge's versatility as a businessman was in full view after the transcontinental railway was finished. Although a heavy favorite to be re-elected to Congress, Dodge did not run for congress in 1868. When work was done on the transcontinental railroad, Dodge became a supplier of goods to the native tribesmen in the West. However, it was not long before he was back in the railroad business of the Texas and Pacific Railroad. The 4th Iowa Infantry and Dodge's old XVI Corps knew that Dodge would help out the soldiers of his old units in times of trouble.[20]

Dodge's financial fortunes sometimes mirrored that of the United States. At a couple of points, Dodge's financial fortunes were at a low ebb, but he always managed to bounce back. However, Dodge was always generous to those in need. When General Grant's chief of staff, General John A. Rawlins, fell on hard times both financially and health-wise, Dodge (at the request of Grant) took Rawlins with him out West to help him recover his health, as he suffered from tuberculosis. Dodge named the Wyoming city of Rawlins after this man who Dodge considered one of the finest he had ever known. Dodge would also payoff Rawlins' mortgage on his house to help his financial situation. Dodge supported scout and mountain man Jim Bridger in his later years. Dodge also helped Grant in his later years when his health and financial conditions failed. One of the few questionable actions Dodge took after the war was his refusal to testify before Congress when the scandal surrounding Durant's Credit Mobiler exploded. The Credit Mobiler was a scheme by Durant to submit fraudulent expenses to the Federal government for payment. Although no friend of Durant, Dodge made himself scarce when congressional subpoenas were issued on this matter. William B. Allison, U.S. senator from the Hawkeye State, Iowa Republican politician James Harlan, and Vice President Schylur Colfax were all implicated in the Credit Mobiler scandal. Allison was a very good friend of Dodge's, and Dodge had known Harlan for some years. Schuyler Colfax's nomination to be Grant's vice president had been put in by Dodge at the Republican National Convention. However, Dodge was at best a very minor player in the matter and in all probability, out of loyalty to these men, he did not want to testify. Most of the 30-some politicians of both parties who were linked to the scandal had no or very little repercussions on their political careers except for Colfax, who was removed from the Republican ticket for the election of 1872. Allison went on to be re-elected U.S. senator from Iowa. In President Chester A. Arthur and President Benjamin Harrison's administrations, Allison was offered the position of secretary of the treasury and in President William McKinley's administration he was offered the position of secretary of state; all these positions Allison declined. James Harlan also suffered no repercussions. James Garfield, who at the time was a U.S. representative from Ohio, was also implicated, but eight years later he was elected president of the United States. One of Dodge's biographers tried to smear his name with the Credit Mobiler scandal, but the truth was that Durant promised Dodge a salary of $10,000 a year plus stock in the Credit Mobiler. As usual, Durant reneged on his promise to give Dodge stock in the Credit Mobiler. The only Credit Mobiler stock the Dodge family owned was through Dodge's wife Anne, who bought a small number of shares from the Union Pacific Railroad out of her own money and kept the dividends in her own accounts. Anne Dodge was

Grenville M. Dodge in his later years. After the war he was very active in the G.A.R., reunions of the Army of the Tennessee and other veteran groups. Because he outlived many of the other Union generals, he was often feted for his outstanding service in the Union army (Library of Congress).

the daughter of a successful banker. However, this same biographer brings up interesting questions about Dodge's role in the building of the railroad bridge between Council Bluffs and Omaha; but again the biographer offers no credible evidence that anything out of the ordinary happened.[21]

By the 1870s, Dodge's reputation as one of the world's greatest builders of railroads was firmly established. When German and Italian engineers were having trouble building the famous St. Gothard tunnel in the Alps, President Grant suggested they confer with Dodge on this matter. The French government conferred with Dodge on building their rail system. Later a group of investors had Dodge go overseas to study the feasibility of building a Siberian Railroad in Russia. Dodge advised against investing in the project, and this Russian rail plan failed, losing investors all their money. Later the Chinese talked to Dodge about their rail system. Dodge was able to build a large amount of railroads in Cuba before an insurrection stopped the building of this rail line. After Grant's term as president was up, he and Dodge spent a lot of time together in Paris with their families.[22]

From 1870 to 1897, Grenville Dodge was director of the Union Pacific Railroad. He held an impressive number of other positions in other railroad companies during his lifetime. Here follows a list of those positions: Dodge served as chief engineer at the Domain Land Company of Pennsylvania (the name of this company was changed to the California and Texas Railway Construction Company); he was appointed capitol commissioner by the State Legislature of Iowa; he built the Iowa School for the Deaf, which was and still is located in Council Bluffs, Iowa; he was chief engineer at the Texas and Pacific Railroad Company; he was president of the Missouri, Kansas and Texas Railroad in 1880; he was associated with the Pacific Railroad Improvement Company organized under the laws of Connecticut; he was associated with the American Railroad Improvement Company, the International Railroad Improvement Company, and the Texas and Colorado Construction Company, all three companies organized under the laws of Colorado; he was president of Oriental Construction Company; he was first agent then vice-president and director of the Fort Worth and Denver City Railway Company; he was president from 1884 to 1892 of the Des Moines Union Railroad Company; he was associated with the Colorado and Texas Construction Company, organized under the laws of the state of Iowa; he was director of the Iron Steamboat Company; he was president from 1889 to 1890 of the Denver, Texas and Fort Worth Railway Company; he was president from 1890 to 1892 of the Des Moines and Northern Railway Company; he was president of Western Industrial Company; he was the director of Wichita Valley Railway Company; he was president of the Union Pacific, Denver and Gulf Railway Company from 1891 to 1892; he was vice-president in 1909 of the Abilene and Southern Railroad; and he was builder of the Cuban Railroad from 1900 to 1903 from Santa Clara to Santiago.[23]

By 1913, of the 80 men who had been Union major-generals, only four remained alive, one of them being Major-General Grenville Dodge. Throughout the years, Dodge had been feted at banquets, conventions and meetings of the Army of the Tennessee and the Grand Army of the Republic (GAR) for his service in the Union army. When Grant's Tomb was dedicated in New York City on April 27, 1897, the Grant family asked General Dodge to be grand marshal of the event and lead the giant parade. After the

Spanish American War, President McKinley asked Dodge to head a commission to look into the conduct of the war, especially the supply of food. Dodge did his usual thorough job and compiled "Report of the Commission Appointed by the President to Investigate the Conduct of the War Department During the War with Spain." Many prominent members of Congress asked Dodge's advice on how to conduct the war against Spain. Dodge's advice against occupying the Philippine Islands proved to be prophetic. He said the occupation of the Philippines by the Americans would draw them into every war in Asia. The Iowa National Guard Camp was named Camp Dodge in his honor. Dodge, remembering the trouble he had had getting the 4th Iowa Volunteer Infantry armed and clothed, took great interest in the organization and preparedness of the Iowa National Guard.[24]

In 1869 and into 1870, General Dodge built a beautiful 14-room mansion in Council Bluffs, Iowa. However, because of his railroad building duties, the Dodge family often had to move to Texas and other locations. By 1875, the Dodge family made their home in a luxury apartment on Park Avenue in New York City, and the general had an office at Number 1 Broadway where he could better track his considerable investment portfolio and his railroad interests. The family made many trips to Europe during this time, as did many wealthy Americans. In 1906, doctors advised Dodge to slow down, and for a change the old warrior followed their advice. In 1907, Dodge longed to move back to the Plains. He and his daughter Lettie, now separated from her husband, moved back to his splendid home in Council Bluffs. Mrs. Dodge and daughter Anne remained in their comfortable apartment in New York City and visited the home in Council Bluffs usually during the springtime. During his later years General Dodge devoted himself to writing about his military career and his building of the transcontinental railroad. The general, because of his health during this time, spent the summers in Glenwood Springs, Colorado. In 1913 and 1915, Dodge had surgery for cancer. An attack of kidney stones sent the general to a specialist in New York City. However, on January 3, 1916, the first citizen of Iowa laid down for the last time. His funeral was one of the more spectacular in the Hawkeye State. The last army and department commander from the Civil War was laid to rest. His body was drawn on a caisson by six black horses, his sword and the cocked hat of a major-general positioned atop the pall; another black horse followed carrying the general's sabre at saddle side and reversed boots in its stirrups. There were 2,000 mourners in the funeral procession and an estimated 10,000 mourners along the procession route. Six hundred Iowa National Guardsmen served as guards of honor. Every military unit Dodge had commanded had a representative at the funeral, including every organization he had headed. Ruth Anne Brown Dodge, the general's beloved wife, followed him in death only nine months later.[25]

Dodge's estate was interesting. The general had already left money to Norwich University, which built and named a dormitory hall in his honor. He left trust funds for the Council Bluffs YMCA and Norwich University, and also a fund for the city of Council Bluffs for the relief of Civil War veterans, their families and charities. The Dodge estate controlled considerable amounts of town properties in Council Bluffs, Omaha, Washington, D.C., Quanah, Texas, Denver, Colorado, and Winnipeg, Canada. He also owned large tracts of land in Saskatchewan, Canada. In Texas, Dodge owned a large ranch of 13,000 acres, which he sold to John Nance Garner, vice-president under Franklin Roosevelt. There were almost 17,000 shares of stock in various corporations, plus 750 bonds, notes, mortgages and contracts. Probably the most interesting aspect of the Dodge estate was the 1,250-acre sugar-cane plantation he bought in Camaguey Province while building the railroad in Cuba. When the Fidel Castro communist government took over in 1960 and broke up large land holdings under their Agrarian Reform law, they paid for the Dodge plantation with bonds that paid 4½ percent over 20 years. The plantation was "valued" by the Castro government at $60,000 and paid an annual income into the Dodge estate of $2,000. All in all the Dodge estate was valued at three and a half million dollars at his death in 1916; it was one of the largest in Iowa at this time. Twenty-one years after the death of the last grandchild in 1984, the Grenville Dodge estate was to be divided, with one half going to the remaining heirs, one fourth to Norwich University and one fourth to the City of Council Bluffs.[26]

# Chapter Notes

## Chapter 1

1. "First Inaugural Address," *Papers of Jefferson Davis*, vol. 7, 45–51.
2. Grenville Dodge, *Biography of Major General Greenville M. Dodge: Written and Compiled by Himself at Different Times and Completed in 1914*, vol. 1, 34. Hereafter cited as CB-Dodge. Unless otherwise noted, all letters are from this collection of material.
3. Carl Sandburg, *Abraham Lincoln: The War Years, vol. 1* (New York: Harcourt, Brace, 1939), 93.
4. CB-Dodge, vol. 1, 33–34.
5. Papers of Peter Anthony Dey, Special Collections Department, University of Iowa Libraries, Biographical Notes. Hereafter cited as "Dey Papers."
6. Fred W. Lorch, "Biography of Orion Clemens," *Palimpsest* 10, no. 10 (October 1929): 353–388.
7. *New York Times*, August 1, 1862; John A. Kasson obituary, *New York Times*, May 19, 1910, John A. Kasson papers, State Historical Society of Iowa, Des Moines; "John A. Kasson Autobiography," *Annals of Iowa*, April 1915, 346–358; Edward Younger, *John A. Kasson: Politics and Diplomacy from Lincoln to McKinley* (Iowa City: Iowa State Historical Society of Iowa, 1955), 59–65, 69.
8. *New York Times*, August 1, 1862; *Metric Act of 1866 (Kasson Act)*, H.R. 596, 15 USC 204 et seq., U.S. Code Title 15, Commerce and Trade, chapter 6, "Weights and Measures and Standard Time," subchapter, "Weights, Measure, and Standards Generally, 204 Metric System"; "John Adam Kasson, 1822–1910," Biographical Directory of the United States Congress 1774–Present, http://bioguide.congress.gov/scripts/biodisplay.pl?index=K000018 (last visited August 29, 2010).
9. Herbert "Hub" Hoxie obituary, *New York Times*, November 24, 1886; "Man of a Frontier Town," *Annals of Iowa*, January 1946, 247–248.
10. *Iowa State Register Morning Edition*, [missing month] 6, 1887, from the files at the Todd House Museum, Tabor, Iowa. The *Iowa State Register* later became the *Des Moines Register*.
11. *Fugitive Slave Act of 1850*, American Historical Documents, 1000–1904, Harvard Classics (New York: P. F. Collier, 1938), 306–312.
12. *Council Bluffs Nonpareil*, August 13 and August 20, 1859; *Council Bluffs Bugle*, n.d., 1859.
13. Abraham Lincoln, letter to G. W. Dole, G. S. Hubbard and W. H. Brown from Springfield, IL, December 14, 1859. The letter expresses Lincoln's confidence in his "faithful friend" Norman Judd. This letter appears in its entirety in Roy P. Basler, ed., *Abraham Lincoln, His Speeches and Writings: Edited with Critical and Analytical Notes* (New York: Da Capo, 2001), 508–509 (hereafter cited as *"Lincoln's Speeches and Writings." Lincoln's Complete Works*, vol. 5 (New York: Francis D. Tandy, 1905), 284. This was an expansion of the two-volume work edited by John G. Nicolay and John Hay (both were Lincoln's secretaries) published by Century Co. in New York in 1894; Albert J. Beveridge, *Abraham Lincoln, 1809–1858*, vol. 4 (Boston and New York: Houghton Mifflin; Cambridge: Riverside Press, 1928), 3, 341.
14. CB-Dodge, vol.1, 32–33.
15. The Mississippi and Missouri Railroad was later absorbed by the Chicago and Rock Island line. The Panic of 1857 and the Civil War ended most railroad building in Iowa until after the Civil War. Even by 1865 the railroad lines in Iowa were still 40 miles east of the state capital in Des Moines. The Mississippi and Missouri line ran into financial difficulties during the Civil War and on July 9, 1866, the M&M merged with the Chicago and Rock Island lines and became the Chicago, Rock Island and Pacific Railroad Company. Some of the officials with the Mississippi and Missouri Railroad were also officials with the Chicago and Rock Island line ("A Brief Historical Overview of the Chicago, Rock Island, and Pacific Railroad," originally published in the Rock Island Lines' *Yard Clerical Manual* in 1970, http://www.rits.org/www/histories/RIHistory.html [last visited July 5, 2010]); CB-Dodge, vol. 1, p. 32. The great bluesman Huddie William Ledbetter, better known as Leadbelly, in 1937 immortalized the Rock Island Line with his rendition of the song "The Rock Island Line."
16. Grenville Dodge, *Personal Recollections of President Abraham Lincoln, General Ulysses S. Grant and General William T. Sherman* (Council Bluffs, IA: Monarch, 1914), 8–9.
17. CB-Dodge, vol. 1, 32–33. Dodge, *Personal Recollections*, 11.
18. CB-Dodge, vol. 1, 33; Dodge, *Personal Recollections*, 11–12.
19. Wiley Britton, *The Civil War on the Border: 1861–1862* (New York, London: G. P. Putnam's Sons, 1891), 6; Eugene Morrow Violette, *A History of Missouri* (Boston, New York, Chicago: D. C. Heath, 1918), 336–38.
20. Hubert (Hub) Hoxie, letter to Grenville Dodge from Dubuque, IA, April 20, 1861; Grenville Dodge, letter to wife Anne Dodge from Washington, D.C., June 18, 1861.
21. Dey Papers.
22. *Omaha Bee*, July 29, 1906.

23. Peter Dey, letter to Grenville Dodge from Iowa City, August 6, 1905, Dey Papers.
24. Samuel J. Kirkwood obituary, *New York Times*, September 3, 1894; Oswald Garrison Villard, *John Brown 1800–1859: A Biography Fifty Years After* (New York: Alfred A. Knopf, 1943; reprint), 570.
25. James Patrick Morgans, *The Underground Railroad on the Western Frontier: Escapes from Missouri, Arkansas, Iowa and the Territories of Kansas, Nebraska and the Indian Nations, 1840–1865* (Jefferson, NC: McFarland, 2010), 106 (hereafter cited as Morgans, *UGRR on Western Frontier*).
26. John Chambers, *Autobiography of John Chambers*, ed. John Carl Parrish (Iowa City: State Historical Society of Iowa, 1908), 127, 240; "John Chambers," Biographical Directory of the United States Congress 1774–Present, http://bioguide.congress.gov/scripts/biodisplay.pl?index=Cooo285 (last visited November 23, 2011); Kenneth G. Martis, *Historical Atlas of Political Parties* (New York: Macmillan, 1989), 93.
27. *The Statue Laws of the Territory of Iowa: Enacted at the First Session of the Legislative Assembly of Said Territory, Held at Burlington A.D. 1838–1839* (Dubuque, IA: Russell and Reeves, 1839); "An Act to Regulate Blacks and Mulattoes," Sec. 1, 2, 4, 5, pp. 65–66.
28. "An Act to Regulate Blacks and Mulattoes," Education Sec. 1, 181, Elections Sec. 12, 188, Militia Sec. 6, 330, Courts Sec. 38, 395, 404, Petit jurors, Sec. 1, 295.
29. John Carl Parrish, *George Wallace Jones* (Iowa City: Iowa Biographical Series, State Historical Society of Iowa, 1912), 127–28; "George Wallace Jones," Biographical Directory of the United States Congress 1774–Present, http://bioguide.congress.gov/scripts/biodisplay.pl?index=j000221 (last visited December 16, 2011).
30. Robert R. Dykstra, *Bright Radical Star: Black Freedom and White Supremacy on Hawkeye Frontier* (Cambridge, MA: Harvard University Press, 1993), 105.
31. *The War of the Rebellion: A Compilation of the Official Records of the Union and Confederate Armies* (Washington, D.C.: Government Printing Office, 1880) (hereafter cited as O.R.), series 3, vol. 1, 127–28; Dan Elbert Clark, *Samuel Jordan Kirkwood* (Iowa City: Iowa State Historical Society, 1917), 187; Allan Nevins, *War for the Union, vol. 1, 1861–1862: The Improvised War* (New York: Konecky and Konecky, 1971), 119.
32. CB-Dodge, vol. 1, 35–36.
33. Ibid., 36.
34. O.R., series 3, vol. 1, 560–61; CB-Dodge, vol. 1, 39.
35. CB-Dodge, vol. 1, 39.
36. *Council Bluffs Bugle*, July 3, 1861.
37. *Council Bluffs Nonpareil*, July 6, 1861.
38. Charles W. Durant, letter to Grenville Dodge from New York, May 9, 1861.
39. *Roster and Record of Iowa Soldiers in the War of the Rebellion: Together with Historical Sketches of Volunteer Organizations 1861–1866*, vol. 1, *1st–8th Regiments Infantry* (Des Moines, IA: Emory H. English State Printer, E. D. Chassell State Binder, 1908), 527–671 (hereafter cited as Roster Iowa Soldiers, 4th Iowa); CB-Dodge, vol. 1, 41.
40. *Roster and Record of Iowa Soldiers in the War of the Rebellion: Together with Historical Sketches of Volunteer Organizations 1861–1866, vol. 5, 22d–48th Regiments Infantry 1st Regiment African Infantry 1st–4th Batteries Light Artillery* (Des Moines: Emory H. English State Printer, E. D. Chassell State Binder, 1908), 1725, 1740; Robert Finney, *Phillips: The First 66 Years* (Bartlesville, OK: Phillips Petroleum Company, 1983), 19–20; O.R., series 3, vol. 1, 344; CB-Dodge, vol. 1, 40.
41. CB-Dodge, vol. 1, 1. In Dodge's typewritten autobiographical material, he states that he was born in Danvers, Essex County, Massachusetts. In the next paragraph he asserts that the house he was born in was in North Danvers. Dodge's secretary John Tileson Granger states that Dodge was born in Putnamville Danvers, Massachusetts (Granger, *A Brief Biographical Sketch of the Life of Major-General Grenville Dodge* [General Books, 2012; reprint], 30). Granger quotes the Phillips Genealogy written by Grenville's brother Nathan P. Dodge in which he states that Grenville was born in Danvers, Massachusetts (31).
42. CB-Dodge, vol. 1, 2. Dodge in his typewritten autobiography states his parents were married in 1827 but gives no month or day. However, Joseph Thompson Dodge declares the couple were married on November 12, 1825, not 1827 (*Genealogy of the Dodge Family of Essex County, Mass., 1629–1894* [Madison, WI: Democrat Publishing Co., 1894, 1898], vol. 1, 335). All other biographic accounts give the date as 1827.
43. CB-Dodge, vol. 1, 1.
44. Dodge, *Genealogy*, vol. 1, 335; Granger, *Brief Biographical Sketch*, 29, 30.
45. Dodge, *Genealogy*, vol. 1, 335; Granger, *Brief Biographical Sketch?*], 31.
46. Granger, *Brief Biographical Sketch*, 2.
47. CB-Dodge, vol. 1, 2–3.
48. Granger, *Brief Biographical Sketch*, 2; CB-Dodge, vol. 1, 34.
49. Gary L. Ecelbarger, *Frederick W. Lander: The Great Natural Soldier* (Baton Rouge: Louisiana State Press, 2000), 6–7.
50. Ecelbarger, *Frederick W. Lander*, 11–12; CB-Dodge, vol. 1, 3–4.
51. U.S. Congress, "Recognizing the Importance of the Role of the Lander Trail in the Settlement of the American West on the 150th Anniversary of the Lander Trail," *Congressional Record*, 110th Cong., 2nd sess. (Thursday, July 22, 2008), vol. 154, no. 122, p. S7301, Senate Resolution 623.
52. Jean Margaret Davenport Lander obituary, *New York Times*, August 4, 1903.
53. "The Late General Lander," *Harper's Weekly*, March 15, 1862, 165–66.
54. Walter W. Pyper, *Grenville Mellen Dodge and 19th Century America's Growing Pains of a Man and a Nation*, unpublished senior thesis submitted to the History Department of Princeton University in partial fulfillment of the degree of Bachelor of Arts (Council Bluffs Library, Council Bluffs, IA), 9.
55. William Arba Ellis, *Norwich University 1819–1911: Her History, Her Graduates, Her Roll of Honor*, vol. 1 (Montpelier, VT: Major-General Grenville Dodge; printed by Capital City Press, 1911), 2; Gary Thomas Lord, *History of Norwich University*.
56. Grenville Dodge, Diaries (Council Bluffs Library, Council Bluffs, IA), May 26, 1849, entry.
57. Ibid., entries for Jan. 18, 1851, and Feb. 26, 1851.
58. William L. Shea, *The Campaign for Pea Ridge: Civil War Series* (Ft. Washington, PA: Eastern National, 2001), 11.

59. Ellis, *Norwich University,* vol. 1, 107.
60. CB-Dodge, vol. 1, 4.
61. Ellis, *Norwich University,* vol. 1, v, vi.
62. Grenville M. Dodge, *How We Built the Union Pacific Railway* (Council Bluffs, IA: Monarch, 1910), 153; Otis A. Singletary, *The Mexican War* (Chicago and London: University of Chicago Press, 1967), 94–96; CB-Dodge, vol. 1, 4.
63. Railroad History Company, *History of the Illinois Central Railroad Company and Representative Employees* (Chicago: Railroad History Company, 1900), 687.
64. CB-Dodge, vol. 1, 5–8; Pyper, *Grenville Mellen Dodge,* 10.
65. CB-Dodge, vol. 1, 12.
66. Grenville Dodge, letter to Sylvanus Dodge from Peru, IL, September 14, 1851; CB-Dodge, vol. 1, 11.
67. CB-Dodge, vol. 1, 13.
68. Ibid., 14–15.
69. "Josiah Bushnell Grinnell," *Biographical Directory of the United States Congress 1774–Present,* http://bioguide.congress.gov/scripts/biodisplay.pl?index=G000478 (last visited February 21, 2013).
70. Charles E. Payne, *Josiah Bushnell Grinnell* (Iowa City: State Historical Society of Iowa, 1938), 27–28.
71. CB-Dodge, vol. 1, 15–16.
72. Ibid., 16–18.
73. James Patrick Morgans, *Letters and Reminiscences from the Iowa Frontier: John Todd and the Tabor Colony 1850–1865* (Tabor, IA: Tabor Historical Society, 2012), 185.
74. Ibid., 194.
75. William E. Ramsey and Betty Dineen Shrier, *Silent Hills Speak: A History of Council Bluffs* (Council Bluffs, IA: Council Bluffs Library Foundation, 2002), 1, 26–27, 35.
76. Pyper, *Grenville Mellen Dodge,* 12.
77. CB-Dodge, vol. 1, 18–20.
78. Grenville Dodge, letter to Sylvanus Dodge from Peru, IL, September 14, 1851; Grenville Dodge, letter to Julia Phillips Dodge, March 7, 1854; CB-Dodge, vol. 1, 21.
79. CB-Dodge, vol. 1, 21.
80. Pyper, *Grenville Mellen Dodge,* 13; CB-Dodge, vol. 1, 20–21; Morgan Kelly and Cormac O'Grada, *Market Contagion: Evidence from the Panics of 1854 and 1857,* www.economics.harvard.edu/files/faculty/98_Kelly-contagion.pdf.
81. Ellis, *Norwich University,* vol. 2, 469; *Council Bluffs Nonpareil,* October 29, 1859.
82. CB-Dodge, vol. 1, 23–26.
83. *Omaha Bee,* July 29, 1906; Melvin Randolph Gilmore, *The True Logan Fontenelle,* a publication of the Nebraska State Historical Society, vol. 19, ed. Albert Watkins (n.p.: Nebraska State Historical Society, 1919), 64–65.
84. CB-Dodge, vol. 1, 26–27.
85. *Council Bluffs Nonpareil,* Sept. 2, 1906, Sept. 2, 1908, Oct. 16, 1927; *History of Pottawattamie County, Iowa* (Chicago: O. L. Baskin, 1883), 123; George G. Wright, "Chief Justice Caleb Baldwin," *Annals of Iowa,* 3rd series, 1 (Oct. 1893): 209–14; Genevieve P. Mauck, "Kanesville," *Palimpsest* 42 (Sept. 1961): 396; CB-Dodge, vol. 1, 27.
86. Peggy Rodina Larson, "New Look at the Elusive Inkpaduta," *Minnesota History Magazine,* Minnesota Historical Society, Spring 1982, 24–35.
87. CB-Dodge, vol. 1, 27–28.
88. Larson, "New Look," 31–35.
89. CB-Dodge, vol. 1, 28–32.
90. John E. Briggs, "The Removal of the Capital from Iowa City to Des Moines," *Iowa Journal of History and Politics* 14, no. 1 (Jan. 1916): 86.
91. Majority Report Special Committee, "Report on Alleged Frauds in the Location of the Capital," Commissioned by Iowa Legislature, 1858, 30, 69; *Keokuk (IA) Daily Gate City,* March 15, 1856.
92. Younger, *John A. Kasson,* 83.
93. Briggs, "Removal," 93.
94. Younger, *John A. Kasson,* 83–84.
95. CB-Dodge, vol. 1, 32.
96. Grenville Dodge, letter to Mother and Julia, from Council Bluffs, December 16, 1860.
97. James Patrick Morgans, *John Todd and the Underground Railroad: Biography of an Iowa Abolitionist* (Jefferson, NC: McFarland, 2006), 92–95.
98. Dodge, letter to Mother and Julia, December 16, 1860.
99. CB-Dodge, vol. 1, 34.

## Chapter 2

1. Grenville Mellen Dodge, *A Sketch of the Life and Services of Brigadier and Brevet Major-General James Alexander Williamson* (Des Moines: Register and Leader, 1903), 4.
2. Ibid., 3–4.
3. Ibid.
4. *Congressional Quarterly's Guide to U.S. Elections* (Washington, D.C.: Congressional Quarterly, 1985), 45–46, 169.
5. Dodge, *Sketch of the Life,* 4.
6. William H. Lyon, "Claiborne Fox Jackson and the Secession Crisis in Missouri," *Missouri Historical Review* 58, no. 4 (July 1964); 431–41; Christopher Phillips, *Missouri's Confederate: Claiborne Fox Jackson and the Creation of Southern Identity in the Border West* (Columbia, Missouri: University of Missouri Press, 2000), 201, 230, 235–36.
7. Albert Castel, *General Sterling Price and the Civil War in the West* (Baton Rouge, LA: Louisiana State University Press, 1968), 11–16; Christopher Phillips, *The Battle of Wilson's Creek.* Civil War Series (Fort Washington, PA: Eastern National in connection with the National Park Service), 9.
8. O.R., series 1, vol. 3, chapter 10; Report of Captain Nathaniel Lyon, 1–2.
9. Castel, *General Sterling Price,* 13–14.
10. Ibid., 18–20.
11. O.R., series 1, vol. 3, chapters 10, 11; Phillips, *Battle,* 16.
12. CB-Dodge, vol. 1, 42; O.R., series 2, vol. 4, 390, 397, 500, 502, 525.
13. E. F. Ware, *The Lyon Campaign and the History of the 1st Iowa Infantry 1861* (Topeka, KS: Crane, 1907), 94–95.
14. O.R., series 1, vol. 3, chapter 10, 425; CB-Dodge, vol. 1, 43.
15. *New York Times,* September 7, 1861.
16. Ken Marks and Lisa Marks, *Hannibal, Missouri: A Brief History* (Charleston, SC: History Press, 2011), 66–67; Catherine Storz Ripley, "Golden Spike Marker Returns for a Brief Visit," Grand River Historical Society Museum, February 17, 2009, http://www.chillicothemuseum.com/press_goldenspike021709.htm. Last visited December 24, 2013.

17. Dodge, *Sketch of the Life*, 4–5.
18. CB-Dodge, vol. 1, 43.
19. Ibid., 44.
20. Ibid., 43.
21. Dodge, *Sketch of the Life*, 5.
22. *Council Bluffs Nonpareil*, October 12, 1861.
23. Dodge, *Sketch of the Life*, 6.
24. Hubert H. Wubben, *Civil War in Iowa and the Copperhead Movement* (Ames, IA: Iowa State University Press, 1980), 68, 123; *New York Times*, August 12, 1863; Benjamin F. Gue, *History of Iowa from the Earliest Times to the Beginning of the Twentieth Century*, vol. 2 (New York: Century History, 1903), 82–89.
25. Dodge, *Sketch of the Life*, 6; Roster Iowa Soldiers, 4th Iowa, 561.
26. O.R., series 1, vol. 3, chapter 10, 236–237.
27. CB-Dodge, vol. 1, insert 44.
28. Phillips, *Battle*, 9.
29. Ware, *The Lyon Campaign*, 80–81, 154–55.
30. O.R., series 1, vol. 3, chapter 10, 47–48.
31. Ware, *The Lyon Campaign*, 206, 216.
32. Phillips, *Battle*, 23–29.
33. Ware, *The Lyon Campaign*, 306–12, 320–22; Phillips, *Battle*, 32–35.
34. O.R., series 1, vol. 3, chapter 10, 115–17.
35. Albert Castel, *Civil War Kansas: Reaping the Whirlwind* (Lawrence: University of Kansas Press, 1997), 177–79, 194, 199, 226; Mark A. Plummer, *Frontier Governor: Samuel J. Crawford* (Lawrence: University Press of Kansas, 1971), 10–11, 27, 43–44, 98.
36. Phillips, *Battle*, 47–51.
37. Britton, *Civil War*, 108–09.
38. O.R., series 1, vol. 3, chapter 10, 108–09.
39. CB-Dodge, vol. 1, insert page 45.
40. Britton, *Civil War*, 120–45.
41. Ibid., 144–48.
42. O.R., series 1, vol. 3, chapter 10, 236, 533.
43. Buel Leopard and Floyd C. Shoemaker, eds., *The Messages and Proclamations of the Governors of the State of Missouri*, vol. 3 (Columbia: State Historical Society of Missouri, 1922), 349, 381; Phillips, *Missouri's Confederate*, 268–70, 295–96; Britton, *Civil War*, 153.
44. O.R., series 1, vol. 8, chapter 18, 442; *New York Times*, November 11, 1861; Grenville M. Dodge, *The Battle of Atlanta: And Other Campaigns, Address, Etc.* (Council Bluffs, IA: Monarch, 1910), 10–13; Stewart Sifakis, *Who Was Who in the Civil War* (New York, Oxford: Facts on File, 1988), 327; Britton, *Civil War*, 152.
45. O.R., series 1, vol. 3, chapter 10, 255, 366; O.R., series 1, vol. 8, chapter 18, 373, 375, 398, 408; CB-Dodge, vol. 1, 45.
46. O.R., series 1, vol. 8, chapter 18, 398, 415, 444, 492.
47. CB-Dodge, vol. 1, 44.
48. Younger, *John A. Kasson*, 128.
49. CB-Dodge, vol. 1, 45.
50. P. H. Sheridan, *Personal Memoirs of P. H. Sheridan*, vol. 1 (Cambridge, MA: Da Capo, 1992), 69–70; Paul Andrew Hutton, *Phil Sheridan and His Army* (Norman: University of Oklahoma Press, 1999), 4, 11; CB-Dodge, vol. 1, 45–46.
51. CB-Dodge, vol.1, 46–47.
52. William L. Shea and Earl J. Hess, *Pea Ridge Civil War Campaign in the West* (Chapel Hill: University of North Carolina Press, 1992), 12–13; Shea, *Campaign*, 6–8; Britton, *Civil War*, 201–03.
53. O.R., series 1, vol. 8, chapter 18, 59; Dodge, *Sketch of the Life*, 7; Dodge, *Battle of Atlanta*, 16.
54. William A. Settle, Jr., *Jesse James Was His Name* (Lincoln: University of Nebraska Press, 1977), 20–23; Cole Younger and D. McCarthy, *The Story of Cole Younger by Himself* (privately published by Thomas Coleman Younger, 1903), 8–9, 15; Daniel O'Flaherty, *General Jo Shelby: Undefeated Rebel* (Chapel Hill: University of North Carolina Press, 1954), 68, 75–88; James I. Robertson, Jr., *Common Soldier* (Fort Washington, PA: Eastern National Publishers in connection with the National Park Service, 2006), 33.
55. O.R., series 1, vol. 8, chapter 18, 611–12.
56. Albert Castel and Thomas Goodrich, *Bloody Bill Anderson: The Short Savage Life of a Civil War Guerrilla* (Mechanicsburg, PA: Stackpole, 1998), 114.
57. Shea and Hess, *Pea Ridge*, 28; CB-Dodge, vol. 1, 47.
58. O.R., series 1, vol. 8, chapter 18, 2; Shea and Hess, *Pea Ridge*, 25.
59. Shea, *Campaign*, 11; Sifakis, *Who Was Who*, 595.
60. O.R., series 1, vol. 8, chapter 18, 60–63, 68–69; Dodge, *Battle of Atlanta*, 17–18; Shea and Hess, *Pea Ridge*, 43; Shea, *Campaign*, 12–19; Henry G. Ankeny, Florence Marie Ankeny Cox, *Kiss Josey for Me!* (Santa Ana, CA: Frils Pioneer, 1974), 47. The Josey referred to in this title was Ankeny's baby son.
61. Sheridan, *Personal Memoirs*, vol. 1, 70–71; CB-Dodge, vol. 1, 47–48, insert 48.
62. Sheridan, *Personal Memoirs*, vol. 1, 72–73; CB-Dodge, vol. 1, 48.
63. O.R., series 1, vol. 8, chapter 18, 74; Britton, *Civil War*, 214–15; Shea and Hess, *Pea Ridge*, 52–58.
64. Britton, *Civil War*, 214–216; Henry Cummings, letter to his wife, March 14, 1862, Cummings Collection, State Historical Society of Des Moines, Iowa; "Henry Johnson Brodhead Cummings," *Biographical Directory of the United States Congress 1774–Present*, http://bioguide.congress.gov/scripts/biodisplay.pl?index=C000986 (last visited January 7, 2014).
65. O.R., series 1, vol. 8, chapter 18, 191; Shea and Hess, *Pea Ridge*, 66–78.
66. O.R., series 1, vol. 8, chapter 18, 198–200, 283; Dodge, *Battle of Atlanta*, 19–21; Dodge, *Sketch of the Life*, 7–8; CB-Dodge, vol. 1, 49; Shea and Hess, *Pea Ridge*, 82–84.
67. O.R., series 1, vol. 8, chapter 18, 203–05; Dodge, *Battle of Atlanta*, 20–22; Dodge, *Sketch of the Life*, 8–9.
68. Addison A. Stuart, *Iowa Colonels and Regiments: Being a History of Iowa Regiments in the War of the Rebellion* (Des Moines, IA: Mills, 1865), 383–88; Dodge, *Battle of Atlanta*, 25, 32.
69. O.R., series 1, vol. 8, chapter 18, 195–200, 284, 305.
70. O.R., series 1, vol. 8, chapter 18, 195–208; Frank Cunningham, *General Stand Waite's Confederate Indians* (Norman: University of Oklahoma Press, 1988), 55–60; Frank Wertheim and Barbara Bair, eds., *The Papers of Will Rogers: The Early Years, vol. 1, November 1879–April 1904* (Norman: University of Oklahoma Press, 1996), 47. Clement V. Rogers and his son Will were a study in contrasts. They did not get along. Clement V. Rogers was a classic in-your-face alpha male, while son Will was more laid-back and introspective.
71. O.R., series 1, vol. 8, chapter 18, 199–201, 284; CB-Dodge, vol. 1, 50; Shea and Hess, *Pea Ridge*, 110–20.

72. O.R., series 1, vol. 8, chapter 18, 199, 284; Shea and Hess, *Pea Ridge*, 140–46, 285.
73. O.R., series 1, vol. 8, chapter 18, 202–03, 283; Dodge, *Battle of Atlanta*, 24, 30, 32, 35; CB-Dodge, vol. 1, 51–52.
74. Roster Iowa Soldiers, 4th Iowa, 534; *Davenport (IA) Daily Gazette*, April 4, 1862; Dodge, *Battle of Atlanta*, 27.
75. United States Census, 1860; Shea, *Campaign*, 59–60.
76. Dodge, *Battle of Atlanta*, 30, 35; CB-Dodge, vol. 1, 53–54.
77. O.R., series 1, vol. 8, chapter 18, 193–95.

## Chapter 3

1. Robert Gaston, *Stoic Soldier*, unpublished manuscript about Alonzo Gaston, 1–3; Roster Iowa Soldiers, 4th Iowa, 534–672.
2. Morgans, *John Todd*, 45.
3. Gaston, *Stoic Soldier*, 2–3.
4. Loren Hume, *Tales of Tabor*, unpublished manuscript about life in Tabor from 1852–1865, prepared by Robert Gaston; Maria Gaston, *Reminiscences*, a record of public meetings in Tabor, Fremont County, Iowa, 100–01.
5. Morgans, *John Todd*, 119; Garrison Oswald Villard, *John Brown 1800–1859: A Biography Fifty Years After* (New York: Alfred A. Knopf, 1943), 267–68, 426–66, 556, 557, 580.
6. Gaston, *Stoic Soldier*, 2–4.
7. CB-Dodge, vol. 1, 54–55; Captain Taylor, 4th Iowa Infantry, letter to Grenville Dodge, dated July 17, 1862, Helena, AR; CB-Dodge, vol. 1, 63; Ankeny, *Kiss Josey*, 55.
8. Gaston, *Stoic Soldier*, 5.
9. John A. Miller, 1st Sergeant, Company G, 4th Iowa Infantry, letter to Thomas S. Beall, Mt. Ayr, IA, December 3, 1862, Special Collections, University of Arkansas Library; James A. Williamson, letter to Grenville Dodge from Helena, Arkansas, November 24, 1862; *Report of the Proceedings of the Society of the Army of the Tennessee Meetings at Columbus, Ohio, 1909, Toledo, Ohio, 1910, Council Bluffs, Iowa, 1911* (Cincinnati, OH: Ebel, 1913), 210. Grenville Dodge was president of the organization.
10. Gaston, *Stoic Soldier*, 5.
11. CB-Dodge, vol. 1, 55–56; Sheridan, *Personal Memoirs*, vol. 1, 91–100.
12. CB-Dodge, vol. 1, 57–58; Grenville Dodge, letter to his wife Anne Brown Dodge, June 8, 1862.
13. O.R., series 2, vol. 4, 290–91; CB-Dodge, vol. 1, 58–60.
14. O.R., series 1, vol. 17, chapter 29, part 1, 29–30, 34–35; *Emancipation Proclamation 1863*. American Historical Documents, 1000–1904. Harvard Classics (New York: P. F. Collier, 1938), 323–25.
15. Biographical notes, John Milton Thayer Papers, Nebraska State Historical Society.
16. Gaston, *Stoic Soldier*, 6–7; Dodge, *Sketch of the Life*, 11.
17. Gaston, *Stoic Soldier*, 7–8.
18. Winston Groom, *Vicksburg 1863* (New York: Alfred A. Knopf, 2009), 203–14; John Y. Simon, *The Personal Memoirs of Julia Dent Grant (Mrs. Ulysses S. Grant)* (Ulysses S. Grant Association: 1975), 107; "The Two Julias," *New York Times*, February 14, 2013.
19. O.R., series 1, vol. 17, chapter 29, part 1, "Reports," 658–60; Gaston, *Stoic Soldier*, 9.
20. O.R., series 1, vol. 17, chapter 29, part 1, "Reports," 658–60; Dodge, *Sketch of the Life*, 11–12; Roster Iowa Soldiers, 4th Iowa, 529; Stuart, *Iowa Colonels*, 119–20.
21. O.R., series 1, vol. 17, chapter 29, part 1, "Reports," 659–60; Dodge, *Sketch of the Life*, 11–12; Roster Iowa Soldiers, 4th Iowa, 529; Stuart, *Iowa Colonels*, 119–20.
22. Gaston, *Stoic Soldier*, 10–11.
23. Ibid., 11.
24. Groom, *Vicksburg*, 227–28.
25. O.R., series 1, vol. 17, chapter 29, part 1, "Reports," 769–70; Groom, *Vicksburg*, 227–28; Gaston, *Stoic Soldier*, 13–14.
26. Dodge, *Sketch of the Life*, 12–13; Groom, *Vicksburg*, 228–29; Gaston, *Stoic Soldier*, 13–14.
27. Gaston, *Stoic Soldier*, 14–16; Dodge, *Sketch of the Life*, 11.
28. Dodge, *Sketch of the Life*, 13–14; Groom, *Vicksburg*, 149–50; Allan Nevins, *War for the Union, 1862–1863: War Becomes Revolution* (New York: Konecky and Konecky, 1960), 412–13.
29. Nevins, *War, 1862–1863*, 463.
30. O.R., series 1, vol. 24, chapter 36, part 1, "Reports," 73–74; Dodge, *Sketch of the Life*, 13.
31. Dodge, *Sketch of the Life*, 13.
32. Nevins, *War, 1862–1863*, 519, 523.
33. O.R., series 1, vol. 24, chapter 36, part 1, "Reports," 506–10; Roster Iowa Soldiers, 4th Iowa, 529.
34. O.R., series 1, vol. 24, chapter 36, part 1, "Reports," 83; Dodge, *Sketch of the Life*, 14; Roster Iowa Soldiers, 4th Iowa, 529.
35. Nevins, *War, 1862–1863*, 426.
36. O.R., series 1, vol. 24, chapter 36, part 1, "Reports," 86, 721–22, 756–57, 770–71.
37. Dodge, *Sketch of the Life*, 10.
38. CB-Dodge, vol. 1, 59.
39. Stephen W. Sears, *George B. McClellan: The Young Napoleon* (New York: Ticknor and Fields, 1988), 107–109, 179; William B. Feis, *Grant's Secret Service: The Intelligence War from Belmont to Appomattox* (Lincoln: University of Nebraska Press, 2002), 129–32.
40. Edward H. Bonekemper III, *A Victor, Not a Butcher: Ulysses S. Grant's Overlooked Military Genius* (Washington, D.C.: Regnery, 2004), 154.
41. H. Donald Winkler, *Stealing Secrets: How a Few Daring Women Deceived Generals, Impacted Battles, and Altered the Course of the Civil War* (Naperville, IL: Sourcebooks, 2010), 287; *Richmond (VA) News Leader*, January 7, 1959; Brent Hamilton Ponsford, *Major-General Grenville M. Dodge: Intelligence Operations During the Civil War*, unpublished manuscript, Iowa State University, 1976; Dodge, *Personal Recollections*, 50–53.
42. Dodge, *Personal Recollections*, 50–51.
43. Thomas Cockrell and Michael B. Ballard, eds., *Chickasaw, A Mississippi Scout for the Union: The Civil War Memoirs of Levi H. Naron* (Baton Rouge: Louisiana State University Press, 2005), 1–9.
44. CB-Dodge, vol. 1, 64, 72.
45. CB-Dodge, vol. 1, 65–66.
46. James A. Williamson, letter to Grenville Dodge, from Helena, AR, July 29, 1862; Grenville Dodge, letter to his brother Nathan P. Dodge, Council Bluffs, IA, from Trenton, TN, August 3, 1862; Grenville Dodge,

letter to Iowa governor Kirkwood, Des Moines, IA, from Trenton, TN, dated August 4, 1862; CB-Dodge, vol. 1, 66–68.

47. CB-Dodge, vol. 1, 70.

48. O.R., series 1, vol. 18, chapter 29, part 1, "Reports," 26–27, 29–30, 31–32, 54–55, 148, 300, 460, 475–76, 541–42; Dodge, *Personal Recollections*, 45, 48; CB-Dodge, vol. 1, 77; Granger, *Brief Biographical Sketch*, 7.

49. O.R., series 1, vol. 18, chapter 29, part 1, "Reports," 547–75, 591; Dodge, *Personal Recollections*, 48; "Death of General Forrest," *New York Times*, October 30, 1877; CB-Dodge, vol. 1, 83; Feis, *Grant's Secret Service*, 132.

50. O.R., series 1, vol. 24, chapter 36, part 1, "Reports," 27; *New York Times*, February 19, 1863; *New York Times*, March 17, 1863; CB-Dodge, vol. 1, 94.

51. Dodge, *Battle of Atlanta*, 111–15; Dodge, *Personal Recollections*, 52.

52. Dodge, *Battle of Atlanta*, 114.

53. O.R., series 1, vol. 23, chapter 35, part 1, "Reports," 243–46, 250–51, 253–58, 281–87, 293–94; Dodge, *Battle of Atlanta*, 114–26; CB-Dodge, vol. 1, 98–102.

54. George Sibley Johns, *Philip Henson, the Southern Union Spy: The Hitherto Unknown Record of a Hero of the War of the Rebellion* (St. Louis: Dixon-Jones, 1887; Google reprint), 26, 31–32, 35–36.

55. Harnett T. Kane, *Spies for the Blue and Gray* (Garden City, NY: Hanover House, 1954), 193–200; Cockrell and Ballard, *Chickasaw*, 87, 100–02, 106, 109; Johns, *Philip Henson*, 44–45.

56. Grenville Mellen Dodge and William Tecumseh Sherman, paper read before the Society of the Army of the Tennessee at its 21st Annual Reunion at Toledo, OH, Sept. 15, 1888, 16–17; Dodge, *Personal Recollections*, 14–17; CB-Dodge, vol. 1, 101–03.

57. CB-Dodge, vol. 1, 104–05.

58. Ibid., 105–07.

59. O.R., series 1, vol. 24, chapter 36, part 1, 152–53; CB-Dodge, vol. 109; *New York Times*, June 1, 1863.

60. O.R., series 1, vol. 24, chapter 36, part 3, 419; *New York Times*, June 27, 1863; Dodge, *Sketch of the Life*, 14.

61. *New York Times*, May 3, 1863; *New York Times*, May 10, 1863; Allan Nevins, *War for the Union 1863–1864: The Organized War* (New York: Konecky and Konecky, 1971), 60–61; Ankeny, *Kiss Josey*, 138.

62. John C. Pemberton, *Pemberton: Defender of Vicksburg* (Chapel Hill: University of North Carolina Press, 2002), 237; O.R., series 1, vol. 24, chapter 36, part 2, 152; O.R., series 1, vol. 24, chapter 36, part 3, 476–79; Roster Iowa Soldiers, 4th Iowa, 529; *New York Times*, July 8, 1863; Ulysses S. Grant, *Personal Memoirs* (Cleveland, OH: World, 1952), 295.

63. A. A. Hoehling, *Vicksburg: 47 Days of Siege* (Mechanicsburg, PA: Stackpole, 1996), 276.

64. Nevins, *War, 1863–1864*, 72.

65. O.R., series 1, vol. 24, chapter 36, part 3, 471, 473–74, 491, 524, 529, 532; Roster Iowa Soldiers, 4th Iowa, 529; Groom, *Vicksburg*, 416–17; Ankeny, *Kiss Josey*, 176.

66. Kane, *Spies*, 200–01; CB-Dodge, vol. 1, 110–11; Johns, *Philip Henson*, 31–32, 35–36, 37.

67. *New York Times*, May 3, 1863; CB-Dodge, vol. 1, 114–15; Nevins, *War, 1863–1864*, 185–92.

68. CB-Dodge, vol. 1, 115–16; Evan S. Connell, *Son of the Morning Star* (San Francisco: North Point, 1984), 281–83.

69. CB-Dodge, vol. 1, 112–14.

70. O.R., series 1, vol. 31, chapter 43, part 2, 22; Roster Iowa Soldiers, 4th Iowa, 529; Dodge, *Sketch of the Life*, 15.

71. *New York Times*, September 21, 1863; *New York Times*, September 22, 1863; *New York Times*, October 21, 1863; *New York Times*, October 22, 1863; *New York Times*, October 25, 1863; Nevins, *War, 1863–1864*, 187–205; CB-Dodge, vol. 1, 115.

72. O.R., series 1, vol. 31, chapter 43, part 1, 17–22, 24; Roster Iowa Soldiers, 4th Iowa, 530; Dodge, *Sketch of the Life*, 15.

73. O.R., series 1, vol. 31, chapter 43, part 2, 599–600, 613–14; Roster Iowa Soldiers, 4th Iowa, 530; Dodge, *Sketch of the Life*, 16; *New York Times*, November 26, 1863.

74. O.R., series 1, vol. 31, chapter 43, part 2, 600–06, 613–19; Roster Iowa Soldiers, 4th Iowa, 530; Dodge, *Sketch of the Life*, 16; *Page County (IA) History* (Des Moines: Iowa Historical, 1880), 643; *New York Times*, November 26, 1863.

75. Dodge, *Sketch of the Life*, 17–18; Roster Iowa Soldiers, 4th Iowa, 530, 563, 565, 653; Stuart, *Iowa Colonels*, 117; Ankeny, *Kiss Josey*, 193–94, 197, 214.

76. CB-Dodge, vol. 1, 118–20.

77. CB-Dodge, vol. 1, 121; Varina Davis, *Jefferson Davis: A Memoir by His Wife*, vol. 2 (Mount Pleasant, SC: Nautical and Aviation, 1991; reprint) 535; Johns, *Philip Henson*, 35–36.

78. Cockrell and Ballard, *Chickasaw*, 106–20.

79. O.R., series 1, vol. 31, chapter 43, part 3, 69, 80, 90; CB-Dodge, vol. 1, 123–24; Cockrell and Ballard, *Chickasaw*, 122.

80. O.R., series 1, vol. 31, chapter 43, part 1, 704–05, 747, 761; O.R., series 1, vol. 31, chapter 43, part 3, 131, 152–53, 179, 220; CB-Dodge, vol. 1, 124–25; Cockrell and Ballard, *Chickasaw*, 123; Dodge, *Personal Recollections*, 138.

81. O.R., series 1, vol. 31, chapter 43, part 3, 98–99, 102; Grant, *Personal Memoirs*, 322–23; CB-Dodge, vol. 1, 125–28; Dodge, *Personal Recollections*, 58, 138–39.

82. O.R., series 1, vol. 31, chapter 43, part 3, 210. Grant, *Personal Memoirs*, 244–45; CB-Dodge, vol. 1, 126–29; Dodge, *Personal Recollections*, 138; Dodge, *Battle of Atlanta*, 165–68.

83. Morgans, *UGRR on Western Frontier*, 20–21, 29, 79, 83–84, 109–10, 187; Frederick H. Dyer, *A Compendium of the War of the Rebellion* (Des Moines, IA: Dyer, 1908), 144, 702, 784, 856, 1183; W. S. Burke, *Official Military History of Kansas Regiments* (Leavenworth, KS: W. S. Burke, 1870), 151–58; Don Russell, *The Lives and Legends of Buffalo Bill* (Norman: University of Oklahoma Press, 1960), 55–72, 185–88, 285–310; CB-Dodge, vol. 1, 131.

84. O.R., series 1, vol. 31, chapter 43, part 3, 203; Cincinnati *Gazette*, December 8, 1863; *New York Times*, April 4, 1915; Dodge, *Battle of Atlanta*, 165–70; CB-Dodge, vol. 1, 131–34; Cockrell and Ballard, *Chickasaw*, 127–30. In Naron's version he had captured Davis. Dodge said it was Hensal of the 7th Kansas Cavalry (Sam Davis Home and Museum, "Who Was Sam Davis?" http://www.samdavishome.org/HISTORY_SAMDAVIS.php). Kane, *Spies*, 252–62.

85. O.R., series 1, vol. 31, chapter 43, part 3, 261–

62; Dodge, *Personal Recollections*, 62; CB-Dodge, vol. 1, 161–62, 167.
   86. O.R., series 1, vol. 31, chapter 43, part 1, 593, 733, 779; O.R., series 1, vol. 31, chapter 43, part 2, 31–43, 125; O.R., series 1, vol. 31, chapter 43, part 3, 12–14, 21, 45, 120, 160, 210–11, 220, 251–52, 308, 412–14; CB-Dodge, vol. 1, 140–41, 148.
   87. Dodge, *Personal Recollections*, 139–42; CB-Dodge, vol. 1, 144–46.
   88. Nathan P. Dodge, letter to Grenville Dodge from Council Bluffs, IA, March 25, 1864; CB-Dodge, vol. 1, 141, 162–63.
   89. O.R., series 1, vol. 32, chapter 44, part 1, 173–79, 350–51; Johns, *Philip Henson*, 58–61; Kane, *Spies*, 201–04; *New York Times*, February 21, 1863; CB-Dodge, vol. 1, 152.
   90. Johns, *Philip Henson*, 63–68; Kane, *Spies*, 204–07.
   91. O.R., series, vol. 38, chapter 50, part 1, 61; Dodge, *Personal Recollections*, 143; *New York Times*, March 15, 1864; Alan Nevins, *War for the Union 1864–1865: The Organized War to Victory* (New York: Konecky and Konecky, 1971), 6–7.
   92. O.R., series 1, vol. 32, chapter 44, part 1, 7, 15–16, 117–20, 492; *New York Times*, March 15, 1864; CB-Dodge, vol. 1, 154, 172.
   93. O.R., series 1, vol. 38, chapter 50, part 4, 16; Dodge, *Personal Recollections*, 145–46.

# Chapter 4

   1. O.R., series 1, vol. 38, chapter 50, part 1, 61, 63, 103; O.R., series 1, vol. 32, chapter 44, part 1, 497–98; Dodge, *Personal Recollections*, 146; Roster Iowa Soldiers, 4th Iowa, 538, 549, 626; CB-Dodge, vol. 1, 186–87, 196.
   2. O.R., series 1, vol. 38, chapter 50, part 1, 64; Robert Underwood Johnson and Clarence C. Buel, eds., "The Struggle for Atlanta," in *Battles and Leaders of the Civil War*, vol. 4 (New York: Century, 1888), 294, 299; Dodge, *Personal Recollections*, 146–47; Albert Castel, *Decision in the West: Atlanta Campaign of 1864*, Modern War Studies (Lawrence: University Press of Kansas, 1992), 139.
   3. O.R., series 1, vol. 38, chapter 50, part 1, 63, part 3, 113; Stuart, *Iowa Colonels*, 121; Dodge, *Sketch of the Life*, 18; "John Alexander Logan," *Biographical Directory of the United States Congress 1774–Present*, http://bioguidecongress.gov/scripts/biodisplay.pl?index=L000403.
   4. O.R., series 1, vol. 38, chapter 50, part 3, 32–33, 151–12; part 4, 184–85, 195–96, 212–13, 218; *New York Times*, May 17, 1864; Dodge, *Sketch of the Life*, 18; CB-Dodge, vol. 1, 205–09; Castel, *Decision in the West: Atlanta*, 137.
   5. O.R., series 1, vol. 38, chapter 50, part 4, 232; CB-Dodge, vol. 1, 210.
   6. CB-Dodge, vol. 1, 215; "Military Pay," Civil War Trust, http://www.civilwar.org/education/history/warfare-and-logistics/logistics/pay.html; Dodge, *Personal Recollections*, 148–49.
   7. CB-Dodge, vol. 1, 208–12.
   8. O.R., series 1, vol. 32, chapter 44, part 3, 828–30; Johns, *Philip Henson*, 69–72; Kane, *Spies*, 207–08; CB-Dodge, vol. 1, 181–82, 184.
   9. Johns, *Philip Henson*, 70–80; Kane, *Spies*, 206–09; CB-Dodge, vol. 2, 336.

   10. O.R., series 1, vol. 38, chapter 50, part 3, 18, 23; CB-Dodge, vol. 1, 211–14.
   11. CB-Dodge, vol. 1, 196–97.
   12. O.R., series 1, vol. 38, chapter 50, part 3, 129–31; Dodge, *Sketch of the Life*, 18; *New York Times*, May 30, 1864; Mary Bobbitt Townsend, *Yankee Warhorse: A Biography of Major-General Peter Osterhaus* (Columbia: University of Missouri, 2010), 154; Ankeny, *Kiss Josey*, 230.
   13. O.R., series 1, vol. 38, chapter 50, part 3, 103; Stuart, *Iowa Colonels*, 196–99, 453–60, 461–66, 467–74; Roster Iowa Soldiers, 4th Iowa, 430.
   14. O.R., series 1, vol. 32, chapter 44, part 3, 411; O.R., series 1, vol. 38, chapter 50, part 1, 23–24; Michael B. Ballard, *The Civil War in Mississippi: Major Campaigns and Battles* (Jackson: University Press of Mississippi, 2011), 197–219; CB-Dodge, vol. 1, 219; *New York Times*, March 27, 1864; *New York Times*, April 1, 1864; *New York Times*, April 14, 1864; *New York Times*, April 15, 1864; *New York Times*, April 16, 1864; *New York Times*, April 18, 1864.
   15. O.R., series 1, vol. 38, chapter 50, part 3, 19–20, 37–38, 99–100, 156; O.R., series 1, vol. 38, chapter 50, part 1, 69; CB-Dodge, vol. 1, 221–22, 227–28; *New York Times*, July 2, 1864; *New York Times*, July 4, 1864; Albert Castel, *The Campaign for Atlanta* (Fort Washington, PA: Eastern National Publishers in connection with the National Park Service, 1996), 26–31; Nevins, *War, 1864–1865*, 56–57.
   16. Castel, *Campaign for Atlanta*, 5.
   17. O.R., series 1, vol. 38, chapter 50, part 3, 617; Castel, *Campaign for Atlanta*, 27.
   18. O.R., series 1, vol. 32, chapter 44, part 3, 409–11; George W. Morgan, letter to H. V. Boynton dated October 8, 1892, from Mt. Vernon, OH. Ironically, Sherman blamed Morgan for the debacle at Chickasaw Bayou in which the 4th Iowa received fire from almost all of the Confederate army. U. S. Grant, letter to William T. Sherman dated April 4, 1864; U. S. Grant, letter to William T. Sherman dated April 19, 1864; CB-Dodge, vol. 1, 225–26.
   19. CB-Dodge, vol. 1, 221; C. Walter Cross, *"Cry Havoc": A History of the 49th Tennessee Volunteer Infantry Regiment* (Franklin, TN: Hillsboro, 2004), 13–17.
   20. CB-Dodge, vol. 1, 230.
   21. O.R., series 1, vol. 38, chapter 50, part 3, 50, 38, 566; O.R., series 1, vol. 38, chapter 50, part 1, 70; CB-Dodge, vol. 1, 230–35; Dodge, *Personal Recollections*, 149–52; *New York Times*, July 6, 1864; Oliver Otis Howard, *Autobiography of Oliver Otis Howard, Major General United States Army*, vol. 1 (New York: Baker and Taylor, 1907), 602.
   22. CB-Dodge, vol. 1, 230; Sifakis, *Who Was Who*, 636–37.
   23. CB-Dodge, vol. 1, 236.
   24. *New York Times*, May 16, 1864; *New York Times*, June 11, 1864; Nevins, *War, 1864–1865*, 57, 196–98.
   25. Dodge, *Personal Recollections*, 152; John P. Dyer, *The Gallant Hood* (New York: Konecky and Konecky, 1993), 251–52; Castel, *Decision in the West: Atlanta*, 62; Richard M. McMurry, *John Bell Hood and the War for Southern Independence* (Lincoln: University of Nebraska Press, 1992), 83; Steven E. Woodworth, *Jefferson Davis and His Generals: The Failure of Confederate Command in the West*, Modern War Studies (Lawrence: University Press of Kansas, 1990), 271; CB-Dodge, vol. 1, 237–38.

26. O.R., series 1, vol. 38, chapter 50, part 3, 203, 369; O.R., series 1, vol. 38, chapter 50, part 1, 72; Dodge, *Battle of Atlanta*, 39–40; CB-Dodge, vol. 1, 238–39; Castel, *Campaign for Atlanta*, 35–39.

27. O.R., series 1, vol. 38, chapter 50, part 1, 73; O.R., series 1, vol. 38, chapter 50, part 3, 371–72; Sifakis, *Who Was Who*, 613; Dodge, *Battle of Atlanta*, 42; Dodge, *Personal Recollections*, 153; Castel, *Campaign for Atlanta*, 41.

28. O.R., series 1, vol. 38, chapter 50, part 1, 73–74; O.R., series 1, vol. 38, chapter 50, part 3, 371; Dodge, *Battle of Atlanta*, 40–44; Dodge, *Personal Recollections*, 153–56; CB-Dodge, vol. 1, 244–45; *New York Times*, July 24, 1864; *New York Tribune*, August 4, 1864; *New York Tribune*, August 8, 1864.

29. O.R., series 1, vol. 38, chapter 50, part 1, 73–75; Dodge, *Personal Recollections*, 154–57; Dodge, *Battle of Atlanta*, 42–44; CB-Dodge, vol. 1, 245; *New York Times*, August 1, 1864; Dyer, *Gallant Hood*, 261.

30. O.R., series 1, vol. 38, chapter 50, part 3, 139–40; O.R., series 1, vol. 38, chapter 50, part 1, 75; Dodge, *Sketch of the Life*, 18–19; Roster Iowa Soldiers, 4th Iowa, 531; CB-Dodge, vol. 1, 247–50; Dodge, *Battle of Atlanta*, 59–60.

31. O.R., series 1, vol. 38, chapter 50, part 3, 140, 157–58; Dodge, *Sketch of the Life*, 19.

32. O.R., series 1, vol. 38, chapter 50, part 1, 23; Dodge, *Personal Recollections*, 157–61, 167; Grenville Dodge, letter to Anne Dodge, Council Bluffs, IA, from near Atlanta, GA, August 4, 1864; William Tecumseh Sherman, *The Memoirs of General W. T. Sherman*, vol. 2 (New York: D. Appleton, 1875), 384; CB-Dodge, vol. 1, 256–57, 263.

33. O.R., series 1, vol. 38, chapter 50, part 5, 252–53; CB-Dodge, vol. 1, 250–53; "Proceedings of the General Court-Martial of Thomas W. Sweeny Convened at Louisville, Kentucky December 3, 1864"; Sifakis, *Who Was Who*, 636–37; Jack Morgan, *Through American and Irish Wars: The Life and Times of General Thomas W. Sweeny, 1820–1892* (Kildare, Ireland: Irish Academic Press, 2006), 102–04, 134–35.

34. O.R., series 1, vol. 38, chapter 50, part 3, 40–42, 642, 1037–38; O.R., series 1, vol. 38, chapter 50, part 5, 568; Dodge, *Sketch of the Life*, 19; Castel, *Campaign for Atlanta*, 43–44; CB-Dodge, vol. 1, 259, 261–63.

35. O.R., series 2, vol. 7, 791–92; Castel, *Campaign for Atlanta*, 44–45; Albert Castel, *Articles of War: Winners, Losers, and Some Who Were Both in the Civil War* (Mechanicsburg, PA: Stackpole, 2001), 114–24; Castel, *Decision in the West: Atlanta*, 436–38. Ironically, General George Stoneman's name was practically forgotten in the mists of history except for a time in the music boom of the late 1960s. Canadian-born songwriter and musician Robbie Robertson wrote of Stoneman in his hit song "The Night They Drove Old Dixie Down." Robertson, whose mother was of the Mohawk First Nations People and whose father was Jewish, first heard live music on the Six Nations Reservation in Canada where his mother was raised. Robertson's song was recorded in 1969 by the group The Band and was a result of Robertson being in the American South for the first time and hearing over and over the phrase "the south will rise again." The lead singer of The Band, Levon Helm, who was raised in Turkey Scratch, Arkansas, gave the song an air of authenticity with his Arkansas drawl. Others including Johnny Cash, Black Crows and the Zac Brown Band have also covered this song.

36. O.R., series 1, vol. 38, chapter 50, part 3, 487; CB-Dodge, vol. 1, 257, 260; Grenville Dodge, letter to his father Sylvanus Dodge, July 31, 1864, from near Atlanta.

37. O.R., series 1, vol. 38, chapter 50, Part 3, 487; CB-Dodge, vol. 1, 264–65; Dodge, *Personal Recollections*, 168–69; *New York Herald*, August 25, 1864; *New York Tribune*, August 25, 1864; Nathan Dodge, letter to General Grenville Dodge, August 26, 1864, from Council Bluffs, IA; Sylvanus Dodge, letter to General Grenville Dodge, August 26, 1864, from Elkhorn City, Nebraska Territory.

38. O.R., series 1, vol. 38, chapter 50, part 3, 135–36, 158–59; Dodge, *Sketch of the Life*, 18–19; Castel, *Campaign for Atlanta*, 48–53; Lincoln actually ran in 1864 under the banner of the National Union Party. The Republican Party used this name to attract War Democrats and Border State Union men. War Democrats and Border Union men would not vote for any Republican.

39. O.R., series 1, vol. 38, chapter 50, part 2, 20; O.R., series 1, vol. 38, chapter 50, part 3, 993; *New York Times*, August 31, 1864; *New York Times*, September 5, 1864; *New York Times*, September 7, 1864; *New York Times*, September 18, 1864; Castel, *Campaign for Atlanta*, 50–51.

40. Amos W. Ames, "A Diary of Prison Life in Southern Prisons," *The Annals of Iowa* 40 (Summer 1969): 1–2.

41. Sifakis, *Who Was Who*, 362–63; Ames, "Diary of Prison Life," 2–3.

42. O.R., series 2, vol. 7, 784–99; Ames, "Diary of Prison Life," 3–4.

43. Roster Iowa Soldiers, 4th Iowa, 565, 598, 627; Ames, "Diary of Prison Life," 4–5.

44. Sherman, *Memoirs*, vol. 2, 144–55; Grant, *Personal Memoirs*, 482–83.

45. Dyer, *Gallant Hood*, 272; Dodge, *Sketch of the Life*, 20; Nevins, *War, 1864–1865*, 154–57; CB-Dodge, vol. 1, 257, 260; Robertson, *Common Soldier*, 36.

46. CB-Dodge, vol. 1, 271–73, 277, 283B, 287; Dodge, *Sketch of the Life*, 20–21; Dodge, *Personal Recollections*, 76–82, 172–73.

47. CB-Dodge, vol. 1, 287–90.

48. O.R., series 1, vol. 44, chapter 56, 6–19; Dodge, *Sketch of the Life*, 21; William T. Sherman, Military Division of the Department of Mississippi, Special Field Order #120, issued November 9, 1864; Sherman, *Memoirs*, vol. 2, 165.

49. O.R., series 1, vol. 44, chapter 56, 99–100, 659; Dodge, *Sketch of the Life*, 21.

50. O.R., series 1, vol. 44, chapter 56, 6–7; Noah Andre Trudeau, *Southern Storm: Sherman's March to the Sea* (New York: HarperCollins, 2008), 508, 510; Nevins, *War, 1864–1865*, 160–61; *New York Times*, December 26, 1864.

51. O.R., series 1, vol. 42, chapter 54, part 2, 1199–1200; Ames, "Diary of Prison Life," 6.

52. Ames, "Diary of Prison Life," 7–9.

53. Ibid., 9–13.

54. O.R., series 1, vol. 47, chapter 59, part 1, 21, 47, 198, 227, 243, 264–66, 269; Dodge, *Sketch of the Life*, 21; Roster Iowa Soldiers, 4th Iowa, 542; Nevins, *War, 1864–1865*, 258–59; *New York Times*, February 18, 1865; *New York Times*, February 20, 1865; Stuart, *Iowa Colonels*, 213–14.

55. O.R., series 1, vol. 47, chapter 59, part 2, 342; O.R., series 1, vol. 44, chapter 56, 798–800; O.R., series 1, vol. 44, chapter 56, 798–800; O.R., series 1, vol. 44, chapter 56, 741; O.R., series 1, vol. 47, chapter 50, part 1, 1044; Nevins, *War, 1864–1865*, 254–62; *New York Times*, February 18, 1865; *Richmond Dispatch*, February 18, 1865.

56. O.R., series 1, vol. 44, chapter 56, 741; O.R., series 1, vol. 47, chapter 60, part 1, 329–30; CB-Dodge, vol. 1, 298–301; John Kasson, letter to Grenville Dodge, dated December 16, 1864, from Washington; James Patrick Morgans, "Furlough," *The Palimpsest: Iowa's Popular History Magazine* 60, no. 3 (May/June 1979): 66–75; Castel, *General Sterling Price*, 188–242; CB-Dodge, vol. 2, 353; Dodge, *Personal Recollections*, 173.

57. O.R., series 1, vol. 45, chapter 57, part 2, 780; O.R., series 1, vol. 44, chapter 56, 741; CB-Dodge, vol. 1, 334–37; CB-Dodge, vol. 2, 334–36; Johns, *Philip Henson*, 82–86; Kane, *Spies*, 209–12.

58. O.R., series 1, vol. 48, chapter 60, part 1, 536; CB-Dodge, vol. 1, 315–20; Brigadier General Ewing, "Order Number 10," Missouri Partisan Ranger Virtual Museum and Archives, http://www.rulen.com/partisan/order10.htm (last visited August 24, 2014); Brigadier General Ewing, "Order Number 11," Missouri Partisan Ranger Virtual Museum and Archives, http://www.rulen.com/partisan/order10.htm (last visited August 24, 2014); "Dave Leip's Atlas of U.S. Presidential Elections," elections of 1860 and 1864, http://uselectionatlas.org/ (last visited August 24, 2014); Dodge, *Personal Recollections*, 22–27; *Lincoln's Speeches and Writings*, 765–66.

59. David McCullough, *Truman* (New York: Simon & Schuster, 1992), 29–36; Settle, *Jesse James*, 26.

60. O.R., series 1, vol. 44, chapter 60, part 1, 33–34, 533, 808; CB-Dodge, vol. 1, 312–26; CB-Dodge, vol. 2, 327–30; Dodge, *Personal Recollections*, 25; Settle, *Jesse James*, 26–31.

61. O.R., series 1, vol. 1, vol. 44, chapter 60, part 1, 3, 10–11, 344–45; O.R., series 1, vol. 44, chapter 60, part 2, 42, 1084; CB-Dodge, vol. 1, 321–24; CB-Dodge, vol. 2, 337; Dodge, *Battle of Atlanta*, 64.

62. O.R., series 1, vol. 48, chapter 60, part 1, 331; Dodge, *Battle of Atlanta*, 71–73; CB-Dodge, vol. 1, 322–24; Genevieve Powlison Mauck, "Grenville Mellen Dodge, 'Destiny Beckons Westward,'" *Palimpsest Magazine*, State Historical Society of Iowa, November 1966, 448–49.

63. O.R., series 1, vol. 47, chapter 59, part 1, 266–69; O.R., series 1, vol. 47, chapter 59, part 2, 797; Stuart, *Iowa Colonels*, 414, 473; Dodge, *Sketch of the Life*, 20–21; Roster Iowa Soldiers, 4th Iowa, 530; *New York Times*, April 29, 1865; *New York Times*, May 24, 1865; *New York Times*, May 25, 1865.

64. Ames, "Diary of Prison Life," 13–14; Roster Iowa Soldiers, 4th Iowa, 563.

65. Ames, "Diary of Prison Life," 14–16.

66. O.R., series 1, vol. 48, chapter 60, part 1, 227–31, 334; O.R., series 1, vol. 48, chapter 60, part 2, 133, 159, 164, 224, 528; Settle, *Jesse James*, 30; CB-Dodge, vol. 2, 338, 345.

67. Dodge, *Personal Recollections*, 26–28; CB-Dodge, vol. 2, 343.

68. O.R., series 1, vol. 48, chapter 60, part 1, 10, 329, 335–37, 348–51; CB-Dodge, vol. 2, 326, 365, 400; Dodge, *Sketch of the Life*, 22; Dodge, *Battle of Atlanta*, 86–101.

69. O.R., series 1, vol. 48, chapter 60, part 1, 351–52; Gideon Wells, *Diary of Gideon Wells: Secretary of the Navy Under Lincoln and Johnson*, vol. 2 (New York: Houghton Mifflin, 1911), 354–55, 357; Dodge, *Battle of Atlanta*, 102–06.

70. O.R., series 1, vol. 48, chapter 60, part 1, 1160–61; CB-Dodge, vol. 2, 387; Dodge, *Battle of Atlanta*, 102–06.

71. CB-Dodge, vol. 2, 444; *Dodge City Daily Globe*, September 10, 1930; Ida Ellen Rath, *Fort Dodge, Ford County, Kansas*, Early Ford County, 1964.

72. Dodge, *Battle of Atlanta*, 100–01; E. F. Ware, *The Indian War of 1864*, introduction and notes by Clyde C. Walton (Lincoln: University of Nebraska Press, 1960), xvii, 398, 407; *Omaha Daily Herald*, January 15, 1866.

73. O.R., series 1, vol. 48, chapter 60, 332, 340; Dodge, *Battle of Atlanta*, 99–108; CB-Dodge, vol. 2, 391–92, 396–97, 466, 468, 480–82; Grenville Dodge, Diaries, Council Bluffs Library, Council Bluffs, IA, entry of September 25, 1865; Stephen E. Ambrose, *Nothing Like It in the World: The Men Who Built the Transcontinental Railroad, 1863–1869* (New York: Simon & Schuster, 2001), 131–32; Dodge, *Sketch of the Life*, 21; Younger, *John A. Kasson*, 178, 184–186.

## Chapter 5

1. Ames, "Diary of Prison Life," 16; Roster Iowa Soldiers, 4th Iowa, 563.

2. Sarah A. M. Ford, "Suffering in Silence: Post Traumatic Stress Psychological Disorders and Soldiers in the American Civil War," *Armstrong Undergraduate Journal of History* 3, no. 2 (April 2013); Damon Adams, "Study Analyzes Physical and Mental Scars of Civil War Vets," *American Medical News*, February 27, 2006, http://www.amednews.com/article/20060227/profession/302279960/7/.

3. Morgans, *UGRR on Western Frontier*, 99–102; *History of Fremont County* (Des Moines, IA: Iowa Historical, 1881), 485, 627; Roster Iowa Soldiers, 4th Iowa, 664.

4. *Tabor (IA) Beacon*, October 22, 1978; Roster Iowa Soldiers, 4th Iowa, 643.

5. Roster Iowa Soldiers, 4th Iowa, 542; John Ely Briggs, *William Peters Hepburn* (Iowa City, IA: State Historical Society of Iowa, 1919), 133–39; "Albert R. Anderson," *Biographical Directory of the United States Congress 1774–Present*, http://bioguide.congress.gov/scripts/biodisplay.pl?index=Cooo285 (last visited September 28, 2014); *New York Times* September 26, 1884; *History of Taylor County, Iowa* (Chicago: S. J. Clarke, 1910), 137.

6. James P. Flick, *Biographical Directory of the United States Congress 1774–Present*, http://bioguide.congress.gov/scripts/biodisplay.pl?index=Cooo285 (last visited September 28, 2014); *History of Taylor County, Iowa* (Chicago: S. J. Clarke, 1910), 372; Roster Iowa Soldiers, 4th Iowa, 582.

7. *History of Fremont County*, 757, 758; Roster Iowa Soldiers, 4th Iowa, 663.

8. Dodge, *Sketch of the Life*, 1–22.

9. Ibid., 22–24; Stuart, *Iowa Colonels*, 117–24; Sifakis, *Who Was Who*, 719–20.

10. Roster Iowa Soldiers, 4th Iowa, 563; N. P. Chipman, *The Tragedy of Andersonville: Trial of Captain Henry Wirz, the Prison Keeper* (Sacramento, CA: published by the author, 1911), 27, 30, 32–36, 275; obit-

uary of Lew Wallace, *New York Times*, February 16, 1905.

11. Chipman, *Tragedy of Andersonville*, 275–76, 288–89, 315; Roster Iowa Soldiers, 4th Iowa, 659.

12. John Stearns Minard and Georgia Drew Merrill, *Allegany County and Its People: A Centennial Memorial History of Allegany County, New York* (Alfred, NY: W. A. Ferguson, 1896), 608.

13. "Iowa in the Civil War: Biographies and Obituaries: Surnames beginning with the letter 'T,'" http://iagenweb.org/civilwar/biographies/biographies_t.htm; Roster Iowa Soldiers, 4th Iowa, 533, 541, 547, 660.

14. Dodge, *Union Pacific*, 16.

15. John A. Kasson obituary, *New York Times*, May 19, 1910, John A. Kasson papers, State Historical Society of Iowa, Des Moines; John A. Kasson Autobiography, *Annals of Iowa*, April 1915, 346–58; Younger, *John A. Kasson*, 204–207; *Cleveland Daily Leader*, May 4, 1866, and July 16, 1866; *Dubuque Herald*, June 20, 1866.

16. Dodge, *Union Pacific*, 21–23; Younger, *John A. Kasson*, 215–16.

17. Dodge, *Union Pacific*, 16, 36–39, 116–19.

18. Dodge, *Union Pacific*, 32–33; *New York Tribune*, April 18, 1868; *American Railroad Journal* 41 (April 25, 1868): 408; Grenville Dodge, Diaries, entries for July 23, 1868, and July 25, 1868; Dodge, *Personal Recollections*, 102–03, 187–88.

19. Dodge, *Union Pacific*, 67–68; Grenville Dodge, letter to Anne Dodge, May 2, 1869; Grenville Dodge, letter to Anne Dodge, May 6, 1869, from Ogden Utah Territory.

20. Dodge, *Union Pacific*, 23; James Harrison Wilson, *The Life of John A. Rawlins* (New York: Neale, 1916), 338; George F. Ashby, *Major-General Grenville M. Dodge (1831–1916): Maker of History in the Great West* (New York: The Newcomen Society of England, American Branch, 1947), 18.

21. Logan Douglas Trent, *The Credit Mobilier* (New York: Arno, 1961), 6; Ambrose, *Nothing Like It*, 93, 374–76; Grenville Dodge, letter to Uriah H. Painter dated January 7, 1873; "James A. Garfield, 1822–1910," *Biographical Directory of the United States Congress 1774–Present*, http://bioguide.congress.gov/scripts/biodisplay.pl?index=K000018 (last visited August 29, 2014); "William B. Allison, 1829–1908," *Biographical Directory of the United States Congress 1774–Present*, http://bioguide.congress.gov/scripts/biodisplay.pl?index=K000018 (last visited August 29, 2014); "James Harlan, 1809–1899," *Biographical Directory of the United States Congress 1774–Present*, http://bioguide.congress.gov/scripts/biodisplay.pl?index=K000018 (last visited August 29, 2014); "Schuyler Colfax, 1823–1885," *Biographical Directory of the United States Congress 1774–Present*, http://bioguide.congress.gov/scripts/biodisplay.pl?index=K000018 (last visited August 29, 2014); *New York Tribune*, February 19, 1873; *New York Sun*, September 4, 1872; *New York Times*, March 30, 1873; *Harper's Weekly*, March 15, 1873.

22. Ashby, *Dodge*, 13; Dodge, *Personal Recollections*, 107–08; author's notes on a tour of the Dodge House in Council Bluffs, Iowa.

23. Granger, *Brief Biographical Sketch*, 81–82; Genevieve Mauck Stoufer, *The Historic General Dodge House, Home of Major-General Grenville Mellen Dodge* (Council Bluffs, IA: General Ladies of the Historic Dodge House, 1981), 29.

24. *Senate Report*, 56th Congress, 1st sess., no. 221, I, 107–2233; Iowa National Guard, "History."

25. Stoufer, *Dodge House*, 12–15, 20–22.

26. Stoufer, *Dodge House*, 22–23; Genevieve Powlison Mauck, "Grenville Mellen Dodge: Last Days in Council Bluffs," *Palimpsest Magazine*, State Historical Society of Iowa, November 1966, 471–75; author's notes on a tour of the Dodge House.

# Bibliography

## Books and Articles

Ambrose, Stephen E. *Nothing Like It in the World: The Men Who Built the Transcontinental Railroad, 1863–1869.* New York, London: Simon & Schuster, 2000.

Ames, Amos W. "A Diary of Prison Life in Southern Prisons." *Annals of Iowa* 40 (Summer 1969), 1–19.

Anderson, Galusha. *The Story of a Border City During the Civil War.* Boston: Little, Brown, 1908.

Ankeny, Henry G., and Florence Marie Ankeny Cox. *Kiss Josey for Me!* Santa Ana, CA: Frils Pioneer, 1974.

Ashby, George F. *Major-General Grenville M. Dodge (1831–1916): Maker of History in the Great West.* New York, NY: The Newcomen Society of England American Branch, 1947.

Ballard, Michael B. *The Civil War in Mississippi: Major Campaigns and Battles.* Jackson, MS: University Press of Mississippi, 2011.

Basler, Roy P., ed. *Abraham Lincoln, His Speeches and Writings: Edited with Critical and Analytical Notes.* New York: Da Capo, 2001; originally published by World Publishing Co., Cleveland, OH, 1946.

Beveridge, Albert J. *Abraham Lincoln, 1809–1858.* Four vols. Boston and New York: Houghton Mifflin; Cambridge: Riverside Press, 1928.

*Biographical Directory of the United States Congress 1774–Present.* http://bioguide.congress.gov.

Bisel, Debra Goodrich. *The Civil War in Kansas: Ten Years of Turmoil.* Charleston, SC: History Press, 2012.

Bonekemper, Edward H., III. *A Victor, Not a Butcher: Ulysses S. Grant's Overlooked Military Genius.* Washington, D.C.: Regnery, 2004.

"A Brief Historical Overview of the Chicago, Rock Island, and Pacific Railroad." Originally published in the Rock Island Lines' *Yard Clerical Manual* in 1970. http://www.rits.org/www/histories/RIHistory.html. Last visited July 5, 2010.

Briggs, John E. "The Removal of the Capital from Iowa City to Des Moines." *Iowa Journal of History and Politics* 14, no. 1 (Jan. 1916): 56–95.

Briggs, John Ely. *William Peters Hepburn.* Iowa City, IA: State Historical Society of Iowa, 1919.

Britton, Wiley. *The Civil War on the Border: 1861–1862.* New York and London: G. P. Putnam's Sons, 1891.

Bruce, Henry Clay. *The New Man: Twenty-Nine Years a Slave, Twenty-Nine Years a Free Man.* Lincoln, NE: University of Nebraska Press, 1996 reprint.

Buel, Leopard, and Floyd C. Shoemaker, eds. *The Messages and Proclamations of the Governors of the State of Missouri.* Columbia, MO: State Historical Society of Missouri, 1922.

Burch, John P. *Charles W. Quantrell: A True History of His Guerrilla Warfare on the Missouri and Kansas Border During the Civil War of 1861 to 1865, as Told by Captain Harrison Trow.* Vega, Texas: n.p., 1923.

Burke, W. S. *Official Military History of Kansas Regiments.* Leavenworth, Kansas: W. S. Burke, 1870.

Castel, Albert. *Articles of War: Winners, Losers, and Some Who Were Both in the Civil War.* Mechanicsburg, PA: Stackpole, 2001.

_____. *The Campaign for Atlanta.* Fort Washington, PA: Eastern National in connection with the National Park Service, 1996.

_____. *Civil War in Kansas: Reaping the Whirlwind.* Lawrence, KS: University Press of Kansas, 1997.

_____. *Decision in the West: The Atlanta Campaign of 1864.* Modern War Studies. Lawrence, KA: University of Kansas Press, reprint 1992.

_____. *General Sterling Price and the Civil War in the West.* Baton Rouge, LA: Louisiana State University Press, 1968.

_____. *William Clarke Quantrill: His Life and Times.* New York: Frederick Fell, 1962.

Castel, Albert, and Thomas Goodrich. *Bloody Bill Anderson: The Short Savage Life of a Civil War Guerrilla.* Mechanicsburg, PA: Stackpole, 1998.

Chambers, John. *Autobiography of John Chambers.* Ed. John Carl Parrish. Iowa City: Historical Society of Iowa, 1908.

Chipman, N. P. *The Tragedy of Andersonville: Trial*

of Captain Henry Wirz, the Prison Keeper. Sacramento, CA: Published by the author, 1911.
Clark, Dan Elbert. *Samuel Jordan Kirkwood.* Iowa City, IA: State Historical Society, 1917.
Cockrell, Thomas, and Michael B. Ballard, eds. *Chickasaw, A Mississippi Scout for the Union: The Civil War Memoirs of Levi H. Naron.* Baton Rouge, LA: Louisiana State University Press, 2005.
Connell, Evan S. *Son of the Morning Star.* San Francisco, CA: North Point, 1984.
Connelley, William Elsey. *Quantrill and the Border Wars.* New York: Pageant, 1956.
Cross, C. Walter. *"Cry Havoc": A History of the 49th Tennessee Volunteer Infantry Regiment.* Franklin, TN: Hillsboro, 2004.
Cunningham, Frank. *General Stand Waite's Confederate Indians.* Norman: University of Oklahoma Press, 1988.
Davis, Varina. *Jefferson Davis: A Memoir by His Wife.* Mount Pleasant, SC: Nautical and Aviation, 1991, reprint.
Dodge, Grenville. *Biography of Major-General Grenville M. Dodge: Written and Compiled by Himself at Different Times and Completed in 1914.* Typescript, letters, and misc. documents. 6 vols. Council Bluffs, IA, library.
_____. *How We Built the Union Pacific Railway.* Council Bluffs, IA: Monarch, 1910.
_____. *Personal Recollections of President Abraham Lincoln, General Ulysses S. Grant and General William T. Sherman.* Council Bluffs, IA: Monarch, 1914.
Dodge, Grenville M. *The Battle of Atlanta: And Other Campaigns, Address, Etc.* Council Bluffs, IA: Monarch, 1910.
Dodge, Grenville Mellen. *A Sketch of the Life and Services of Brigadier and Brevet Major-General James Alexander Williamson.* Des Moines: Register and Leader, 1903.
Dodge, Joseph Thompson. *Genealogy of the Dodge family of Essex County, Mass., 1629–1894.* Madison, WI: Democrat Printing, 1894, 1898.
Dyer, Frederick H. *A Compendium of the War of the Rebellion.* Des Moines, IA: Dyer, 1908.
Dyer, John P. *The Gallant Hood.* New York: Konecky and Konecky, 1993.
Dykstra, Robert R. *Bright Radical Star: Black Freedom and White Supremacy on the Hawkeye Frontier.* Cambridge, MA: Harvard University Press, 1993.
Ecelbarger, Gary L. *Frederick W. Lander: The Great Natural Soldier.* Baton Rouge: Louisiana State Press, 2000.
Feis, William B. *Grant's Secret Service: The Intelligence War from Belmont to Appomattox.* Lincoln: University of Nebraska Press, 2002.
Finney, Robert. *Phillips: The First 66 Years.* Bartlesville, OK: Phillips Petroleum, 1983.
Gilmore, Melvin Randolph. "The True Logan Fontenelle." *Publications of the Nebraska State Historical Society,* 19 (1919), ed. Albert Watkins: 64–65.
Granger, John Tileston. *A Brief Biographical Sketch of the Life of Major-General Grenville M. Dodge.* General Books, reprint 2001. Original published in New York by Press of Styles and Cash in 1893. John Tileston Granger was Dodge's private secretary.
Gue, Benjamin F. *History of Iowa from the Earliest Times to the Beginning of the Twentieth Century.* Vol. 2. New York: Century History, 1903.
Hirshson, Stanley P. *Grenville M. Dodge: Soldier, Politician, Railroad Pioneer.* Bloomington, IN, and London: Indiana University Press, 1967.
*History of Fremont County.* Des Moines, IA: Iowa Historical, 1881.
*History of Pottawattamie County, Iowa.* Chicago: O. L. Baskin, 1883.
*History of Taylor County, Iowa.* Chicago: S. J. Clarke, 1910.
Hoehling, A. A. *Vicksburg: 47 Days of Siege.* Mechanicsburg, PA: Stackpole, 1996.
Howard, Oliver Otis. *Autobiography of Oliver Otis Howard, Major General United States Army.* Vol. 1. New York: Baker and Taylor, 1907.
Johns, George Sibley. *Philip Henson, the Southern Union Spy: The Hitherto Unknown Record of a Hero of the War of the Rebellion.* St. Louis: Dixon-Jones, 1887; Google reprint.
Johnson, Jack T. *Peter Dey: Integrity in Public Service.* Iowa City: State Historical Society of Iowa, 1939.
Johnson, Robert Underwood, and Clarence C. Buel, eds. *Battles and Leaders of the Civil War.* Vol. 4. New York: Century, 1888.
Jones, Archer. *Civil War Command and Strategy: The Process of Victory and Defeat.* New York: Free Press, 1992.
Kane, Harnett T. *Spies for the Blue and Gray.* Garden City, NY: Hanover House, 1954.
Larson, Peggy Rodina. "New Look at the Elusive Inkpaduta." *Minnesota History Magazine,* Minnesota Historical Society, Spring 1982, 24–35.
"The Late General Lander." *Harpers Weekly,* March 15, 1862, 165.
Lincoln, Abraham. *Complete Works of Abraham Lincoln.* 12 vols. New York: Francis D. Tandy, 1905. This was an expansion of the 2-vol. work edited by John G. Nicolay and John Hay (both were Lincoln's secretaries) published by Century in New York in 1894.
Lyon, William H. "Claiborne Fox Jackson and the Secession Crisis in Missouri." *Missouri Historical Review* 58, no. 4 (July 1964): 422–41.
Marks, Ken and Lisa. *Hannibal, Missouri: A Brief History.* Charleston, SC: History Press, 2011.
Martis, Kenneth G. *Historical Atlas of Political Parties.* New York: Macmillan, 1989 reprint.
Mauck, Genevieve P. "Kanesville." *Palimpsest* 42 (Sept. 1961).
Mauck, Genevieve Powlison. "Grenville Mellen

Dodge: Destiny Beckons Westward." *Palimpsest Magazine,* State Historical Society of Iowa, November 1966.

_____. "Grenville Mellen Dodge: Last Days in Council Bluffs." *Palimpsest Magazine,* State Historical Society of Iowa, November 1966.

McCullough, David. *Truman.* New York and London: Simon & Schuster, 1992.

McMurry, Richard M. *John Bell Hood and the War for Southern Independence.* Lincoln: University of Nebraska Press, 1992.

Minard, John Stearns, and Georgia Drew Merrill. *Allegany County and Its People: A Centennial Memorial History of Allegany County, New York.* Alfred, NY: W. A. Ferguson, 1896.

Morgan, Jack. *Through American and Irish Wars: The Life and Times of General Thomas W. Sweeny, 1820–1892.* Kildare, Ireland: Irish Academic Press, 2006.

Morgans, James Patrick. "Furlough." *The Palimpsest: Iowa's Popular History Magazine* 60, no. 3 (May/June 1979).

_____. *John Todd and the Underground Railroad: Biography of an Iowa Abolitionist.* Jefferson, NC: McFarland, 2006.

_____. *Letters and Reminiscences from the Iowa Frontier: John Todd and the Tabor Colony, 1850–1865.* Tabor, IA: Tabor Historical Society, 2012.

_____. *The Underground Railroad on the Western Frontier: Escapes from Missouri, Arkansas, Iowa and the Territories of Kansas, Nebraska and the Indian Nations, 1840–1865.* Jefferson, NC: McFarland, 2010.

Nast, Thomas. Credit Mobiler political cartoon. *Harper's Weekly,* March 15, 1873.

Nevins, Allan. *War for the Union. 1861–1862: The Improvised War.* New York: Konecky and Konecky, 1971.

_____. *War for the Union. 1862–1863: War Becomes Revolution.* New York: Konecky and Konecky, 1960.

_____. *War for the Union, 1864–1865: The Organized War to Victory.* New York: Konecky and Konecky, 1971.

O'Flaherty, Daniel. *General Jo Shelby: Undefeated Rebel.* Chapel Hill, NC: University of North Carolina Press, 1954.

*Page County (IA) History.* Des Moines: Iowa Historical, 1880.

Parrish, John Carl. *George Wallace Jones.* Iowa Biographical Series. Iowa City: State Historical Society of Iowa, 1912.

Payne, Charles E. *Josiah Bushnell Grinnell.* Iowa City: State Historical Society of Iowa, 1938.

Pemberton, John C. *Pemberton: Defender of Vicksburg.* Chapel Hill: University of North Carolina Press, 2002; reprint.

Perkins, Jacob R. *Trails, Rails and War: The Life of G. M. Dodge.* Indianapolis: Bobbs-Merrill, 1929.

Phillips, Christopher. *The Battle of Wilson's Creek.* Civil War Series. Fort Washington, PA: Eastern National in connection with the National Park Service, 2008.

_____. *Missouri's Confederate: Claiborne Fox Jackson and the Creation of Southern Identity in the Border West.* Columbia: University of Missouri Press, 2000.

Plummer, Mark A. *Frontier Governor: Samuel J. Crawford.* Lawrence: University Press of Kansas, 1971.

Poirier, Robert G. *By the Blood of Our Alumni: Norwich University Citizen Soldiers in the Army of the Potomac, 1861–1865.* Cambridge, MA: Da Capo, 1999.

Railroad History Company. *History of the Illinois Central Railroad Company and Representative Employees.* Chicago: Railroad History Company, 1900.

Ramsey, William E., and Betty Dineen Shrier. *Silent Hills Speak: A History of Council Bluffs.* Council Bluffs: Council Bluffs Library Foundation, 2002.

*Report of the Proceedings of the Society of the Army of the Tennessee Meetings at Columbus, Ohio, 1909, Toledo, Ohio, 1910, Council Bluffs, Iowa, 1911.* Cincinnati, OH: Ebel, 1913.

Russell, Don. *The Lives and Legends of Buffalo Bill.* Norman: University of Oklahoma Press, 1960.

Sandburg, Carl. *Abraham Lincoln: The War Years.* 4 vols. New York: Harcourt, Brace, 1939.

Sears, Stephen W. *George B. McClellan: The Young Napoleon.* New York: Ticknor and Fields, 1988.

Settle, William A., Jr. *Jesse James Was His Name.* Lincoln and London: University of Nebraska Press, 1977.

Shea, William L. *The Campaign for Pea Ridge: Civil War Series.* Ft. Washington, PA: Eastern National, 2001. Eastern National, a non-profit publisher, provides educational materials to America's National Parks.

Shea, William L., and Earl J. Hess. *Pea Ridge Civil War Campaign in the West.* Chapel Hill and London: University of North Carolina Press, 1992.

Sheridan, P. H. *Personal Memoirs of P. H. Sheridan.* Cambridge, MA: Da Capo, 1992.

Sherman, William Tecumseh. *The Memoirs of General W. T. Sherman.* Vols. 1 and 2. New York: D. Appleton, 1875.

Sifakis, Stewart. *Who Was Who in the Civil War.* New York and Oxford: Facts on File, 1988.

Simon, John Y. *The Personal Memoirs of Julia Dent Grant (Mrs. Ulysses S. Grant).* New York: G. P. Putnam, 1975.

Stoufer, Genevieve Mauck. *The Historic General Dodge House, Home of Major-General Grenville Mellen Dodge.* Council Bluffs, IA: General Ladies of the Historic Dodge House, 1981.

Stuart, Addison A. *Iowa Colonels and Regiments: Being a History of Iowa Regiments in the War of the Rebellion,* Des Moines, IA: Mills, 1865.

Singletary, Otis A. *The Mexican War.* Chicago and London: University of Chicago Press, 1967.

Trent, Logan Douglas. *The Credit Mobiler.* New York: Arno, 1961.

Trudeau, Noah Andre. *Southern Storm: Sherman's March to the Sea.* New York: HarperCollins, 2008.

Townsend, Mary Townsend. *Yankee Warhorse: A Biography of Major-General Peter Osterhaus.* Columbia: University of Missouri, 2010.

Villard, Oswald Garrison. *John Brown, 1800–1859: A Biography Fifty Years After.* New York: Alfred A. Knopf, 1943; reprints of 1910 original by Houghton Mifflin.

Violette, Eugene Morrow. *A History of Missouri.* Boston, New York, and Chicago: D. C. Heath, 1918.

Ware, E. F. *The Indian War of 1864.* Introduction and notes by Clyde C. Walton. Lincoln: University of Nebraska Press, 1960.

———. *The Lyon Campaign and the History of the 1st Iowa Infantry, 1861.* Topeka, KS: Crane, 1907.

Wells, Gideon. *Diary of Gideon Wells: Secretary of the Navy Under Lincoln and Johnson.* Vol. 2. New York: Houghton Mifflin, 1911.

Wertheim, Frank, and Barbara Bair, eds. *The Papers of Will Rogers: The Early Years. Vol. 1, November 1879–April 1904.* Norman and London: University of Oklahoma Press, 1996.

"William B. Allison, 1829–1908." *Biographical Directory of the United States Congress 1774–Present.* http://bioguide.congress.gov/scripts/biodisplay.pl?index=K000018. Last visited August 29, 2014.

Wilson, James Harrison. *The Life of John A. Rawlins.* New York: Neale, 1916.

Winkler, H. Donald. *Stealing Secrets: How a Few Daring Women Deceived Generals, Impacted Battles, and Altered the Course of the Civil War.* Naperville, IL: Sourcebooks, 2010.

Woodworth, Steven E. *Jefferson Davis and His Generals: The Failure of Confederate Command in the West.* Modern War Studies. Lawrence: University Press of Kansas, 1990.

Wright, George G. "Chief Justice Caleb Baldwin." *Annals of Iowa*, 3rd series, 1 (Oct. 1893).

Wubben, Hubert H. *Civil War in Iowa and the Copperhead Movement.* Ames: Iowa State University Press, 1980.

Younger, Edward. *John A. Kasson: Politics and Diplomacy from Lincoln to McKinley.* Iowa City: State Historical Society of Iowa, 1955.

## Original Documents, Court Cases, Government Publications, Web Sites and Miscellaneous

Civil War Trust. "Military Pay." http://www.civilwar.org/education/history/warfare-and-logistics/logistics/pay.html.

Cummings Collection. State Historical Society of Iowa. Des Moines, IA.

Curtis, Saml. R. "Report of Brigadier General Samuel R. Curtis, U.S. Army, Commanding Army of the Southwest." *Official Records of the Union and Confederate Armies.* http://www.civilwararchive.com/RESEARCH1/1862/peausa.htm.

"Dave Leip's Atlas of U.S. Presidential Elections." Elections of 1860 and 1864. http://uselectionatlas.org/. Last visited August 24, 2014.

Davis, Jefferson. "First Inaugural Address." *The Papers of Jefferson Davis.* Vol. 7, pp. 45–51. Rice University, Houston, Texas. Last visited September 5, 2011.

Dey, Peter Anthony. Papers. Special Collections Department, University of Iowa Libraries, Biographical Notes.

Dodge, Grenville. Diaries. Council Bluffs Library, Council Bluffs, IA.

Dodge, Grenville Mellen, and William Tecumseh Sherman. Paper read before the Society of the Army of the Tennessee at its 21st Annual Reunion at Toledo, OH, September 15, 1888.

Ewing, Brigadier General. "Order Number 10." Missouri Partisan Ranger Virtual Museum and Archives. http://www.rulen.com/partisan/order10.htm. Last visited August 24, 2014.

———. "Order Number 11." Missouri Partisan Ranger Virtual Museum and Archives. http://www.rulen.com/partisan/order10.htm. Last visited August 24, 2014.

*Fugitive Slave Act of 1850.* American Historical Documents, 1000–1904. Harvard Classics. New York: P. F. Collier, 1938.

Gaston, Maria. *Reminiscences.* Record of public meetings in Tabor, Fremont County, Iowa.

Gaston, Robert. *Stoic Soldier.* Unpublished manuscript about Alonzo Gaston.

Hume, Loren. *Tales of Tabor.* Unpublished manuscript about life in Tabor (Iowa), 1852–1865, prepared by Robert Gaston.

John A. Kasson Papers. State Historical Society of Iowa, Des Moines, Iowa.

John Milton Thayer Papers. Biographical notes. Nebraska State Historical Society.

Lord, Gary Thomas. *History of Norwich University.* 1995.

Majority Report Special Committee. "Report on Alleged Frauds in the Location of the Capital." Commissioned by Iowa Legislature, 1858.

Morgan, Kelly, and Cormac O'Grada. *Market Contagion: Evidence from the Panics of 1854 and 1857.* www.economics.harvard.edu/files/faculty/98_Kelly-contagion.pdf.

Ponsford, Brent Hamilton. "Major-General Grenville M. Dodge: Intelligence Operations During the Civil War." Unpublished manuscript, Iowa State University, 1976.

"Proceedings of the General Court-Martial of

Thomas W. Sweeny Convened at Louisville, Kentucky December 3, 1864."

Pyper, Walter W. *Grenville Mellen Dodge and 19th Century America: Growing Pains of a Man and a Nation*. Unpublished senior thesis submitted to the History Department of Princeton University in partial fulfillment for the degree of Bachelor of Arts. Council Bluffs Library, Council Bluffs, IA.

Ripley, Catherine Storz. "Golden Spike Marker Returns for a Brief Visit." Grand River Historical Society Museum. February 17, 2009. http://www.chillicothemuseum.com/press_golden spike021709.htm. Last visited December 24, 2013.

*Roster and Record of Iowa Soldiers in the War of the Rebellion: Together with Historical Sketches of Volunteer Organizations 1861–1866*. Vol. 1, *1st–8th Regiments Infantry*. Des Moines: Emory H. English State Printer, E. D. Chassell State Binder, 1908.

*Roster and Record of Iowa Soldiers in the War of the Rebellion: Together with Historical Sketches of Volunteer Organizations 1861–1866*. Vol. 5, *22d–48th Regiments Infantry 1st Regiment African Infantry 1st–4th Batteries Light Artillery*. Des Moines: Emory H. English State Printer, E. D. Chassell State Binder, 1908.

Sam Davis Home and Museum. "Who Was Sam Davis?" http://www.samdavishome.org/HISTORY_SAMDAVIS.php.

Sherman, William T. Military Division of the Department of Mississippi. Special Field Order #120, issued November 9, 1864.

*The Statue Laws of the Territory of Iowa: Enacted at the First Session of the Legislative Assembly of Said Territory, Held at Burlington A.D. 1838–1839*. Dubuque, IA: Russell and Reeves, 1839.

U.S. Congress. *Congressional Record*. 110th Cong., 2nd sess., Thursday, July 22, 2008. Vol. 154, no. 122, p. S7301. Senate Resolution 623, "Recognizing the Importance of the Role of the Lander Trail in the Settlement of the American West on the 150th Anniversary of the Lander Trail."

U.S. Congress. *Congressional Quarterly's Guide to U.S. Elections*. Washington, D.C.: Congressional Quarterly, 1985.

U.S. Congress. House. *The Metric Act of 1866 (Kasson Act)*. H.R. 596. 15 USC 204 et seq., U.S. Code Title 15, Commerce and Trade, Chapter 6, "Weights and Measures and Standard Time," Subchapter, "Weights, Measure, and Standards Generally, 204 Metric System."

U.S. Congress. Senate. *Senate Report*. 56th Congress, 1st sess., no. 221, I, 107–233.

*The War of the Rebellion: A Compilation of the Official Records of the Union and Confederate Armies*. Washington, D.C.: Government Printing Office, 1880.

Younger, Cole, and McCarthy, D. *The Story of Cole Younger by Himself*. Privately published by Thomas Coleman Younger, 1903.

# Newspapers

*Cincinnati Gazette*
*Cleveland Daily Leader*
*Council Bluffs Bugle*
*Council Bluffs Nonpareil*
*Davenport (IA) Daily Gazette*
*Des Moines (IA) State Register*
*Dodge City Daily Globe*
*Dubuque Herald*
*Keokuk (IA) Daily Gate City*
*New York Herald*
*New York Sun*
*New York Times*
*New York Tribune*
*Omaha Bee*
*Omaha Daily Herald*
*Richmond (VA) Dispatch*
*Richmond (VA) News Leader*
*Richmond (VA) Whig*
*Tabor (IA) Beacon*

# Index

Abbott, Charles 123
Abilene and Southern Railroad 169
Abolitionist 4, 8, 14, 16, 21, 23, 40, 42, 76, 111
*Achieves of General Psychiatry* 160
Adair County, Iowa 42
Adairsville, Georgia 119
Adams County, Iowa 19, *40*, 108
Addington, Joseph 164
Afton, Iowa 137, 159
Agrarian Reform law 171
Alabama 7, 89, 93–96, 98, 101–103, 105–106, 108, 113–114, 117–118, 120–121, 136, 144, 148, 163–164
Alabama Colored Infantry 95, 105
Alabama River 113
Albany, Georgia 144, 153
Allatoona, Georgia 141
Allegheny Arsenal 17, 19, 47
Allison, William B. 13, 168
Alton, Illinois 84, 155
American Railroad Improvement Company 169
Ames, Cpl. Amos 5, 137–138, 143–144, 153–154, 159
Anderson, Maj. Albert R. (A.R.) 145, 153, 161
Anderson, Bloody Bill 61, 146–147, 150
Anderson, Jim 150, 152, 154
Andersonville, Georgia 5, 117, 133, 137, 144–145, 153, 159, 163–164
Ankeny, Capt. Henry G. *40*, 64, 76, 100, 102, 108, 122
Anthony, Lt. Col. Daniel R. 111
Apache (tribe) 150
Appomattox Courthouse 153
Arapaho 150, 155
Arkansas 2, 5, 10–11, 19, 46, 51–53, 55, 57–58, 62–66, *68–69*, 71–*73*, 75–77, 79, 83, 86, 88, 94, 104–105, 137, 150–151, 154–156, 160–162

Arkansas Post 83, *86*, 105, 161
Arkansas River 5, 57, 79, 83, 150–151, 155–156
Army Medical Museum *165*
Army of Hood Corps 120
Army of Northern Virginia 145, 152
Army of Tennessee 105, 128, 133, 141
Army of the Cumberland 105, 110, 112, 118–122, 126, 128, 140, 147
Army of the Ohio 118, 128, 140
Army of the Potomac 141
Army of the Southwest 4, *59*–60, 62–67, 71
Army of the Tennessee 77, 89, 92, 98, 104, 106, 113, 117–118, 120–122, 126–132, 136, 157, 162, 169
Army of the West 55, 65–67, 72
Arthur, Pres. Chester A. 168
Asboth, Gen. Alexander 64, 71
Asia 100, 170
Atlanta, Georgia 4–5, 89, 97, 105, 115–118, 122–125, 127–134, 136–137, *139*–141, 143, 146, 155, 160–161
Atlanta Campaign 121–123, 125, 131, 136
Atlantic and Pacific Railroad 162
Atlantic Ocean 152
Augusta, Georgia 124, 130
*Augusta Chronicle* 97

Bacon, Reverend Dr. 29
Bailey, Gideon S. 50
Baker, Col. Edward D. 130
Baker, 1st Lt. Charles W. 107
Baker, J.D. 108
Baldwin, Judge Caleb 17, 35, 42, 47, 59
Baldwin, John 34, 36, 38, 41, 77
Baldwin, Dodge and Co. 34, 39–40, 78
Baldwin, Pegram and Co. 39–40, 78

Ball, Sarah E. 159
*Baltimore* 26
Baltimore, Maryland 43, 136
Barton Station 106
Bates, Edward 8–9
Batesville, Arkansas 19, 76
Baton Rouge 45, 54
"Battle Above the Clouds" 106
Battle at Arkansas Post 161
Battle at Chattanooga 101
Battle at Chickamauga 105, 106
Battle at Ezra Church 132
Battle at Wilson's Creed 53, 55
Battle of Atlanta 5, 113, 118, 130, 131, *135*, *139*, 155, 160–161
Battle of Bull Run 53
Battle of Carthage 61
Battle of Champion Hill 70, 99
Battle of Corinth 92, 102
Battle of Dallas 122
Battle of Jonesboro 5, 137
Battle of Pea Ridge 2, 28, 67, 72, *76*, *80*
Battle of the Little Big Horn 36
*Bay State* 25
Beauregard, Pierre G.T. 146
Bedford, Iowa 140, 161
*Ben Hur: A Tale of Christ* 163
Benteen, Frederick W. 103
Bentonville, North Carolina 64–66, 152
Bentonville Detour 4, 66, 70–71
"Billy the Kid" 163
Birmingham, Iowa 43
Black Hawk 96, 103
Black Hills 157–158
*Black Prince* 22
Black River, Mississippi 102, 140
Blair, Gen. Francis P. 118, 120, 129, 132
Blair, Montgomery 9
"Bleeding Kansas" 51, 75, 111
Bloomer, Amelia 14
Bloomer, Dexter 14
"bloodhound law" 10
"Bloody Hill" 53–55, 61

# Index

Blount, Alabama 148
Bonney, William H. 163
Boone, Daniel 28
Boonville, Missouri 46, 52
Booth, John Wilkes 48
Boston, Massachusetts 24, 40, 42, 142
Boston Mountains 64–65, 70
Boutwell, George W. 91
Bowen, Lt. Col. William D. 103
"Boy Colonel" 119
Bozeman Trail 155
Bradford, William 27
Bragg, Gen. Braxton 4, 93–94, 103, 152
Breckinridge, John 146
Brice's Crossroads 123
Bridger, James 155, 168
*Bridges of Madison County* 19
Briggs, Lewis 164
"Brothels of Boston" 22
Brown, Elizabeth 122
Brown, Gratz 8
Brown, John C. 14, 76, 122, 130
Brown, Joseph E. 140
Brown, Joshua 111–112
Brown, Oliver 76
Brown, (Ruth) Anne 26–27, 31, 170
Brown, Watson 76
Brule Sioux tribe 33
Buffalo, New York 25
"Buffalo Bill Cody's Wild West" 111
Bull Run 53, 55–56
Burke, William S. 166
Burnside, Gen. Ambrose 13
Burnt Bridge 92
Burton, George 73, 104, 106, 117

Caldwell, Billy 30
Calhoun, James 137
Calhoun, John C. 16
California 8, 10, 22, 30, 33, 51, 156, 169
California and Texas Railway Construction Company 169
Camaguey Province 171
Cambridgeshire 161
Cameron, Simon 16–18, 20
Camp Dodge 1, 156, 170
Camp Douglas 125
Camp Jackson 44–45
Camp Kirkwood 18–19
Camp Lawton 140
Campbell, Rufus 108
Canada 10, 13–14, 42, 69, 131, 151, 160, 170
Carpenter, Captain 104
Carr, Colonel 60, 67–68, 70–71
Carskaddon, David 123
Carthage, Missouri 51–52, 62
Cass County, Iowa 19

Cassville Road 119–120
Castle Sorghum 145–146
Castro, Fidel 171
Central Pacific 167
Centralia, Missouri 146–147
Chambers, John 15
Chaney, Sgt. John B. 108, 140, 144
Chapultepec 25
Charleston, South Carolina 13, 43, 94, 138, 146, 152
Charleston *Mercury* 152
Chase, Lydia A. 164
Chattahoochee River 124, 126, 133
Chattanooga 4, 89, 94, 105–106, *108*, 110, 116–117, 124, 140
Chattanooga Creek 107
Cherokee 58, 70
Cherokee Station 106, 123
Chesapeake 38
Cheyenne (tribe) 36, 150, 155, 157–158
Cheyenne, Wyoming 166–167
Chicago, Illinois 7, 10, 12, 25–27, 30, 34, 40, 42, 113, 125, 160, 162
Chicago and Rock Island Railroad 8, 12
Chickamauga Creek 4
Chickasaw (tribe) 70, 91
Chickasaw Bayou, Mississippi 4, 80–84, *86*, 94, 105, 160, 162
Chickasaw Bluffs, Tennessee 81, 162
Chickasaw County, Mississippi 91
Chipman, Norton P. 163
Chivington, Col. John 5, 150, 156
*Choctaw*(tribe) 70, 86
City Point, Virginia 141
Clarinda, Iowa 145, 161
Clark, Captain 74
Clark, Colonel 131
Clark, Ezekiel 18
Clark, Meriwether 74
Clay, Henry Dean 50
Claysville, Alabama 117, 144, 163–164
Clemens, John Marshall 48
Clemens, Orion 8
Clemens, Sam 8, 48
Clement, Archie 146–147, 150, 152, 154
Cleveland, Ohio 25, 69
Cody, "Buffalo Bill" 111
Coe, E.D. 98–99
Coleman, Captain 112
Coleman, E. 112
Colfax, Vice Pres. Schylur 168
Colorado 7, 33, 39, 70, 150, 155, 157, 162, 170

Colorado and Texas Construction Company 169
Columbia, Kentucky 42–43, 162
Columbia, South Carolina 145–146, 161
Columbus, Kentucky 78
Columbus, Mississippi 89, 92, 96, 109
Columbus, Nebraska 32–33
Comanche 150
Confederacy 1, 10, 13, 44, **45**, 46, 49, 52, 56–58, 60, 72, 79, 87, **90**, 91, 98, 105, 110, 115, 120–121, 127, 133, 140, 144–145, 147–149
Confederate flag 46, 57, 101
Confederate guerrilla(s) 3, 78, 85, 104, 109, 113, 116, 147, 150, 152
Confederate State Guards 55
Confederate States 7, 46, 57, 60–61, 72
Confederate States Army 55
Congress of the Confederate States 61
Connecticut 169
Connor, Gen. Patrick E. 5, 155, 157–158
Cooper, Capt. Daniel E. 124
Coosa River 113
Copperhead movement 13, 49–50, 105, 127, 135
Coppoc, Barclay 14
Coppoc, Edwin 14
Corinth, Mississippi 78, 89–90, 92–97, 99, 104–105, 109
Cornyn, Col. F.M. 103
"Corps of Scouts" 58
Corse, Brig.-Gen. J.M. 134
Council Bluffs, Iowa 3, 5, 7, 11–13, 16, 30, 67, 69–70, 72, 104, 141, 170
*Council Bluffs Bugle* 11, 18
Council Bluffs Guards 16, 19, 36
*Council Bluffs Nonpareil* 11, 18, 49, 166
Council Bluffs YMCA 170
Cramer, Joseph 108
Cramer, Thomas H. 108
Crane Creek 63
Crandall, Wilford W. (Bill) 153, 163–164
Crawford, Capt. Samuel J. 54
Crazy Horse 36
Credit Mobiler railroad-building scandal 32, 142, 168
Crockett, J.B. 8
Cross Hollows, Arkansas 64–66
Cuba 169, 171
Cuban Railroad 169
Cummings, Hannah Maria 76
Cummings, Capt. Henry J. B. 66

# Index

Cuppy, Ad  29
Cuppy's Grove  28
Curtis, Gen. Samuel  4, 28, 31, 40, 47, 49, 59–67, 70–72, 74, 76, 92, 150
Custer, Lt. Col. George Armstrong  36, 103, 123, 157
Custer's Last Stand  36

*Daily Gazette*  72
Dallas, Georgia  122
Dallas County, Iowa  19, 61
Dalton, Georgia  4, 117–118, 141
Dalton Station, Alabama  106
"Damn the Dutch"  45
Dana, Charles A.  91, 148
Danvers, Massachusetts  20–21, 26, 35, 142
Dartmouth College  23
Darwin, Joseph Z.  144, 153
Davenport, Jean Margaret  22
Davenport, Iowa  11, 27, 69, 72, 123, 141, 153, 163–164
Davis, Benjamin  121
Davis, George B.  153
Davis, Jefferson  7, **45**–46, 56, 60, 91, 100, 105, 121, 125, 128, 140–141, 144
Davis, Samuel  111–112
Debusk, Elihu  72
Debusk, Isaac  72
Debusk, William S.  72
Decatur, Georgia  128–130
Decatur County, Iowa  19, 47
"De Costa Syndrome"  159
Deer Creek Valley Expedition  87
DeGrasse, Capt. F.  130
Democrat  21, 42, 118, 127, 133, 136, 161, 166
Democratic National Convention  43, 162
Denver, Colorado  5, 39, 150–151, 157, 160, 166, 170
Denver, Texas and Fort Worth Railway Company  169
Department of Kansas  5, 150, 155–156, 158
Department of Missouri  5, 142, 146, 149–150, **152**, 158
Department of the West  45–46, **51**, 57
Derby, Elias Haskett  21–22
Derby, Elizabeth West  22
De Smet, Father Pierre-Jean  30
Des Moines, Iowa  7, **8**, 9–10, 12, 19, 25, 28, **35**, 37–38, **40**, 42, **43**, 59, 108, 117, 141, 162–**163**, 166
Des Moines and Northern Railway Company  169
Des Moines Union Railroad Company  169
Detroit, Michigan  25
Dey, Peter  7–8, 13–14, 27, 29, 30–31, 34, 36–37, 78, 91, 114, 142
Diocese of Louisiana  121
District of Columbia, Washington (D.C.)  7
District of Columbus, Mississippi  92
District of the Trans-Mississippi  60
Dixon, Illinois  26
Dodge, Augustus Caesar  16
Dodge, Julia  20
Dodge, Lettie  33, 170
Dodge, Nathan Phillips  20, 30, 36, 41, 77
Dodge, Richard  21
Dodge, (Ruth) Anne (Brown)  13, 26, 31, 33, 77–78, 108, 131, 135, 168, 170
Dodge, Capt. Solomon  21
Dodge, Sylvanus  20–21, 27, 31, 39, 157
Dodge, William  21
Dodge City, Kansas  156
Dodge House  5
Dodge's Order #7  148
Domain Land Company of Pennsylvania  169
Doolittle, James R.  156
Douglas, Stephen A.  11, 25, 43
Dubuque, Iowa  15, 50
Durant, Charles W.  19, 32, 97
Durant, Thomas C.  12, 32, 97, 109, 114, 119, 142, 158, 164, 167–168
Durham, New Hampshire  23
Dyersville, Tennessee  78

East Chickamauga Creed  4, 107
East Nishnabotna River  28
East Point, Georgia  138
Eastern Railroad  22
Eastern Theater  5, 55, 64, 89, 105, 159
Eastport, Mississippi  95, 105
"Eastsiders"  38
Edwards Ferry  22
Eliot, the Rev. Dr. William Greenleaf  166
Eliot, T.S.  166
Elk River Valley  110
Elkhorn, Nebraska  31–34, 158
Elkhorn Tavern, Pea Ridge, Arkansas  67, **69**, 70–72
Elliot, Capt. W.L.  48
Ellis, Prof. William Arba  24
Elson, Sgt. James M.  123
Emancipation Proclamation  79
*Emile*  47
England  21–22, 79, 131, 161
Essex County, Massachusetts  20–21
Etowah River  121
Europe  9, 39, 63, 162, 170

Everett, Edward  142
Ewing's Orders #10 and #11  148–149
Ezra Church  130, 132

Fairbanks Scale Company  9
Faneuil Hall  142
Farnam, Harry/Henry  12, 27–28, 32, 34, 37, 39, 97
Farnam and Durant Company  32
Fayetteville, Arkansas  64
Featherstone, Jane  89
Federal Missouri Home Guards  62
Fees, Sergeant Jacob  144
Fetterman Massacre  157, 167
Fifield, Samuel  32–34, 158
Fillmore, Millard  10
"First at Chickasaw Bayou"  82, 105
Flat Creek  63
Fletcher, Gov. Thomas  150
Flick, James P.  161
Flint River  136
Florence, Nebraska  37
Florence, South Carolina  145
Florida  7, 145, 154
Fontenelle, Logan  33
Fontenelle, Lucien  33
Ford, Capt. George E.  107
Ford Road  70, 71
Forrest, Nathan Bedford  78, 80, 93, 106, 113–117, 120, 123, 141
Forsyth, Missouri  76
Fort Calhoun, Nebraska  31–32
Fort Cottonwood  39–40, **135**, 157
Fort Croghan  30
Fort Des Moines  38, 43
Fort Dodge, Iowa  35, 156
Fort Donelson  79, 125
Fort Fisher, South Carolina  152
Fort Hindman, Arkansas  4, 83, **86**, 94
Fort Kearney  17, 157
Fort Laramie  157
Fort Leavenworth  17, 150, 158
Fort McAllister  143
Fort McPherson  39, 135, 157
Fort Pillow  93, 123
Fort Randolph  93
Fort Scott, Kansas  56, 58
Fort Smith, Arkansas  53, 104
Fort Sumter  10, 13
Fort Worth and Denver City Railway Company  169
France  9, 63, 79, 144
Frank, Albert  159
Freeman, Col. Thomas R.  58
Fremont, John C.  3, 33, 48–49, 56–58
Fremont, Nebraska  33
Fremont County, Iowa  19, 161

## Index

Fugitive Slave Act of 1850 10–11, 16
Fuller, General 131

Galena and Chicago Railroad 114
Galesburg, Illinois 42, 162
Galligan, Lt. Col. John 55, 73
"Galvanized Yankees" 155
Gamble, Hamilton R. 44
Garfield, Gen. James A. 105, 168
Garner, John Nance 170
Garrard, Gen. Kenner 126
Gasconade Bridge 46
Gaston, Alex 75
Gaston, Alonzo 4, 75–77, 79, 82, 84, **86**
Gaston, George 75, 84
Gaston, Loren 76
Gaston, Maria 75–76
Gebbins, Sam 121
General Hospital 84
General Order # 2 62
General Order #43 86
Gentryville, Missouri 47
Georgia 4, 5, 7, 43, 91, 98, 101, 105–107, 115–120, 122–123, 126, 128, 130, 132–133, 136–138, 140–146, 153
Georgia Railroad 124
Germany 9, 24, 63
Gettysburg, Pennsylvania 4, 101, 105
Geyer, Henry S. 8
Gholson, Confederate general 114–115
Gilson, George W. 25–27
Glenwood, Iowa 108
Glenwood Springs, Colorado 170
Goldsboro, North Carolina 152–153
Goodwin, Thomas 145
*Gospel of Peace* 142
Government Hospital for the Insane 159
Grand Army of the Republic (G.A.R.) 118, 162, **168**–169
Grant, Julia Dent 80, **83**
Great Britain 39, 128
"Great Natural American Soldier" 23
Great Salt Lake Valley 35
Green, Preston 72
Greenville, Indiana 135, 142
Greer, Col. Elkanah 71
Gregory, Ann W. 43
Grenada, Mississippi 80, 103
Greusel, Colonel 58, 70, 71
Griffin, Georgia 137
Griffin, Mary 161
Grimes, James W. 36, 38, 40, 109, 167
Grinnell, Josiah Bushnell 10, 28

Grinnell, Iowa 10, 28
guerrilla 3, 5, 47, 49, 58, 60–62, 78, 85, 104, 109–110, 113, 116, 143, 147–150, 152, 154
Guthrie County, Iowa 19, 50, 117

Hall, Susanna 162
Halleck, Gen. Henry W. 57, 59, 60, 62–63, 78, 86, 101, 103, 127, 141, 146–147
*Hamlet* 113
Hampton, Gen. Wade 146
Hannibal, Missouri 8, 28, 47–48, 146
Hannibal-St. Joseph Railroad 47–48
Hardee, Gen. William J. 119–121, 125, 129, 136–137, 143
Harlan, James 141–142, 168
Harney, Gen. William S. 17, 45–46
Harney-Price agreement 46
Harpers Ferry assault 14
Harris, Gen. Thomas 56
Harrison, Pres. Benjamin 168
Harrison, William Henry 15
Harrison County, Iowa 19
Hatchie River 92
Hawthorne, Nathaniel 20–21
Hazen, General 143
Hebert, Col. Louis 71
Helena, Arkansas 77, 79, 82
Hensal, James 110–111, 141
Henson, Philip 4, 90, 95–96, 102, 109, 114–115, 120–121, 148
Hepburn, William P. 161
Hill, Ed 75–76
Holly Springs, Mississippi 80–81, 93
Hood, Gen. John Bell 5, 120, 128–130, **132**–133, 136, 141, 148
Hooker, Gen. Joe 106, 130, 136
House of Representatives 40, 78
Howard, Gen. Oliver O. 126, 130–132, 143, 153
Hoxie, Herbert "Hub" 9–11, 13, 47, 49–50, 59, 109, 114, 134, 164, 166
Hulbert, Gen. Stephen A. 89
Humboldt, Tennessee 92–93
Hunter, Maj.-Gen. David 57–58
Hutton, Samuel 140, 153

Illinois 11, 12, 25–27, 30–31, 42–43, 57, 72, 84, 92, 98–99, 118–119, 154–155, 160–162
Illinois Central 25–27
Illinois River 26
India 21
Indian Creek 29

Indian Nations 10–11, 58, 62, 65, 75, 150, 160
Indian Wars 111, 156–157
Indiana 1, 16, 19, 41–42, 95, 135, 140, 142
Indianapolis, Indiana 42
Inkpaduta 35–37
International Railroad Improvement Company 169
Iowa Brigade 5, 105–106, 123, 130, 132, 136, 143, 145, 152–153
Iowa City, Iowa 13, 18, 27, 29, 34, 37–38, 43
*Iowa Colonels and Regiments* 108
Iowa legislature 36–37, 108
Iowa National Guard 1, 5, 170
Iowa School for the Deaf 169
*Iowa State Register* 59
Iowa Steamboat Company 169
Iowa Supreme Court 17, 35, 42, 47
Ireland 22, 24, 73, 104, 123, 126, 131
"Irritable Heart Syndrome" 159
Ish-got-up 33

Jackson, Claiborne 44–**45**, 56–57
Jackson, Gen. "Red" 133
Jackson, William "Red" Hicks 78, 133
Jackson, Mississippi 87, 89, 102
Jackson, Tennessee 93, 102
Jackson County, Missouri 13, 149
Jackson Hospital 84
Jacksonville, Florida 154
James, Frank 61, 146, 149
James, Jesse 61, 146–147
James River 53, 101
James-Younger gang 62, 146
Janis, Frenchman Nick 158
Jasper County, Iowa 37
Jayhawkers 149
*J.C. Swan* 45
Jefferson Barracks 47–48
Jefferson City, Missouri 46, 56–58
Jennison, Col. Charles R. 110–111
"Jennison's Jayhawkers" 111
*John J. Roe* 79, 82
Johnsey, Jesse 96
Johnson, A.J. 103
Johnson, Andrew 113, 158, 166–167
Johnson, Maj. A.V.E. 147
Johnson, Herschel V. 43
Johnston, Joseph 5, 96, 99–100, 102, 109, 114–115, 117–121, 124–125, 127–128, 140, 146, 152–154
Jones, George Wallace 16, 50

# Index

Jonesboro, Georgia 5, 136–137
Judd, Norman 11–12
Julesburg, Colorado 157

Kagi, John 76
Kane, Thomas Leipe 30
Kanesville, Iowa 30
Kansas 5, 10, 12–13, 17, 44, 51–54, 56, 58, 75–76, 111, 146, 148–151, 156, 160, 169
Kansas City, Missouri 55–56, 58, 97, 148–149
Kansas Pacific 150
Kasson, John *8*, 9, 38, 59, 91, 119, 141, 147, 157, 166
Kasson Act 9
Kearney, Missouri 61
Keetsville, Missouri 65
Kennesaw Mountain 122–125, 130
Kentucky 5, 15–16, 42–*43*, 56, 78–79, 123, 131, 150, 153, 162
Keokuk, Iowa 8, 19, 47, 52, 123
Keokuk County, Iowa 42
Kil-Cavalry 138, 143
Kilpatrick, Gen. Hugh Judson 136, 138, 143
King, Aden 19
King, Sarah 161
Kinsman, Capt. William H. 67, 69, 91, 99
Kingston, Georgia 4, 117, 119, 120
Kiowa (tribe) 150
Kirkwood, Samuel J. 3, 13–*18*, 20, *35*, 47–49, 73, 92, 166
Kittoe, Dr. 134
Knights of the Golden Circle 49
Knox College, Illinois 42, 162
Knoxville, Tennessee 141

Lafayette County, Missouri 13, 55–56
Lake City, Florida 154
Lancaster, Iowa 42
Lander, Charles 22
Lander, Edward 22
Lander, Mrs. Eliza (West) 21–22
Lander, Frederick W. 12, 22–23, 31, 33
Lander, Wyoming 22
Lane, James 57, 149, 151
Lane, Wiley 28
Laramie, Wyoming 166
LaSalle, Illinois 26
Leavenworth, Col. Jesse H. 156
Leavenworth, Kansas 110
Lebanon, Missouri 51, 57–58, 73
Le Claire, Antoine 27
Lee, Robert E. 89, 106, 115, 125, 127–128, 133, 144–146, 152–154

Lee, Stephen D. 120–121, 132, 136
Lexington, Missouri 55–56, 58
Libby Prison 95
Liberty, Missouri 13
Lincoln–Douglas debates 11
*Lion's Whelp* 21
Little Bear Creek 95
Little Big Horn 36, 103
"Little Dixie" 56
Little Platte River 47
Little Sugar Creek 63, 66–67, 70
Lockett, Maj. Samuel 87
Loess Hills 30
Logan, Gen. John 101, 117–118, 123–124, 126, 130–132, 141, 153
London, England 162
Lookout Creek 106
Lookout Mountain 106–107, 110, 123, 160
Louisiana 7, 45, 54, 63, 71, 79–80
Louisville, Kentucky 5, 131, 153
Lovejoy Station, Georgia 136–137
Lynn, Massachusetts 20
Lyon, Capt. Nathaniel 45–46, 51–55
Lyon, Iowa 104
Lyon and Iowa Central Line 27, 31

M & M Railroad 12, 32, 34, 36–37, 39, 114
MacArthur, Maj. Arthur, Jr. 119
MacArthur, Douglas 119
Macon, Georgia 98, 132–133, 137–138, 144
Macon and Western Railroad 124, 128, 133–134, 136, 143
Madison County, Iowa 19, 66, 72
Mahoney, D.A. 50
Mainard, Mary 89
Malone, Mary 89
Manifest Destiny 151
Marietta, Georgia 4, 117, 124
Marion, Iowa 123
Marion County, Missouri 28
Maryland 43, 86
Massachusetts 20–22, 24, 26, 31–32, 34–35, 91, 142
*Mayflower* 27
McCarty, William Henry 163
McClellan, George B. 22–23, 89, 125, 136, 144
McClernand, John A. 82–83, 87–88
McCook, Edward M. 133
McCulloch, Brig. Ben 51–53, 55, 57–58, 60, 63–65, 70–71
McIntosh, James 55, 66, 70–71
McKinley, Pres. William 168, 170

McKinney, Capt. T.J. 65
McKissick's Creek 65
McPherson, Gen. James 5, 101, 116–118, 120, *124*, 127–131, *135*
McRae, Lucy 101
Me-um-bane 33
Medal of Honor 111, 123, 129, 162
Memphis, Tennessee 81, 84, 93–94, 105, 114, 123
Meridian, Mississippi 89–90, 94, 98–99, 114, 145, 148
Merewether's Ferry 92
Metric Act of 1866 9
Mexican Military Academy 25
Mexican War 24–25, 27, 30, 44, 51–52, 91, 108, 118, 126
Mexico City, Mexico 24–25
Michigan 26, 157
Millen, Georgia 140
Miller, 1st Sergeant John A. 77
Milliken's Bend, Louisiana 80
Mills County, Iowa 19
Minnesota 14, 36
Missionary Ridge 107, 110
Mississippi 7, 22, 63, 77, 89, 91, 96–98, 101, 109, 114, 123
Mississippi and Missouri Railroad 11, 12, 27, 31
Mississippi Central Railroad 80, 103
Mississippi River 11, 25, 27, 46, 62, 72, 77, 79, 83–84, 94–95
Mississippi Valley 85, 102
Missouri 8, 10, 13, 15–17, 19, 28–30, 44, *45*, 46–48, 51–58, 60, 63–64, 72, 75, 77, 79–80, 82–83, 86, 88, 103, 111, 142, 146–150, *152*, 154, 156, 158, 160
Missouri, Kansas and Texas Railroad 169
Missouri River 11–12, 25, 28–32, 47, 55–56, 75, 97, 114, 146, 156, 160
Missouri State Guards 44, *45*, 46, 50, 53–58, 60–61
Missouri Valley 56, 58, 75
Mitchell, Thomas 10
Mobile, Alabama 90, 94, 97–99, 113, 121, 148
Mobile and Ohio Railroad 78, 93
Mobile Harbor, Alabama 101
Mobile River 113
Montgomery, Alabama 7, 90, 99
Montgomery County, Iowa 19
Morgan, Gen. George W. 125
Morgan's Woods 71
Mormon(s) 30, 33, 157
Mormon Battalion 30
Morrill, Maj. Edmund Needham 111

Moscow 140
Mosquito Creek 18
Mount Pleasant, Iowa 123
*Mountain Howitzer* 68
Mounted Confederate Cherokees 70
Muscatine, Iowa 8

Naron, Levi Holloway 91, 97, 105, 109, 112
Nashville, Tennessee 95, 109, 112–113, 128, 135, 140–141, 147
National Republican Convention 162
Native American 10, 16–17, 27, 29–30, 33–34, 36, 39, 51, 54, 65, 69, 70–71, 150–152, 156, 167
Nauvoo, Illinois 30
*Nebraska* 77
Nebraska 10, 13, 17, 31–33, 37, 40, 44, 75, 79, 97, **135**, 146, 150, 158, 160
Nebraska City, Nebraska 40, 160
Nelson, Cpl. Charles 140
Neosho, Missouri 57
Neuse River 153
Nevada 8, 22
New Hope Church 122, 130
New Jersey 117, 127
New Mexico 163
New Orleans, Louisiana 33, 113
New York 10, 16, 18–19, 25, 29, 63, 97, 126–127, 134, 138, 160, 163–164
New York City, New York 18, 37, 42, 98, 109, 142, 162, 169–170
*New York Herald* 134
*New York Times* 93, 103
*New York Tribune* 17, 29, 91, 130, 134
Newbury, Vermont 23
Newton County, Georgia 91
Newton County, Missouri 57
Niagara Falls, New York 25
Nichols, Captain 82
Nichols, Lt. Colonel 130, 153
Nichols, Samuel D. 50, 66, 73, 107, 117, 119, 143, 145
Nickajack Creek 124
North, Maj. Frank 151
North Carolina 5, 98, 146, 152–153
North Dakota 14
North Danvers, Massachusetts 142
North Platte, Nebraska 39
North Platte River 150
Norwich (Vermont) Military School 18–19
Norwich University 3, 22–25, 32, 126, 134, 170–171

Nova Scotia, Canada 69
Nucholls, Stephen 40
Nye, James Warren 8

Oberlin, Ohio 75, 79
Oberlin College 4, 75
Official Record of the War of the Rebellion 101
Ogeechee River 143
Oglesby, General 102, 119
Ohio 1, 13, 16, 19, 41, 98, 107, 160–161, 168
Oklahoma 10–11, 20, 58, 62, 75, 150
"Old Pap" 44, 56
Omaha, Nebraska 5, 30–34, 37, 97, 114, 150–151, 157, 164, 166, 169–170
*Omaha Daily Herald* 157
Oostanaula River, 118
Ord, Maj.-Gen. Edward 102
Order # 67 137
Oregon 33
Oriental Construction Company 169
Osage River 57
Osceola, Missouri 57
Osterhaus, Gen. Peter 70–71, 105–107, 117, 119, 122–123, 136, 143
Otoe (tribe) 29
Owens, Doctor 98–99
Ozarks 52, 59, 152

Pacific Ocean 12
Pacific Railroad Improvement Company 169
Page County, Iowa 19, 47, 108, 140, 161
Page County Rangers 17
Palmer, Francis W. 59, 166
Palmetto Station 140
Panic of 1854 31
Panic of 1857 12, 39
Panora, Iowa 107, 117
Paris, France 9, 102, 169
Partisan Ranger Act 61
Partridge, Captain 18, 23–25
Pawnee 5, 31–34, 75, **86**, 151, 155, 157–158
Pea Ridge, Arkansas 53, 58, 62–64, 67–**69**, 72–**73**, 74–75, 77, 104–105, 123, 160–163
Pea Ridge Plateau 70
Peabody, Massachusetts 20, 35, 142
Peabody, Danvers and Rowley 35
Pegram, Benjamin R 35, 38, 41
Pegram, Charles 77
Pelican Rangers 53
Pemberton, John C. 80–81, 87, 96, 99–101, 105, 125
Pennsylvania 1, 19, 41, 161

Peru, Illinois 25–26, 31
Philadelphia, Pennsylvania 87
Philippine Islands 170
Phillips, Colonel 113, 134
Phillips, Frank 20
Phillips, Lt. Col. Jesse 103
Phillips, Julia Theresa (Dodge) 20–21
Phillips, Lee Eldas 20
Phillips, Lewis F. 20
Phillips, Wendell 21
Phillips Petroleum Company 20
Pierce, Pres. Franklin 10, 24, 36
Pigeon Creek 29
Pike, Gen. Albert 65, 70–71, 74
Pine Mountain 125
Pinkerton, Allan 17, 88–89
Pittsburg Landing, Tennessee 97, 109
Pittsburgh, Pennsylvania 17
Platte River Valley 12, 31, 114, 166
Plymouth Colony, Massachusetts 27
Pocahontas, Arkansas 62–63
Poindexter, Colonel 47
Polk, James K. 21
Polk, Gen. Leonidas 115, 120–121, 125
Polk County, Iowa 19, 35, 37, 61
Ponca tribe 33
Ponder House *139*
Pony Express 48
Pool, Dave 146–147, 150, 152, 154
Pope, General 56–57, 155, 158
Popular Corners, Tennessee 92
Porter, Adm. David 83–84, 87, 94, 100
Potawatomi tribe 30
Pottawattamie County, Iowa 16, 19, 37, 39
Powder River Expedition 155, 157
P.O.W.s 84, 101, 117, 125, 133, 138, 144–146, 155, 159, 164
Presbyterian 42
Price, Cmdr. Sterling 4, 44–46, 49–53, 55–58, 60–65, 67–72, 92, 147
Promontory Summit, Utah 167
Pulaski, Tennessee 110, 122
Pumpkin Vine Creek 121

Quanah, Texas 170
Quantrill, William 61, 146, 150
"Queen of the Cow-towns" 156
Quimby, General 78
Quincy, Iowa 40, 140, 144

Raccoon River 28, 36
Rains, Brig. Gen. James S. 53
Raleigh, North Carolina 153
Ransom, Ned 27

# Index

Ransom, Thomas E.G. 134–135, 142
Ransom, Truman B. 24–25
Ransom, Mrs. Truman B. 24
Rawlins, Gen. John A. 141–142, 167–168
Rawlins, Wyoming 168
Red Cloud War 155
"Redlegs" 111
Reed, Pete 13
Republican 3, 7–11, 14, 24, 37, 40, 42, 47, 49, 51, 60, 102, 109, 118, 136, 161–162, 166–168
Republican National Convention 11, 136, 162, 168
Resaca, Georgia 4, 117–119, 122, 130
Revolutionary War 21
Reynolds, Lieutenant Governor 46
Rhode Island 162
Richmond, VA 57, 89, 95, 103, 127–128, 133, 145
Ringgold, Georgia 4, 117, 140
Robbins, Dr. Mynn W. 106
Rochester, New York 29
Rock Island Railroad 8, 12, 26–27
"Rock of Chickamauga" 105
Rockies 12, 158, 166–167
Rocky Face 117
Roddey, Philip 94–96, 113, 116, 120–121
Rogers, Clement V. 70
Rogers, Will 70
Rolla, Missouri 3, 46, 48, 51–52, 55, 57–59, 66, 72–73, 140
Rome, Georgia 120, 140
Roosevelt, Franklin 170
Roseau, General 113
Rosecrans, Gen. William 4, 92, 103, 105–106, 142, 147, 149
Ross Grove, Iowa 144
Rossville, Georgia 107, 110
Roswell, Georgia 126
*Roughing It* 8
Rowley, Massachusetts 35, 142
Ruggles, General 96, 102–103
Russia 169

Sac tribe 35
Saddle Creek 31
St. Joseph, Missouri 12, 44, 47–48, 84, 146
St. Joseph Mission 30
St. Louis, Missouri 8–9, 13, 17, 39, 44–53, 59, 62–63, 65, 67, 72–73, 77, 84, 142, 146–148, 150, 154, 166
Salem, Massachusetts 20–22, 31, 142
Samuel, Dr. Reuben 149
Sand Creek Massacre 150, 156
Sandburg, Carl 7

Santa Clara, Cuba 169
Santa Fe Trail 150
Santee Sioux 35
Santiago, Cuba 169
Saskatchewan, Canada 170
Sauganash 30
Savannah, Georgia 5, 138, 140, 143–145, 153
Schofield, General 120, 128–129, 134, 140
Scott, Gen. Winfield 23, 25
Secretary of the Treasury 91, 168
Secretary of War 16–17, 20, 59, 91, 155
Sedalia, Missouri 57
Seddon, James 144
Selma, Alabama 89, 99, 148
Seminoles (tribe) 70
Shaw, Col. Henry (aka Capt. Coleman) 111–112
Sheffield, Joseph 27
Shelby, Jo 62
Shelby County, Iowa 19
Sheldon, Benjamin "Ben" O. 75–76, 83, 161
Shepherd, George 150, 152
Sheridan, Gen. Phillip 2–3, 59–60, 64–66, 76, 78, 105, 115, 167
Sherman, William T. 2, 5, 79–83, 87, 89, 93, 95–96, 100–102, 105–106, 109–115, 116–120, 123–128, 129–136, 138–143, 145–147, 152–153, 155, 157–158, 160, 167
Shields, Lt. Lemuel 108, 153
Shiloh, Tennessee 79, 132, 134
Siberian Railroad 169
Sidney, Iowa 161
Sigel, Col. Fritz 51–55, 61, 63–66, 70, 72
Silver, PHD Roxanne Cohan 160
Simonson, Capt. Peter 125
Sintominaduta 35–36
Sioux (tribe) 30, 33–34, 36–37, 75, **86**, 155, 157–158
Sioux City, Iowa 97
Sitting Bull 36
Slocum, Maj. Gen. Henry R. 136, 143
Smith, J.A. 108
Smith, Col. Milo 87
Smith, Morgan L. 130
Smith, Gen. William Sooy 114
Smithland, Iowa 36
Smyth, William 123
Snake Creek Gap 118
Society of the Army of the Tennessee 162
"Soldier's Heart" 159
South Carolina 5, 7, 16, 145–146, 164
South Dakota 14, 161

South Danvers, Massachusetts 20–21
South Pass 12, 150
South Platte 150
"South Wester" 82
Spain 170
Spanish-American War 5, 170
Special Field Order #120 142
Special Order #44 151
Spencer, George 94
spies 3–5, 58–59, 66, 88–91, 93–95, 97–99, 109–112, 115, 127, 141, 148
Spirit Lake Massacre 36
Spoor, Capt. Nelson T. 19
Sprague, John 129
Springdale, Iowa 14
Springfield, Illinois 12, 154
Springfield, Massachusetts 24
Springfield, Missouri 4, 51–55, 57–58, 60–65
spy network 4, 58, 90–91, 94, 100, 102, 104, 109–111
Stanton, Edwin M. 85, 91, 155
Steele, Gen. Frederick 79, 85–87, 100–102
Stevens, Aaron 76
Stoll, Henry 153
Stone, Col. George C. 123, 145, 152
Stone, William W. 132
Streight, Col. A.D. 95
Stuart, Capt. Addison A. 1, 108
Sturgis, Maj. Samuel 55, 123, 149
Sturgis, South Dakota 123
*Sucker State* 47
Sugar Creek 63
Surgeon General's Office **165**
Sweeny, Gen. Thomas 5, 52, 118, 126–127, 131, 134

Tabor, Iowa 40, 75–76, 79, 84, 160–161
*Tabor Beacon* 83
Talbot, Benjamin 164
Taylor County, Iowa 19, 161
Taylor's Ridge 107, 110
Teal, Frederick K. 47, 58, 77, 153
Tennessee 4, 57, 72, 79, 86, 88, 92, 94, 103, 105–106, 109–113, 115, 122–123, 134, 141–142
Tennessee River 79, 93–94, 102, 106, 109, 112
Tennessee River Valley 4, 93–95, 105
Texas 7, 65, 70–71, 79, 150, 152, 170
Texas and Colorado Construction Company 169
Texas and Pacific Railroad 122, 167, 169
Texas County, Missouri 58
Texas Rangers 52, 55

# Index

Thayer, Brig. John M. 79, 81–82, 100, 104
Thetford College 23
Thomas, A.D. 108
Thomas, Gen. George 105, 120, 123–125, 130, 140, 147
Thomas, Gen. Lorenzo 85–86, 91, 115
Thomasville, Georgia 153
Thompson, Jeff 154
Tibbles, Charles E. 164
Tichenor, George C. 166
Todd, George 146, 150
Tongue River 155
Torrence, Col. William M.G. 123
Totten, Capt. James 55
transcontinental railroad 2–3, 7, 12, 31, 34, 48, 78, 91, 97, 109, 164, 166–167, 170
Trenton, Tennessee 78
tribesmen 5, 30–34, 150–151, 155–157, 167
Troublesome Creek 28
Truman, Harry S. 149
Truman, John Anderson 149
Tupelo, Mississippi 93, 115, 121
Tuscaloosa, Alabama 120
Tuscumbia, Alabama 93, 95, 98, 106
Tuttle, James M 166
Twain, Mark 8, 48

Underground Railroad 4, 10, 14, 28, 40, 42, 75, **86**, 160
Union 42–44, 52, 54, 56–58, 61–63, 66–67, 70, 72, 91, 166, 169
Union Pacific, Denver and Gulf Railway Company 169
Union Pacific Railroad 5, 97, 109, 114, 119, 142, 150, 155, 157–158, 167–169
U.S. Army 5, 44, 48, 57, 111, 156, 162
U.S. Cavalry 59
United States Congress 5, 36, 66, 142, 161
U.S. Sanitary Commission 144
United States Senate 119
United States Supreme Court 25
United States Volunteers 162
Universalist minister 31
University of Iowa 38
Utah 30, 33, 35, 150, 157

Vallandingham, Clement L 13
Van Buren, Arkansas 72
Van Buren County, Iowa 43
Vandever, William 123
Van Dorn, Gen. Earl 4, 60–63, 65–67, 70–72, 74, 80, 92–94
Van Lew, Elizabeth 89
veterans 113, 121, 159–160, 167, 170
Vicksburg, Mississippi 4, 79–82, 84, 86, 87–88, **90**, 93–103, 105, 114, 123–124, 132, 134, 142, 160–162
Virginia 14, 53, 87, 145, 148, 153

Walker's Landing 92
Wallace, Gen. Lew 163
Waller, Robert James 19
War Department 57, 88, 92, 131, **165**
War of 1812 15
Ware, E.F. 52, 54, 156–157
Warren, Fitz Henry 17, 33
Warren County, Iowa 19, 61
Washington County, Iowa 107
Washington, D.C. 3, 7, 16–17, 19–20, 40, 48, 57, 59, 97–98, 107, 141–142, 146, 153, 155, 157–159, 166–167, 170
Washington University 166
Weavers, George 75–76, 161
Wells, Sec. of Navy Gideon 155
Wenham Lake 22
West, Elizabeth 22
West, Nathaniel 22
West Nishnabotna River 28
West Point 3, 18, 51–52, 59–60, 76, 83, 87, 114, 120–121, 126, 128, 130
Western and Atlanta Railroad 124
Western Department 57, 59
Western Industrial Company 169

Western Theater 1, 17, 53, 58, 88
"Westsiders" 38
Wheeler, Captain 26
Wheeler, General 106, 129, 133–134, 143
Wheeler, Joe 146
White River 76, 79, 83
Whitesville, New York 164
Wichita Valley Railway Company 169
Wilder, General 105
Williams, Reuben 160
Williams, Sturgis 75, 160–161
Williamson, Col. James A. 2, 3, 5, 38, 40, 42–43, 48–50, 61, 67, 73, 76–77, 81–85, 87–88, 91–92, 104–107, 117, 119, 122–123, 130, 132, 136, 141, 143, 145, 155, 157–158, 160, 162, 166
Williamson, John 40, 160
Wilmington, North Carolina 152
Wilson's Creek 53, 55–57, 61–62
Winnipeg, Canada 170
Winterset, Iowa 66, 72, 124, 163–164
Wirz, Capt. Henry 145, 153, 163–164
Wisconsin 16, 78, 156
Woodbury, Levi 25
Woods, Gen. Charles 117, 143
Woodville, Alabama 108, 117
World War II 119
Wright, Gen. Marcus J. 101
Wright County, Missouri 58
Wyoming 22, 79, 150, 157, 162, 168

Yale University 29
Yazoo River 80, 82, 84
Young, Brigham 157
Young, Harrison 149
Young, Martha Ellen 149
Young, Solomon 149
Younger, Cole 61–62
Younger, Henry 62
Young's Point 84

www.ingramcontent.com/pod-product-compliance
Ingram Content Group UK Ltd.
Pitfield, Milton Keynes, MK11 3LW, UK
UKHW050525150426
5217IPUK00026B/1798